Student Study Guide

to accompany

Educational Psychology

Effective Teaching, Effective Learning

Third Edition

Elliott • Kratochwill
Littlefield Cook • Travers

Prepared by

Joan Littlefield Cook
University of Wisconsin—Whitewater

McGraw
Hill

Boston   Burr Ridge, IL   Dubuque, IA   Madison, WI   New York   San Francisco   St. Louis
Bangkok   Bogotá   Caracas   Lisbon   London   Madrid
Mexico City   Milan   New Delhi   Seoul   Singapore   Sydney   Taipei   Toronto

McGraw-Hill Higher Education

A Division of The McGraw-Hill Companies

Student Study Guide to accompany
EDUCATIONAL PSYCHOLOGY: EFFECTIVE TEACHING, EFFECTIVE LEARNING, THIRD EDITION

 This book is printed on recycled, acid-free paper
containing 10% postconsumer waste.

2 3 4 5 6 7 8 9 0 QPD QPD 9 0 3 2 1 0
ISBN 0-697-37580-3

www.mhhe.com

CONTENTS

Preface to the Student iv

1. An Introduction: Educational Psychology and Effective Teaching Interactions   *1*

Section One: The Development of Students

2. Cognitive and Language Development   *23*

3. Psychosocial and Moral Development   *55*

4. Diversity in the Classroom: Culture, Class, and Gender   *83*

5. Exceptional Students   *113*

Section Two: Learning Theories and Implications for Practice

6. Behavioral Psychology and Learning   *145*

7. Cognitive Psychology and the Construction of Knowledge   *178*

8. Thinking Skills and Problem-Solving Strategies   *212*

9. Motivation and Student Learning   *239*

Section Three: Effective Teaching and the Evaluation of Learning

10. Classroom Management: Creating Effective Learning Environments   *272*

11. Assessment of Students' Learning Using Teacher-Constructed Methods   *303*

12. Standardized Tests and Behavior Rating Scales   *335*

13. Effective Teaching Strategies and the Design of Instruction   *361*

Appendix A: Research Methods and the Practice of Education   *405*

PREFACE TO THE STUDENT

This study guide was designed to help you master the material in the text *Educational Psychology: Effective Teaching, Effective Learning,* by Elliott, Kratochwill, Littlefield, and Travers. Used along with your textbook, this guide will help you learn, review, retrieve, and evaluate course material. By working on each corresponding chapter in your textbook, you will become an active participant in the learning process. Active participation involves more than just attending class and reading the textbook—it means that you ask questions, hypothesize, doubt some of the research findings, and wonder how psychological principles apply to you and to teaching. This study guide is intended to help you become a critical thinker of educational psychology. Be actively engaged in this learning process!

LEVELS OF THINKING AND STUDY

In studying the material, make sure you study at different levels—i.e., do not focus all your efforts on memorizing definitions, stages, and other factual material as many students tend to do. Make sure you consider the higher-level aspects of the material. For example, for each key term and concept listed or identified from the chapter, focus not only on the definition but also on what the concept means for teaching and learning, and what it means to you personally (e.g., Is it reasonable? How could you use it to improve your own learning and teaching?), and be able to give a clear, detailed example. Use some system (Bloom's taxonomy, covered in the text, is a good one) to ensure that you have studied at higher as well as lower levels.

The material in the study guide will help you study at different levels. The Guided Review and many items on the Practice Test focus on lower levels, asking for mastery of factual information. Though some items in the Guided Review and Practice Tests also require higher levels of thinking, the following sections are geared specifically toward higher levels of thought: Summarize the Main Point, Why Should You Care?, Discussion Questions, Take it Personally!, Case In Point, and Big Ideas in Educational Psychology. Even if the assessments in the course are multiple choice in nature, completing these other sections will be helpful in preparing you for those aspects of the assessment that focus on comparing, contrasting, and considering the implications of the material. The Suggested Readings included in each chapter provide more details on topics presented in or relevant to the text. In addition to providing summaries and guides to the text information, this study guide offers some general tips on how to improve your study habits. These suggestions should help you improve your comprehension and performance not only in this class, but in others as well.

HOW TO USE THIS STUDY GUIDE

Each chapter in this study guide has 13 sections to help you learn the text material. The following is an explanation of how to utilize the sections.

1. **Learning Objectives.** Before you read each chapter, scan the objectives to see what you are going to read. The objectives lists presented in the *Student Study Guide* include those from the text, but also add a few others. Formulate questions as you look through the objectives, and return to them after reading the material and again after studying the chapter to see if you have adequately covered each one. A thorough review and understanding of the material covered in each objective will prepare you for your examinations and help you learn the material.

2. **Chapter Highlights.** Read the Chapter Highlights before you read the chapter to provide an overview of the main points in the chapter. These highlights also are presented at the end of each textbook chapter to provide a built-in review of the text. Use the highlights actively: Jot down additional points you (or the instructor) feels are important. Doing so ensures that you will not forget any major points and helps you

step back and look at the whole picture after you have immersed yourself in studying the details of the chapter.

3. **Detailed Chapter Outline.** Each chapter includes a detailed outline. The outline helps you develop a framework around which to organize the material that you will be learning and provides a helpful preview of key terms and concepts to be addressed in the chapter. Before reading the text, scan the outline so that you can preview the topics that you will read about. Studying the outline should also motivate you to begin asking questions about the material before you start to read it. Use these questions to guide your learning. The outline also serves as a useful comprehensive summary following your reading of the chapter. A warning, though: Do not use the outline to replace reading the text! By definition, an outline omits many details. Examples, caveats, and applications of the material often are not included, but are important to your understanding and use of the material.

4. **Key Terms.** The key terms and concepts are those that are basic to an understanding of the important theories and issues involved in educational psychology. To test your understanding of the terms, you should be able to put the definitions in your own words. Also, be able to give an example of the term when an example is appropriate, and discuss why the term or concept is important for teaching and learning. If you understand a concept well enough to provide an example, you probably understand it well enough to answer questions about it and use it in answers to questions about key theories.

5. **Guided Review.** The Guided Review consists of fill-in-the-blank items to help you through your reading of the chapter. If you plan to use this Guided Review more than once in studying, do not write out your answers in the blanks until your final review. Read a sentence that has a word or phrase missing and fill in the missing word or phrase. Keep the answer that follows the sentence covered while you fill in the blank. Immediate feedback is given when you uncover the answer, so you can quickly discover what you know and what you may need to study some more. If you do not understand why your answer is wrong or why the answer given is right, go back to the text. These items most often are geared toward understanding the factual details of the material. It will also be useful to ask yourself as you go through the review, or on a subsequent review, why the information in that item is important and how you could use it in your teaching and learning.

6. **Summarize the Main Points.** This section of your study guide is designed to help you identify and understand the main points in each chapter. You will have already reviewed the details using the Guided Review and will consider the importance, relevance, and usefulness of the information in later sections. The focus in this section is on summarizing the main point and the evidence presented in the text to support and/or discuss it. Prompting questions are provided to help you structure your review.

7. **Why Should You Care?** The purpose of this section is to help you understand how and why the information in the chapter is relevant for you personally. You'll be asked to think about the relevance of the main points for teachers and for yourself and to identify specific examples for which the ideas presented in this chapter are relevant.

8. **Discussion Questions.** Discussion questions help facilitate critical thinking, and help you become a critical evaluator of educational and psychological theory, research, and application. You also may want to add your own questions for further study. Attempting to answer the questions should help prepare you for questions focusing on higher levels of thought on an examination, as well.

9. **Take It Personally!** The questions in this section are designed to help you personalize, integrate, and apply the information from the text. Personalization questions ask you to consider the personal relevance and usefulness of concepts, and consider how they might be useful in your life now and in the future. Integration questions ask you to pull together information from the text to evaluate it, summarize it, or synthesize a recommendation on the basis of it or express an opinion about it. Application questions ask you to think about how the concepts might be useful to address real problems or situations you may find

yourself in. All three question types will help you consider the information at a deeper conceptual level, understand it more fully, and remember it.

10. **Case In Point.** The textbook presents in detail three cases that can be useful to help you identify and apply the textbook concepts to real-life teaching situations. This section helps you use the text cases as contexts for identifying examples of main concepts from the chapter, and as contexts for solving educational problems.

11. **Big Ideas in Educational Psychology.** This section of your study guide is designed to help you integrate the content of each chapter and relate the separate concepts to the five main themes of this text (assessment, communication, learning, motivation, time) and identify additional general principles and specific strategies that will help you improve these five main elements of your own teaching skill. I also hope the format of the TIPS in the text (i.e., identifying main concepts, stating them as principles, and identifying specific strategies that follow from each principle) will give you an organizational framework for use in integrating and applying your knowledge.

12. **Suggested Readings.** Each chapter includes a list of suggested readings. These readings were provided by the authors of the text and represent several different sources, including books and book chapters, magazines, and professional journals. Use the readings to obtain more details on topics included in or relevant to the text. They are also useful as a starting point for further information on topics for student projects and reports.

13. **Practice Tests.** Each chapter provides two multiple-choice practice tests. Each test provides a sampling of the entire chapter material. There are three types of questions included in the tests: factual, conceptual, and applied. Factual questions ask you to remember—either by recall or recognition—words, definitions, or concepts as they appeared in the text. Factual questions facilitate your knowledge of remembering the facts. Conceptual questions test your ability to analyze, evaluate, or synthesize information you read in the text. Answering a conceptual question involves actively attempting to understand the material, rather than just memorizing. Applied questions test your ability to apply or use what you have learned in the text to arrive at a solution to a problem.

STUDY TIPS

Included below are some suggestions for how to improve your study habits. These suggestions are gleaned from several sources, including my own experience as a student and an instructor of college students; students in my classes; and the literature on problem-solving and study skills. It also may be helpful for you to read chapter 9 of the text ("Thinking Skills and Problem Solving Strategies") for other useful ideas.

The main reason for taking a course such as this one is to gain information that will improve your teaching and learning. The best way to study to achieve this goal is to engage in activities that will increase your comprehension of the material, see its usefulness, and understand how to use it. Most of you have this goal, but there is another more immediate concern: good performance on an assessment of some sort. While performance on an assessment clearly should not be the main goal in studying, it is a fact of college life. Therefore, I have organized the following suggestions around preparing for, participating in, and learning from an assessment. The suggestions offered should be helpful regardless of the form of assessment you will be taking, though in most places they are phrased in terms of preparing for a typical classroom examination (i.e., answering instructor-generated questions presented in a multiple-choice and/or essay and/or short-answer format under some degree of time constraint, without reference to notes or the text). Find out what assessment format is being used in your course and adjust the suggestions accordingly.

Before an Assessment

1. *Keep up.* The first step in preparing for an assessment is to keep up with the reading, course notes, and any other assignments and activities. You all know you should do this; doing it consistently is another matter. The literature on effective studying unequivocally supports the conclusion that distributed practice (spread out over several weeks or months) is more effective in retention, recall, and comprehension of material than massed practice (also known as "cramming for the exam"). Make a real effort to distribute your study efforts.

2. *Review your class notes* at least briefly each day after class. Doing this immediately is best, but if you can't do it immediately, do it sometime that day. Take 10 to 20 minutes and go over the notes. Using a highlighter or contrasting pen color, mark places where the notes are incomplete (either because you didn't have time to get it all down or because the instructor didn't provide enough information), places where you aren't clear on the point being made, places where the information seems inconsistent to you, and places where you simply have questions (e.g., "I wonder why . . . ?"; "What if . . . ?"; "Why is it like that?"; etc.). Before the next class, ask a classmate, the teaching assistant, or the instructor your questions. If you have extensive questions, make an appointment with the instructor to get them answered.

3. *Read actively.* When reading the chapters in the text, use some method to ensure that you actively question and process the information as you go. The SQ3R system described in chapter 12 of the text is a good one. This involves several steps. *Survey* the text briefly before reading, looking at the headings, reading the notes, definitions, and questions in the margins, skimming the objectives and highlights and outline in the chapter and the *Student Study Guide*, and glancing over the list of key terms. Next, ask a few *questions* about the content, such as what these terms mean, what that figure is illustrating, what that table is all about, etc. Jot the questions down in the margin of the text. *Read* the text, addressing the questions you have come up with as well as those in the text margins and in the *Student Study Guide*. *Recite* after you read; this means that you try to answer the questions you developed and those in the text margin and in the *Student Study Guide* without looking at the text. *Review* the text by skimming the outline, highlights, objectives, and key terms. Also, use the Guided Review in the *Student Study Guide* at this point, then the Practice Test. Identify areas you are unclear or incorrect about and go back over these areas in detail. Identify questions for which you need clarification from the instructor. Finally, I would add a fourth R to the strategy: *Relate* the material to your specific situation and interests. You'll be doing some of this as you answer the Embedded Questions in the text margin and the Personalization, Integration, and Application Questions in the *Student Study Guide*, but take some time to systematically consider each main point and ask what it means for you personally.

4. *Be an active class member.* As you are listening to lectures and participating in class activities, always consider: Can I define and give an example of this concept? What does this really mean? Who cares (meaning, how is this useful to teachers in general and to me personally)? Discover (or ask about) the instructor's structure for presenting material. By this I mean look for patterns in how the instructor formats the material, how transitions are made between points, how the main points are emphasized, etc. Understanding and using the structure will help you take clearer and more organized class notes. Finally, ask questions! If you didn't hear or see something, didn't understand it, or simply need another example or a clearer definition, be sure to ask.

During Studying

1. *Look for patterns.* Often there are underlying themes in the material you are studying. Look for historical timelines to identify changes in the dominant theories, which are usually related to changes in concepts and practice. Such timelines will help you understand why current practice is as it is and will help you remember details about the different theorists. Also, look for commonalities in the underlying themes of different theorists. For example, the "active organism" assumption is common to many of the

theories covered in developmental and educational psychology (Piaget, cognitive psychology) and the role of interaction with the environment is emphasized in several theories as well (Piaget, Vygotsky, and Erikson, to name a few). After identifying a common theme, consider how the different theorists deal with it. For example, although several of the theorists discuss the importance of interaction with the environment for development to proceed, some theorists emphasize the social environment, while others talk more about interacting with objects in the physical environment. Use the common themes as a basis for comparing and contrasting theories.

2. *Ask why* concepts, stages, etc., are proposed as they are. You certainly should be able to describe different theories and concepts, but if you consider why the theories were proposed as they were, or why the concepts were developed, you will gain a better understanding of them. For example, Piaget had a strong background in the biological sciences, and many of his concepts are essentially biological concepts applied to psychological development. Also ask why concepts and processes work. For example, if you can not only define and give examples of elaboration but also describe why it enhances memory, you are moving beyond a descriptive level of knowledge and moving toward using the concept to explain memory functioning.

3. *Ask who cares.* Most instructors certainly want students to be able to define, describe, and give examples of the concepts studied. Most, though, also want students to be able to discuss how the concepts are useful, either to educators in classrooms or to researchers trying to understand classroom processes better. One of the best ways to evaluate practical utility of concepts is to simply ask yourself, "Who cares? Why is this concept important, and how could I use it in my particular situation?" Some prompts to use when considering the usefulness of the material are (a) Why is this concept, theory, etc., important? Why did the authors/instructor include it? (b) What does this concept, theory, etc., contribute? Facts, a framework, a specific tool? (c) Why should I personally care about this? How can I use it to improve my own teaching, learning, or outlook?

4. *Compare and contrast.* When studying different theorists or approaches, always compare and contrast them to identify specific points of similarity and difference. List the main concepts from each approach, or write a brief summary paragraph that explains the perspective and any important terminology. Then address a standard list of questions from each perspective (e.g., What is "learning" from this perspective? What are the three most important elements for good teaching from this perspective? What develops from this perspective?) and compare the answers.

5. *Make charts, graphs, concept maps, etc.* Use visuals to summarize the text material and as a way of comparing and contrasting the perspectives. Doing so forces you to summarize and clarify. Often, when making charts, you must come up with headings for the rows and columns; this automatically provides dimensions for comparing the approaches.

6. *List any questions you still have.* A week or two before the assessment, meet with the instructor, teaching assistant, and/or other students and ask your questions. Review the questions just before your meeting to make sure you haven't already answered them and to make sure that you still understand what your question was. If available, you can use e-mail to send your list to the TA or instructor ahead of time so your meeting time can be used more efficiently.

7. *Use the learning objectives and chapter highlights.* Most texts have a list of learning objectives and some way of summarizing the highlights from each chapter. This text includes both Learning Objectives and Chapter Highlights in the text and in the *Student Study Guide.* Use these instructional aids by reviewing them before you read (as noted above) and by reviewing them after you finish studying the chapters. Doing so will ensure that you have covered the material completely and hit all the major points. It also gives you one more opportunity to self-evaluate and consider whether there are still concepts you do not completely understand and questions you still have.

The Assessment Itself

1. *Find out about the assessment.* Get as much information as you can concerning the format of the assessment, the types of questions likely, and the level of knowledge expected. The best way to do this is to ask if the instructor has any example assessment items, or examples of previous students' performances, portfolios, projects, etc. Also ask if there are any options—most students assume that they must do the assessment in one and only one format, but this is often not the case. There may be different formats for exams (essay, multiple-choice), or options for doing projects, portfolios, performances, etc., for all or part of an assessment. Ask what the range of choices is.

2. *Level of questions.* Find out the level of question that is likely. Is it likely that you will be expected to know factual information, or will you need to know also how to apply the facts and concepts to specific types of problems? Will you be expected to synthesize material and present your own theories and solutions to problems? Will you be expected to evaluate the theoretical soundness and practical usefulness of theories and concepts? Get examples of previous test questions, if possible. Use Bloom's taxonomy of cognitive objectives (or some other taxonomy) to evaluate systematically the level of knowledge the questions require. If example assessment items are not available, ask the instructor and/or teaching assistant about the level of knowledge they expect, perhaps posing a sample question of your own and asking whether it is a good example of what to expect. Also ask for sample answers, especially for essay items, and samples of what should be included in projects and portfolios.

3. *Assessment conditions.* Get information on the physical conditions of the testing situation. Will there be time pressure, i.e., will you have to complete the exam in a certain time period? Is extra time allowed under any circumstances? What is the room like where the assessment will take place? Is it likely to be noisy, poorly lit, cold, hot, etc.? If you think the physical conditions may be problematic, discuss this ahead of time with the instructor. If appropriate, alternative testing conditions may be possible.

4. *Instructor's role.* What will the instructor do during the assessment? Monitor only? Provide feedback, and if so, what kind and to what extent? Can the instructor answer questions about the assessment items, clarify terms, etc.? Instructors vary in how active they are during an assessment; it may help you relax a bit if you know that you can ask questions and/or get feedback during the assessment.

5. *Be physically and mentally prepared.* Make sure you are rested (no late-night cramming sessions the night before!) and are not hungry, thirsty, or otherwise distracted when you arrive for the assessment. Some students like to take a 10- to 15-minute walk before an assessment, while others prefer to sit quietly and relax. If you feel comfortable looking over your notes one last time, then do so, but some students find last-minute reviews anxiety producing. If so, then do your last review an hour or so before the assessment and spend the time just before the assessment relaxing.

During the Assessment

1. *Get there early* and choose a seat that is comfortable for you. Some students get very distracted by people around them who finish early. The noise of these students' packing up of their belongings and leaving is bad enough, but students also sometimes begin to feel panicky, as if because others are finishing earlier it must be an easy assessment and they themselves ought to be almost done. Don't set yourself up for this; sit in the back or the front or somewhere where you won't be painfully aware of others finishing earlier than you. Also remember that finishing early very often does not mean students have done well, and it definitely does not mean you should be done.

2. *Relax!* Take a few deep breaths at the beginning, again in the middle, and at the end.

3. *Keep an eye on the time, but not too close an eye.* You need to pace your efforts, but you don't want to become so aware of the time that you begin to feel panicky about getting finished.

4. *Identify key elements in the question.* When taking a multiple-choice exam, identify the key elements in a question and get a sense of what the question is asking as a whole. Underline parts of the question you think are central; jot down questions and notes about the question as needed. Then make sure you review *all* the alternatives. I know you've heard this one before, but it really is true that many students find one plausible-sounding answer and never go further. There often is a better, clearer, more specific answer further along in the alternatives.

5. *Briefly outline your answer.* When taking an essay or short-answer exam, first jot down a brief outline of your answer, noting key points you plan to include. Just write this in the margins of the paper on which you are writing your answers (or at the beginning of the file, if you are doing a computerized essay) and turn it in with your answers. That way, if you start to run short on time, you can list quickly the rest of the points you planned to make and a description of key details. The instructor will get some sense of what you know, what you planned to discuss, and where you were headed with your answer.

After the Assessment

This is the stage of assessment preparation that many students leave out, but it is critical for improved performance on the next assessment. You must take time to reflect on your preparation, your performance, and what you learned from the assessment.

1. *Get more than the score.* Find out which items you missed or did not receive full credit for, what the correct answer was, and/or what else should have been done or included. Understand *why* your answer was wrong or your performance incomplete.

2. Then *evaluate your preparation procedure.* Did you feel prepared? What parts of your preparation could be improved? Did you feel prepared, but not do well? Analyze why. You might want to meet with the professor to discuss this, describing how you prepared and asking for suggestions. Go over the aspects of the assessment you didn't do well on and ask whether you interpreted the task correctly; discuss as well your procedure for selecting a test item or completing an aspect of the assessment.

Chapter 1

AN INTRODUCTION: EDUCATIONAL PSYCHOLOGY AND EFFECTIVE TEACHING INTERACTIONS

LEARNING OBJECTIVES

After completing this chapter, you should be able to:

1. Define educational psychology and discuss how educational psychology can answer the questions that novice teachers often have.

2. Define reflective teaching and identify how it contributes to effective teaching.

3. Describe qualities that contribute to excellent teaching.

4. Compare teaching as an art and as a science.

5. Define constructivism and explain its implications for teaching.

6. Define developmental contextualism and discuss its relationship to teaching.

7. Identify and discuss out-of-school influences that impact teaching and learning.

8. List and define the five themes of educational psychology.

CHAPTER HIGHLIGHTS

Educational Psychology

- Educational psychology is the application of psychology and psychological methods to the study of learning and teaching.
- Educational psychology is a broad discipline that focuses on the interaction of human development, cognitive science, instructional methods, measurement, and assessment.

So You Want to Teach

- Teachers have their own unique expectations as they enter the classroom.
- Novice teachers ask several key questions about their beginning days.
- Reflective teachers think about their teaching and use their conclusion to improve their skills.
- Research consistently has shown that effective teachers exhibit several behaviors or practices. These include: lesson clarity, instructional variety, task involvement, careful use of praise, consistent classroom guidelines, and periodic feedback about learning.

What Teachers Need To Know

- Teachers need three types of knowledge: teaching knowledge, subject matter knowledge, and teaching subject matter knowledge
- Teaching knowledge refers to the principles and strategies of subjects.
- Good teachers are masters of their subjects.
- Teaching subject matter knowledge refers to the best manner of presenting content.
- Good teachers display the characteristics of both artist and scientist.

Important Topics in Educational Psychology Today

- Educational psychology has maintained its vitality by addressing important and practical issues, three of which are constructivism, diversity, and out-of-school influences.
- Constructivism refers to the manner in which students construct their personal views of the world.
- Effective teachers have learned to capitalize on the diversity in their classrooms and to design instructional environments that accommodate a wide range of learners with varying backgrounds and experiences.
- For students to achieve their maximum potential, teachers should be aware of the impact of out-of-school experiences.

Themes for Organizing and Building Knowledge of Educational Psychology

- The five core themes of educational psychology offer practical guidance and help to teachers. These themes focus on communication skills, understanding of the learning process, motivating learners, using time well, and using assessment methods to provide feedback to students and educators.

DETAILED CHAPTER OUTLINE

I. Educational psychology: A definition and key concepts
  A. Educational psychology is the application of psychology and psychological methods to the study of development, learning, motivation, instruction, assessment, and related issues that influence the interaction of teaching and learning.
  B. Educational psychology is a vital discipline that is contributing to the education of teachers and learners.
  C. Key concepts and their relationship to instruction and learning
    1. Understanding the meaning of teaching
    2. Knowledge of pupils
    3. Understanding the learning process
    4. Understanding instructional strategies
    5. Understanding assessment strategies

II. So you want to teach
  A. To be the best teacher you can be, you must have clear objectives in mind, understand students' developmental characteristics, select materials and methods, and assess students' knowledge and skills appropriately.
  B. Questions teachers ask
    1. Will I be able to maintain discipline in my classroom?
    2. When are students ready for certain experiences?
    3. Are there specific teaching techniques that are better suited to some students than to others?
      a. Reflective teachers learn from their experiences and speculate about the implications for their future teaching.
    4. Does a knowledge of learning theory help in the classroom?

C. Qualities of outstanding teachers
    1. Boyer (1990) identified several characteristics of effective teachers.
        a. They employ language clearly and efficiently.
        b. They are well-informed and comfortable with the history and frontiers of their disciplines.
        c. They relate what they know to their learners.
    2. Other research has identified additional key behaviors associated with good teaching.
        a. Lesson clarity, meaning that your students understand you.
        b. Instructional variety, or being able to use a variety of techniques.
        c. Task involvement, or keeping students actively engaged with tasks.
        d. Careful use of praise. Avoid noncontingent praise (i.e., not linked to a specific behavior), and don't let a student's personal qualities be the occasion for praise.
        e. Consistent classroom guidelines. Avoid double-standards, don't use threats and intimidation, try to understand the purpose of misbehavior, emphasize the positive, and refuse to take misbehavior personally.
        f. Periodic feedback. Give periodic feedback about work efforts and performances.
    3. Skilled teachers:
        a. Try to understand students' behavior, their problems, and their solutions from their perspective.
        b. Create a learning environment that encourages motivation, learning, and transfer of that learning.
        c. Use instructional techniques that lead to problem-solving activities for students.
        d. Establish a positive learning environment and monitor it carefully.
        e. Provide frequent feedback about students' efforts and performances.

III. What teachers need to know
  A. All the ideas you have about children, subject matter, and teaching are filtered through your network of personal beliefs.
  B. The knowledge base of teaching is important, especially familiarity with developmental psychology, motivation, classroom management, teacher expectations, learning, and learning strategies.
  C. Teaching knowledge refers to how the basic principles and strategies of a subject are best acquired and retained.
    1. Classroom management is critical, but depends on many things, including your personality.
    2. Instructional strategies refer to how you structure activities in your classroom. You will need an arsenal of strategies to meet the widely varied needs of your students.
    3. Knowledge of learners and learning is important.
  D. Subject matter knowledge refers to a teacher's comprehension of a subject when compared to that of a specialist.
    1. Do not be content with the basic facts and information of a subject, but acquire familiarity with the ideas, facts, and concepts of a subject, and how they are organized.
    2. Research indicates that knowledgeable teachers can better detect student difficulties and seize opportunities for meaningful learning.
  E. Teaching subject matter knowledge refers to the most appealing manner in which you organize and present content.
    1. Think about the following questions that help to shape your personal teaching style.
        a. Why are you teaching what you're teaching?
        b. What are your students' typical understandings and misunderstandings of a subject?
        c. How much do you know about curriculum and curricular materials?
        d. Have you thought about the strategies and representations you could use for particular topics?
  F. Your task is to help your pupils learn as much as their potential permits. There are several principles of learning that will help.
    1. Be sure you know what you want to accomplish.
    2. Encourage as much student activity as possible.
    3. Guard against student anxiety.
    4. Teach for understanding, and encourage the use of learning strategies.

G. Teaching as an art and as a science
  1. Teaching as an art
     a. You must know your subject, including the material you currently are presenting in class, the core of the subject, and what researchers are discovering at the frontiers of the discipline. This necessitates constant independent study.
     b. To devote hours of study beyond the demands of duty requires a commitment to the discipline and to the students.
     c. Veteran secondary teachers studies by Cohen (1992) showed passion and enthusiasm for the subject taught and development of their own unique teaching style, which was constantly modified.
  2. Teaching as a science
     a. Teachers adopt the role of experimenters as they try new instructional methods and classroom procedures.
     b. There are four steps in the role of teacher as scientist:
        (1) Identifying the problem.
        (2) Formulating a logical series of steps to reach a goal.
        (3) Gathering the data.
        (4) Interpreting the data.

IV. Important topics in educational psychology today
  A. Constructivism
     1. Constructivism means that students construct their own understanding of the world. The two key words are *active* and *meaning*. Learners take their own knowledge and interpret it according to what's already known.
     2. Different interpretations have arisen. Some argue that the individual alone constructs meaning, while others argue that individuals in a social situation construct meaning.
     3. Constructivist teachers often wrap their teaching in a cloak of problems for their students, use students' perspectives to interpret responses and solutions, know that responses reflect current levels of understanding, and accept the conflicts and confusion that initially accompany the search for meaning.
  B. Student diversity in the classroom
     1. Developmental contextualism holds that all a student's characteristics, psychological as well as biological, interact with the environment (the context).
     2. There are four major forces of development.
        a. The physical settings through which students move.
        b. Social influences.
        c. The personal characteristics of students.
        d. The influence of time.
     3. The crucial element in learning and development is the changing relationship between the complexity your students bring to the classroom and a multilayered context.
  C. Out-of-school influences
     1. Understanding the wellsprings of students' achievement demands that we know more about their lives beyond the classroom.
     2. Steinberg et al. (1996) concluded that school is only one influence that affects what students learn and how well they do on tests. Though their study identified the same pattern of ethnic differences as others, they also looked at the reasons why the differences existed.
        a. Students of different ethnic backgrounds differed in their belief that failing in school would have negative consequences.
        b. Parents exert a profound and lasting effect on their children's achievement in three ways:
           (1) Deliberately or casually, parents communicate specific messages about teachers, schools, and learning.
           (2) Parental behavior sends clear and unmistakable signals about the importance the parents place on schooling.
           (3) Parenting style encourages, or discourages, engagement in school.

V. Themes for organizing and building knowledge of educational psychology into your teaching-learning interactions

    A. TIPS: Teaching Interaction Principles and Strategies

        1. TIPS are presented in each chapter to help you relate the theories and research you'll be reading about to the everyday world of teaching. They focus on five themes.

            a. Communication and the role it plays in the establishment of learning and behavior expectations, teacher-student interpersonal relationships, and delivery of quality instruction.

            b. Learning, as an interactive enterprise. These TIPS help you create environments where routines are smooth and efficient, instruction facilitates personal connections between new and existing knowledge, attention is maintained, and students are asked to act upon and use information.

            c. Motivation, to promote excellence and positive personal interactions between teachers and students, which in turn impacts achievement and behavior.

            d. Time, and how to increase the proportion of actual learning or engaged time in classrooms.

            e. Assessment, and the role it plays in planning instruction and documenting the effects of teaching.

    B. Case studies of teachers in action

        1. Three case studies have been included in the text for you to analyze and discuss.

        2. Each case contains five components: a case description, a case opening box, case notes, case reflections, and a teacher's case conference.

        3. Case One is about Marsha Warren, a 3rd grade teacher overwhelmed by her heterogeneous class of students. This case is used to structure and integrate information on development and special learners.

        4. Case Two is about Mark Siegel, a 4th grade teacher puzzled by the learning problems of one of his students and challenged by the student's parent to do more to help her child. This case is used to structure and integrate information on learning theories and practices.

        5. Case Three is about Melissa Williams, a novice 7th grade teacher feeling pressure from her teaching team members to maintain the existing superior end-of-year test scores. This case is used to structure and integrate information on instruction and assessment.

VI. Chapter highlights

VII. What do you think? questions

VIII. Key terms

KEY TERMS

artist	out-of-school influences
constructivism	reflective teachers
developmental contextualism	scientist
diversity	subject matter knowledge
educational psychology	teaching knowledge
noncontingent praise	teaching subject matter knowledge

GUIDED REVIEW

1. _____ involves the application of psychology to the study of development, learning, motivation, instruction, assessment, and any related issues that influence the interaction of teaching and learning.

Educational psychology

2. The first key concept in educational psychology is the need to understand the meaning of _____ . Teachers must also have as much knowledge of _____ as possible and understand the _____ . Teachers must concentrate on learning those instructional _____ that research has shown to be effective, and they must develop skill in _____ students' knowledge and skills.

teaching, pupils, learning process, strategies, assessing

3. To be the best teacher you can be, you must have clear _____ in mind, understand students' _____ characteristics, select _____ , and _____ students' knowledge and skills appropriately.

objectives, developmental, materials and methods, assess

4. Novice teachers typically ask whether they'll be able to maintain _____ , how to determine when students are _____ for certain experiences, whether there are specific teaching _____ that are better suited to some students than to others, and whether knowledge of _____ helps in the classroom.

discipline, ready, techniques, learning theory

5. _____ teachers learn from their experiences and speculate about the implications for their future teaching.

Reflective

6. Boyer (1990) identified several characteristics of effective teachers, including clear use of _____ , being well-informed and comfortable with the _____ of their disciplines, and _____ what they know to their learners.

language, history and frontiers, relating

7. Other research has identified additional key behaviors associated with good teaching. They include lesson _____ , instructional _____ , task _____ , using _____ carefully, and using consistent classroom _____ .

clarity, variety, involvement, praise, guidelines

8. Lesson clarity means that your students _____ you. It is achieved by _____ materials carefully, giving precise _____ , _____ the present lesson to past work, and using _____ instructional strategies.

understand, organizing, directions, linking, developmentally appropriate

9.   Effective teachers are able to use a variety of _____ , experiment, _____ , use student _____ , and _____ techniques when needed.

techniques, evaluate, feedback, change

10.   Good teachers keep students _____ with tasks and are aware of their students' task _____ and engagement.

actively engaged, orientation

11.   Good teachers use _____ carefully, avoiding _____ praise, i.e., praise not linked to a specific behavior.

praise, noncontingent

12.   Good teachers use _____ classroom guidelines, avoiding _____ . They emphasize the _____ and refuse to take misbehavior personally.

consistent, double standards, positive

13.   Effective teachers give frequent _____ about work efforts and performances.

feedback

14.   _____ refers to how the basic principles and strategies of a subject are best acquired and retained. It is sometimes called pedagogical knowledge.

Teaching knowledge

15.   Important aspects of teaching knowledge include: classroom _____ , which is critical but depends on many things, including your personality; _____ , or how you structure activities in your classroom; and knowledge of _____ .

management, instructional strategies, learners and learning

16.   _____ refers to a teacher's comprehension of a subject when compared to that of a specialist. Do not be content with the basic facts and information of a subject, but acquire familiarity with the ideas, facts, and _____ of a subject, and how they are _____ . Keep up with current _____ .

Subject matter knowledge, concepts, organized, research

17.   _____ refers to the most appealing manner in which you organize and present content. To better understand your personal teaching style, consider _____ you are teaching what you're teaching, identify your students' typical understandings and _____ of a subject, consider how much you _____ about curriculum and curricular materials, and think about the strategies and _____ you could use for particular topics.

Teaching subject matter knowledge, why, misunderstandings, know, representations

18. There are several principles of learning to help you help students learn as much as possible, including: Be sure you know _____, encourage as much student _____ as possible, guard against student _____ , and teach for understanding and encourage the use of _____ .

what you want to accomplish, activity, anxiety, learning strategies

19. Veteran secondary teachers studies by Cohen (1992) showed passion and _____ for the subject taught and development of their own _____, which was constantly modified.

enthusiasm, unique teaching style

20. Teachers adopt the role of _____ as they try new instructional methods and classroom procedures. There are four steps in the role of teacher as scientist: _____ the problem, _____ a logical series of steps to reach a goal, _____ the data, and _____ the data.

experimenters, Identifying, formulating, gathering, interpreting

21. _____ means that students construct their own understanding of the world. The two key words are _____ and _____ . Learners take their own knowledge and _____ it according to what's already known.

Constructivism, active, meaning, interpret

22. Different interpretations of constructivism have arisen. Some argue that the _____ constructs meaning, while others argue that individuals in a _____ construct meaning.

individual alone, social situation

23. Constructivist teachers often wrap their teaching in a cloak of _____ for their students, use students' _____ to interpret responses and solutions, know that responses reflect current _____ , and accept the _____ that initially accompany the search for meaning.

problems, perspectives, levels of understanding, conflicts and confusion

24. _____ holds that all a student's characteristics, psychological as well as biological, interact with the environment (the context).

Developmental contextualism

25. Developmental contextualism attempts to understand development in the light of the multiple _____ between individuals and their environments. There are four major forces of development: the _____ settings through which students move, _____ influences, the _____ of students, and _____. The crucial element in learning and development is the _____ between the complexity your students bring to the classroom and a multilayered context.

levels of interactions, physical, social, personal characteristics, time, changing relationship

26. Steinberg et al (1996) concluded that school is only one influence that affects what students learn. Though their study identified the same pattern of _____ as others, they also looked at the reasons why the differences existed. Students of different ethnic backgrounds differed in their belief that _____ in school would have negative consequences.

ethnic differences, failing

27. _____ exert a profound and lasting effect on their children's achievement by three things: Communicating specific _____ about teachers, schools, and learning; sending signals about the _____ the parents place on schooling; and the way their _____ encourages, or discourages, engagement in school.

Parents, messages, importance, parenting style

28. The text discusses five themes for organizing and building knowledge of educational psychology into your teaching-learning interactions. The first is _____, which plays an important role in the establishment of learning and behavior _____ , teacher-student interpersonal _____ , and delivery of quality _____ .

Communication, expectations, relationships, instruction

29. Learning is an _____ enterprise. It is desirable for teachers to create environments where routines are _____ , instruction facilitates personal _____ between new and existing knowledge, _____ is maintained, and students are asked to act and use information.

interactive, smooth and efficient, connections, attention

30. Teachers must know about _____ to promote excellence and positive personal interactions between teachers and students, which in turn impacts achievement and behavior.

motivation

31. Teachers must do more with the _____ allocated for instruction and learn how to increase the proportion of actual learning or _____ in classrooms.

time, engaged time

32. _____ plays an important role in planning instruction and documenting the effects of teaching.

Assessment

33. Three case studies have been included in the text for you to analyze and discuss. The purpose of the cases is to facilitate _____ between educational psychology and teaching. For each, the text offers observations, _____ , and possible _____ designed to illustrate how the content of each chapter applies to the case being considered.

connections, hypotheses, actions

SUMMARIZE THE MAIN POINTS

This section of your study guide is designed to help you identify and understand the main points in each chapter. You've already reviewed the details using the Guided Review (above), and will consider the importance, relevance, and usefulness of the information in later sections. For now, focus on summarizing the main ideas.

For each major section in the chapter, summarize the main point and the evidence presented in the text to support and/or discuss it. If there are key terms presented in the section, define them. Some prompting questions are provided to help you structure your review.

The main sections of Chapter 1 are:

- Educational psychology: A definition and some concepts
- So you want to teach
- What teachers need to know
- Important topics in educational psychology today
- Themes for organizing and building knowledge of educational psychology into your teaching-learning interactions
- Case studies of teachers in action

For each section, answer the following questions:

1. In two sentences or less, **summarize** what the **main point** of this section was.

2. Briefly **summarize the evidence** for and against each point (a simple list of details the authors use to support each of their points is sufficient). If the authors discuss research studies to support the point, summarize the findings in one sentence. If the authors are presenting a logical argument to support the point (i.e., not citing data from research studies), briefly list the supporting points they made. Use the detailed chapter outline to help you identify the supporting points.

3. Briefly review the **definitions of any key terms** in each main section.

WHY SHOULD YOU CARE?

The purpose of this section of your study guide is to help you understand how and why the information in the chapter is relevant for you personally. You'll be asked to think more about the relevance and usefulness of the information in later sections of this study guide.

Look back at the work you did in summarizing the main points in the section above and answer the following questions:

1. For each section you summarized, why or how is the **main point** you identified **important to and/or relevant for teachers in general**? Try to limit your answer to only one or two sentences so you don't get bogged down in details, but focus on general usefulness.

2. Now think about the chapter as a whole. **Identify two specific events, contexts, or problems** for which the ideas presented in this chapter are relevant. Briefly discuss how they're relevant and how they could be useful.

3. Now **identify three concepts** from the chapter that **YOU find useful** in some way. Discuss how/why these concepts are useful, and specify how you will actually use them in your teaching and/or your daily life. (It's okay if there is some overlap between your answers for numbers 2 and 3.)

DISCUSSION QUESTIONS

The following "What do you think?" questions are printed in the text.

1. If you are thinking about becoming a teacher, you probably have several ideas about teaching and what you hope to accomplish. These ideas are known as teacher expectations. What are they? Compare your expectations with those of your classmates. How similar are they?

2. When you consider the relationship between teaching and learning, are there other characteristics of good teachers that you would mention? Think about a teacher you have had who you really thought was effective. What characteristics made him or her effective for you?

3. After reading about several issues that have captured the interest of educational psychologists, do you agree with their importance in teaching and learning? Why?

Additional discussion questions:

4. Explain what is meant by "teaching as an art" and "teaching as a science." How do these two aspects of teaching interact or complement one another?

5. List and explain the characteristics of effective teachers. How do these characteristics contribute to effective teaching, and to effective learning in students?

6. Define what is meant by "reflective teaching." Discuss how and why reflectivity is important for teaching and learning.

7. Distinguish between teaching knowledge, subject matter knowledge, and teaching subject matter knowledge. Give an example of each kind of knowledge.

8. Define constructivism and describe a constructivist approach to teaching.

9. What is the difference between knowing *why* and knowing *that*. Is it an important difference? Why or why not?

TAKE IT PERSONALLY!

The questions in this section are designed to help you personalize, integrate, and apply the information from the text. Personalization questions ask you to consider the personal relevance and usefulness of concepts, and consider how they might be useful in your life now and in the future. Integration questions ask you to pull together information from the text to evaluate it, summarize it, synthesize a recommendation on the basis of it, or express an opinion about it. Application questions ask you to think about how the concepts might be useful to address real problems or situations you may find yourself in. All three question types will help you consider the information at a deeper conceptual level, understand it more fully, and remember it.

1. Identify the core concepts of educational psychology and list questions you would like to have answered that pertain to each concept during the course. Keep the list and review it periodically to see if you have addressed your questions.

2. What is teaching? What is educational psychology? How will educational psychology help you in your teaching?

3. Why are you going into teaching as a profession? What characteristics of outstanding teachers do you have? Which do you still need to develop?

4. Identify current topics you think are important in education. Keep the list and review it at the end of the course, using it to reflect on what you have learned from the course and how it is useful. How does your list compare with the topics discussed in Chapter 1?

5. Identify an example of teaching as an art, then an example of teaching as a science. Explain how each example illustrates the art or the science of teaching.

6. State your personal theories of teaching and learning. Review these as you go through the course to see how they are similar to and different from those in the course.

7. How has the cultural, racial, and ethnic mix changed in your area? How and why are such changes important to you as a teacher? Are there any programs you know of that have been implemented to assist in developing positive outcomes from such changes? Have they been useful?

8. Identify one good classroom and one poor classroom in which you have been a student. Analyze each classroom, identifying which key teaching behaviors the teacher showed/did not show and which of the five themes of educational psychology were effectively addressed/not well addressed. Describe how these aspects affected your learning.

9. Which of the questions that teachers ask are ones you also have? Keep the list and jot down concepts and notes as you encounter material in the text that is relevant for answering your questions.

10. Which of the three types of knowledge (teaching knowledge, subject matter knowledge, and teaching subject matter knowledge) have you already developed, at least to a moderate degree? Which kinds do you still need to develop? How will educational psychology help you develop your knowledge?

11. Briefly define each of the five themes of educational psychology presented in the text (assessment, communication, learning, motivation, and time). Do you think they are important? Why/why not? How is each one relevant and important for good teaching and learning?

CASE IN POINT....

Your textbook presents three cases in detail. The cases can be useful to help you identify and apply the textbook concepts to real-life teaching situations. Different instructors will use the cases in different ways, with some instructors heavily emphasizing them during instruction and perhaps even providing additional cases for you to think about in class or as homework. Even if your instructor doesn't use a "case-based" approach to teaching, try using the cases in the following two ways on your own. Also, think about other real-life cases you have experienced or know of as contexts for applying the information from this chapter.

• **Contexts for identifying examples** — Use the text case as a context from which to identify concepts from the book chapters. Examples of the general types of things you can look for include teacher behaviors and strategies; characteristics of student development, behaviors, and individual differences; and other things such as contextual variables, interactions, home variables, and administrative practices, any of which can affect teaching and learning. For each chapter, I have listed several major concepts you can look for.

• **Contexts for solving educational problems** — Use the case as a context to develop your educational problem-solving skills. Try to use a standard format across all the chapters, such as the DUPE model from Chapter 8 of the text, as an organizing framework. Use the DUPE model to structure a "Mini-Case Report." Each report would include the following information:

> Definition of the problem — A clear statement of the problem/issue in the case, what the nature of the problem/issue is;

> Understand the problem — Hypotheses about what is causing the problem and/or what is keeping the problem going;

> Plan for problem solution — Suggestions for a course of action that might help solve the problem, along with a clear statement of why this course of action is being recommended. This section could also contain a discussion of other alternative solutions that were considered and why they were rejected;

> Evaluation of the plan — Explanations of the expected effects of the proposed actions and suggestions for how one can determine whether the recommended course of action worked.

The CASE NOTES presented in the text (beginning with Chapter 2) are one way to think about using the text information to solve the problems presented in each case. Remember that each case presented is complex and probably involves more than one simple problem, just as in real-life instructional problems. Also as in real-life problems, there are usually multiple pieces of information and skills that might be useful to address the problem and often more than one possible strategy for solving the problem. So for each case, it might be useful and interesting to talk with other students in your class (or in other classes) and exchange ideas about what the problem(s) is(are) and which textbook concepts might be helpful in addressing it(them).

qualities of outstanding teachers
key behaviors of skilled teachers
constructivism
diversity
reflective teachers
teacher as artist/as scientist
subject matter knowledge
teaching knowledge
teaching subject matter knowledge

Read through all three of the cases in the textbook and consider how the information from Chapter 1 relates to each case. Then consider the following questions:

1. Which key qualities and behaviors of skilled teachers do the teachers in these cases show?

2. How well do these teachers deal with the diversity of their students? Is their handling of diversity causing any problems?

3. Do these teachers show evidence of being reflective teachers? How could being more reflective help them?

BIG IDEAS IN EDUCATIONAL PSYCHOLOGY

Thinking about the "big ideas" in educational psychology will help you organize and apply your newly acquired knowledge. This section of your study guide is designed to help you integrate the content of each chapter and relate the separate concepts to the five main themes of this text (assessment, communication, learning, motivation, time) and identify additional general principles and specific strategies that will help you improve these five main elements of your own teaching skill. I also hope the format of the TIPS in the text (i.e., identifying main concepts, stating them as principles, and identifying specific strategies that follow from each principle) will give you an organizational framework for use in integrating and applying your knowledge.

Use the following steps to identify your own principles and strategies from the chapter and to relate them to the five main themes of the text (i.e., the "big ideas").

1. Review the TIPS from the text.

2. List some of the main concepts from the chapter. Use the work you did in prior sections of the study guide to help generate this list. Also look at the list of key terms from the chapter.

3. Select what you think are two or three of the most important concepts from your list.

4. For each concept you select, try to state it as a principle (use the TIPS format in the text and the example shown below as a guide for how to state principles).

5. Develop two or three specific teaching strategies that follow from each stated principle.

6. Relate your work to the five main themes from the text, identifying which theme(s) are relevant for each principle and strategy. This step will help you see how the information in each chapter contributes to improved teaching for each of these five critical aspects of instruction.

7. Think about and discuss with classmates how the principles and strategies you identify will help you improve your teaching for each theme you listed as relevant.

The five main themes from the text are:
ASSESSMENT, COMMUNICATION, LEARNING, MOTIVATION, AND TIME

Some example concepts, principles, and strategies for Chapter 1:

> teaching as an art, as a science
> reflective teachers
> scientist
> kinds of knowledge (subject matter, teaching, teaching subject matter)

Principle   *Reflectivity in teaching helps teachers learn from their experiences and improve their teaching. (ASSESSMENT, COMMUNICATION, LEARNING, MOTIVATION, TIME)*

Strategy   Analyze how well your classroom activities met your stated learning targets. If an activity's purpose or intended target isn't clear, revise it. (ASSESSMENT, LEARNING, TIME)

Strategy   Clarify the goals of your teaching. Develop written statements of your long- and short-term goals, then plan sample activities to address each goal. (ASSESSMENT, COMMUNICATION, LEARNING)

Strategy   Think about how your classroom feels, i.e., the emotional climate of your classroom. If you have a supportive climate conducive to learning, try to understand how you have achieved it. If your climate is not what you'd like, brainstorm ways to improve it. (LEARNING, MOTIVATION)

SUGGESTED READINGS

Beyond Effective Teaching. (1992). *Educational Leadership, 49* (7). (Whole issue.)

Brown, A., & Campione, J. (1990). Communities of learning and thinking: A context by any other name. *Contributions to Human Development, 21,* 108-126.

Gage, N. L. (1977). *The scientific basis of the art of teaching.* New York: Teachers College Press.

Goodlad, J. (1984). *A place called school.* New York: McGraw-Hill.

PRACTICE TEST 1

1. Greg noticed that his class was getting restless, and even though he had another 20 minutes of lecture left to present, he decided to take a break. This is an example of which type of knowledge that teachers must have?
   a. teaching knowledge
   b. subject matter knowledge
   c. teaching subject matter knowledge

2. Which of the following is the correct sequence of steps when teachers adopt the role of teacher as scientist?
   a. Formulate a series of steps to reach a goal, gather the data, identify the problem, interpret the data.
   b. Identify the problem, formulate a series of steps to reach a goal, gather the data, interpret the data.
   c. Identify the problem, gather the data, interpret the data, formulate a series of steps to reach a goal.
   d. Gather the data, identify the problem, formulate a series of steps to reach a goal, interpret the data.

3. Educational psychology involves the application of psychology to the study of
   a. development.
   b. learning.
   c. motivation.
   d. All of these things.

4. Which of the following is typical of the types of questions novice teachers ask about teaching?
   a. Will I be able to improve my level of subject matter knowledge during my first year of teaching?
   b. Will knowledge of specific teaching methods be helpful in the classroom?
   c. Will I be able to maintain order and use appropriate disciplinary techniques?
   d. When will I be ready to try more innovative teaching techniques?

5. Janine is a teacher who often spends time thinking about how her classes are going, trying to identify what is working and what isn't, and what could be done differently to make things go better. These behaviors indicate that Janine is a/an
   a. reflective teacher.
   b. novice teacher
   c. impulsive teacher.
   d. experienced teacher.

6. Which of the following has been indicated by research to be a characteristic of outstanding teachers?
   a. The ability to teach subjects they do not really know very well.
   b. The ability to use noncontingent praise effectively.
   c. The ability to relate information to students without encouraging them to relate it to their prior knowledge.
   d. The tendency to use only one style of instruction regardless of the content and students being taught.

7. Mark has an unusual approach to teaching history in which he often dresses as the "character of the day" to help students personalize the information. He loves teaching history, and it shows. Mark is a good example of the teacher as
   a. an experimenter.
   b. an artist.
   c. a disciplinarian.
   d. a novice.

8. Which of the following statements best illustrates a constructivist approach to teaching?
   a. Students' perspectives and prior beliefs do not influence what they learn from a lesson.
   b. It is better to avoid conflict and confusion when teaching a lesson because they indicate poor instructional management.
   c. It is better to give students all the relevant information they need to solve a problem before they attempt to solve it.
   d. Students will often show some initial confusion when attempting to solve problems, but this is an essential part of learning.

9. Constructivist teachers often do which of the following?
   a. Use a problem-based approach to teaching
   b. Use students' answers as an indication of current level of understanding
   c. Recognize that initial attempts to learn sometimes involve conflicts and confusion
   d. All of the above are characteristics of a constructivist approach to teaching.
   e. None of the above are characteristics of a constructivist approach to teaching.

10. According to developmental contextualism, the most important factor in learning and development is which of the following?
   a. The physical settings through which students move
   b. The social influences a student experiences
   c. The changing relationship between the students and their contexts.
   d. The stable personal characteristics that students develop.

11. Which of the following is most consistent with the concept of developmental contextualism?
   a. An interest in understanding the many different settings with which a student interacts.
   b. An emphasis on problem-based teaching strategies
   c. Lack of interest in students' home environments
   d. Lack of interest in students' peer groups and outside-school interests.

12. Mark's parents do not emphasize school achievement very much, placing more emphasis on social and athletic activities. Which of the following can be said about the effect that his parents' attitudes have on Mark?
   a. His parents' attitudes will likely have little influence on Mark's school achievement.
   b. His parents' attitudes will likely have an important and lasting effect on Mark's school achievement.
   c. Mark's school achievement is likely to be much more influenced by his friend's attitudes toward school than his parents' attitudes.
   d. Mark is likely to become more concerned with his school performance because his parents emphasize social and athletic activities rather than school performance.

13. Which of the following is one of the ways the text describes by which parents influence their children's school achievement?
   a. Not taking part in school functions and volunteer efforts does not affect a child's attitudes toward school.
   b. Maintaining a physical presence at a child's school makes little difference in the child's achievement.
   c. Intense involvement in homework activities by parents makes a big difference in the child's achievement.
   d. Talking about the importance of school activities communicates that school is important.

14. Teachers interested in improving their skills relevant for the learning theme of educational psychology should do which of the following?
    a. Understand that learning is often social in nature.
    b. Create a learning environment with smoothly functioning and clearly understood routines.
    c. Develop instruction that helps students see the personal relevance of the material being taught.
    d. All of the above will strengthen a teacher's skills relevant for the learning theme.
    e. None of the above are relevant for the learning theme.

PRACTICE TEST 2

1. When a teacher evaluates whether a student's speech has met the desired objectives of the assignment, the teacher is involved in
   a. problem identification.
   b. data interpretation.
   c. data gathering.
   d. formulating a logical series of steps to reach a goal.

2. The study of development, learning, motivation, instruction, assessment, and related issues that affect teaching and learning interactions is called
   a. psychology.
   b. individual differences.
   c. educational psychology.
   d. reflective teaching.

3. Effective teachers
   a. consistently use only one or two teaching techniques sot they don't confuse their students.
   b. react intuitively to problems, rather than having to spend time thinking about the causes of problems.
   c. are knowledgeable, enthusiastic, and supportive.
   d. keep themselves at a distance from their students so that high academic standards can be maintained.

4. Martin is a novice teacher who has lots of questions about teaching. According to the text, which of the following questions would Martin be MOST likely to ask?
   a. How can I know when students are ready to move on to new learning experiences?
   b. How will I know which teaching techniques are best for which particular students?
   c. Will all those theories of learning really be helpful to me when teaching?
   d. All of the above are common questions of novice teachers.
   e. None of the above are common questions of novice teachers.

5. Reflective teachers are teachers who
   a. think carefully before answering student questions during class.
   b. find it difficult to learn from experience and consider implications for future situations.
   c. use time wisely during lessons.
   d. periodically analyze their own strengths and weaknesses and try to learn from their experiences.

6. Which of the following is true regarding lesson clarity?
   a. Lesson clarity is a characteristic that both better and worse teachers typically show.
   b. Lesson clarity refers to how much variety a teacher shows in the instructional techniques used to teach lessons.
   c. Lesson clarity results in students being able to understand the lesson better.
   d. Lesson clarity means that teachers emphasize the positive in students and do not take misbehaviors personally.

7. Performing as an "artist" in the classroom means that the teacher
   a. carefully follows the four steps of experimentation when making changes in the classroom.
   b. restrains his/her enthusiasm for content to help maintain discipline.
   c. seeks to keep his/her personality out of classroom interactions to avoid unintentional bias.
   d. develops and continually modifies his/her own personal teaching style.

8. A teacher says, "Teaching basically means simply telling students information, then seeing how well they remember it on a test." This teacher clearly
   a. is a constructivist in his/her educational philosophy.
   b. is not a constructivist in his/her educational philosophy.
   c. believes that students interpret information on the basis of their prior knowledge.
   d. believes that students build their own personal knowledge representations.

9. Which of the following statements best illustrates a constructivist philosophy of teaching and learning?
   a. Students interpret information on the basis of their prior knowledge and build their own personal representations of information.
   b. If a lesson is well-structured and well-organized, all students will learn the same information.
   c. Students do not attempt to understand new information in relation to what they already know.
   d. Students are passive rather than active in their attempts to understand new information.

10. Developmental contextualism refers to understanding development by
    a. considering the many levels and types of interactions an individual experiences.
    b. emphasizing and carefully analyzing only the social influences an individual experiences.
    c. focusing mostly on students' personal characteristics and how they affect achievement.
    d. separating enduring personal characteristics from the contexts an individual interacts with.

11. As a teacher, Tara does not feel that she needs to know much about the backgrounds and cultures of her students. She believes that all students are equally capable, given good instruction. Which of the following could be said about Tara?
    a. Tara is likely to provide relevant, meaningful instruction to all her students.
    b. Tara is a developmental contextualist.
    c. Tara is not a developmental contextualist.
    d. Tara is ensuring that all her students have equal opportunities to succeed by removing cultural biases and preferences from her teaching.

12. Which of the following is the best summary of the Steinberg et al (1996) study on high school students' views of what affects school performance?
    a. Most students do not believe that doing well in school has positive consequences.
    b. Students differed in whether they believed that doing well in school has positive consequences.
    c. Students differed in whether they believed that doing poorly in school has negative consequences.
    d. Most students believed that doing poorly in school has negative consequences.

13. Which of the following is true regarding the effect of out-of-school influences on children's school achievement?
    a. Parents have a strong effect on a child's school achievement.
    b. The effect that parents have on student attitudes toward school and learning is long-lasting.
    c. Peers and one's social context both influence a child's school achievement.
    d. All of the above are true.

14. A teacher is careful to clearly discuss classroom rules and procedures, listens carefully when students are discussing academic and social problems, and plans and delivers her instructions clearly. Which of the five themes is this teacher illustrating?
    a. Communication
    b. Motivation
    c. Time
    d. Assessment

ANSWER KEY

Practice Test 1

1.   ANSWER: C, Applied; OBJECTIVE: 3; PAGE: 12
2.   ANSWER: B, Factual; OBJECTIVE: 4; PAGE: 14
3.   ANSWER: D, Factual; OBJECTIVE: 1; PAGE: 2
4.   ANSWER: C, Factual; OBJECTIVE: 1; PAGE: 4-5
5.   ANSWER: A, Applied; OBJECTIVE: 2; PAGE: 5
6.   ANSWER: B, Factual; OBJECTIVE: 3; PAGE: 6-7
7.   ANSWER: B, Applied; OBJECTIVE: 4; PAGE: 14
8.   ANSWER: D, Conceptual; OBJECTIVE: 5; PAGE: 15
9.   ANSWER: D, Factual; OBJECTIVE: 5; PAGE: 16
10. ANSWER: C, Factual; OBJECTIVE: 6; PAGE: 16
11. ANSWER: A, Conceptual; OBJECTIVE: 6; PAGE: 16
12. ANSWER: B, Applied; OBJECTIVE: 7;   PAGE: 18
13. ANSWER: D, Factual; OBJECTIVE: 7;   PAGE: 18
14. ANSWER: D, Factual; OBJECTIVE: 8;   PAGE: 20

Practice Test 2

1.   ANSWER: B, Applied; OBJECTIVE: 4; PAGE: 14
2.   ANSWER: C, Factual; OBJECTIVE: 1; PAGE: 2
3.   ANSWER: C, Factual; OBJECTIVE: 3; PAGE: 6-12
4.   ANSWER: D, Applied; OBJECTIVE: 1; PAGE: 4-5
5.   ANSWER: D, Factual; OBJECTIVE: 2; PAGE: 5
6.   ANSWER: C, Factual; OBJECTIVE: 3; PAGE: 6
7.   ANSWER: D, Factual; OBJECTIVE: 4; PAGE: 14
8.   ANSWER: B, Applied; OBJECTIVE: 5; PAGE: 15
9.   ANSWER: A, Conceptual; OBJECTIVE: 5; PAGE: 15
10. ANSWER: A, Factual; OBJECTIVE: 6; PAGE: 16
11. ANSWER: C, Applied; OBJECTIVE: 6; PAGE: 16
12. ANSWER: C, Factual; OBJECTIVE: 7; PAGE: 18
13. ANSWER: D, Factual; OBJECTIVE: 7; PAGE: 18
14. ANSWER: A, Applied; OBJECTIVE: 8; PAGE: 20

Chapter 2 COGNITIVE AND LANGUAGE DEVELOPMENT

LEARNING OBJECTIVES

After completing this chapter, you should be able to:

1. Explain how biopsychosocial elements influence students' learning and achievement.

2. Explain the basics of Piaget's theory.

3. Use Piaget's ideas to describe how students pass through his four cognitive stages.

4. State and evaluate criticisms of Piaget's theory of cognitive development.

5. Summarize the key ideas in Vygotsky's theory.

6. Analyze Vygotsky's belief that culture powerfully shapes cognitive development.

7. Identify the major points on which Piaget and Vygotsky disagree.

8. Suggest techniques using Piaget's and Vygotsky's ideas that could improve classroom instruction.

9. Analyze the path of language development.

10. Compare and contrast Piaget's and Vygotsky's views of language development.

CHAPTER HIGHLIGHTS

The Meaning of Development

- The Biopsychosocial model helps to illustrate the many forces influencing students' development.
- Knowledge of cognitive development will help you with instructional decisions.

Piaget and Cognitive Development

- Piaget's basic ideas help teachers to decide on developmentally appropriate materials and instructions.
- Piaget's theory helps us understand that "children think differently from adults."
- His stages of cognitive development help us to understand what we can expect cognitively from pupils of different ages.
- Piaget's belief that students must interact with the environment for learning to occur has classroom implications.

Vygotsky and Cognitive Development

- Vygotsky's interpretation of development is at the heart of his theory.
- His use of inner speech and social interactions help to explain his belief in the relationship between thought and language.
- Vygotsky's concept of a zone of proximal development offers insight into the relationship among learning, development, and social processes.

Language Development

- Like other cognitive processes, language development follows a predictable sequence in children of all cultures.
- Language acquisition offers definite clues to a pupil's developmental progress, which can help you in working with your pupils.

Language Development in Infancy

- Infants immediately begin to distinguish the sounds of their language and react to the context of their language.

Language Development in Early Childhood

- Vocabulary development proceeds at a rapid rate.
- Whole language is a relatively modern method of teaching language skills.

Language Development in Middle Childhood

- Students become quite skillful in their use of language in settings such as the classroom.

DETAILED CHAPTER OUTLINE

I. The meaning of development
   A. The biopsychosocial model
      1. If you think of students' development as the product of the interaction of biological, psychological, and social forces, you can better understand and appreciate the complexity of development, and it provides an opportunity to explore cross-cultural and sociocultural issues.
      2. The biopsychosocial model illustrates the constant interaction of heredity and environment that explains the complexity of development.
      3. Questions that can guide your thinking and help you form classroom applications are:
         a. In what way does a specific age group see the world differently from you?
         b. How can you recognize signs of developmental growth in students and use these signs to determine their readiness to acquire new skills?
         c. Do the theorists provide any insights into the relationship between the abilities of students and their classroom performance?
      4. Case Notes: Marsha Warren's class

II. Piaget and cognitive development
    A. Key concepts in Piaget's theory
        1. Functional invariants
            a. Piaget identified two psychological mechanisms, adaptation and organization, that are responsible for the development of our cognitive structures. These mechanisms are called functional invariants because we use them constantly throughout our lives.
            b. Adaptation consists of assimilation and accommodation.
                (1) Assimilation involves mentally taking in ideas and shaping them to fit your cognitive structures.
                (2) Accommodation is the change in your cognitive structures that will produce corresponding behavioral changes.
                (3) Equilibration is the process of trying to "fit" new material into existing cognitive structures, trying to balance between assimilation and accommodation.
            c. Organization refers to the idea that cognitive structures are formed. These organizational structures enable us to engage in ever-more-complex thinking.
            d. Case Notes: Marsha Warren's class
            e. Schemes
                (1) Schemes are organized patterns of thought and action. They are the cognitive structures and behaviors that help us adapt to our environment. They may be best thought of as the inner representation of our activities and experiences.
                (2) A scheme is named by its activity.
                (3) Stimuli come from the environment and are filtered through the functional invariants, which use the stimuli to form new structures or change existing structures. Your content or behavior now changes because of the changes in your cognitive structures.
                (4) Cognitive structures change with age, so subject matter must be presented in a form that matches the cognitive structure of your pupils.

III. Piaget's four stages of cognitive development
    A. Piaget's theory is stage invariant, age variant.
    B. Four interacting influences aid passage through the stages.
        1. Maturation means physical development, especially that of the muscular and nervous systems.
        2. Experience—Piaget felt there are two types of experience. One involves acting on objects to learn about them, while the second refers to what we learn from using objects.
        3. Social interactions mean that children acquire knowledge from others in their culture.
        4. Equilibration refers to a process of self-regulation in which there is constant interplay between assimilation and accommodation.
    C. The sensorimotor period
        1. Extends from birth to about 2 years.
        2. Cognitive development of infants and toddlers comes mainly through their use of their bodies and senses as they explore the environment.
        3. Features of the sensorimotor period
            a. Egocentrism—the child's universe is initially egocentric, entirely centered on self.
            b. An object or person removed from an infant's visual field ceases to exist because the child has not yet acquired object permanence.
            c. Children learn about space and the time it takes to move from object to object.
            d. Children begin to distinguish their own actions as causes and to discover events that have their causes elsewhere.
            e. Infants pass through six subdivisions of the sensorimotor period: reflexive actions, primary circular reactions, secondary circular reactions, coordinating secondary schemata, tertiary circular reactions, and representation.

4. Educational implications
    a. Provide multiple objects of various sizes, shapes, and colors for them to use.
    b. If infants are to develop cognitively as fully as their potential permits, they must actively engage environmental objects.
    c. TIPS on Learning: The sensorimotor period
D. The preoperational period
    1. Extends from 2 years to about 6 or 7 years.
    2. Operations are actions that we perform mentally in order to gain knowledge.
    3. Preoperational refers to a child who has begun to use symbols but is not yet capable of mentally manipulating them.
    4. Features of the preoperational period
        a. Realism: slowly distinguishing and accepting a real world.
        b. Animism: considering a large number of objects that adults consider inert to be alive and conscious.
        c. Artificialism: assuming that everything is the product of human creation.
        d. Transductive reasoning: reasoning that is neither deductive nor inductive, but from particular to particular.
    5. Limitations of the preoperational period
        a. Centering, or concentrating on only part of an object or activity and ignoring the relationships among the various parts.
        b. Egocentrism.
        c. Irreversibility, or the inability to reverse one's thinking.
    6. Educational implications
        a. Deferred imitation
        b. Symbolic play
        c. Drawing
        d. Mental images
        e. Language
    7. TIPS on Learning: The preoperational period
E. The concrete operational period
    1. Extends from 7 to 11 years of age.
    2. Children can perform mental operations, but only on concrete (tangible) objects or events and not on verbal statements.
    3. Features of concrete operational thought
        a. Conservation, or the realization that the essence of something remains constant although surface features may change. Three arguments children use to conserve are the arguments of identity, reversibility, and compensation.
        b. Seriation, or the ability to arrange objects by increasing or decreasing size.
        c. Classification, or the ability to group objects with some similarities within a larger category.
        d. Number concept, or the ability to understand the "oneness of one."
    4. Educational implications
        a. Elementary school children up to the age of 10 or 11 are capable of representational thought, but only with concrete substances. Consequently, they cannot comprehend abstractions fully.
    5. TIPS on Assessment: The concrete operational period
    6. Case Notes: Marsha Warren's class
F. The formal operational period
    1. Begins at about 11 or 12 years.
    2. The period's great achievement is a release from the restrictions of the tangible and concrete, though learning to use formal operational thought takes time and practice.
    3. Features of adolescent thought include adolescent egocentric thinking, in which adolescents assume that everyone else thinks as they do and shares their concerns. Adolescents create the imaginary audience, asking "Why is everyone looking at me?"

4. Features of formal operational thought
   a. The adolescent's ability to separate the real from the possible.
   b. The adolescent's thinking is propositional, which means using concrete data as well as statements or propositions that contain the concrete data.
   c. The adolescent attacks a problem by gathering as much information as possible and then making all the possible combinations of the variables that he or she can.
5. Educational implications
   a. Teachers should be careful not to exaggerate adolescents' abilities. Provide concrete examples and discuss how students sequence material.
   b. Activities should challenge a student's thinking but not be so difficult as to frustrate and cause failure.
   c. Try first to have the student understand the facts and the reasons for them, and then guide students to draw implications from the data.
   d. Keep in mind that many adolescents and adults never reach the stage of formal operations.
6. TIPS on Learning: The formal operational period

G. Piaget and language development
   1. Piaget believed that language emerges not from a biological timetable, but rather from existing cognitive structures and in accordance with a child's needs.
   2. The language function differs at each of the four cognitive levels.
   3. The first two years are a preparation for the appearance and growth of language during the preoperational years.
   4. Piaget identified two major speech categories of the preoperational child:
      a. Egocentric speech is when children do not care to whom they speak, or whether anyone is listening to them. There are three types: repetition, monologue, and collective monologue.
   5. The early childhood years see the slow and steady disappearance of egocentrism, except in verbal thought. Usage and complexity of language increase dramatically.
   6. Case Notes: Marsha Warren's class

H. Criticisms of Piaget
   1. Acquisition of cognitive structures may be more gradual than Piaget believed.
   2. By changing the nature of the task, by allowing children to practice, and by using material familiar to children, researchers have found that children can accomplish specific tasks at earlier ages than Piaget believed.
   3. Gelman and Baillargeon (1983) questioned the idea of broad stages of development, though they supported the notion of cognitive structures that assimilate and accommodate the environment.
   4. Piaget contributed a deeper understanding of children's cognitive development and made us more alert to the need for greater comprehension of the processes children use in thinking.

I. For the classroom
   1. Assess the level of a student's cognitive development. By observing your students closely, you can link behavior to cognitive level and utilize appropriate subject matter.
   2. Piaget's ideas on cognitive development have been used to develop programs in other fields, such as health and AIDS prevention.
      a. To be most effective, such programs should be developmentally based because children understand themselves and their world according to their level of cognitive development.
      b. Children seem to follow Piaget's sequence of cognitive development in understanding AIDS, moving from a very egocentric understanding at younger ages, to greater differentiation of causes, to the possibility of many interacting elements at older ages.
   3. Piaget always insisted that his theory stressed the interaction between the individual and the environment.
   4. Carefully consider how much direction and guidance each pupil needs.
   5. Be careful concerning the materials that you use.
   6. Use instructional strategies appropriate to your students' ethnic and racial backgrounds.

J. Current Issues and Perspectives: Should Piaget's theory of cognitive development drive public school curricula?

IV. Vygotsky and cognitive development
    A. Basic themes in Vygotsky's theory
        1. Vygotsky believed that children's behaviors emerge from the intertwining of two paths of cognitive development: elementary processes that are basically biological, and higher psychological processes that are sociocultural.
        2. Vygotsky's concept of development
            a. Changes are best viewed as a series of transformations brought about by developmental processes. We focus too often on the products of development rather than the processes that caused them.
        3. The social origin of mind
            a. To understand cognitive development, we must examine the social and cultural processes shaping children.
            b. Any function in a child's cultural development appears twice, on two separate planes: first, in an interpsychological category, and second, within the child as an intrapsychological category.
            c. Internalization is the process that transforms an external activity to an internal one. This transformation is the result of a long series of developmental events.
        4. Vygotsky believed that speech is one of the most powerful tools humans use to progress developmentally.
    B. Vygotsky and language development
        1. Speech, especially inner speech, plays a critical role.
        2. Vygotsky believed there are four stages in language development:
            a. Preintellectual speech, the biological sources that gradually develop into more sophisticated forms of speech and behavior (e.g., crying, cooing, babbling, bodily movements).
            b. Naive psychology, in which children explore the concrete objects in their world. They begin to label objects and acquire the syntax of their speech.
            c. Egocentric speech, in which they carry on lively conversations, whether or not anyone is present or listening to them. This is speech on its way inward, but still mostly overt. The more complex the task, the greater the amount of egocentric speech.
            d. Inner speech. Speech turns inward and serves an important function in guiding and planning behavior.
    C. The zone of proximal development
        1. The ZPD is the distance between a child's actual developmental level, as determined by independent problem solving, and the higher level of potential development, as determined by problem solving under adult guidance or in collaboration with more capable peers.
        2. Scaffolding
            a. This is a way of helping students move from initial difficulties with a topic to a point where they perform the task independently. Support is needed in the early stages, but is gradually removed.
            b. Instruction is only effective when it proceeds ahead of development. Teaching awakens those functions that are already maturing and that are in the zone of proximal development.
        3. Literary lunches
            a. This is an example of the value of the zone of proximal development.
            b. Teachers invite several senior citizens to read the same book as middle school students, then they meet for lunch and to discuss the book.
            c. The seniors help the students grasp the more subtle themes in the story, while the students help the seniors gain knowledge and confidence about young people.
        4. Case Notes: Marsha Warren's class

V. Language development
    A. Language accomplishments
        1. All children manifest similar patterns of speech development at about the same age, regardless of the language they learn or where they live. Almost no direct instruction seems to be needed.
        2. Most children have completed the greater part of the process of language acquisition by the age of 4 or 5.
        3. Innate ability isn't enough to explain language acquisition, but requires interactions with other language users to flourish.
    B. The language components
        1. The phoneme is the smallest language unit, while the smallest unit of language to have meaning is the morpheme.
        2. Morphemes are arranged in the grammar or syntax of a language. The task of any syntax is to arrange morphemes in meaningful sentences.
        3. Semantics refers to the relationship between ideas and words. Fast mapping is a technique that enables children to use context for a word's meaning, helping them to continue rapid vocabulary development.
        4. Pragmatics refers to the fact that children learn how to use their language to communicate.
        5. All children, regardless of their native tongue, manifest similar patterns of language development.

VI. Language development in infancy
    A. Sequence of infant language development
        1. Infants tune into the speech they hear and immediately begin to discriminate distinctive features, and seem to be sensitive to the context of the language they hear.
        2. The origins of language appear immediately after birth in infants' gazes and vocal exchanges with those around them.
        3. Motherese is a simplified form of speech with short sentences, a high-pitched tone, and frequent pauses, which adults use with babies. It probably indicates a desire to hold babies' attention and attempt to further understanding.
        4. Newborns vocalize by crying and fussing. Cooing appears at 6 to 8 weeks.
        5. At about 4 months, children begin to babble, that is, to make sounds that approximate speech.
        6. At about 1 year, the first words appear and holophrastic speech appears.
        7. Between the age of about 1 year and 18 months, children begin to use these single words to convey multiple meanings.
        8. When the two-word stage appears, at about 18 months, youngsters initially struggle to devise some means of indicating tense and number, and they typically experience difficulty with grammatical correctness.
        9. At about 2 years of age, children's vocabularies expand rapidly, and simple sentences, or telegraphic speech, appear.
        10. Vocabulary constantly expands.

VII. Language development in early childhood
    A. Once language appears, it is difficult to retard its progress. Usually only some traumatic event or dramatically deprived environmental conditions will hinder development.
    B. To encourage language development, teachers can give students something real to talk about and then listen carefully to their stories, and encourage as much conversation as possible.
    C. Metalinguistic awareness refers to children's realization that they are language users and understand what this means for interacting with their environments.

D. Speech irregularities
   1. Youngsters who consistently miss the milestones should receive a more detailed examination—but don't confuse a serious language problem with temporary setbacks or speech irregularities that are a normal part of development.
   2. Overextensions, or using one label for several objects, make up children's beginning words.
   3. Overregularities, or applying recently learned grammatical rules in situations where they do not apply, occur when youngsters begin to use two- and three-word sentences and struggle to convey more precise meanings by mastering the grammatical rules of their language.
E. The whole language movement
   1. Refers to a technique by which all language processes are studied in a more natural context, as a whole.
   2. The basic premise is that children learn their language by actually using it, and this should be the acquisition model for reading and writing.
   3. Proponents believe it is consistent with Piaget's theory because the student's use of language materials matches his or her level of cognitive development, and with Vygotsky's theory because of the role of the context. Others believe it builds on earlier educational beliefs of integrated curriculum and individualized reading.
   4. The whole language concept works by having students experience the literature, expand the literature concepts, respond to the literature by completing a story form, and extend their reading experiences.
   5. Tchudi summarized the main features of whole language:
      a. the level of students' language development is the starting point;
      b. language skills develop naturally;
      c. instruction uses the natural connection between literature and language;
      d. integration of all components of language arts is critical;
      e. it builds on a student's personal experiences; and
      f. language is viewed as a whole structure, not discrete units.
   6. Critics believe children can miss many necessary fundamentals because of the lack of a structured curriculum, especially instruction in phonics.

VIII. Language development in middle childhood
   A. Changes in language usage
      1. Students begin to use language for their own purposes
      2. Language becomes less literal
         a. Metalinguistic awareness refers to the capacity to think about and talk about language.
      3. Students are able to communicate with others more effectively. They understand relationships and can express these relationships accurately.
   B. For children between 6 and 10 years old, the relationship of language development to reading is crucial.
   C. TIPS on Learning: Language in the classroom
   D. Case Notes: Marsha Warren's class

IX. Case reflections

X. Chapter highlights

XI. "What do you think?" questions

XII. Key terms

KEY TERMS

accommodation
adaptation
animism
artificialism
assimilation
biopsychosocial
causality
centering
classification
conservation
constructivism
content
egocentric speech
egocentrism
equilibration
fast mapping
functional invariants
inner speech
internalization
irreversibility
metalinguistic awareness
morpheme
motherese

naive psychology
number concept
object permanence
operations
organization
phonemes
phonology
pragmatics
preintellectual speech
psycholinguistics
realism
reversibility
scaffolding
schemes
semantics
seriation
structure
syntax
telegraphic speech
transductive reasoning
whole language
zone of proximal development

GUIDED REVIEW

1.   Development is a continuous series of _____ changes involving complex interactions of _____, _____, and _____ forces.

biopsychosocial, biological, psychological, social

2.   The biopsychosocial model provides a _____ to help you understand and remember the need for _____ materials and methods. This model emphasizes _____ features.

tool, developmentally appropriate, sociocultural

3.   Jean Piaget was born in Switzerland in 1896. His training in _____ had a major impact on his theory. He was a self-described _____, interested in age-related changes in the process of acquiring knowledge and the processes that lead to _____ answers.

biology, genetic epistemologist, incorrect

4.   Piaget believed that we inherit a method of intellectual functioning that enables us to respond to our environment by forming _____. Two psychological mechanisms responsible for the development of our cognitive structures are _____ and _____. Because we use these two mechanisms constantly throughout our lives, Piaget named them _____.

cognitive structures, adaptation, organization, functional invariants

5.   Adaptation to the environment occurs in two ways: _____ and _____. The adaptive process is the heart of Piaget's explanation of learning. Students begin by trying to "fit" new material into existing cognitive structures by a process called _____.

assimilation, accommodation, equilibration

6.   Assimilation involves mentally taking in ideas and shaping them to _____.

fit one's cognitive structures

7.   Accommodation is the _____ in an individual's cognitive structures that produce corresponding _____ changes.

change, behavioral

8.   Organization refers to the idea that cognitive _____ are formed that enable us to engage in more _____ thinking.

structures, complex

9.   Organization and adaptation are _____. As Piaget stated, they are two complementary processes of a _____.

inseparable, single mechanism

10.   Organized patterns of thought and action are called _____. They help us adapt to our environment and may be thought of as the _____ of our activities and experiences.

schemes, inner representation

11.   Cognitive structures change with _____; therefore, subject matter must be presented in a form that matches the _____ of pupils.

age, cognitive structure

12.   For Piaget, cognitive development means passage through four periods: _____, _____, _____, and _____. The age at which children reach the four stages varies, but the sequence of the stages never varies.

sensorimotor, preoperational, concrete operational, formal operational

13. Four interacting influences aid passage through the stages. _____ means physical development, especially that of the muscular and nervous systems. Piaget felt there are two types of _____: _____ to learn about them and what we _____ objects. _____ mean that children acquire knowledge from others in their culture. _____ refers to a process of self-regulation in which there is constant interplay between assimilation and accommodation.

Maturation, experience, acting on objects, learn from using, Social interactions, Equilibration

14. The sensorimotor period extends from _____ to about _____. The cognitive development of infants and toddlers comes mainly through their use of their _____ and their _____ as they explore their environment.

birth, 2 years, bodies, senses

15. One feature of this period includes _____, meaning that the child's universe is entirely centered on self. Another feature of this period is that an object or person removed from an infant's field of vision ceases to exist; this refers to the concept of _____. Gradually, as children begin to crawl and walk, they realize that there is distance between the objects that they are using to steady themselves. This helps them develop concepts of _____ and _____. As children use their growing sensorimotor intelligence, they begin to find order in the universe and establish _____.

egocentrism, object permanence, space, time, causality

16. Infants pass through _____ subdivisions of the sensorimotor period. As they do, they progress from reliance on _____ to a basic understanding of the world around them and the beginning of the ability to _____ the world through language.

six, reflex actions, represent

17. If infants are to develop cognitively as fully as their potential permits, they must _____ environmental objects. Provide _____ objects of various sizes, shapes, and colors for them to use.

actively engage, multiple

18. Actions that we perform mentally in order to gain knowledge are called _____. Piaget refers to a child who has begun to use symbols but is not yet capable of mentally manipulating them as _____.

operations, preoperational

19. For Piaget, knowledge is not just a _____; it requires the ability to modify the object.

mental image

20.   During the preoperational period, children exhibit _____, the ability to distinguish and accept the real world. _____ is the tendency to consider a large number of objects that adults consider inert to be alive and conscious. _____ is the assumption that everything is the product of human creation. Another characteristic is _____, which is reasoning that is neither deductive nor inductive; rather, it moves from particular to particular. Several important limitations exist during the preoperational period. _____ is concentrating on only part of an object or activity. _____ is a kind of thinking focused only on the self. The inability to reverse one's thinking is called _____.

realism, Animism, Artificialism, transductive reasoning, Centering, Egocentrism, irreversibility

21.   Kindergarten- and first-grade-level teachers should encourage the _____ of materials. Activities that help preoperational children improve their representational skills include deferred _____, in which children recreate some event or activity they previously witnessed; _____ play, or pretending; drawing, in which children project their _____; _____ images, in which they represent objects and events; and _____, which becomes a vehicle for thought.

manipulation, imitation, symbolic, mental representations, mental, language

22.   The concrete operational period extends from _____ to _____ years. Children accomplish true _____; they can _____ their thinking and group objects into _____.

7, 12, mental operations, reverse, classes

23.   There are still limitations at the concrete operational stage, however. Children can perform mental operations only on _____ objects or events, and not on verbal statements.

concrete

24.   The realization that the essence of something remains constant although surface features may change is called _____. Piaget believed that youngsters use three arguments to conserve. _____ means that children realize that since nothing has been removed or added, it is still the same. _____ indicates an understanding that one just replaces the water and it is the same as before. _____ means that changes in one aspect are compensated for by changes in another.

conservation, Identity, Reversibility, Compensation

25.   The ability to arrange objects by increasing or decreasing size is called _____.

seriation

26.   The ability to group objects with some similarities within a larger category is called _____.

classification

27.	After children acquire the concepts of seriation and classification, they are able to understand the "oneness of one," which is called _____.

number concept

28.	Children during the concrete operational period have become _____ and more _____ in their thinking; their _____ improves, and memory becomes more _____ as they develop new strategies.

logical, abstract, attention, efficient

29.	Up to age 10 or 11, children are capable of _____ thought, but only with the _____. They cannot be expected to comprehend fully any abstract subtleties.

representational, concrete

30.	The _____ period, during which the beginning of logical, abstract thinking appears, begins at about 11 or 12 years. The greatest achievement is a release from the restrictions of the _____.

formal operational, concrete

31.	One feature of adolescent thought is adolescent _____ thinking, in which adolescents assume that everyone else thinks as they do and shares their concerns. Adolescents create the _____, asking "Why is everyone looking at me?"

egocentric, imaginary audience

32.	A feature of formal operational thinking is the adolescent's ability to separate the _____ from the _____; this distinguishes the concrete operational from the formal operational child.

real, possible

33.	The adolescent's thinking is _____; this means that the adolescent uses not only concrete data but also statements or propositions that contain the concrete data.

propositional

34.	The adolescent attacks a problem by gathering as much information as possible and then making all the possible combinations of the variables that he or she can. Piaget often refers to this process as _____.

hypothetico-deductive thinking

35. Teachers should be careful to not _____ students' abilities. Provide many _____ examples before asking students to formulate general principles, and _____ students' thinking without _____ them and causing failure. The ability to _____ propositions and speculate about the future can't be forced, but it can be encouraged by having students _____ facts and reasons first, then _____ them to draw implications from data.

exaggerate, concrete, challenge, frustrating, combine, understand, guiding

36. Piaget believed that language emerges from _____ and in accordance with the child's needs. The language function _____ at each of the four levels of cognitive development.

existing cognitive structures, differs

37. Piaget believed that the first two years were a _____ for the appearance and growth of language during the preoperational years.

preparation

38. Piaget identified two major speech categories of the preoperational child. Children engage in _____ when they do not care to whom they speak or whether anyone is listening to them. This type of speech has three types: Children engage in _____ for the sheer pleasure of talking, _____ when they talk to themselves as if thinking aloud, and in the _____ when other children are present but not listening to the child who is speaking. The other major speech category is _____ speech.

egocentric speech, repetition, monologue, collective monologue, socialized

39. Critics of Piaget's theory note that the acquisition of cognitive structures is _____ rather than abrupt, and that by modifying the task and/or materials, children can accomplish specific tasks at _____ than Piaget believed.

gradual, earlier ages

40. Piaget's two major contributions are a _____ of children's cognitive development and a greater comprehension of _____ children think, and not just what they think.

deeper understanding, how

41. Children seem to follow Piaget's sequence of cognitive development in understanding AIDS, moving from a very _____ understanding at younger ages, to greater _____ of causes, to the possibility of many _____ elements at older ages.

egocentric, differentiation, interacting

42. During Piaget's first two stages, children should constantly interact _____ with their environments. During the concrete operational period, students should use as many _____ as possible. During formal operations, adolescents should encounter _____ problems, master _____, and _____ their solutions.

physically, tangible objects, verbal, learning strategies, test

43. Piaget always insisted that his theory stressed the _____ between the individual and the environment. When applying Piaget's theory to teaching, you should carefully consider how much _____ each pupil needs, be careful concerning the _____ that you use, and use instructional strategies _____ to your students' ethnic and racial backgrounds.

interaction, direction and guidance, materials, appropriate

44. Lev Vygotsky was born in Russia in 1896. He believed that children's behaviors emerge from the intertwining of two paths of cognitive development: _____ processes that are basically _____, and _____ processes that are _____ .

elementary, biological, higher psychological, sociocultural

45. Vygotsky's concept of development was that elementary biological processes are _____ into higher psychological functioning by development processes. He thought we too often focus on the _____ of development rather than the _____ that caused them.

qualitatively transformed, products, processes

46. Vygotsky believed that to understand cognitive development, we must examine the _____ processes shaping children. Every function in a child's cultural development appears twice, on two separate planes: first, in an _____ category, and second, within the child as an _____ category. _____ is the process that transforms an external activity to an internal one. This transformation is the result of a long series of developmental events.

social and cultural, interpsychological, intrapsychological, Internalization

47. Vygotsky believed that _____ is one of the most powerful tools humans use to progress developmentally.

speech

48. Vygotsky believed there are four stages in language development: (a) _____ speech refers to the biological sources that gradually develop into more sophisticated forms of speech and behavior; (b) _____ , in which children explore the concrete objects in their world and begin to label objects and acquire the syntax of their speech; (c) _____ , in which they carry on lively conversations whether or not anyone is present or listening to them; and (d) _____ , in which speech turns inward and serves an important function in guiding and planning behavior.

Preintellectual, naive psychology, egocentric speech, inner speech

49. The _____ is the distance between a child's actual developmental level, as determined by _____ problem solving, and the higher level of potential development as determined by problem solving under adult _____ or in _____ with more capable peers.

zone of proximal development, independent, guidance, collaboration

50. _____ is a way of helping students move from initial difficulties with a topic to a point where they perform the task independently. Support is needed in the early stages, but is _____.

Scaffolding, gradually removed

51. Instruction is only effective when it _____ development. Teaching awakens those functions that are _____ and that are in the zone of proximal development.

proceeds ahead of, already maturing

52. _____ are an example of the zone of proximal development. Teachers invite senior citizens to read the same book as middle school students, then they meet for lunch and to discuss the book.

Literary lunches

53. All children show _____ patterns of speech development at about the same age, regardless of the language they learn or where they live. Almost no _____ seems to be needed. Most children have completed the greater part of the process of language acquisition by the age of _____ . Innate ability isn't enough to explain language acquisition, but requires _____ with other language users to flourish.

similar, direct instruction, 4 or 5, interactions

54. When linguists examine a language, they identify four major components: sound, or _____; meaning, or _____; grammar, or _____; and use, or _____.

phonology, semantics, syntax, pragmatics

55. _____ are the smallest language unit, while the smallest unit of language to have meaning is the _____.

Phonemes, morpheme

56. Morphemes are arranged in the grammar or _____ of a language. Grammar seems to be designed to convert ideas into word combinations. The relationship between ideas and words is the source of meaning, or _____.

syntax, semantics

57. _____ is a technique that enables children to use context for a word's meaning, helping them to continue rapid _____ development.

Fast mapping, vocabulary

58. Children also must learn how to use their language, which requires the development of _____ skills.

pragmatic

59. During the first year, adults speak to their children using _____ , a simplified form of speech that probably indicates a desire to hold the baby's _____ and attempt further understanding.

motherese, attention

60. The language sequence is as follows: At about 4 months, children begin to _____, that is, to make sounds that approximate speech. Late in this period, children use consistent sound patterns to refer to objects and events. These sound patterns are called _____, and seem to indicate that children have discovered that meaning is associated with sound.

babble, vocables

61. At about 1 year, the first words appear. Often called _____ speech, these first words are difficult to analyze. They are usually nouns, adjectives, or self-invented words, and they may even represent multiple meanings. Between 1 year and 18 months, children begin to use these single words to convey _____ meanings.

holophrastic, multiple

62. When the two-word stage appears, at about ____ months, youngsters initially struggle to devise some means of indicating tense and number, and they typically experience difficulty with grammatical correctness.

18

63. At about _____ of age, children's vocabularies expand rapidly, and simple sentences appear. _____ speech contains considerably more meaning than the sum of its words. For example, "milk gone" means "my milk is all gone."

2 years, Telegraphic

64. When speech emerges, certain irregularities appear that are quite normal and to be expected. _____ mark children's beginning words. A child who has learned the name of the family pet may for a while use that label for a cat, horse, donkey, cow, or any other animal with a head, tail, body, and four legs.

Overextensions

65. _____ occur when youngsters begin to use two- and three-word sentences; they struggle to convey more precise meanings by mastering the grammatical rules of their language.

Overregularities

66. Whole language is a technique in which all language processes (speaking, listening, reading, and writing—including spelling and handwriting) are studied in a more _____. The basic premise is that infants learn their language by _____ it.

natural context, using

67. Using the whole language concept, students read a story that illustrates a selected theme. This is known as _____. Next, the teacher _____ the concepts; then students may _____ to the literature by completing a story form. Finally, students _____ their reading experiences.

experiencing the literature, expands, respond, extend

68. Proponents of the whole language approach believe it is consistent with Piaget's theory because the language materials _____ the level of cognitive development, and with Vygotsky's theory because of the role of the _____. Others believe it helps _____ the curriculum and individualize reading. Critics believe children can miss many necessary fundamentals because of the lack of a structured curriculum, especially instruction in _____.

match, context, integrate, phonics

69. Three types of change in language usage occur during middle childhood. Students begin to use language for their _____, language becomes less literal because of changes in _____, and students are able to _____ with others more effectively because they are understand relationships and can express these relationships accurately.

own purposes, metalinguistic awareness, communicate

SUMMARIZE THE MAIN POINTS

This section of your study guide is designed to help you identify and understand the main points in each chapter. You've already reviewed the details using the Guided Review (above), and will consider the importance, relevance, and usefulness of the information in later sections. For now, focus on summarizing the main ideas.

For each major section in the chapter, summarize the main point and the evidence presented in the text to support and/or discuss it. If there are key terms presented in the section, define them. Some prompting questions are provided to help you structure your review.

The main sections of Chapter 2 are:

- The meaning of development
- Piaget and cognitive development
- Piaget's four stages of cognitive development
- Piaget and language development
- Criticisms of Piaget
- For the classroom
- Vygotsky and cognitive development
- Language development
- Language development in infancy
- Language development in early childhood
- Language development in middle childhood

For each section, answer the following questions:

1. In two sentences or less, **summarize** what the **main point** of this section was.

2. Briefly **summarize the evidence** for and against each main point (a simple list of details they use to support each of their points is sufficient). If the authors discuss research studies to support the point, summarize the findings in one sentence. If the authors are presenting a logical argument to support the point (i.e., not citing data from research studies), briefly list the supporting points they made. Use the detailed chapter outline to help you identify the supporting points.

3. Briefly review the **definitions of any key terms** in each main section.

WHY SHOULD YOU CARE?

The purpose of this section of your study guide is to help you understand how and why the information in the chapter is relevant for you personally. You'll be asked to think more about the relevance and usefulness of the information in later sections of this study guide.

Look back at the work you did in summarizing the main points in the section above and answer the following questions:

1. For each section you summarized, why or how is the **main point** you identified **important to and/or relevant for teachers in general**? Try to limit your answer to only one or two sentences so you don't get bogged down in details, but focus on general usefulness.

2. Now think about the chapter as a whole. **Identify two specific events, contexts, or problems** for which the ideas presented in this chapter are relevant. Briefly discuss how they're relevant and how they could be useful.

3. Now **identify three concepts** from the chapter that **YOU find useful** in some way. Discuss how/why these concepts are useful, and specify how you will actually use them in your teaching and/or your daily life. (It's okay if there is some overlap between your answers for numbers 2 and 3.)

DISCUSSION QUESTIONS

The following "What do you think?" questions are printed in the text.

1. From your present knowledge of children, do you think Piaget's stages give a realistic picture of a child's cognitive development? Why or why not?

2. Do you think Piaget placed enough emphasis on culture in his explanation of cognitive development? Give specific reasons for your answer.

3. Why do you think Vygotsky has become such a popular figure in psychology? Be specific.

4. How would you use the heredity-environment controversy to explain language development? In other words, do you think language development is mainly biological? Or is it learned? Or is there another explanation?

Additional discussion questions:

5. What is the biopsychosocial model of development? How is this model useful for teachers?

6. For each of Piaget's stages of cognitive development, list the major accomplishments and major limitations for that stage. For each stage, give two suggestions for how teachers can foster cognitive development at that stage.

7. What would Piaget recommend that teachers do to foster their students' language development? What would Vygotsky recommend?

8. Define and give an example of assimilation and accommodation.

9. Define and give an example of the language components, overextension, and overregularization.

10. For Piaget, what are the four forces that interact to aid passage through the four stages of cognitive development? Define each force and describe an example that shows how the four interact.

11. Define inner speech. Describe its role in cognitive development according to Piaget, then according to Vygotsky. How can teachers make positive use of inner speech in a classroom?

TAKE IT PERSONALLY!

The questions in this section are designed to help you personalize, integrate, and apply the information from the text. Personalization questions ask you to consider the personal relevance and usefulness of concepts, and consider how they might be useful in your life now and in the future. Integration questions ask you to pull together information from the text to evaluate it, summarize it, synthesize a recommendation on the basis of it, or express an opinion about it. Application questions ask you to think about how the concepts might be useful to address real problems or situations you may find yourself in. All three question types will help you consider the information at a deeper conceptual level, understand it more fully, and remember it.

1. Pages 30 to 31 list several questions to guide your thinking and help you form classroom applications. Answer each of the questions.

2. Define the zone of proximal development. Discuss its implications for teachers in classrooms. How will you use the ZPD to design instruction?

3. How have you adapted or organized your cognitive structures? What are schemes and why are they important to teachers?

4. For each of Piaget's stages, explain why the stage has the label it does, describe a child in that stage in terms of skills and limitations, and describe three teaching strategies that would be appropriate for a child in that stage. Specify why each is appropriate. If you wish, it might be helpful to organize this information in a chart.

5. Does Piaget's theory make sense to you? Does it seem to be a reasonable account of development? How would you respond to his critics?

6. If you were designing an AIDS program, what would it consist of? How would you consider students' cognitive levels?

7. Describe, compare, and contrast the theories of language development. Which do you agree with, and why?

8. Describe the whole language approach. Discuss how you would use it to teach a certain theme. Do you like this approach or not? Why?

9. According to Vygotsky, speech is one of the most powerful tools humans use to progress developmentally. Why does he say this? Do you agree or disagree? Why?

CASE IN POINT...

Remember to use the cases from the text as contexts for identifying examples of concepts from the text and as contexts for solving educational problems. Also remember to use a consistent framework (like the DUPE model or the CASE NOTES in the text) to structure your "Mini-Case Report." Review the "Case in Point..." section of Chapter 1 in this study guide for more details.

SOME CONCEPTS TO IDENTIFY FOR CHAPTER 2

- accommodation
- adaptation
- assimilation
- equilibration
- features of thought at different cognitive stages
- functional invariants
- inner speech
- mediation
- metalinguistic awareness
- organization
- scaffolding
- schemes
- semantics
- syntax
- zone of proximal development

In this section of the text, you were introduced to Marsha Warren, a third-grade teacher (Case #1). Review Case #1 in your text and use the following questions to prompt your thinking about this case.

1. How well does Marsha seem to mediate for her students? How could she do better? Would this help her solve her instructional problems?

2. Would consideration of the zone of proximal development for each student help improve the effectiveness of Marsha's instruction?

3. Could knowledge of Piaget's functional invariants and their instructional implications be useful for improving how well the students in this cases respond and learn?

4. Is the text information on language development (e.g., vocabulary development, metalinguistic awareness, knowledge of syntax and semantics) relevant? How could this knowledge be useful?

BIG IDEAS IN EDUCATIONAL PSYCHOLOGY

Thinking about the "big ideas" in educational psychology will help you organize and apply your newly acquired knowledge. Use the following steps to identify your own principles and strategies from the chapter and to relate them to the five main themes of the text (i.e., the "big ideas").

1. Review the TIPS from the text.

2. List some of the main concepts from the chapter. Use the work you did in prior sections of the study guide to help generate this list. Also look at the list of key terms from the chapter.

3. Select what you think are two or three of the most important concepts from your list.

4. For each concept you select, try to state it as a principle (use the TIPS format in the text and the example shown below as a guide for how to state principles).

5. Develop two or three specific teaching strategies that follow from each stated principle.

6. Relate your work to the five main themes from the text, identifying which theme(s) are relevant for each principle and strategy. This step will help you see how the information in each chapter contributes to improved teaching for each of these five critical aspects of instruction.

7. Think about and discuss with classmates how the principles and strategies you identify will help you improve your teaching for each theme you listed as relevant.

The five main themes from the text are:
ASSESSMENT, COMMUNICATION, LEARNING, MOTIVATION, AND TIME

Some example concepts, principles, and strategies for Chapter 2:

accommodation	metalinguistic awareness
adaptation	object permanence
assimilation	organization
classification	preintellectual speech
conservation	scaffolding
egocentrism	schemes
equilibration	telegraphic speech
holographic speech	zone of proximal development
inner speech	

Principle   *Humans are active processors of information, always trying to understand.*
              (ASSESEMENT, LEARNING, MOTIVATION)

Strategy   Encourage students to get actively involved with the information and material. Use role plays in reading and social studies, manipulative in math and science. (LEARNING, MOTIVATION)

Strategy   Let students conduct experiments and do projects to learn about new topics. Use assessments that let students actually demonstrate their knowledge and use it to solve problems. (ASSESSMENT, LEARNING, MOTIVATION)

SUGGESTED READINGS

Baillargeon, R. (1987). Object permanence in 3-and 4-month-old infants. *Developmental Psychology, 23,* 655-664.

Flavell, J. (1985). *Cognitive development.* Englewood Cliffs, NJ: Prentice Hall.

Garcia Coll, C. (1990). Developmental outcome of minority infants: A process-oriented look into our beginnings. *Child Development, 61,* 270-289.

Goodman, Y. (1989). Roots of the whole language movement. *Elementary School Journal, 90,* 113-127.

Rogoff, B. (1990). *Apprenticeship in thinking.* New York: Oxford.

PRACTICE TEST 1

1. The difference between what John can read independently and what he can read with help is called
   a. metalinguistic awareness.
   b. the whole language method.
   c. the language acquisition device.
   d. the zone of proximal development.

2. According to Vygotsky, what is required for an understanding of human development?
   a. Assimilation and accommodation of cognitive structures.
   b. Psychological mechanisms of adaptation and organization.
   c. Perception of one's inner reality in relation to the external world.
   d. Knowledge of the culture in which development occurs.

3. What interpretation of mental development is adhered to by both Vygotsky and Piaget?
   a. psychoanalytic
   b. behavioral
   c. cognitive
   d. information processing

4. Adaptation and organization are psychological mechanisms known as
   a. cognitive structures.
   b. functional invariants.
   c. schemes.
   d. content.

5. Cody solved the math problems in school using a strategy he learned last year. He rearranged the numbers in the problem, and then he carried out the operations. He was so used to doing it this way, he really didn't have to think about it very much. This is an example of
   a. organization.
   b. assimilation.
   c. accommodation.
   d. cognitive structure.

6. Marty tried to solve her math problems in school using a strategy she learned last year. She rearranged the numbers in the problem, then tried to carry out the operations, but it didn't work. She then modified the strategy, and now she usually is successful in solving the problems. This is an example of
   a. organization.
   b. assimilation.
   c. accommodation.
   d. cognitive structure.

7. The formal operational period occurs at what approximate ages?
   a. birth to 18-24 months
   b. 2 to 7 years
   c. 7 to 11 years
   d. over 11 years

8. Piaget discussed four interacting influences that aid passage through his stages. One of the influences, equilibration, refers to
   a. muscular and nervous system development.
   b. what we learn from using objects.
   c. knowledge acquired from others in the culture.
   d. the constant interplay between assimilation and accommodation.

9. Egocentrism, causality, object permanence, and concepts of space and time are features of which Piagetian period?
   a. sensorimotor period
   b. concrete operational period
   c. formal operational period
   d. preoperational period

10. A preschooler witnesses other children making sounds like monkeys. Later that day, the child imitates his peers. This illustrates
    a. deferred imitation.
    b. animism.
    c. coordination of secondary schemata.
    d. mental images.

11. One of the main implications of Piaget's theory is that
    a. it is useful for understanding the influence of one's culture on development.
    b. it is useful for understanding the reasons for students' academic interests.
    c. it is useful for assessing students' levels of development.
    d. it is useful for assessing teachers' areas of strength and weaknesses.

12. A preschooler asks his parents if his stuffed bear can go on vacation with them, so that it "won't be lonely." This illustrates
    a. artificialism.
    b. animism.
    c. transductive reasoning.
    d. realism.

13. A concrete operational child is able to solve a conservation problem. She explains that since no water has been removed or added to either jar, it is still the "same thing." Which conservation argument has this youngster used?
    a. the argument of reversibility
    b. the argument of identity
    c. the argument of artificialism
    d. the argument of compensation

14. What distinguishes the concrete operational from the formal operational?
    a. The adolescent's ability to reverse his or her thinking.
    b. The adolescent's ability to represent.
    c. The adolescent's ability to separate the real from the possible.
    d. The adolescent's ability to conserve.

15. Researchers have found that when they _____, children can accomplish tasks at earlier ages than Piaget believed.
    a. strictly control the nature of the task
    b. do not allow children to practice
    c. use more familiar materials
    d. prevent students from interacting with the materials

16. When Gelman and Baillargeon (1983) replicated Piaget's three-mountain problem, they found that by showing cards with different pictures on each side to 3-year olds, the children
    a. correctly reported what they saw and what the tester would see.
    b. correctly reported what they saw, but incorrectly reported what the tester would see.
    c. correctly reported what the tester would see, but incorrectly reported what they saw.
    d. incorrectly reported what they saw and what the tester would see.

17. Walsh and Bibace's AIDS/HIV educational program is based on
    a. Chomsky's language acquisition device.
    b. Vygotsky's zone of proximal development.
    c. Piaget's theory of cognitive development.
    d. the whole language movement.

18. What is the smallest language unit?
    a. morpheme
    b. phoneme
    c. syntax
    d. semantic

19. What is the first form of communication?
    a. babbling
    b. cooing
    c. crying
    d. single words

20. In the whole-language movement, all language processes are studied
    a. as a series of facts.
    b. bilingually.
    c. using "chunking" to facilitate language acquisition.
    d. in a more natural context.

21. Which of the following is true about the whole-language approach to language learning?
    a. It is based on Skinner's theory of learning.
    b. It is based on the premise that people learn language by using it in a natural context.
    c. It is based on learning the components of language separately and in succession.
    d. It involves learning language in a controlled environment.

22. Kindergartner Tanya talks out loud to no one in particular while playing with blocks in the classroom play area. Even though other children are playing next to her, no one is listening. This illustrates which type of egocentric speech?
    a. collective monologue
    b. parallel
    c. monologue
    d. repetition

23. The biopsychosocial model views development as
    a. a continuous series of biological changes.
    b. a series of unrelated changes in one's biological, social, and psychological characteristics.
    c. complex interactions among one's biological, social, and psychological features.
    d. determined mostly by one's sociocultural background.

PRACTICE TEST 2

1. Lev Vygotsky introduced the concept of
    a. the language acquisition device.
    b. the whole language movement.
    c. telegraphic speech.
    d. the zone of proximal development.

2. Who claimed that human mental processes can be understood only by considering how, where, and with whom they occur?
    a. Noam Chomsky
    b. Jean Piaget
    c. Lev Vygotsky
    d. Robbie Case

3. Ben's teacher encourages students to work together and talk about their ideas because she believes that the interpersonal interaction helps students learn and fosters their cognitive development. The teacher's philosophy most closely resembles the ideas of
    a. Vygotsky.
    b. Chomsky.
    c. Case.
    d. Piaget.

4. According to Piaget, how do we adjust to the environment?
    a. through the processes of assimilation and accommodation
    b. through schemes
    c. through content
    d. through the zone of proximal development

5. Maria has a system for dealing with the large volumes of mail in her business. She set the system up years ago, and it has been successful in handling even the largest amounts of mail. Maria is successfully _____ the environment.
    a. classifying
    b. assimilating
    c. accommodating
    d. conserving

6. Years ago, Kim set up a system for dealing with the large volumes of mail in her business. Lately, Kim's system has become overloaded, and mail is not being handled as it should be, so she has changed how mail is sorted and routed. Kim is trying to _____ the environment.
    a. classify
    b. assimilate
    c. accommodate
    d. conserve

7. An infant learns about the size of a ball when she reaches to hold the ball. This illustrates
    a. schema.
    b. content.
    c. organization.
    d. object permanence.

8. What is the major accomplishment of the preoperational period?
    a. understanding of reversibility
    b. ability to separate the real from the possible
    c. ability to represent
    d. ability to conserve

9. Piaget discussed four interacting influences that aid passage through his stages. One of the influences, experience, refers to
    a. muscular and nervous system development.
    b. learning about objects and what we learn from using objects.
    c. knowledge acquired from others in the culture.
    d. the constant interplay between assimilation and accommodation.

10. Nine-month-old Andrew was playing ball with his father. When it rolled out of sight, Andrew searched for it. This illustrates the concept of
    a. space.
    b. causality.
    c. object permanence.
    d. egocentrism.

11. A teacher asks a class of fifth-graders to imagine how they would walk home if their usual route were blocked and they had to take another route. Students are asked to draw a map depicting how they would arrive home. This activity demonstrates concrete operational students' ability to
    a. classify events.
    b. reverse their thinking.
    c. seriate.
    d. test hypotheses.

12. One of the main implications of Piaget's theory is that
    a. it is useful for understanding each student's background culture.
    b. it is useful for assessing students' academic interests.
    c. it is useful for planning a developmentally appropriate curriculum.
    d. it is useful for assessing teachers' levels of expertise.

13. Which of the following exemplifies egocentrism during the preoperational period?
    a. Ted learned that 2 + 2 = 4, but he cannot yet grasp that 4 - 2 = 2.
    b. Ted explained to his mother that the rainbow was following him wherever he went.
    c. Ted said to his friend that the wind was angry.
    d. Ted reasoned that the sun was out because it was yellow.

14. The concrete operational child's ability to arrange objects by increasing or decreasing size is called
    a. conservation.
    b. number concept.
    c. seriation.
    d. classification.

15. At what stage does abstract logical thinking become possible?
    a. sensorimotor period
    b. formal operational period
    c. preoperational period
    d. concrete operational period

16. Piaget believed the acquisition of cognitive structures is _____, but recent work indicates the acquisition is _____.
    a. abrupt; gradual
    b. gradual; abrupt
    c. not dependent on experience; dependent on experience
    d. none of the above are correct

17. Which of the following have been found to be TRUE when investigating Piaget's theory?
    a. There is strong support for the idea of broad stages of development.
    b. The existence of cognitive structures has not been supported by research.
    c. Modifying the task in Piaget's experimental tasks does not affect the outcomes.
    d. Using materials that are more familiar to children reveals cognitive competencies at earlier ages than Piaget suggested.

18. At what Piagetian stage would a student understand AIDS/HIV prevention and need detailed biological explanations of preventive behavior and conditions under which it operates and that affect use?
    a. sensorimotor
    b. preoperational
    c. formal operational
    d. concrete operational

19. What is the task of any syntax?
    a. To arrange morphemes in meaningful sentences
    b. To understand the relationship between ideas and words
    c. To understand the distinctive, fundamental sounds of language
    d. To develop pragmatic skills

20. Will says, "Mommy goed to the store." This illustrates
    a. overextensions.
    b. overregularities.
    c. telegraphic speech.
    d. holophrastic speech.

21. Proponents of whole language believe that it is consistent with
    a. Chomsky's theory.
    b. Piaget's theory.
    c. Piaget's and Chomsky's theories.
    d. Piaget's and Vygotsky's theories.

22. Whole-language approaches involve
    a. reading.
    b. writing.
    c. speaking.
    d. all of the above.

23. One implication of the biopsychosocial model is that
    a. sociocultural factors become less important in understanding students.
    b. teachers no longer have to consider whether their methods and materials are developmentally appropriate for their students.
    c. it becomes critical for teachers to learn about the biological background of their students, but their psychological background is not important to know about.
    d. None of the above are implications of the biopsychosocial model.

24. Piaget and Vygotsky _disagree_ about which of the following?
    a. That children engage in some form of egocentric speech.
    b. That egocentric speech represents the transition to inner speech.
    c. That egocentric speech represents a lower level of cognitive functioning than inner speech.
    d. That egocentric speech is the stage of speech development used when children talk regardless of whether anyone else is listening or responding.

ANSWER KEY

Practice Test 1

1.   ANSWER: D, Factual; OBJECTIVE: 5; PAGE: 55
2.   ANSWER: D, Factual; OBJECTIVE: 6; PAGE: 53
3.   ANSWER: C, Factual; OBJECTIVE: 7; PAGE: 51
4.   ANSWER: B, Factual; OBJECTIVE: 2; PAGE: 32
5.   ANSWER: B, Applied; OBJECTIVE: 2; PAGE: 32
6.   ANSWER: C, Applied; OBJECTIVE: 2; PAGE: 33
7.   ANSWER: D, Factual; OBJECTIVE: 3; PAGE: 44
8.   ANSWER: D, Factual; OBJECTIVE: 2; PAGE: 33
9.   ANSWER: A, Factual; OBJECTIVE: 3; PAGE: 36-37
10. ANSWER: A, Applied; OBJECTIVE: 3; PAGE: 40
11. ANSWER: C, Conceptual; OBJECTIVE: 8; PAGE:51
12. ANSWER: B; Applied; OBJECTIVE: 3; PAGE: 39
13. ANSWER: B, Applied; OBJECTIVE: 3; PAGE: 42
14. ANSWER: C, Conceptual; OBJECTIVE: 3; PAGE: 43-44
15. ANSWER: C, Factual; OBJECTIVE: 4; PAGE: 48
16. ANSWER: A, Factual; OBJECTIVE: 4; PAGE: 49
17. ANSWER: C, Factual; OBJECTIVE: 8; PAGE: 49
18. ANSWER: B, Factual; OBJECTIVE: 9; PAGE: 59
19. ANSWER: C, Factual; OBJECTIVE: 9; PAGE: 61
20. ANSWER: D, Factual; OBJECTIVE: 9; PAGE: 64
21. ANSWER: B, Factual; OBJECTIVE: 9; PAGE: 64-65
22. ANSWER: A, Applied; OBJECTIVE: 10; PAGE: 47
23. ANSWER: C, Factual; OBJECTIVE: 1; PAGE: 30

Practice Test 2

1. ANSWER: D, Factual; OBJECTIVE: 5; PAGE: 55
2. ANSWER: C, Factual; OBJECTIVE: 6; PAGE: 52-53
3. ANSWER: A, Conceptual; OBJECTIVE: 5; PAGE: 53
4. ANSWER: A, Factual; OBJECTIVE: 2; PAGE: 32-33
5. ANSWER: B, Applied; OBJECTIVE: 2; PAGE: 32-33
6. ANSWER: C, Applied; OBJECTIVE: 2; PAGE: 32-33
7. ANSWER: A, Applied; OBJECTIVE: 2; PAGE: 34
8. ANSWER: C, Factual; OBJECTIVE: 3; PAGE: 38-39
9. ANSWER: B, Factual; OBJECTIVE: 2; PAGE: 35
10. ANSWER: C, Applied; OBJECTIVE: 3; PAGE: 36
11. ANSWER: B, Applied; OBJECTIVE: 3; PAGE: 40, 43
12. ANSWER: C, Conceptual; OBJECTIVE: 8; PAGE: 51
13. ANSWER: B, Conceptual; OBJECTIVE: 3; PAGE: 40
14. ANSWER: C, Factual; OBJECTIVE: 3; PAGE: 43
15. ANSWER: B, Factual; OBJECTIVE: 3; PAGE: 44
16. ANSWER: A, Factual; OBJECTIVE: 4; PAGE: 48-49
17. ANSWER: D, Conceptual; OBJECTIVE: 4; PAGE: 48-49
18. ANSWER: C, Factual; OBJECTIVE: 8; PAGE: 49, 51
19. ANSWER: A, Factual; OBJECTIVE: 9; PAGE: 59
20. ANSWER: B, Applied; OBJECTIVE: 9; PAGE: 64
21. ANSWER: D, Factual; OBJECTIVE: 10; PAGE: 65
22. ANSWER: D, Factual; OBJECTIVE: 9; PAGE: 64
23. ANSWER: D, Conceptual; OBJECTIVE: 1; PAGE: 30
24. ANSWER: B, Conceptual; OBJECTIVE: 7; PAGE: 47 & 54

Chapter 3 PSYCHOSOCIAL AND MORAL DEVELOPMENT

LEARNING OBJECTIVES

After completing this chapter, you should be able to

1. Describe Erikson's theory of psychosocial development and identify the stages of the theory.

2. Identify and describe Marcia's four identity statuses.

3. Formulate ways in which the strengths of each of Erikson's stages help students adjust to the crises inevitably awaiting them.

4. Summarize the key ideas in Kohlberg's theory.

5. Summarize Gilligan's theory of moral development.

6. Suggest techniques that enhance the moral development of your students.

7. Describe the major forces influencing socialization and explain how they affect student achievement.

8. Describe the development of self.

9. Suggest specific ways to help students acquire a positive and realistic self-esteem.

CHAPTER HIGHLIGHTS

Psychosocial Development

- Erik Erikson's eight stages of psychosocial development provide a structure for analyzing the crises and strengths in students' lives.
- Understanding the meaning of these stages in your pupils' lives can only help to enhance and enrich teacher-learner interactions.

Moral Development

- Children begin to understand the moral consequences of their actions.
- To explain moral development, Kohlberg has formulated a cognitive interpretation that incorporates Piagetian thinking.
- Using the technique of moral dilemmas and analyzing an individual's reasoning, Kohlberg has traced progress through stages of moral development.
- Kohlberg's ideas have been challenged, especially by Carol Gilligan, who proposes a different path for a woman's moral development.
- Many educators believe that the concepts of moral development can be translated into classroom practice.

Socialization and Development

- Changes in the family have caused changes in parenting practices.
- The number of divorces remains high, causing children to adapt to transitions in their living conditions.
- The number of children in day care has risen steadily as family styles have become more diverse.
- Firm conclusions are still elusive with regard to the developmental outcomes of day care.

Individuation and Development

- Children usually acquire a sense of self by the age of 18 months.
- Children's sense of self changes noticeably with age.
- The emergence of self-control is a critical feature of psychosocial growth as children develop their ideas of right and wrong.

DETAILED CHAPTER OUTLINE

I. Psychosocial development
   A. Definitions
       1. Socialization means the need to establish and maintain relations with others and to regulate behavior according to society's demands.
       2. Individuation refers to the fullest development of one's self.
   B. Children are deeply affected by the social agents that surround them. Erikson linked children's development to the interactions and interrelationships with the critical agents in their environment.
   C. Erikson's psychosocial stages
       1. Erikson believed that personality emerges from a series of inner and outer conflicts that, if resolved, result in a greater sense of self. These crises arise at each of eight stages of life. Each crisis results in a period of increased vulnerability and heightened potential, which can lead to either maladjustment or increased psychic strength.
       2. Erikson believed that personality develops according to one's ability to interact with the environment, and society invites this interaction with the environment and encourages the successive appearance of the stages.
       3. The early years
           a. Stage 1: Trust versus Mistrust (birth to one year)
               (1) Erikson believed that a healthy personality requires a sense of trust toward one's self and the world, which develops during the first year. Cold parental care and rejection cause mistrust and affect all later development.
               (2) Attachment (usually to the mother) appears during the last half of the first year. If attachment is not nurtured by the mother or other caregiver, children may not develop the trust necessary to establish lasting relationships with others.
               (3) Other factors contribute to the development of attachment, such as the child's inborn temperamental tendencies.
               (4) Reciprocal interactions refers to the fact that children immediately seek stimulation from their environment and instantly interpret and react to how they are being treated.
           b. Stage 2: Autonomy versus Shame and Doubt (2-3 years)
               (1) Usually appears during toilet training. Personality is shaped by learning the meaning of self-control. This stage is decisive for establishing a proper balance between standing on one's own feet and being protected.
               (2) Parental reactions are crucial, since the objective of this stage is self-control with no loss of self-esteem.

c. Educational implications-The early years
   (1)   Ideally, youngsters should achieve self-control as well as control of their bodies during these years.
   (2)   Young children require consistent and reasonable discipline.
   (3)   Young children need ample opportunities to do things for themselves.
   (4)   Young children need good models and should be protected from unwarranted fears.
d. Stage 3: Initiative versus Guilt (4-5 years)
   (1)   Children in Erikson's third stage show greater freedom of movement, perfection of language, and expansion of imagination. A sense of initiative emerges that will serve as a basis for realistic ambitions and purposes.
   (2)   Parents who encourage children to do things encourage a sense of initiative. Scoffing at children's ideas and efforts produces a sense of guilt.
   (3)   Play aids cognitive development, helps social development, and provides an emotional release.
   (4)   The role of conscience emerges during these years. If children face too many restrictions, they can acquire emotional problems early in life.
   (5)   Educational implications
      (a)   These characteristics of children have led to a concern for developmentally appropriate curricula.
      (b)   Youngsters who acquire a sense of initiative will bring to the classroom a healthy desire to face challenges.
      (c)   Schooling must capitalize on a child's spontaneous learning, thus aiding the development of competence and security.
      (d)   TIPS on Learning: Erikson's early stages

4. The middle years
a. Stage 4: Industry versus Inferiority (6-11 years)
   (1)   Children now possess a sense of being able to do things well; they want to win recognition by producing things, which is the meaning of industry.
   (2)   Some degree of success contributes to both personal adjustment and social acceptance. Conversely, children who despair of their skills and their status with their peers can easily acquire a sense of inadequacy.
   (3)   Industry and inferiority are particularly relevant for students of diverse backgrounds. The language and customs of the classroom may seem strange, and these pupils may feel overwhelmed by self-doubt. The teacher's behavior is important in enhancing their self-esteem and setting an example for the rest of the students.
   (4)   Educational implications-The middle years
      (a)   For youngsters at this stage, learning occurs from almost everything they do.
      (b)   Elementary school youngsters are eager to use the abilities that they developed during their first six or seven years. They will inevitably encounter failure as well as success, especially in their schoolwork. The balance between these two outcomes will decisively affect a child's self-esteem.
      (c)   Teachers can help students gain a sense of mastery over the environment by matching content with ability so that they can achieve at their level.
      (d)   Social interactions and educational technology
         (i)   Students working on computers often show more social interaction than students working on non-computer activities, increases in turn-taking, and increases in providing explanations.
        (ii)   Networked research projects encourage social development and can improve knowledge and acceptance of different cultures.
      (e)   Case Notes: Marsha Warren's class
      (f)   TIPS on Learning: Erikson's middle years

5. The adolescent years
   a. Stage 5: Identity versus Identity Confusion (12-18 years)
      (1) This is the beginning of adulthood. Peer opinion plays a large part in how youngsters think of themselves.
      (2) Minority children may be particularly susceptible to identity concerns.
      (3) By the end of adolescence, those who have resolved their personal crises have achieved a sense of identity. Those who remain locked in doubt and insecurity experience what Erikson calls identity confusion.
      (4) Marcia (1966, 1980) noted that adolescents seem to respond to the need to make choices about their identity in one of four ways.
         (a) Identity diffusion, or inability to commit themselves to choices.
         (b) Identity foreclosure, or making a commitment only because someone else has prescribed a particular choice.
         (c) Identity moratorium, or desiring to make a choice at some time in the future but being unable to do so.
         (d) Identity achievement, or committing oneself to choices about identity and maintaining that commitment under all conditions.
      (5) TIPS on Communication: Erikson's adolescent years
      (6) Educational applications-The adolescent years
         (a) Help adolescents integrate the physical, sexual, and cognitive changes of adolescence by: treating them as almost adult; challenging them with realistic goals; using materials that challenge, not defeat; and constantly addressing the issue of identity vs. identity diffusion.
6. The later years
   a. Stage 6: Intimacy versus Isolation (18-35 years)
      (1) Intimacy goes beyond being sexual and involves the capacity to develop psychosocial intimacy with friends, and the ability to care for others without fearing a loss of self-identity.
      (2) Young people of this age continue to develop their identity by close relationships with others.
   b. Stage 7: Generativity versus Stagnation (35-65 years)
      (1) Individuals think about the future of both society and their own children.
      (2) Care for others is an outstanding characteristic of this period. If a sense of generativity is lacking, individuals may stagnate, suffering from morbid self-concern.
   c. Stage 8: Integrity versus Despair (over 65 years)
      (1) A sense of integrity means that one looks back and sees meaning in life.
      (2) Basic to a sense of integrity is wisdom, a detached yet active concern with life and its meaning.
7. For the classroom
   a. Children require systematic instruction.
   b. Effective teachers know how to alternate work with play, and how to pace their instruction to maximize learning.
      (1) Optimal scheduling and time on task demands a good knowledge of students' cognitive levels, attention spans, interests, and motivation.
      (2) Student attitudes toward school itself will affect a teacher's pacing.
      (3) If you encourage students to express their opinions about psychosocial issues and if you model high levels of moral behavior, you will help to advance your students' insights into matters of right and wrong.
8. Case Notes: Marsha Warren's class

II. Moral development
   A. The pattern of moral growth
      1. Moral behavior is a complex mixture of cognition, emotion, and behavior.
      2. Initially, young children begin to learn about right and wrong from their parents. Modeling is especially effective.
      3. From about 2 to 6 years, children interact with a variety of authority figures other than parents. These individuals assume great importance in children's lives.
      4. From about 6 to 11 years, children learn about making and following regulations, as well as deriving insights into those children who don't.
      5. Beginning with adolescence, children learn to tame impulsive actions that clash with rules and regulations of society. Adults now become firmer in dealing with children. Students must begin to evaluate the values of friends and make decisions on their own.
   B. Kohlberg's theory of moral development
      1. Lawrence Kohlberg attempted to apply Piaget's cognitive rationale to moral development.
      2. Kohlberg believed that moral stages emerge from a child's active thought about moral issues and decisions. He presented children with a series of moral dilemmas and asked them what they would do and why.
      3. His view of moral development extends from about 4 years of age through adulthood, and traces moral development through three levels that encompass six stages. Passage through the six stages occurs by successive transformations of a child's cognitive structures.
      4. Kohlberg believed that moral judgment requires us to weigh the claims of others against self-interest. Many children and adults become fixated at one of the lower levels.
      5. Knowing the right answers to the moral dilemmas doesn't guarantee moral behavior.
      6. Level 1. Preconventional morality (about 4 to 10 years).
         a. During these years, children respond mainly to cultural control to avoid punishment and attain satisfaction.
         b. TIPS on Assessment: Moral development—the early years
         c. Case Notes: Marsha Warren's class
      7. Level 2. Conventional morality (about 10 to 13 years).
         a. During these years, children desire approval.
      8. Level 3. Postconventional morality (13 years and over)
         a. If true morality (an internal moral code) is to develop, it appears during these years. The individual does not appeal to other people for moral decisions; they are made by an "enlightened conscience."
         b. TIPS on Communication: Moral development—the later years
   C. Using Kohlberg's work in the classroom
      1. Using moral dilemmas
         a. Moral dilemmas are thought-provoking dialogues that probe the moral basis of people's thinking. They are real or imaginary conflicts involving competing claims, for which there are no clear, morally correct solutions.
         b. Some specific suggestions for using moral dilemmas more effectively:
            (1) Ask "why," to help students identify the dilemma and discover their level of moral reasoning.
            (2) Complicate the circumstances to add a new dimension to the problem.
            (3) Present examples, based on incidents at school.
            (4) Effective discussions of moral dilemmas require a conducive atmosphere of trust and fairness, respect for students, and valuing of their opinions. This atmosphere does not appear overnight, and teachers must be sensitive to students' experiences.
   D. Criticisms of Kohlberg's theory
      1. Parenting practices, years of schooling, and industrialization of one's society all impact moral development.
      2. Gilligan has questioned the validity of Kohlberg's theory for women.
         a. Gilligan believes the qualities the theory associates with the mature adult are qualities traditionally associated with "masculinity" rather than "femininity."
         b. She argued that different images of self lead to different interpretations of moral behavior. Girls are raised to believe that attachment is desirable, while boys are raised to believe that separation and independence are desirable.

c. Women's moral decisions are based on an ethic of caring rather than a morality of justice. Gilligan argues for a different sequence for the moral development of women.

d. For males, separation from mothers is essential for the development of masculinity. For females, femininity is defined by attachment to mothers.

e. Gilligan does not argue for the superiority of either the male or the female sequence, but urges that we recognize the difference between the two.

3. Current issues and perspectives: Schools and character development

III. Socialization and development

A. The changing family

1. As families change, they exercise different effects on a child's development.

2. The very idea of what constitutes parenting has been drastically altered for both men and women. Children of different ages, with different problems, and from different cultures need different types of parenting.

B. Children of divorce

1. The United States has a larger number of single parents than any other developed country.

2. For these children, their physical way of life changes and they are psychologically immersed in an emotionally charged home environment.

3. Learning is usually affected, with more frequent absences from school, more disruptiveness in the classroom, deterioration in peer relationships and social behavior, and a decline in academic competence.

C. Day Care

1. Facts about day care

a. A wide variety of circumstances exist. The best centers are staffed by teachers who specialize in day-care services.

2. Developmental outcomes of day care

a. No definite conclusions have been reached concerning the long-term developmental consequences of day care because careful follow-up of children is not yet available.

b. Several general conclusions are possible:

(1) Children typically maintain their normal course of physical development.

(2) Children in good day care centers during the early childhood years manifest more advanced cognitive and language development than those who stay at home. Effects of poorer quality care on cognitive and language development aren't known.

(3) Children in day care seem to be more assertive, independent, and self-confident, less pleasant, less polite, and less compliant with adults' requests.

D. Homelessness

1. Families with young children may be the fastest-growing segment of today's homeless.

2. The impact of homelessness on development

a. Homeless children have much higher rates of acute and chronic health problems, which may have their roots in the prenatal period.

b. They suffer from hunger and poor nutrition.

c. They experience a higher than normal degree of developmental delays.

d. They suffer more from psychological problems such as depression, anxiety, and behavioral problems.

e. Parental stress often translates into poor parenting practices which can lead to behavioral and emotional problems and academic difficulty. Homeless children often witness, and are the victims of, violence.

f. Homeless children show educational underachievement, doing poorly on reading and mathematics tests. School is especially critical for these students because it often produces a sense of stability that is otherwise lacking.

3. Homeless children cannot directly solve the problem of homelessness, so they often concentrate on coping with the emotions that arise from becoming homeless, perhaps by restructuring the circumstances surrounding their homelessness.

4. Case Notes: Marsha Warren's class

IV. Individuation and development
   A. The emerging self
      1. William James believed that the "I" part of the self was the knower that thinks, makes judgements, recognizes it is separate from everything it sees, and controls the surrounding world. The "Me" is the object of the "I's" thinking.
      2. A practical example of the relationship between I and Me is the case of Julia Ming Gale, who was born in Taiwan of Chinese parents but adopted and raised by American Caucasian parents.
   B. The development of self
      1. A sense of self refers to the sense of who you are and what makes you different from everyone else.
      2. Children will usually have acquired a sense of self by 18 months of age.
      3. Children change from identifying themselves by physical characteristics at younger ages to more social and emotional characteristics and comparisons with others at older ages.
      4. Physical, cognitive, and psychological influences are all active forces in self development.
   C. The changing self
      1. Self-esteem refers to a feeling of confidence and self-satisfaction with one's self. Several elements contribute to it.
         a. A sense of physical safety
         b. A sense of emotional security
         c. A sense of identity
         d. A sense of belonging
         e. A sense of competence
      2. Concern with competence appears at about 7 or 8 years. Children begin to measure themselves against their classmates, and confidence in their own abilities becomes more realistic.
   D. Self-esteem and competence
      1. Harter identified five types of competence central to a child's level of self-esteem: scholastic competence, athletic competence, social acceptance, behavioral conduct, and physical appearance.
      2. Most children in Harter's study showed a "sawtooth" profile of these competencies, indicating they feel good about themselves in some activities and not in others. Some children with very different profiles had quite similar levels of self-esteem, while others with similar profiles had very different levels of self-esteem.
      3. Children who receive considerable support from the important people in their environment had a high regard for themselves.
      4. Harter discovered that those who believed their looks determined their self-esteem felt worse about their appearance, had lower self-esteem, and suffered more depression.
      5. Teachers and parents need to praise and recognize children's honest achievements.
      6. Case Notes: Marsha Warren's class
   E. The self in self-control
      1. Children must learn to control their impulses to be successful.
      2. Children who are reflective as opposed to impulsive seem destined to achieve at higher levels, attain greater emotional maturity, and gain popularity.
      3. Children who displayed impulsivity at four years of age were more troubled adolescents, with fewer friends, more psychological difficulties, more irritable and aggressive, and less able to cope with frustration.
      4. Impulsivity and the classroom
         a. Teachers can help preschool students develop self-control by helping students distract themselves.
         b. "Transformation" appears by around first grade, in which children learn to think about what they shouldn't do in different terms. Students are then better at devising their own strategies for self-control.
         c. Three measures taken during fifth grade will predict later problems (Sylwester, 1991):
            (1) teachers' ratings of social skills
            (2) negative playground behavior
            (3) disciplinary contacts with the principal's office
         d. Teachers should play a critical role in obtaining early help for troubled students.

F. Adolescents and individuation
    1. Teachers may be the first to observe changes in behavior.
    2. Teachers should encourage, support, and participate in pertinent intervention programs.
    3. Good programs include a school's leadership role in establishing the program, and a brief training program for parents.

V. Case reflections

VI. Chapter highlights

VII. What do you think? questions

VIII. Key terms

KEY TERMS

attachment
autonomy
conventional level
day care
divorce
generativity
identity achievement
identity confusion
identity crisis
identity diffusion
identity foreclosure

identity moratorium
industry
initiative
integrity
intimacy
moral dilemma
postconventional level
preconventional level
reciprocal interactions
self
self-esteem

GUIDED REVIEW

1. _____ means the need to establish and maintain relations with others and to regulate behavior according to society's demands. _____ means the fullest development of one's self.

Socialization, Individuation

2. Erikson believed that personality emerges from a series of inner and outer conflicts, which, if resolved, result in a greater sense of _____. These crises arise at each of _____ stages identified by Erikson. Each crisis results in a period of increased vulnerability and heightened potential, which can lead to possible _____ or to _____.

self, eight, maladjustment, increased psychic strength

3. Erikson stated that personality develops according to one's ability to _____ with the environment.

interact

4.   Stage 1 of Erikson's psychosocial stages is the stage of _____.

trust versus mistrust

5.   Attachment (usually to the mother) appears during the _____.

last half of the first year

6.   _____ is the process in which we respond to those around us and they change; their changed behavior then causes changes in us. Students are not merely _____ recipients in any exchange.

Reciprocal interactions, passive

7.   For Erikson, the theme of the second stage is _____, a concept that usually appears during toilet training. During this period, personality is shaped by learning the meaning of _____.

autonomy versus shame and doubt, self-control

8.   Young children during Erikson's second stage require consistent and reasonable _____, need opportunities to _____, and need good _____.

discipline, do things for themselves, models

9.   In Erikson's third stage, a sense of _____ emerges that serves as a basis for realistic ambitions and _____. The child's sense of purpose for _____ is freed. Scoffing at children's efforts and ideas can cause them to develop a sense of _____.

initiative, purposes, adult tasks, guilt

10.   Play aids _____ by allowing children to explore their environment. It helps _____ by teaching the basics of forming relationships. It also provides an _____.

cognitive development, social development, emotional release

11.   In Stage 4, called _____, children possess a sense of being able to do things well; they want to win recognition by producing things, which is the meaning of _____.

industry versus inferiority, industry

12.   Erikson's ideas of industry and inferiority are particularly relevant for students of _____. The classroom _____ and _____ may seem strange, and these students may feel overwhelmed by _____.

diverse backgrounds, language, customs, self-doubt

13. Elementary school students approach tasks eagerly, which means they will encounter both _____. The balance between these two outcomes will affect the child's _____. The teacher's task is to _____ a child's energy and talents in positive directions, and to help students gain a sense of mastery over the environment by _____ content with ability.

successes and failures, self-esteem, channel, matching

14. Computer usage by young students often results in a _____ amount of social interaction by students using computers than by those not using computers. Computer users showed increases in _____ and in providing _____ to other students. Involvement in networked research projects may encourage students' social development due to increased _____ with others in different locations. Students' knowledge and acceptance of _____ may be increased as well.

higher, turn-taking, explanations, collaboration, different cultures

15. Erikson's Stage 5 is called _____. _____ children may be particularly susceptible to these concerns.

identity versus identity confusion, Minority

16. Adolescence is the period Erikson is most often associated with, mainly because of his speculations about the adolescent _____.

identity crisis

17. In Erikson's stage of identity versus identity confusion, those who remain locked in doubt and insecurity experience what Erikson calls _____.

identity confusion

18. Marcia notes that adolescents seem to respond to the need to make choices about their identity in one of four ways: _____, or the inability to commit themselves to choices—the lack of a sense of direction; _____, or making a commitment only because someone else has prescribed a particular choice—being "outer-directed"; _____, or desiring to make a choice at some time in the future but being unable to do so; and _____, or committing oneself to choices about identity and maintaining that commitment under all conditions.

identity diffusion, identity foreclosure, identity moratorium, identity achievement

19. For teachers working with adolescents, _____ the physical, sexual, and cognitive changes and focusing on particular and clearly defined _____ is the crucial task. You can help students achieve psychosocial maturity by treating them as _____, challenging them with _____, using materials that challenge but do not _____, and constantly addressing the issue of _____.

integrating, goals, almost adult, realistic goals, defeat, identity

20.   Erikson's Stage 6 is called _____.

intimacy versus isolation

21.   Erikson believes that a sense of _____ goes beyond being sexual and involves the capacity to develop a true and mutual psychosocial intimacy with friends, the ability to care for others without fearing a loss of self-identity.

intimacy

22.   Stage 7 of Erikson's psychosocial development is the stage of _____.

generativity versus stagnation

23.   During middle age, individuals think about the future of both society and their own children. An outstanding characteristic of this period is _____, which implies an obligation to guide the next generation by passing on desirable social values. If a sense of _____ is lacking, individuals may stagnate, suffering from morbid self-concern.

care for others, generativity

24.   Stage 8 of Erikson's psychosocial stages is called _____.

integrity versus despair

25.   The person who can view his or her life with satisfaction and accept its ups and downs has achieved a sense of _____; this term implies that one looks back and sees meaning in life.

integrity

26.   Basic to a sense of integrity is _____, a detached yet active concern with life and its meaning.

wisdom

27.   Erikson believes that children require _____ instruction. Good teachers alternate _____ with _____, work well with students to whom school is _____, and know how to _____ their instruction to maximize learning.

systematic, work, play, not important, pace

28.   Moral behavior is a complex mixture of _____, or thinking about what to do; _____, or feelings about what to do or what was done; and _____, or what is actually done.

cognition, emotion, behavior

29.   Lawrence Kohlberg attempted to apply Piaget's cognitive rationale to _____. Kohlberg believed that moral stages emerge from a child's _____ about moral _____ and _____.

moral development, active thought, issues, decisions

30.   Kohlberg presented children with _____ and asked them what they would do and _____ they would do it. These real or imaginary conflicts forced children to _____ based on their moral reasoning.

moral dilemmas, why, make decisions

31.   Kohlberg found that children begin thinking about moral issues at about ___ years of age, and they pass through six stages of moral reasoning, which are organized into three levels of development. The first level is _____ (from 4 to 10 years), the second level is _____ (from 10 to 13 years), and the third level is _____ (from 13 years).

four, preconventional, conventional, postconventional

32.   When making moral judgements, students weigh the _____ against their own _____. Some children don't progress too far in Kohlberg's levels, and even those children who progress to the third level may not always _____ in a moral manner. Knowing the "right" answers to moral dilemmas doesn't _____ moral behavior.

claims of others, self-interest, act, guarantee

33.   At the preconventional level of moral development, children respond mainly to _____. They are trying to _____ and obtain _____.

control, avoid punishment, personal satisfaction

34.   At the conventional level, children are looking for _____ for doing the right thing. Urge them to move beyond this level by helping them be more _____ to others' feelings.

approval, sensitive

35.   At the postconventional level of moral reasoning, moral behavior is determined by an individual's _____, not by _____ and others' _____. This constitutes _____, but _____ people make it to this stage because it requires a high level of complex and abstract _____ .

enlightened conscience, laws, approval, true morality, few, thought

36.   To use moral dilemmas effectively in the classroom, act as a _____ during discussions and then later introduce more complex issues. Ask _____ to help students identify the dilemma and discover their level of moral reasoning. Add a new dimension to the dilemma by _____, and use _____ examples. To establish an atmosphere conducive to moral instruction, teachers should create an atmosphere of _____ and _____, _____ students and their opinions, give the process enough _____, and be _____ to what students are experiencing.

guide, why, complicating the circumstances, school, trust, fairness, respect, time, sensitive

37.   Questions have been raised about the applicability of Kohlberg's theory to all _____. _____ practices, years of _____, and how _____ the society is all seem to affect the level of moral maturity demonstrated.

cultures, Parenting, schooling, industrialized

38.   Gilligan has questioned the validity of Kohlberg's theory for _____.

women

39.   Noting that women's moral decisions are based on an _____ rather than on a _____, Gilligan argues for a different sequence for the moral development of women. For males, _____ is essential for the development of masculinity, while for females, _____ defines femininity.

ethic of caring, morality of justice, separation from mothers, attachment to mothers

40.   The very idea of what constitutes _____ has altered dramatically for both men and women. Parents and children actually _____ their relationships, and no one model fits all.

parenting, construct

41.   The United States has a larger number of single parents than any other developed country, with about _____ of children living with one parent. For these children, their _____ way of life changes and they are psychologically immersed in an _____ home environment.

25 percent, physical, emotionally charged

42.   After a divorce, children's _____ is usually affected, with more frequent _____ from school and more _____ in the classroom. There is often deterioration in peer relationships and _____, and academic _____ declines. Teachers and fellow students can offer needed _____ during this time of distress.

learning, absences, disruptiveness, social behavior, competence, support

43.   The best day care centers are staffed by teachers who specialize in _____ . No _____ have been reached concerning the long-term developmental consequences of day care because careful _____ of children is not yet available.

day-care services, definite conclusions, follow-up

44.   Children typically _____ their normal course of physical development when in day care. Children in good day care centers show more advanced _____ and _____ development than those who stay at home. Effects of poorer quality care on cognitive and language development aren't known. Children in day care seem to be more _____, independent, and _____, but less pleasant, less _____, and less _____ with adult's requests.

maintain, cognitive, language, assertive, self-confident, polite, compliant

45.   Families with young children may be the _____ segment of today's homeless. They are characterized by few _____, poor _____, and a high level of contact with the _____.

fastest-growing, social contacts, health, criminal justice system

46.   Homeless children have much higher rates of _____ problems. They also suffer from hunger and _____, experience a high degree of _____, and suffer more from _____ problems. Parental stress often leads to poor _____ . Homeless children often witness, and are the targets of, _____. Homeless children show educational underachievement, but school is especially critical for them because it often produces a sense of _____ that is otherwise lacking.

health, poor nutrition, developmental delays, psychological, parenting practices, violence, stability

47.   Homeless children cannot directly solve the problem of homelessness, so they often concentrate on _____ that arise from becoming homeless, perhaps by _____ the circumstances surrounding their homelessness.

coping with the emotions, restructuring

48.   William James believed that the "I" part of the self was the _____ that thinks, makes judgements, recognizes it's _____ from everything it sees, and _____ the surrounding world. The "Me" is the _____ of the "I's" thinking.

knower, separate, controls, object

49.   A sense of _____ refers to the sense of who you are and what makes you different from everyone else. Children will usually have acquired a sense of self by _____ of age. Children change from identifying themselves by _____ characteristics at younger ages to more _____ characteristics and comparisons with others at older ages.

self, 18 months, physical, social and emotional

50.   _____ refers to a feeling of confidence and self-satisfaction with one's self. Several elements contribute to it, including a sense of _____ safety, _____ security, _____, belonging, and _____.

Self-esteem, physical, emotional, identity, competence

51.   Harter identified five types of competence central to a child's level of self-esteem: _____ competence, _____ competence, _____ acceptance, _____ conduct, and physical _____ . Most children in Harter's study showed a " _____ " profile of these competencies, indicating they feel good about themselves in some activities and not in others. Children who receive _____ from the important people in their environment had a high regard for themselves.

scholastic, athletic, social, behavioral, appearance, sawtooth, support

52.   Harter discovered that those who believed their _____ determined their self-esteem felt _____ about their appearance, had lower self-esteem, and suffered more _____ .

looks, worse, depression

53.   Children who are _____ seem destined to achieve at higher levels, attain greater emotional maturity, and gain popularity. Some studies indicate that children who displayed _____ at four years of age were more troubled adolescents, with fewer friends, more _____ difficulties, more irritable and aggressive, and _____ with frustration.

reflective, impulsivity, psychological, less able to cope

54.   Teachers can help preschool students develop self-control by helping students _____ themselves. _____ appears by around first grade, in which children learn to think about what they shouldn't do in different terms. Students are then better at devising their _____ for self-control.

distract, Transformation, own strategies

55.   One study found that three measures taken during fifth grade will _____ later problems: teachers' ratings of _____, negative _____ behavior, and _____ with the principal's office. Teachers play a critical role in obtaining early help for troubled students.

predict, social skills, playground, disciplinary contacts

56.   Teachers may be the _____ to observe changes in behavior. Teachers should encourage, support, and participate in _____. Good programs include a school's _____ role in establishing the program, and a brief _____ for parents.

first, intervention programs, leadership, training program

SUMMARIZE THE MAIN POINTS

This section of your study guide is designed to help you identify and understand the main points in each chapter. You've already reviewed the details using the Guided Review (above), and will consider the importance, relevance, and usefulness of the information in later sections. For now, focus on summarizing the main ideas.

For each major section in the chapter, summarize the main point and the evidence presented in the text to support and/or discuss it. If there are key terms presented in the section, define them. Some prompting questions are provided to help you structure your review.

The main sections of Chapter 3 are:

- Psychosocial development
- Erikson's psychosocial stages
- For the classroom
- Moral development
- Kohlberg's theory of moral development
- Using Kohlberg's work in the classroom
- Criticisms of Kohlberg's theory
- Socialization and development
- Individuation and development

For each section, answer the following questions:

1. In two sentences or less, **summarize** what the **main point** of this section was.

2. Briefly **summarize the evidence** for and against each main point (a simple list of details they use to support each of their points is sufficient). If the authors discuss research studies to support the point, summarize the findings in one sentence. If the authors are presenting a logical argument to support the point (i.e., not citing data from research studies), briefly list the supporting points they made. Use the detailed chapter outline to help you identify the supporting points.

3. Briefly review the **definitions of any key terms** in each main section.

WHY SHOULD YOU CARE?

The purpose of this section of your study guide is to help you understand how and why the information in the chapter is relevant for you personally. You'll be asked to think more about the relevance and usefulness of the information in later sections of this study guide.

Look back at the work you did in summarizing the main points in the section above and answer the following questions:

1. For each section you summarized, why or how is the **main point** you identified **important to and/or relevant for teachers in general**? Try to limit your answer to only one or two sentences so you don't get bogged down in details, but focus on general usefulness.

2. Now think about the chapter as a whole. **Identify two specific events, contexts, or problems** for which the ideas presented in this chapter are relevant. Briefly discuss how they're relevant and how they could be useful.

3. Now **identify three concepts** from the chapter that **YOU find useful** in some way. Discuss how/why these concepts are useful, and specify how you will actually use them in your teaching and/or your daily life. (It's okay if there is some overlap between your answers for numbers 2 and 3.)

DISCUSSION QUESTIONS

The following "What do you think?" questions are printed in the text.

1. Controversy continues to surround the consequences of day care. Do you think there are both positive and negative outcomes, or are you firmly on one side or the other? Consider such variables as age of placement and the personalities of children in your answer.

2. Assume that you are a middle-school teacher and have just discovered one of your pupils flagrantly cheating. You have heard that this student has a history of cheating, but because of parental pressure and influence, little has been done. What would you do?

3. Divorce causes an emotional upheaval in the lives of children. If the parents of one of your students were in the midst of a divorce, what would you do? Remember: Some students may not want to discuss it at all. Would you still try to offer emotional support?

4. In this chapter, you read about the conditions that contribute to high self-esteem. What do think you can do in your classroom to further your students' self-esteem in a realistic manner?

Additional discussion questions:

5. For each of Erikson's stages, list the crisis faced during that stage. Then give two suggestions for each stage for how teachers and parents can help students work toward a positive resolution.

6. Discuss educational implications for a preschool teacher working with 2- and 3-year-olds, according to Erikson's developmental stage theory.

7. Give an example of each of Marcia's four identity outcomes.

8. List, define, and give an example of each of Kohlberg's stages of moral development.

9. List, explain, and evaluate the criticisms of Kohlberg's theory.

10. Compare and contrast Kohlberg's and Gilligan's theories of moral development.

11. What are the important aspects of day care to consider? How does good or poor day care affect students when they get to later grades in school?

12. What can teachers do to help ease the impact of divorce on students in their classes?

13. Define and give examples of reflectivity and impulsivity. How are these concepts relevant for teaching and learning? How can teachers help foster reflectivity and help students learn to control impulsivity?

14. William James distinguished between the "I" and the "me." Explain what the distinction is and why it is important for teaching and learning.

15. Define self-esteem and discuss how it affects school performance.

16. What is individuation? What can teachers do to foster healthy individuation in adolescents?

17. Discuss how play relates to psychosocial and moral development.

TAKE IT PERSONALLY!

The questions in this section are designed to help you personalize, integrate, and apply the information from the text. Personalization questions ask you to consider the personal relevance and usefulness of concepts, and consider how they might be useful in your life now and in the future. Integration questions ask you to pull together information from the text to evaluate it, summarize it, synthesize a recommendation on the basis of it, or express an opinion about it. Application questions ask you to think about how the concepts might be useful to address real problems or situations you may find yourself in. All three question types will help you consider the information at a deeper conceptual level, understand it more fully, and remember it.

1. Bill Brown was faced with the moral dilemma of whether to tell the authorities who set the fire at his school. What would you do in Bill's place, and why? How can you help students think through moral dilemmas like this?

2. How have you resolved the Eriksonian crises that you have faced so far? What impact are your prior resolutions having on how you're dealing with whatever your current socioemotional crisis is?

3. Do you agree with the purposes of and need for moral education programs? Why or why not? Describe a moral education program you would put together.

4. Create your own hypothetical moral dilemma, and apply the dilemma to Kohlberg's stages of moral development. Identify how students at the preconventional, conventional, and postconventional levels might respond to this dilemma.

5. For each of Erikson's stages, list three implications for teaching. How will you foster students' positive resolutions of each stage?

6. What impact does homelessness have on students' school achievement and motivation? How will you as a teacher deal with homeless students? What invalid assumptions might you make that put these students at a disadvantage?

7. What will you as a teacher do to foster students' self-esteem? Why should you worry about this?

8. Identify a moral dilemma that is relevant to you. What would you do (or what are you doing) in this situation, and why? Relate your responses to Kohlberg's levels. Do you think Kohlberg's theory is a valid description of your moral reasoning, or is an alternative (e.g., Gilligan's theory) more appropriate? Does forgiveness play a role in this dilemma? How?

9. Describe Gilligan's theory. Is this a more or a less "valid" description of your moral reasoning than the other theories presented?

10. What kind of "model" are you for your students' moral behavior and development? How can you become a better model? Should this issue be of concern for teachers?

11. Harter described five types of competencies that are involved in a person's overall sense of self-esteem. What is your "profile" of competencies for these five types of competencies? How does this particular profile affect your overall sense of self-esteem?

CASE IN POINT...

Remember to use the cases from the text as contexts for identifying examples of concepts from the text and as contexts for solving educational problems. Also remember to use a consistent framework (like the DUPE model or the CASE NOTES in the text) to structure your "Mini-Case Report." Review the "Case in Point..." section of Chapter 1 in this study guide for more details.

SUGGESTED CONCEPTS TO IDENTIFY FOR CHAPTER 3

attachment
cultural differences in moral and/or socioemotional development
Erikson's eight crises and possible outcomes
gender differences in moral and/or socioemotional development
identity crisis and possible outcomes
individuation
Kohlberg's three levels of moral development
moral dilemma
play
reciprocal interactions
self-esteem

Review Case #1 in your text about Marsha Warren. Use the following questions to prompt your thinking about this case.

1. Could knowledge of Erikson's theory help Marsha change the classroom structure and/or activities so that there are fewer problems in this class? How?

2. Suggest teaching strategies that might foster positive socioemotional and moral development for the students in Marsha's classroom. What is she doing well, and what can she do better?

BIG IDEAS IN EDUCATIONAL PSYCHOLOGY

Thinking about the "big ideas" in educational psychology will help you organize and apply your newly acquired knowledge. Use the following steps to identify your own principles and strategies from the chapter and to relate them to the five main themes of the text (i.e., the "big ideas").

1. Review the TIPS from the text.

2. List some of the main concepts from the chapter. Use the work you did in prior sections of the study guide to help generate this list. Also look at the list of key terms from the chapter.

3. Select what you think are two or three of the most important concepts from your list.

4. For each concept you select, try to state it as a principle (use the TIPS format in the text and the example shown below as a guide for how to state principles).

5. Develop two or three specific teaching strategies that follow from each stated principle.

6. Relate your work to the five main themes from the text, identifying which theme(s) are relevant for each principle and strategy. This step will help you see how the information in each chapter contributes to improved teaching for each of these five critical aspects of instruction.

7. Think about and discuss with classmates how the principles and strategies you identify will help you improve your teaching for each theme you listed as relevant.

The five main themes from the text are:
ASSESSMENT, COMMUNICATION, LEARNING, MOTIVATION, AND TIME

Some example concepts, principles, and strategies for Chapter 3:

attachment	integrity
autonomy	intimacy
conventional level	moral development
generativity	moral dilemma
identity crisis	reciprocal interactions
individuation	self-esteem
industry	
initiative	

Principle *The adolescent identity crisis is a time when adolescents must address questions of who they are and who they want to become. (ASSESSMENT, COMMUNICATION, LEARNING, MOTIVATION)*

Strategy Have adolescents (younger and older) select, read, and do projects on topics of current relevance to the choices they are grappling with (e.g., friendships, emerging sexuality, loneliness and connectedness, etc.). (LEARNING, MOTIVATION, COMMUNICATION)

Strategy Help students learn to analyze their own strategies for dealing with problem-solving, making difficult choices, etc., by keeping journals, role playing, etc. (ASSESSMENT, LEARNING, MOTIVATION)

SUGGESTED READINGS

Ainsworth, M. (1979). Infant-mother attachment. *American Psychologist, 34*, 932-937.

Bowlby, J. (1969). *Attachment*. New York: Basic.

Brooks, D., & Kann, M. (1993). What makes character education programs work? *Educational Leadership, 51*(3), 19-21.

Clarke-Stewart, A. (1993). *Daycare*. Cambridge, MA: Harvard University Press.

Damon, W. (1995). *Greater expectations: Overcoming the culture of indulgence in America's homes and schools*. Old Tappan, NJ: The Free Press.

Lickona, T. (1993). The return of character education. *Educational Leadership, 51*(3), 6-11.

Walsh, M. (1992). *Moving to nowhere*. New York: Auburn House.

PRACTICE TEST 1

1. According to Erik Erikson, personality develops according to one's ability to interact with
   a. society.
   b. peers.
   c. parents.
   d. the environment.

2. What is the psychosocial crisis of young adulthood?
   a. industry vs. inferiority
   b. intimacy vs. isolation
   c. generativity vs. stagnation
   d. identity vs. identify confusion

3. Play serves to
   a. create emotional tension within children.
   b. inhibit children's language skills.
   c. increase assertiveness in children.
   d. foster cognitive development.

4. Two-year-old Charlyce's parents believe that their daughter requires consistent and reasonable discipline in order to help her gain
   a. identity.
   b. initiative.
   c. industry.
   d. autonomy.

5. According to Erikson, children need
   a. early intervention programs to foster their cognitive and social development.
   b. better health and nutrition programs, such as Head Start.
   c. systematic instruction and teachers who are trusted and respected.
   d. teachers who strongly emphasize work rather than playing.

6. Infants have as much influence on adults as the adults have on them. What is this called?
   a. attachment
   b. complementarity
   c. sensitive responsiveness
   d. reciprocal interactions

7. After Al graduated from high school, he decided to go to work for his father because of family pressure. With respect to his identity, Al has reached
   a. identity achievement.
   b. identity moratorium.
   c. identity foreclosure.
   d. identity diffusion.

8. How children feel about themselves and how they value themselves is called
   a. self-esteem.
   b. self-enhancement.
   c. self-awareness.
   d. self-actualization.

9. Kohlberg's theory of moral development extends from
   a. birth through old age.
   b. 4 years of age through adulthood.
   c. childhood through adolescence.
   d. adolescence through late adulthood.

10. Kohlberg's moral dilemmas involve
    a. a conflict of two or more equally good choices.
    b. children playing a game of marbles.
    c. a conflict causing subjects to justify the morality of their choices.
    d. None of the answers is correct.

11. Gilligan's theory describes the moral development of
    a. women.
    b. men.
    c. teachers.
    d. children.

12. When presented with "Kohlberg-like" moral dilemmas, Paula consistently gives answers and reasons at the highest level. Based on this information, what can we expect about Paula?
    a. She will consistently reason at Piaget's formal operational level.
    b. She will consistently behave at the highest moral level.
    c. She will tend to offer forgiveness to those who hurt her.
    d. None of the answers is correct.

13. Sandy's class was not participating to the degree he had hoped in the discussion of moral issues he was conducting. He had identified and presented a moral dilemma around which to structure the discussion, but the students were not responding. What could Sandy do to make the discussion more effective?
    a. Focus on the behavior students said they would engage in the dilemma situation rather than the reasons for the behavior.
    b. Keep the circumstances simple so students did not become confused.
    c. Present examples that were not related to this school to avoid students' feeling threatened.
    d. None of the above would be likely to make the discussion more effective.

14. Studies of day care indicate that
    a. in general, day care has positive effects on children's long-term cognitive development.
    b. in general, day care has positive effects on children's long-term social development.
    c. day care has an overall negative effect on children's development.
    d. there are no definite conclusions concerning the effects of day care on children's development.

15. Daniel looks forward to going to school every day because of the predictable routine it offers. His family lives in a homeless shelter right now, but he's not sure where they will be from week to week. For Daniel, school
    a. provides a sense of stability.
    b. is stressful.
    c. helps his parents work through feelings of helplessness.
    d. encourages his academic overachievement.

16. Michael and Jane's parents are getting a divorce. What effects on the children can be expected?
    a. Michael will show few effects, since he is not very close to his father.
    b. Jane will show few effects, since she is not very close to her mother.
    c. The children's school achievement and behavior will probably not be affected.
    d. Both children will be negatively affected to some degree.

17. Most intervention programs for the treatment of delinquent behavior
    a. are successful.
    b. are unsuccessful.
    c. require too much parental involvement.
    d. are implemented too late.

PRACTICE TEST 2

1. Which theorist assumes that personality emerges from a series of inner and outer conflicts, that, if resolved, result in a greater sense of self?
    a. Piaget
    b. Gilligan
    c. Erikson
    d. Kohlberg

2. What is the environmental influence during the psychosocial crisis of industry versus inferiority?
    a. peers
    b. school
    c. parents, family, friends
    d. both parents or adult substitutes

3. Play serves to
    a. teach children cognitive and behavioral skills.
    b. decrease egocentrism.
    c. increase a willingness to share.
    d. all the answers are correct.

4. At what stage must schooling capitalize on a child's spontaneous learning, thus aiding the development of competence and security?
    a. initiative vs. guilt
    b. autonomy vs. shame and doubt
    c. trust vs. mistrust
    d. industry vs. inferiority

5. According to Erikson, good teachers are those who
    a. pace their instruction to maximize learning.
    b. strongly emphasize work rather than playing.
    c. downplay students' attitudes toward school.
    d. refer those students not interested in school to a psychologist for therapy.

6. When Chris cries constantly, he can provoke impatient responses from his parents; parental impatience only further annoys Chris. What does this illustrate?
   a. autonomy
   b. strange situation
   c. sensitive responsiveness
   d. reciprocal interactions

7. Helen decided that she would go to work with the poor at a homeless shelter following high school graduation. She worked there for years and eventually became the director. Which identity status did Helen adopt?
   a. identity foreclosure
   b. identity diffusion
   c. identity moratorium
   d. identity achievement

8. According to Harter's (1993) work on self-esteem, which of the following children would be most likely to have HIGH self-esteem?
   a. A child who believes that physical appearance determines his/her worth.
   b. A child who has learned to take care of herself because she received little support from others.
   c. A child who believes that athletic ability determines his/her worth.
   d. A child who receives a great deal of support from her parents.

9. According to Kohlberg, what must children overcome in order to make moral judgments?
   a. identity
   b. societal mores
   c. egocentrism
   d. parental expectations

10. Which of the following is true regarding Gilligan's theory of moral development?
    a. It proposes that women's moral decisions are based on an ethic of caring.
    b. It proposes that attachment to mothers is the overriding concern for males.
    c. It proposes that the sequence of female moral development is better than that of males.
    d. It proposes that consideration of dependence, helping, and caring represent lower levels of moral reasoning.

11. According to the text, teachers who use moral dilemmas in the classroom should
    a. ask questions to help students identify the nature of the problem and their level of thinking about it.
    b. be passive during the discussion.
    c. quickly define the stages of moral development and identify better and worse levels.
    d. start by presenting complex issues that require resolution at the stage above the students' present moral level.

12. When presented with "Kohlberg-like" moral dilemmas, Gina consistently gives answers and reasons at the second (conventional) level. Which of the following can be said about Gina?
    a. She is not capable of reasoning at higher levels about moral issues.
    b. She may reason at a high moral level, but may have more of a caring orientation than a justice orientation.
    c. She will consistently behave at the conventional moral level.
    d. She will tend to forgive those who hurt her.

13. Kerry uses moral dilemmas to structure discussion of moral issues and reasoning in her class. She presents a real or hypothetical example, then gradually introduces other, sometimes more subtle and less clearcut, factors to consider. Kerry's discussions are likely to be effective because she
    a. focuses on the behavior students say they would engage in the dilemma situation, rather than on the reasons for the behavior.
    b. complicates the circumstances so students must consider the interactions of multiple factors.
    c. presents examples that are not related to this school, to avoid students' feeling threatened.
    d. works hard to retain her position of authority in resolving the issues.

14. Which of the following is true regarding the effects of day care on children's development?
    a. The physical development of children in day care is negatively affected.
    b. Children in day care show slower cognitive development than those not in day care.
    c. Children in day care are more independent than those not in day care.
    d. Children in day care are more polite than those not in day care.

15. Homeless children often
    a. have a stronger sense of self-competence than non-homeless children.
    b. develop greater creativity than non-homeless children.
    c. become educational overachievers.
    d. have difficulty with depression and anxiety.

16. Michael and Jane's parents were divorced several years ago, and now their mom is getting remarried. What effects of the remarriage can be expected?
    a. Michael will become withdrawn.
    b. Jane's behavior problems probably will increase, while Michael's may decrease slightly.
    c. Michael's behavior problems probably will increase, while Jane's may decrease slightly.
    d. The children's school achievement and behavior probably will not be affected.

17. Walker and Sylvester (1991) concluded that many later problems of delinquent boys
    a. could be predicted by three simple measures.
    b. cannot be remediated once the behavior patterns begin.
    c. are caused by inadequate parental discipline.
    d. are associated with high amounts of television watching during the preschool years.

ANSWER KEY

Practice Test 1

1. ANSWER: D, Factual; OBJECTIVE: 1; PAGE: 72
2. ANSWER: B, Factual; OBJECTIVE: 1; PAGE: 81
3. ANSWER: D, Factual; OBJECTIVE: 3; PAGE: 75
4. ANSWER: D, Applied; OBJECTIVE: 1; PAGE: 74
5. ANSWER: C, Factual; OBJECTIVE: 3; PAGE: 81
6. ANSWER: D, Factual; OBJECTIVE: 1; PAGE: 72-73
7. ANSWER: C, Applied; OBJECTIVE: 2; PAGE: 79
8. ANSWER: A, Factual; OBJECTIVE: 8; PAGE: 101
9. ANSWER: B, Factual; OBJECTIVE: 4; PAGE: 86
10. ANSWER: C, Factual; OBJECTIVE: 4; PAGE: 85
11. ANSWER: A, Factual; OBJECTIVE: 5; PAGE: 91
12. ANSWER: D, Applied; OBJECTIVE: 4; PAGE: 87, 89
13. ANSWER: D, Applied; OBJECTIVE: 6; PAGE: 90-91
14. ANSWER: D, Factual; OBJECTIVE: 7; PAGE: 95
15. ANSWER: A, Applied; OBJECTIVE: 7; PAGE: 98
16. ANSWER: D, Applied; OBJECTIVE: 7; PAGE: 95
17. ANSWER: D, Factual; OBJECTIVE: 9; PAGE: 106-107

Practice Test 2

1. ANSWER: C, Factual; OBJECTIVE: 1; PAGE: 71
2. ANSWER: B, Factual; OBJECTIVE: 1; PAGE: 77
3. ANSWER: D, Factual; OBJECTIVE: 3; PAGE: 75
4. ANSWER: A, Factual; OBJECTIVE: 3; PAGE: 76
5. ANSWER: A, Factual; OBJECTIVE: 3; PAGE: 81
6. ANSWER: D, Applied; OBJECTIVE: 1; PAGE: 72-73
7. ANSWER: D, Applied; OBJECTIVE: 2; PAGE: 79
8. ANSWER: D, Conceptual; OBJECTIVE: 8; PAGE: 102-103
9. ANSWER: C, Conceptual; OBJECTIVE: 4; PAGE: 86
10. ANSWER: A, Conceptual; OBJECTIVE: 5; PAGE: 92
11. ANSWER: A, Factual; OBJECTIVE: 6; PAGE: 90
12. ANSWER: B, Applied; OBJECTIVE: 4; PAGE: 92
13. ANSWER: B, Applied; OBJECTIVE: 6; PAGE: 90
14. ANSWER: C, Factual; OBJECTIVE: 7; PAGE: 96
15. ANSWER: D, Factual; OBJECTIVE: 7; PAGE: 98
16. ANSWER: B, Applied; OBJECTIVE: 7; PAGE: 95
17. ANSWER: A, Factual; OBJECTIVE: 9; PAGE: 106

Chapter 4 DIVERSITY IN THE CLASSROOM: CULTURE, CLASS, AND GENDER

LEARNING OBJECTIVES

After completing this chapter, you should be able to

1. Apply your knowledge of cultural differences to the methods and materials you introduce into your classroom.

2. Identify potential sources of bias in classroom interactions, curriculum, and materials.

3. Describe and evaluate approaches to educating bilingual students.

4. Analyze the ways in which social class differences can affect a student's behavior and achievement.

5. Describe the cycle of poverty, its causes, and effects.

6. Describe and discuss theories of and influences on gender development.

7. Detect any gender biases that influence participation, classroom success, and testing results.

8. Evaluate the relationships in a classroom on the basis of culture, class, and gender.

CHAPTER HIGHLIGHTS

Different Cultures, Difficult Adjustments

- Awareness of cultural differences helps teachers to avoid misjudgments in working with a diverse group.

Culture and the Schools

- Cultural differences imply the transmission of ideas from generation to generation by significant members of older generations. Differences are not deficits, nor do differences imply something "wrong" or "bad."
- The cultural compatibility hypothesis suggests that when instruction is compatible with cultural patterns of problem solving, learning improves.
- Four variables that have been manipulated to bring about greater compatibility with different cultures are: social organization, sociolinguistics, cognition, motivation, and sociolinguistics.
- The growing diversity in the nation's classrooms highlights the need for a greater emphasis on multicultural education.
- In an effort to help students with limited language proficiency to succeed in schools, the number of bilingual education programs has grown rapidly.

Social Class and Academic Achievement

- Socioeconomic status (SES) is a reliable predictor of school achievement and suggests that students from the same social class will perform in a similar manner.
- Parents can have a profound influence on their children's view of school and learning.

Gender, Development, and the Classroom

- Gender refers to psychosocial aspects of maleness and femaleness, whereas sex refers to biological maleness and femaleness.
- Gender identity is a conviction that one belongs to the sex of birth.
- Gender stereotypes reflect those beliefs about the characteristics associated with being male or female.
- Gender role refers to culturally acceptable sexual behavior.
- Researchers have consistently reported that teachers pay more attention to boys than girls. Boys simply demand more attention than girls. These findings are particularly applicable to math and science classes.
- The quality of the relationships between teachers and students will influence the success of instruction, classroom management, and students' learning.

DETAILED CHAPTER OUTLINE

I. Different cultures, difficult adjustments
  A. Misconceptions and misjudgments
    1. It is valuable to understand the attitudes, customs, and behaviors of individuals if we are to interact positively with them.
    2. Understanding cultures
      a. Hispanics possess a unique set of cultural beliefs that distinguish them from Asian-Americans or African-Americans, often preferring authority figures (such as teachers) who are understanding and nurturing.
      b. As a teacher, be aware of the learning styles of your students.
        (1) For example, Hispanic students often function more effectively when working in groups.
        (2) The learning styles of African-American students include responding to the whole picture rather than parts; tendency to approximate space, numbers, and time; proficiency in nonverbal communication; focus on people rather than things.
      c. There is a subtle form of racism in classrooms that is often inadvertent and not intended to hurt, but racist nevertheless.
      d. General suggestions
        (1) The experiences of culturally diverse students will enrich everyone they encounter.
        (2) Take time to become familiar with the characteristics that make children from other cultures unique.
        (3) Try to recognize any of your own preconceived notions and ideas of different cultures.
        (4) Case Notes: Marsha Warren's class

II. Culture and the schools
  A. Appreciating your students' behavior demands an understanding of their culture at three levels.
    1. Superficial level, or knowing facts about a cultural history.
    2. Intermediate level, or understanding the central behaviors at the core of a student's psychosocial life.

3. Significant level, or grasping the values, beliefs, and norms that structure a student's view of the world and how to behave in it.

B. Merging cultures
1. Members of one group use standards from their own cultural backgrounds to form opinions about those from other cultures.
2. Relationships with others can move to a level of mutual understanding in all settings if the effort is made to understand the differences.
3. As companies become more global and as the number of international markets increases steadily, the workplace is beginning to resemble the classroom as a meeting place of cultures.
4. If you adopt a multicultural perspective, you will come to realize that different people have different world views that decisively influence their thinking, and will be able to work, play, or study more congenially with others.

C. Cultural compatibility in our changing classrooms
1. Helping children of various cultures to achieve as fully as possible, while simultaneously adapting to each other, demands innovative strategies on the part of parents, teachers, and administrators.
2. Children may be socialized to think and behave one way at home and another at school.
3. Forces for compatibility
   a. Today's focus has moved from a cultural deficit belief to an appreciation of cultural differences. When instruction is compatible with cultural patterns, learning improves.
   b. Tharp identified four variables that seem to produce greater compatibility between students' classroom experiences and their different cultural background.
      (1) social organization—when the social structure of the classroom is changed, achievement scores and motivation increase.
      (2) cognition—children whose pattern of cognitive functioning is compatible with the school's are usually successful, while those whose cognitive patterns do not match the school's usually do poorly.
      (3) motivation—providing an understanding, supportive environment will foster successful integration and accomplishment of multicultural students, as well as improving their self-concept, self-esteem, and academic confidence.
      (4) sociolinguistics—conversational practices that reflect students' backgrounds.
         (a) Bilingual students—the better both languages are spoken, the better the cognitive attainment, and the native language does not interfere with second language development.
         (b) Two approaches to help Limited English Proficiency students are available: English as a Second Language programs remove students from class and give special English instruction; the bilingual technique teaches students partly in English and partly in their native language.
         (c) Proponents of bilingual education programs believe that students in these programs are not penalized because of a language deficit, stay current with their studies, and thus maintain their self-esteem. Opponents say bilingual education wastes time reinforcing students' native languages instead of teaching them English.
         (d) English as a second language (ESL) programs are an alternative. Proponents say ESL is desirable because most of the student's coursework is in English, with separate time allotted for specific English language instruction.
         (e) For either approach, other important questions arise, such as: what level of English proficiency is needed to end participation in the program; what subjects are taught in each language; how can each language be used most effectively; and should English be gradually phased in, or should students be totally immersed in the second language?

       (f)   A dialect is a variety of a language distinguished by vocabulary, grammar, and pronunciation that differs from a standard language. Schools with culturally different populations must be sufficiently flexible to accommodate a range of dialects.

  D. Interactions in the classroom
     1. Rejection because a child is a member of a particular group can frustrate the development of positive self-regard.
     2. Interaction with individuals from other cultures helps students accept those with different customs, languages, and ideas.
     3. TIPS: Improving interactions with students.

  E. Cultural differences and testing practices
     1. In an effort to insure equity in testing, a new national system of authentic assessment has been proposed in which students engage in real-world tasks rather than multiple-choice tests.
     2. Since social and cultural groups differ in the extent to which they share the values that underlie testing and the values that testing promotes, any national testing system raises questions of equity.
     3. Multicultural children need information about why the test is being given, when it is being given, what material will be tested, and what kinds of items will be used.
     4. Helping multicultural and economically disadvantaged students in this way means extra time and effort for teachers, but it is part of teaching.

  F. Multicultural education
     1. Multicultural education programs should
       a. teach children to recognize, accept, and appreciate cultural, ethnic, social class, religious, and gender differences.
       b. instill in learners a sense of responsibility and a commitment to work toward the democratic ideals of justice, equality, and democracy.
       c. further students' fundamental skills and provide opportunities for them to exercise them in practical situations.
     2. Multicultural education and educational technology
       a. Networking and web-based instruction help students communicate and work cooperatively with others from sites all over the world.
       b. A more diverse store of information and expertise becomes available to students than would otherwise be possible.
       c. Cooperative projects on the World Wide Web can lead to greater appreciation that cultures vary in how they approach problems and in what solutions are considered adequate and acceptable, and that a person's views are always shaped in some way by culture.
       d. Technology is useful in helping classroom teachers deal with students who differ in levels of knowledge, interest, motivation, and learning styles. Different learning preferences are taken into account.
       e. Technological capabilities require intelligent utilization and planning by teachers if they are to consider diversity and foster understanding.
     3. TIPS for improving instruction: Building positive attitudes
     4. Case Notes: Marsha Warren's class

III. Social Class and Academic Achievement
  A. The culture of poverty
     1. Poverty is not the same as disadvantage—most vulnerable children are not poor, and all the poor are not alike.
     2. Children of poverty have more health problems, have more accidents, and are exposed to greater stress and violence than other children.

3. Poverty can become a self-perpetuating cycle. Poverty conditions put children at an immediate disadvantage, with school difficulties, low self-esteem, troublesome behavior, limited job opportunities, and encounters with the law. Erratic employment contributes to poverty and the cycle commences again.
4. Analyses of the children of poverty typically focus on income, education, occupation, and social status, yet other, potentially more powerful, psychological forces are also at work, such as feelings of powerlessness.
5. Socioeconomic status, more than any other variable, predicts educational outcome, but it consists of many components.

B. Social class and education
1. In some school districts, particularly in urban and rural communities, the dropout rate ranges from 20 percent to 40 percent.
2. Too many poor and minority students continue to attend schools that do not address their needs and in which they learn little.
   a. The differential high school graduation rate for white and black populations is closely related to the economic success of the population as a whole in a particular school building.
   b. Not every student can adjust to the role of white middle-class America.
   c. Students who in previous generations were expected to leave school before graduation and get jobs with livable wages now are expected to finish high school and move into the middle class.
   d. Children who come to school hungry and listless are not overly concerned about academic achievement.
   e. The schools themselves are not prepared for learning, with too few texts and other materials and concerns other than teaching taking precedence.

C. Teaching, learning, and social class
1. Kozol drew vivid comparisons between schools populated with poor students and those of a more affluent district with regard to materials, physical facilities, access to technology, overcrowding, and the surrounding communities.
2. The extent to which the family supports the school objectives directly affects its children's academic performance.
3. Comer schools represents a successful attempt to improve education under trying economic conditions.
   a. Comer formed a school-based management team of principal, parents, and teachers who jointly ran the school, meshed with a mental health team.
   b. Several principles led to effective education for vulnerable children, including: emphasis on academic achievement, capacity to react swiftly to student needs, safe and orderly but not restrictive school atmosphere, open and encouraging attitude to parent participation, true partnership between school administrators and staff personnel, close relationship with the community.
4. Case Notes: Marsha Warren's class
5. Head Start was originally conceived as part of President Lyndon Johnson's War On Poverty, and was intended to provide educational and developmental services to preschool children from low-income families to prepare them for entrance into first grade.
   a. Head Start programs had six components: preschool education, health screening and referral, mental health services, nutrition education and hot meals, social services for the child and family, and parental involvement.
   b. Early claims about the gains to be realized from Head Start programs revolved around changes in IQ, and were unrealistic. Studies showed a "fadeout effect" among Head Start children, with immediate gains in test scores being lost after several months in the public schools.

  c. Even if Head Start graduates do not maintain academic gains, they have improved their readiness for school. Advantages extend to other parts of their lives, with significant effects on school achievement, grade retention, special ed placement, and social adjustment.

 6. Resilient children are those who grow up in chaotic and adverse conditions, yet manage to thrive.

  a. Competence, confidence, and caring can flourish if children encounter persons who provide them with the secure basis for the development of trust, autonomy, and initiative.

  b. Resilient children often mention teachers who offered them support and guidance.

IV. Gender, Development, and the Classroom

 A. Gender equity

  1. Sex refers to biological maleness or femaleness, while gender suggests psychosocial aspects of maleness and femaleness.

  2. Gender identity is a conviction that one belongs to the sex of birth.

  3. Gender stereotypes reflect those beliefs about the characteristics associated with male or female.

  4. Gender role refers to culturally acceptable sexual behavior.

  5. Many people are still treated according to stereotypical characteristics, severely limiting their potential.

  6. At an early age, children construct social categories from the world around them, attach certain characteristics to these categories, and then label the categories. This helps children organize the world, but can be negative if the characteristics associated with a category are limiting.

  7. TIPS on Learning and Motivation: Avoiding gender stereotyping

 B. Becoming boys and girls

  1. A reciprocal interaction model of development is accepted today, in which we respond to those around us and they change, then they respond to us and we change, in an ongoing process.

  2. Reactions to ideas of gender, particularly if they are stereotypical, can influence gender identity and also behavior.

  3. Children have the cognitive competency to acquire their own gender identity by 2 to 3 years of age. Lott (1989) reported a study in which children as young as 2 years assigned traditionally male occupations to male dolls.

  4. Martin, Wood, and Little found a developmental sequence to the appearance of gender stereotypes: children learn what kinds of things are associated with each sex, then they learn the more complex associations for their own sex, then later make the same kinds of associations for the opposite sex.

  5. Evidence clearly suggests that parents treat boy and girl babies differently from birth, but may be unaware of the extent to which they engage in this type of reinforcement. Siblings also influence gender development via their interactions with one another.

  6. By the age of 3, children reinforce each other for sex-typed play and criticize and tend to isolate children showing gender-inappropriate behavior. During development, children of the same sex tend to play together, a custom called sex cleavage, and one that is encouraged by parents and teachers.

  7. TV, a powerful influence on children's socialization, consistently portrays gender-specific stereotypes as positive and desirable. Children learn the cues that signal "male" or "female": music, scene changes, sound effects, and type of cuts used.

  8. Theories of gender development

   a. Social learning theorists believe that parents, as the distributors of reinforcement, reinforce appropriate gender role behaviors, and that children also learn appropriate gender behavior from other male and female models.

     b.   Cognitive-developmental explanation says that around 2 years, children use their symbolic thinking ability to acquire gender identity, then begin acquiring gender-appropriate behavior.

     c.   Gender schema theory says that children develop an integrated schema or picture of what gender is and should be.

  9.   Gender similarities and differences

     a.   There is a growing consensus that the differences between the sexes are not as great as they were once thought to be.

     b.   Differences do exist, however—for example, in verbal abilities and spatial skills. The differences are not fixed, but change as more sophisticated research techniques produce new data.

C. Gender and classroom achievement

  1.   Case Notes: Marsha Warren's class

  2.   Many teachers treat boys differently than they treat girls. Boys are reinforced for intellectual pursuits; girls, for nurturing activities. Teachers more frequently attribute failure in boys to lack of motivation, while girls more frequently are seen as lacking ability.

  3.   Regardless of the level of schooling, teachers pay more attention to boys than to girls even though the teachers often report having similar expectations.

  4.   Although teachers may believe they hold all of their students accountable to classroom rules, their observed behavior shows they do not, with boys' infractions tolerated more.

  5.   Differences also appear in the nature of the interactions, with boys receiving more comments in general and particularly more precise teacher reactions (e.g., praise, criticism, and remediation).

  6.   Gender and educational technology

     a.   Girls tend to show less favorable attitudes to technology than boys, a finding seen at both younger and older ages and across countries. This may be because girls have less experience with technology than boys, or because computers are often seen as a more male-appropriate activity.

     b.   This gender gap may be narrowing.

     c.   All students should be encouraged from an early age to view computers as an integral and natural part of their lives; adults should model positive attitudes and should reinforce both genders for interest in and work with technology.

  7.   Current Issues and Perspectives: Equal education for all: Does that include girls?

D. Gender and the curriculum

  1.   The curriculum conveys a school's position on matters of culture, class, and gender in what is covered and what is not.

  2.   Examine the curriculum materials available for suggestions for specific resources that address the issue of gender and achievement.

  3.   Banks identified four levels of integration of gender material into the curriculum:

     a.   contributions approach

     b.   additive approach

     c.   transformational approach

     d.   social action approach

  4.   Pullin argued that the potential for gender differences resides in almost any testing or assessment program. Allegations of gender bias in assessment could be subject to legal challenge.

  5.   Examples of possible bias in access to educational opportunity include: Girls are more likely than boys to go to college, but scholarships based on test scores are twice as likely to go to boys. SAT scores underpredict women's success and overpredict men's.

  6.   Adopt testing practices that help girls feel more at ease with science and mathematics and help to give them equal access to opportunity.

E. Teacher-student relationships: A summary
   1. Remember that regardless of students' actual abilities, teachers form certain expectations for their students. They then, subtly or otherwise, communicate these feelings to the individual students, who quickly grasp the messages and react to them accordingly.
   2. TIPS on Communication: Valuing relationships
   3. Case Notes: Marsha Warren's class

V. Case reflections

VI. Chapter highlights

VII. What do you think? questions

VIII. Key terms

KEY TERMS

bilingual education
chromosomal sex
Comer schools
cultural compatibility
culture
dialect
gender identity
gender role
gender schema

gender stereotype
genital sex
gonadal sex
Head Start
hormonal sex
interactions
poverty level
resilient children
sex cleavage

GUIDED REVIEW

1.   It is valuable to understand the _____, customs, and _____ of individuals if we are to _____ with them.

attitudes, behaviors, interact positively

2.   As a teacher, be aware of the _____ of your students. Hispanic students often prefer authority figures who are _____ and nurturing and often function more effectively when working in _____.

learning styles, understanding, groups

3.   The learning styles of African-American students include responding to the _____; tendency to _____ space, numbers, and time; proficiency in _____ communication; and focus on _____ rather than things.

whole picture, approximate, nonverbal, people

4. Asian-American students are often reluctant to _____ their opinions, sometimes remaining _____ when they know the answer to a teacher's question. They may do less well in _____, and seem to prefer a _____ , orderly environment.

express, silent, group discussions, structured

5. The experiences of culturally diverse students will _____ everyone they encounter. Take time to _____ with the characteristics that make children from other cultures unique. Try to recognize any of your own _____ notions and ideas of different cultures.

enrich, become familiar, preconceived

6. Appreciating students' behavior demands an understanding of their culture at three levels. The _____ level, or knowing _____ about a cultural history; the _____ level, or understanding the central _____ at the core of a student's psychosocial life; and the _____ level, or grasping the values, beliefs, and norms that structure a student's _____ and how to behave in it.

superficial, facts, intermediate, behaviors, significant, view of the world

7. Adopting a multicultural perspective in your classroom will help you come to realize that different people have different _____ that decisively influence their thinking. Understanding this will enable you to work, play, or study more _____ with others.

world views, congenially

8. Today's focus has moved from a cultural _____ belief to an appreciation of cultural _____. When instruction is _____ with cultural patterns, learning improves.

deficit, differences, compatible

9. Tharp identified four variables that produce greater compatibility between classrooms and cultural backgrounds. First was _____: When the social structure of the classroom is changed, achievement scores and motivation increase. Second was _____: Children whose pattern of cognitive functioning is compatible with the school's are usually successful, while those whose cognitive patterns do not match the school's usually do poorly. Third was _____: Providing an understanding, supportive environment will foster successful integration and accomplishment of multicultural students and will improve their self-concept, self-esteem, and academic confidence. Finally is _____: Discernable differences exist in the conversational practices of the classroom.

social organization, cognition, motivation, sociolinguistics

10. Research has indicated that for bilingual students, the _____both languages are spoken, the better the _____. The native language _____interfere with second language development.

better, cognitive attainment, does not

11.   Two approaches to help Limited English Proficiency students are available: English as a
_____ programs remove students from class and give _____; the _____technique
teaches students partly in English and partly in their native language.

Second Language, special English instruction, bilingual

12.   Proponents of bilingual education programs believe that students in these programs are not
penalized because of a _____, stay _____ with their studies, and thus maintain their
_____. Opponents say bilingual education _____ reinforcing students' native languages
instead of teaching them English.

language deficit, current, self-esteem, wastes time

13.   English as a second language (ESL) programs are an alternative. Proponents say ESL is
desirable because most of the student's coursework is in _____, with separate time allotted for
specific _____.

English, English language instruction

14.   A _____ is a variety of a language distinguished by vocabulary, grammar, and pronunciation
that differs from a standard language. Schools with culturally different populations must be sufficiently
flexible to accommodate a _____.

dialect, range of dialects

15.   Rejection because a child is a member of a particular group can frustrate the development of
_____. Interaction with individuals from other cultures helps students _____ those with different
customs, languages, and ideas.

positive self-regard, accept

16.   In an effort to insure _____ in testing, a new national system of authentic assessment has
been proposed in which the tests engage students in _____ rather than multiple-choice tests. But
since social and cultural groups differ in the extent to which they share the _____ that underlie testing
and the values that testing promotes, any national testing system raises questions of equity.

equity, real-world tasks, values

17.   Children need information about _____ a test is being given, _____ it is being given,
_____ will be tested, and what _____ will be used. This enables them to feel more _____,
and so do better.

why, when, what material, kinds of items, comfortable

18.   Multicultural education programs should teach children to recognize, _____, and _____ cultural, ethnic, social class, religious, and gender differences; instill in learners a sense of responsibility and a commitment to work toward the democratic ideals of _____, equality, and _____; and further students' _____ and provide opportunities for them to exercise them in practical situations.

accept, appreciate, justice, democracy, fundamental skills

19.   Networking and Web-based instruction help students _____ and work _____ with others from sites all over the world. A more diverse store of information and _____ becomes available to students than would otherwise be possible.

communicate, cooperatively, expertise

20.   Cooperative projects on the World Wide Web can lead to greater appreciation that cultures vary in how they _____ and in what _____ are considered adequate and acceptable, and that a person's views are always shaped in some way by _____.

approach problems, solutions, culture

21.   Technology is useful in helping classroom teachers deal with students who differ in levels of _____, interest, motivation, and _____. Different learning _____ are taken into account.

knowledge, learning styles, preferences

22.   Technological capabilities require intelligent _____ and _____ by teachers if they are to consider _____ and foster understanding.

utilization, planning, diversity

23.   Children of _____ have more health problems, have more accidents, and are exposed to greater stress and violence than other children. Poverty conditions put children at an immediate disadvantage and can result in a _____.

poverty, self-perpetuating cycle

24.   _____ of all types are overrepresented in poverty, but especially high numbers of _____ children live in poverty.

Children, African-American

25.   _____, more than any other variable, predicts educational outcome. Children of lower SES levels score _____ IQ points below middle-class children, a difference that is present by the _____ and that _____ throughout the school years.

Socioeconomic status, 10 to 15, first grade, persists

26.	In some school districts, particularly in urban and rural communities, the _____ ranges from 20 percent to 40 percent. The chances of these children for _____ in a technological society are limited.

dropout rate, employment

27.	Renyi found that differential success rates for white and black populations were closely related to the _____ of the population as a whole in a particular school building. The critical difference for any child was whether that child attended a school with others who were _____.

economic success, affluent

28.	Students who in previous generations were expected to _____, but get jobs with livable wages now are expected to finish high school and move into the _____.

not graduate, middle class

29.	One way that economic differences among school systems is reflected is in access to _____. The "technology gap" between school may _____ the already existing gap in _____ between students in poorer versus wealthier areas.

educational technology, widen, quality of schooling

30.	A family's _____ toward education makes a significant difference in their children's classroom achievement. Parents have a profound influence on the ways their children _____ school and learning.

attitude, view

31.	Comer formed a school-based management team of _____, _____, and _____ who jointly ran the school, meshed with a mental health team.

principal, parents, teachers

32.	Several principles led to effective education for vulnerable children, including emphasis on academic _____, capacity to _____ to student needs, safe and orderly but not _____ school atmosphere, open and encouraging attitude to _____, true _____ between school administrators and staff personnel, and a close relationship with the _____.

achievement, react swiftly, restrictive, parent participation, partnership, community

33.	_____ was intended to provide educational and developmental services to preschool children from low-income families to prepare them for entrance into first grade. It had six components: _____ education, _____ screening and referral, mental health services, _____ education and hot meals, _____ for the child and family, and _____ involvement.

Head Start, preschool, health, nutrition, social services, parental

34.   Studies showed a _____ among Head Start children, with immediate gains in test scores being lost after several months in the public schools. However, these students improved their _____ for school, and the advantages extended to other parts of their lives, with significant effects on school _____, grade _____, placement in special education classes, and social _____.

"fadeout effect", readiness, achievement, retention, adjustment

35.   _____ children are those who grow up in chaotic and adverse conditions, yet manage to thrive.

Resilient

36.   Competence, confidence, and caring can flourish if children encounter persons who provide them with the _____ for the development of _____, autonomy, and _____. Resilient children often mention _____ who offered them support and guidance.

secure basis, trust, initiative, teachers

37.   Sex refers to _____ maleness or femaleness, while _____ suggests psychosocial aspects of maleness and femaleness. Gender _____ is a conviction that one belongs to the sex of birth. Gender _____ reflect those beliefs about the characteristics associated with males or females. Gender _____ refers to culturally acceptable sexual behavior.

biological, gender, identity, stereotypes, role

38.   Concern about gender equity has become more prevalent, but many people are still treated according to _____ characteristics, which severely limits their _____. At an early age, children construct social _____ from the world around them, attach certain characteristics to these categories, and then label the categories. This helps children _____ the world, but can be _____ if the characteristics associated with a category are limiting.

stereotypical, potential, categories, organize, negative

39.   In the _____ model of development, we respond to those around us and they change; their responses to us then change, and we in turn change.

reciprocal interaction

40.   Martin, Wood, and Little found a developmental sequence to the appearance of gender _____: Children learn what _____ are associated with each sex; then they learn the more complex associations for _____; later they make the same kinds of associations for _____.

stereotypes, kinds of things, their own sex, the opposite sex

41.   Evidence clearly suggests that parents treat boy and girl babies _____ from birth, but may be unaware of doing so. _____ also influence gender development via their interactions with one another. TV is a powerful influence on children's socialization, but consistently portrays _____ as positive and desirable.

differently, Siblings, gender-specific stereotypical behavior

42.   By the age of 3, children reinforce each other for _____ and criticize and tend to _____ children showing gender-inappropriate behavior. During development children of the same sex tend to play together, a custom called _____, and one that is encouraged by parents and teachers.

gender-typed play, isolate, sex cleavage

43.   _____ theorists believe that parents reinforce appropriate gender role behaviors, and that children also learn appropriate gender behavior from other male and female _____. A cognitive-developmental explanation says that children use their _____ ability to acquire gender identity, then begin acquiring gender-appropriate behavior. Gender schema theory says that children develop an integrated _____, or picture, of what gender is and should be.

Social learning, models, symbolic thinking, schema

44.   The differences between the sexes are _____ as they were once thought to be, and those that do exist are not necessarily caused by _____ and are not fixed.

not as great, biological forces

45.   Boys are reinforced for _____ pursuits; girls, for _____ activities. Teachers more frequently attribute failure in boys to _____, while girls more frequently are seen as lacking _____. Teachers pay more attention to boys than to girls, and give boys more _____ teacher reactions.

intellectual, nurturing, lack of motivation, ability, precise

46.   There are subtle consequences of gender inequality in the classroom, including possible effects on later feelings of academic _____, powerlessness, and lack of scholarly _____.

helplessness, initiative

47.   Girls tend to show _____ attitudes to technology than boys, a finding seen at both younger and older ages and _____. This may be because girls have _____ with technology than boys, or because computers is often seen as a more _____ activity. This gender gap may be narrowing, however. All students should be encouraged from an early age to view computers as a natural part of their lives; adults should _____ positive attitudes and should _____ both genders for interest in and work with technology.

less favorable, across countries, less experience, male-appropriate, model, reinforce

48.   Banks identified four levels of integration of gender material into the curriculum: The _____ approach, which involves using heroic figures as curricular illustrations; the additive approach, in which _____ are added to the existing curriculum; the _____ approach, in which the goals, structures, and perspectives of the curriculum are changed; and the social action approach, in which students are encouraged to undertake _____ and _____ after being taught decision-making skills.

contributions, themes, transformational, social criticism, social change

49.   Pullin argued that the potential for gender differences resides in almost any _____ or _____ program. Allegations of gender bias in assessment could be subject to _____.

testing, assessment, legal challenge

50.   Examples of possible bias in access to educational opportunity include: Girls are more likely than boys to go to college, but scholarships based on test scores are _____ as likely to go to boys; SAT scores _____ women's success and _____ men's.

twice, underpredict, overpredict

51.   Teachers need to _____ of differences between girls and boys in math and science scores, make certain to distribute _____ evenly to boys and girls, involve girls in math and science _____ learning activities, adopt _____ that help girls feel more at ease with science and mathematics, and help give them _____ to opportunity.

be aware, questions, cooperative, testing practices, equal access

52.   Teachers form certain _____ for their students, then _____ these feelings to the individual student, who quickly grasps the message and reacts to it accordingly.

expectations, communicate

SUMMARIZE THE MAIN POINTS

This section of your study guide is designed to help you identify and understand the main points in each chapter. You've already reviewed the details using the Guided Review (above), and will consider the importance, relevance, and usefulness of the information in later sections. For now, focus on summarizing the main ideas.

For each major section in the chapter, summarize the main point and the evidence presented in the text to support and/or discuss it. If there are key terms presented in the section, define them. Some prompting questions are provided to help you structure your review.

The main sections of Chapter 4 are:

- .Different cultures, difficult adjustments
- Culture and the schools
- Social class and academic achievement
- Gender, development, and the classroom

For each section, answer the following questions:

1. In two sentences or less, **summarize** what the **main point** of this section was.

2. Briefly **summarize the evidence** for and against each main point (a simple list of details they use to support each of their points is sufficient). If the authors discuss research studies to support the point, summarize the findings in one sentence. If the authors are presenting a logical argument to support the point (i.e., not citing data from research studies), briefly list the supporting points they made. Use the detailed chapter outline to help you identify the supporting points.

3. Briefly review the **definitions of any key terms** in each main section.

WHY SHOULD YOU CARE?

The purpose of this section of your study guide is to help you understand how and why the information in the chapter is relevant for you personally. You'll be asked to think more about the relevance and usefulness of the information in later sections of this study guide.

Look back at the work you did in summarizing the main points in the section above and answer the following questions:

1. For each section you summarized, why or how is the **main point** you identified **important to and/or relevant for teachers in general**? Try to limit your answer to only one or two sentences so you don't get bogged down in details, but focus on general usefulness.

2. Now think about the chapter as a whole. **Identify two specific events, contexts, or problems** for which the ideas presented in this chapter are relevant. Briefly discuss how they're relevant and how they could be useful.

3. Now **identify three concepts** from the chapter that **YOU find useful** in some way. Discuss how/why these concepts are useful, and specify how you will actually use them in your teaching and/or your daily life. (It's okay if there is some overlap between your answers for numbers 2 and 3.)

DISCUSSION QUESTIONS

The following "What do you think?" questions are printed in the text.

1. The expression "different is not deficit" has received wide acceptance. When you think of your friends who have cultural backgrounds that differ from yours, do you understand why this concept needs to be emphasized? Explain your answer.

2. Some individuals have stated that cultural compatibility is just another fad. Students will learn, regardless of their culture. How do you respond to this?

3. Do you agree with the statement that since all students are expected to graduate from high school, schools must adapt to their changing population to lower the dropout rate? Why?

4. From your own classroom experiences, would you agree that there is a difference in how boys and girls are treated?

Additional discussion questions:

5. Define culture and discuss how it affects education.

6. List and discuss Tharp's four important psychocultural variables. Discuss how these variables differ for different cultural groups.

7. How does one's gender affect one's education?

8. Describe the developmental sequence of gender identity development. What variables contribute to the development of gender identity?

9. Summarize the literature on gender inequities in the classroom and discuss the short- and long-term effects of such inequities.

10. Summarize the literature on gender differences and similarities.

11. List and discuss the characteristics of Comer Schools. Why do these schools work well?

12. What is bilingual education? Summarize the advantages and disadvantages of the ESL and the bilingual approaches to educating students with limited English proficiency.

13. How can educational technology be useful in achieving successful multicultural education?

TAKE IT PERSONALLY!

The questions in this section are designed to help you personalize, integrate, and apply the information from the text. Personalization questions ask you to consider the personal relevance and usefulness of concepts, and consider how they might be useful in your life now and in the future. Integration questions ask you to pull together information from the text to evaluate it, summarize it, synthesize a recommendation on the basis of it, or express an opinion about it. Application questions ask you to think about how the concepts might be useful to address real problems or situations you may find yourself in. All three question types will help you consider the information at a deeper conceptual level, understand it more fully, and remember it.

1. What steps can you take to prepare for a class you are culturally different from?

2. How can you ensure that your testing practices are culture- and gender-fair?

3. What effects does poverty have on learning and education? If possible, identify an example of these effects from your own experience.

4. Summarize Kozol's findings and consider what impact this information will have on your teaching.

5. Describe Head Start, including its goals, components, and results. If you were in charge, would you continue funding it? Why or why not? To what extent? Would you make any changes in its components or implementation?

6. Identify an example of the influence of family, peers, and the media on the development of your gender identity.

7. Identify and describe gender stereotypes and expectations you hold. What functions do they serve (positive or negative)? How might these stereotypes and expectations affect your teaching?

8. Describe, compare, and contrast the social learning, cognitive-developmental, and schema theories of gender development.

9. Discuss how you as a teacher will deal with inequities of culture, social class, and gender in your classroom.

10. Discuss Banks' four levels of integration of gender, cultural and social class content into the curriculum. Give an example of how you will accomplish integration at each level for a class you will one day teach.

11. Are tests gender-biased? Give support from the literature for your answer. If they are, how can you as a teacher make them more fair?

12. Have you known any "resilient children?" What characteristics did they show and what protective factors did they experience?

13. Have you ever experienced any form of bilingual education? What type of program was it? Do you think these programs work? How will you work with bilingual students in your classes?

CASE IN POINT...

Remember to use the cases from the text as contexts for identifying examples of concepts from the text and as contexts for solving educational problems. Also remember to use a consistent framework (like the DUPE model or the CASE NOTES in the text) to structure your "Mini-Case Report." Review the "Case in Point..." section of Chapter 1 in this study guide for more details.

SUGGESTED CONCEPTS TO IDENTIFY FOR CHAPTER 4

   bilingual education
   cultural compatibility
   gender identity
   gender role
   gender schema
   gender stereotype
   interactions
   poverty level
   resilient children
   Tharp's cultural variables

Review Case #1 in your text about Marsha Warren. Use the following questions to prompt your thinking about this case.

1. Is misunderstanding of cultural background (including social class) creating a problem in Marsha's class? How?

2. Are gender differences creating problems or inequities in these classes? How, and what would you suggest Marsha do about it?

3. What teaching behaviors and strategies could Marsha adopt that would help insure fair and consistent treatment and expectations for all students?

BIG IDEAS IN EDUCATIONAL PSYCHOLOGY

Thinking about the "big ideas" in educational psychology will help you organize and apply your newly acquired knowledge. Use the following steps to identify your own principles and strategies from the chapter and to relate them to the five main themes of the text (i.e., the "big ideas").

1. Review the TIPS from the text.

2. List some of the main concepts from the chapter. Use the work you did in prior sections of the study guide to help generate this list. Also look at the list of key terms from the chapter.

3. Select what you think are two or three of the most important concepts from your list.

4. For each concept you select, try to state it as a principle (use the TIPS format in the text and the example shown below as a guide for how to state principles).

5. Develop two or three specific teaching strategies that follow from each stated principle.

6. Relate your work to the five main themes from the text, identifying which theme(s) are relevant for each principle and strategy. This step will help you see how the information in each chapter contributes to improved teaching for each of these five critical aspects of instruction.

7. Think about and discuss with classmates how the principles and strategies you identify will help you improve your teaching for each theme you listed as relevant.

The five main themes from the text are:
ASSESSMENT, COMMUNICATION, LEARNING, MOTIVATION, AND TIME

Some example concepts, principles, and strategies for Chapter 4:

> bilingual education
> cultural compatibility
> gender identity
> gender role
> gender schema
> gender stereotype
> interactions
> learning style
> resilient children

Principle　　*Students differ tremendously in their preferred learning styles. If teaching style is consistent with preferred learning styles of students, learning can be easier and more effective for students. (ASSESSMENT, COMMUNICATION, LEARNING, MOTIVATION)*

Strategy　　Observe how different students react to different classroom setups and activities. When reasonable, give students choices as to the format and setting of their work. (ASSESSMENT, COMMUNICATION, LEARNING, MOTIVATION)

Strategy　　Try to use a variety of learning formats and activities to better accommodate differences in preferred learning styles. (LEARNING, MOTIVATION)

SUGGESTED READINGS

Banks, J. (1993, September). Multicultural education: Development, dimensions, and challenges. *Phi Delta Kappan*, 22-28.

Billingsley, A. (1992). *Climbing Jacob's ladder: The enduring legacy of African-American families.* New York: Simon & Schuster.

Educating for Diversity. (1994). *Educational Leadership, 51*(8).

Kozol, J. (1991). *Savage inequalities.* New York: Crown.

Pipher, M. (1994). *Reviving Ophelia.* New York: Putnam.

Ramsey, P. (1987). *Teaching and learning in a diverse world.* New York: Teachers College Press.

Sadker, M., & Sadker, D. (1994). *Failing at fairness: How America's schools cheat girls.* New York: Scribners.

Zigler, E., & Styfco, S. (1994). Head Start: Criticisms in a constructive context. *American Psychologist, 49*(2), 127-132.

PRACTICE TEST 1

1. The bilingual technique for educating students with limited language proficiency
   a. gives students special English instruction in classes separate from content area instruction.
   b. helps students learn content knowledge and English at the same time.
   c. is the fastest way to help students learn to speak English.
   d. does not support students in their native language.

2. Gender stereotypes may be positive, since they help children
   a. classify the acceptability of gender-specific behaviors.
   b. organize their world.
   c. develop differential expectations about boys' and girls' capabilities.
   d. develop differential attitudes toward boys and girls.

3. Gender-based differences in teacher-student interactions are important because
   a. they foster feelings of increased academic competence in girls.
   b. they can contribute to attributions of lack of effort in girls.
   c. they foster positive gender stereotypes.
   d. none of the answers is correct.

4. A multicultural perspective is important in education because
   a. it enables educators to provide a better education to all students.
   b. it enables educators and students to interact in more positive ways with one another.
   c. it fosters an atmosphere of mutual respect among students.
   d. all the answers are correct.

5. Mr. Abundio was having difficulty with his tenth-grade English class. The students, who were mostly Native Americans, did not participate well in the discussion portions of the class. Mr. Abundio was trying to teach a fast-paced, energetic class, with students answering questions and offering comments quickly and with enthusiasm, but the students often did not respond to questions or offered only partial answers. Perhaps Mr. Abundio is forgetting
   a. that students may be socialized to think and respond in ways different from his own.
   b. that these students are used to the faster-moving pace of MTV, and he is moving too slowly for them.
   c. to assign the reading, so that students haven't read the material when they come to class.
   d. to offer feedback on students' answers and encourage them to express their opinions.

6. Tharp's four psychocultural variables are useful to teachers
   a. to help improve their classroom organization.
   b. to help improve the cultural compatibility of their instruction and their students.
   c. to help culturally different students adopt the values of the dominant culture.
   d. to explain why culturally different students have less academic ability than those of the dominant culture.

7. "Immigrant students need to catch up. They seem to have less ability to understand the material, and need to be taught in special, segregated classes to help them develop to their potential. They cannot handle regular classroom instruction." This statement exemplifies
   a. the cultural compatibility hypothesis.
   b. a cultural deficit belief.
   c. Vygotsky's social processes orientation.
   d. Bruner's emphasis on language as a symbolic system.

8. One attempt to insure equity in testing involves a new national testing system of authentic assessment. This type of assessment involves
   a. real-world tasks.
   b. multiple-choice tests.
   c. standardization of test items.
   d. compatibility between the values underlying the test and the students' values.

9. Poverty puts children at an immediate disadvantage in school, which can lead to poor job prospects and erratic employment, and to continued poverty. This process is referred to as the _____ of poverty.
   a. powerlessness
   b. occupational discrimination
   c. low self-esteem
   d. self-perpetuating cycle

10. Which variable is the best predictor of educational outcome?
    a. health status
    b. gender
    c. socioeconomic status
    d. parental intelligence levels

11. One of the most devastating potential effects of poverty is the _____ that easily can develop.
    a. distrust of authority
    b. feeling of powerlessness
    c. lowering of teacher expectations
    d. dependence on social programs

12. A major factor in the academic success of black students seems to be
    a. the degree of violence present in the school district.
    b. the type of curriculum materials used in the school.
    c. the salaries of the teachers in the school.
    d. the economic success level of the school population.

13. Jean came from a very poor area in which the high school dropout rate approached 40 percent. Her teachers all came from a middle-class background and did not make special attempts to modify their teaching to be more compatible with Jean's background. Jean's parents were strong advocates for her education, however, and Jean went on to do very well in school. This is an example of
    a. the positive effects of a family's belief in education.
    b. modifying one's cultural background to be more compatible with the school's values.
    c. assimilation into the dominant culture.
    d. the positive effects of a strongly ethnocentric style of teaching.

14. The purpose of Head Start is to
    a. increase disadvantaged students' IQs.
    b. provide children with nutritious meals.
    c. better prepare disadvantaged children for school entrance.
    d. prevent high rates of teenage pregnancy.

15. Studies of the effects of Head Start indicate that it
    a. produces gains in intelligence and achievement test scores that continue throughout these students' school years.
    b. produces immediate gains in intelligence and achievement test scores that are not sustained beyond the first few months in school.
    c. does not produce any measurable gains in intelligence and achievement test scores.
    d. produces significant gains in student achievement in some subject areas but not all.

16. According to Martin, Wood, and Little's description of the development of gender stereotypes, children first
    a. learn associations between objects and gender.
    b. learn associations between activities and their own gender.
    c. learn associations between activities and the opposite gender.
    d. learn associations between themselves and their opposite-gender parent.

17. One parent said, "It's interesting to me that my son is so interested in playing with cars, trucks, and guns. According to my son, girls can't play with these toys, girls have to play with dolls and dishes. I'm not sure where that came from, since we have never said or done anything to encourage this attitude." This could be an example of
    a. parents' lack of awareness that they differentially reinforce gender-specific behavior.
    b. the child's immature gender identity.
    c. sex cleavage.
    d. reciprocal interactions.

18. According to Lips, television
    a. emphasizes positive aspects of both sexes.
    b. teaches gender acceptance.
    c. teaches gender stereotypes.
    d. emphasizes non-stereotypic behavior.

19. The cognitive-developmental theory of gender development emphasizes
    a. reinforcement of appropriate gender-role behaviors.
    b. use of symbolic thinking to acquire gender identity and sex-appropriate behavior.
    c. a mental blueprint for organizing gender information.
    d. learning appropriate gender behavior from male and female models.

20. Ms. Banks has modified her teaching to make it more gender-sensitive by including themes and perspectives relevant to women in her instruction. This approach to curriculum reform is called the
    a. contributions approach.
    b. additive approach.
    c. transformational approach.
    d. social action approach.

PRACTICE TEST 2

1. The English as a Second Language (ESL) program educating students with limited language proficiency
   a. gives students special English instruction in classes separate from content area instruction.
   b. helps students learn content knowledge and English at the same time.
   c. interferes with the development of English proficiency.
   d. helps maintain students' self-esteem by helping them keep up with their peers in content instruction.

2. Gender stereotypes are often negative since
   a. they help children organize their world.
   b. they reflect the social categories constructed by children.
   c. the categories are labeled as male and female.
   d. the characteristics associated with the categories are limiting.

3. Which of the following is true about teacher interactions with boys versus girls?
   a. Boys are held more accountable than girls for following classroom rules.
   b. Boys receive less precise teacher comments than girls.
   c. Boys are reinforced for intellectual pursuits more than girls.
   d. Boys' failure is attributed to lack of ability more often than is girls'.

4. Adopting a multicultural perspective helps teachers
   a. become more organized in their instruction.
   b. recognize different world views and interact more positively with others.
   c. make up for a lack of consistent discipline and parental involvement in students' home lives.
   d. identify and modify instruction to compensate for biologically based difficulties such as learning disabilities and mental retardation.

5. Ms. Kendrick was appalled at discovering that some of her students cheated on their homework problems. Even worse, the students involved seemed to see nothing wrong with working together on the problems, and even said their parents encouraged them to do so. Ms. Kendrick does not realize that
   a. parents have a strong influence on children's cheating behavior.
   b. students may be socialized to respond in ways different from her own.
   c. working together is not cheating.
   d. the problems she is assigning are so difficult that a group effort is necessary.

6. Use of Tharp's four psychocultural variables to make the classroom more culturally compatible with students' backgrounds hopefully will result in
   a. better achievement by students.
   b. higher levels of students' self-esteem.
   c. greater motivation for academic tasks by students.
   d. all of the answers are correct.

7. "Immigrant students need to catch up. They come from different cultures with different languages and different value systems. To be effective, teachers need to consider these factors and modify their instruction accordingly." This statement exemplifies
   a. the cultural compatibility hypothesis.
   b. a cultural deficit belief.
   c. Vygotsky's social processes orientation.
   d. Bruner's emphasis on language as a symbolic system.

8. Giving multicultural children information about why and when a test is given and the kinds of items used is important because
   a. it helps them feel more comfortable, and so perform better.
   b. it helps them master the language in which the test is given, and so perform better.
   c. it provides them with items from the test to be studied.
   d. it emphasizes for them how difficult the test will be and encourages them to study harder.

9. Children of poverty are at an immediate disadvantage in school because
   a. they have more health problems than children who are not poor.
   b. they are exposed to greater physical and emotional stress than children who are not poor.
   c. they experience more violence than children who are not poor.
   d. all of the answers are correct.

10. Which of the following is true concerning the relationship between socioeconomic status and educational outcome?
   a. Socioeconomic status predicts educational outcome better than any other variable.
   b. Socioeconomic status does not predict educational outcome as well as psychosocial variables, such as powerlessness and self-esteem.
   c. Socioeconomic status predicts educational outcome as well as other variables, such as health status.
   d. There is no consistent relationship between socioeconomic status and educational outcome.

11. Children of poverty often have a lower _____ than more affluent children.
   a. rate of involvement with the law
   b. sense of self-esteem
   c. amount of stress in their lives
   d. degree of learned helplessness

12. One possible reason for high dropout rates among urban and rural schools is that
   a. little value is placed on education by students and parents.
   b. the schools do not address the needs of these students.
   c. there is little discipline in these schools.
   d. teachers in these schools are underpaid.

13. The academic disadvantages experienced by children living in poverty can be improved by
   a. teachers' sensitivity to these students' backgrounds.
   b. their families' support of school objectives.
   c. high parental expectations for academic performance.
   d. all the answers are correct.

14. Head Start is designed to
   a. foster students' self-esteem.
   b. increase parental expectations for their children's academic achievement.
   c. prevent students' becoming involved in the legal system.
   d. prepare disadvantaged children for first grade.

15. Studies of the effects of Head Start indicate that Head Start students
   a. have more positive self-concepts than non-Head Start disadvantaged students.
   b. are less likely to be retained than non-Head Start disadvantaged students.
   c. have more positive attitudes toward self and school than non-Head Start disadvantaged students.
   d. all the answers are correct.

16. According to Martin, Wood, and Little's description of the development of gender stereotypes, children in the third (last) stage are learning
    a. associations between objects and gender.
    b. associations between activities and their own gender.
    c. associations between activities and the opposite gender.
    d. associations between themselves and their opposite-gender parent.

17. Parents treat boys and girls differently
    a. often without being aware of it.
    b. because of sex cleavage.
    c. usually from about age two.
    d. because of reciprocal interactions.

18. Some 5-year-olds are playing at their preschool. One boy begins rocking a baby doll, singing a lullaby. At this age, what reaction might be expected from the other boys in the class?
    a. They will likely join in and also sing the lullaby.
    b. They will be more likely to play with this boy in the future.
    c. They will make fun of the boy and say he's not supposed to play with dolls.
    d. They will complain to the teacher that this boy is not letting them have a turn rocking the doll.

19. The gender schema theory of gender development emphasizes
    a. reinforcement of appropriate gender role behaviors.
    b. a mental blueprint for organizing gender information.
    c. use of symbolic thinking to acquire gender identity and gender-appropriate behavior.
    d. learning appropriate gender behavior from male and female models.

20. Mr. Camina has made extensive changes in his teaching approach to try to eliminate gender bias. He involves students in active discussions about social change, and encourages them to constructively criticize materials, situations, and concepts to identify and understand gender, cultural, and social class bias. They are encouraged to consider and support social changes that decrease bias. This approach to curriculum reform is called the
    a. contributions approach.
    b. additive approach.
    c. transformational approach.
    d. social action approach.

ANSWER KEY

Practice Test 1

1. ANSWER: B, Factual; OBJECTIVE: 3; PAGE: 117
2. ANSWER: B, Factual; OBJECTIVE: 7; PAGE: 134
3. ANSWER: D, Conceptual; OBJECTIVE: 7; PAGE: 140-141
4. ANSWER: D, Conceptual; OBJECTIVE: 1; PAGE: 111; 115
5. ANSWER: A, Applied; OBJECTIVE: 8; PAGE: 114
6. ANSWER: B, Conceptual; OBJECTIVE: 2; PAGE: 116
7. ANSWER: B, Applied; OBJECTIVE: 2; PAGE: 116
8. ANSWER: A, Factual; OBJECTIVE: 7; PAGE: 120
9. ANSWER: D, Factual; OBJECTIVE: 5; PAGE: 125
10. ANSWER: C, Factual; OBJECTIVE: 4; PAGE: 127
11. ANSWER: B, Factual; OBJECTIVE: 5; PAGE: 126
12. ANSWER: D, Factual; OBJECTIVE: 4; PAGE: 127
13. ANSWER: A, Applied; OBJECTIVE: 4; PAGE: 129
14. ANSWER: C, Factual; OBJECTIVE: 4; PAGE: 130
15. ANSWER: B, Factual; OBJECTIVE: 4; PAGE: 130
16. ANSWER: A, Factual; OBJECTIVE: 6; PAGE: 135
17. ANSWER: A, Applied; OBJECTIVE: 6; PAGE: 135
18. ANSWER: C, Factual; OBJECTIVE: 6; PAGE: 137
19. ANSWER: B, Factual; OBJECTIVE: 6; PAGE: 138
20. ANSWER: B, Applied; OBJECTIVE: 7; PAGE: 142

Practice Test 2

1. ANSWER: A, Factual; OBJECTIVE: 3; PAGE: 117
2. ANSWER: D, Factual; OBJECTIVE: 7; PAGE: 133
3. ANSWER: C, Factual; OBJECTIVE: 7; PAGE: 140
4. ANSWER: B, Conceptual; OBJECTIVE: 1; PAGE: 114-115
5. ANSWER: B, Applied; OBJECTIVE: 8; PAGE: 114
6. ANSWER: D, Conceptual; OBJECTIVE: 2; PAGE: 116
7. ANSWER: A, Applied; OBJECTIVE: 2; PAGE: 116
8. ANSWER: A, Factual; OBJECTIVE: 1; PAGE: 121
9. ANSWER: D, Factual; OBJECTIVE: 4; PAGE: 125
10. ANSWER: A, Factual; OBJECTIVE: 4; PAGE: 127
11. ANSWER: B, Factual; OBJECTIVE: 5; PAGE: 125
12. ANSWER: B, Factual; OBJECTIVE: 5; PAGE: 128
13. ANSWER: D, Factual; OBJECTIVE: 4; PAGE: 129
14. ANSWER: D, Factual; OBJECTIVE: 4; PAGE: 130
15. ANSWER: D, Factual; OBJECTIVE: 4; PAGE: 130
16. ANSWER: C, Factual; OBJECTIVE: 6; PAGE: 135
17. ANSWER: A, Applied; OBJECTIVE: 6; PAGE: 135
18. ANSWER: C, Applied; OBJECTIVE: 6; PAGE: 136-137
19. ANSWER: B, Factual; OBJECTIVE: 6; PAGE: 138
20. ANSWER: D, Factual; OBJECTIVE: 7; PAGE: 142

Chapter 5   EXCEPTIONAL STUDENTS

LEARNING OBJECTIVES

After completing this chapter, you should be able to

1. Explain IDEA and summarize guidelines for implementing least restrictive services.

2. Identify the various types of exceptionalities.

3. Contrast educational programs for specific exceptionalities.

4. Discuss guidelines for and issues in assessing and classifying students with special needs.

5. Define and assess the effectiveness of mainstreaming and inclusion.

6. Appraise the progress of mainstreamed students in your class.

7. Formulate appropriate classroom techniques for students to address their specific exceptionalities.

8. Define and give examples of assistive technologies.

CHAPTER HIGHLIGHTS

Exceptional Children in the Classroom

- You can expect to find a wide range of individual differences in your classroom: physical, cognitive, and behavioral.
- Federal law requires that students with handicaps be placed in the environment that is "least restrictive" for them.

The Categories of Exceptionality

- Students who are gifted and/or talented have often been overlooked in our classrooms, but today we realize they deserve special attention to further their abilities in a manner calculated to provide normal social and emotional development.
- Students with sensory impairments (visual and hearing) require early detection to prevent lingering problems that may affect performance. The cognitive ability of these students will be in a normal range. Be sure you understand each child's strengths and limitations. Be familiar with the student's IEP goals.
- Students with communication disorders may experience a developmental delay in language acquisition or find difficulty in expressing themselves. Your knowledge of language development should help you to identify these students.
- Students with medical, physical and multiple disabilities need your help in physically adjusting to the classroom and participating in all class activities.
- Students with behavior disorders present a range of problems that are caused by some interaction of personal, environmental, and even physical factors. You will need considerable sensitivity in working with these students to help them achieve as fully as possible.

- Students with learning disabilities are now identified by applying an exclusion component; that is, the difficulty is not attributed to some other cause, such as mental retardation or a physical problem. In your work with these students, be careful that some other surface difficulty does not mask the learning disability.
- Students with cognitive disabilities will be in your class; they require a carefully sequenced program and a lack of stress as they work.
- Several support systems, ranging from a student's family to professional staff, operate to help exceptional students adjust to their placement.

The Assessment and Classification of Children

- Assessment plays a critical role in placement decisions about students.
- Any classification system of students with handicaps must avoid the dangers of labeling.

Mainstreaming and Inclusion

- Mainstreaming (or inclusion) is a policy of placing students with handicaps into regular classrooms whenever possible.
- You will undoubtedly be involved at some point in educational decisions about these students: their identification, evaluation, and placement.
- Your informed input requires knowledge from reading, classroom visits, and workshops (among other sources).

Multicultural Students and Special Education

- Considerable sensitivity is needed in making decisions about multicultural students, since many factors may affect their performance.

Technology and Exceptional Students

- Technology often allows students with exceptional needs to do things that were previously impossible.

DETAILED CHAPTER OUTLINE

I. Exceptional children in the classroom
    A. Children at risk
        1. At-risk children are considered to have a high probability of becoming disabled.
        2. Risk factors include low academic achievement, grade retention, low socioeconomic status, social behavior problems, and poor school attendance.
        3. Slavin and Madden (1989) summarized effective programs for students at risk. The programs include intensive resources, tutors, and small-group instruction; cooperative learning programs and continuous-progress models; frequent assessment of student progress; many supportive materials. Ineffective strategies include retention and special pull-out programs.
    B. Children in need of special education
        1. Public Law 105-17 extends PL 94-142. Some highlights include:
            a. All children must be provided with a free, appropriate public education, regardless of the severity of their handicap.
            b. Children with disabilities must be included in general state- and district-wide assessments and with appropriate accommodations.
            c. All children who are potentially disabled must be fairly and accurately evaluated.

      d.   The education of children who are exceptional must "match" individual capacities and needs. Each exceptional child must receive an individualized educational plan (IEP).

      e.   Children who are exceptional must be educated in the least restrictive, most normal educational environment possible.

      f.   Students' and parents' rights must be protected throughout all stages of evaluation, referral, and placement.

2. TIPS on Learning: The importance of individual differences

3. Case Notes: Marsha Warren's class

4. "Least restrictive" means that students are to be removed from the regular classroom, home, and family as infrequently as possible.

5. TIPS on Motivation: The importance of individualizing

6. The Americans with Disabilities Act (ADA) of 1990 is a civil rights law that protects individuals from discrimination solely on the basis of disability in employment, public services, and accommodations.

7. Section 504 of the Rehabilitation Act of 1973 (called 504) is a civil rights law that prohibits discrimination on the basis of disability in programs and activities, public and private, that receive any financial assistance.

II. The areas of exceptionality

   A. The federal IDEA has identified 13 categories of exceptionality.

   B. Incidence and prevalence

      1. Incidence refers to the number of new cases of exceptionality during a given period.

      2. Prevalence refers to the total number of existing cases (new and old) in the population at a particular time.

         a.   High-prevalence categories usually include students with learning disabilities, gifted and talented abilities, and those with speech and language problems.

         b.   Moderate-prevalence categories are students with cognitive disabilities and emotional disturbances.

         c.   Low-prevalence categories include students with hearing and visual problems, health and orthopedic handicaps, and multiple handicaps.

   C. The gifted/talented

      1. The term "gifted" describes children and youth who are identified at the preschool, elementary, or secondary level as possessing demonstrated or potential abilities that give evidence of high performance capabilities in specific areas and who require services or activities not ordinarily provided by the school.

      2. They are a minority, characterized by their exceptional ability, who come from all levels of society, all races, and all national origins, and who represent both sexes equally.

      3. For every Einstein that is identified and flourishes, there are probably dozens of others whose gifts are obscured.

      4. In spite of a concentrated effort to insure equality in our schools, minority students remain underrepresented in programs for the gifted.

         a.   Problems in identifying minority gifted adolescents are the major cause.

         b.   The environments of those homes that foster intellectual achievement are quite similar, regardless of income level.

         c.   The concept of relative functionalism says that high levels of achievement can be explained by the understanding that behavior (including achievement) patterns result from a combination of cultural values and status in society.

         d.   Screening procedures have inherent limitations built into them for multicultural students, and should be changed. Techniques that broaden the concept of giftedness in multicultural populations should be used.

         e.   Other attempts to identify potential include seeking nominations, using behavior indicators, collecting data from multiple sources, and delaying decision making until all pertinent data can be collected in a case study.

      5. Once children are identified, the schools usually adopt one of three different techniques: acceleration, enrichment, or some form of special grouping.

         a.   Acceleration means some modification in the regular school program that permits a gifted student to complete the program in less time or at an earlier age than usual. Reactions to acceleration are mixed, but recent reactions have turned more positive.

      b.   Enrichment is a term designating different learning experiences in the regular classroom.
          (1) Enrichment techniques: try to challenge gifted students by assigning extra readings and activities; group gifted students together occasionally; provide special offerings; employ a special teacher.
          (2) The chief advantage is that enrichment can provide challenging, meaningful work for gifted youngsters while they remain with their peers.
          (3) The major disadvantage is the tendency to provide the gifted with busy work and call it enrichment.
      c.   Case Notes: Marsha Warren's class
      d.   Special grouping implies self-contained special classes, or even special schools, and not the temporary groupings mentioned under enrichment. There is considerable controversy surrounding self-contained units for the gifted, and research is inconclusive.
      e.   TIPS on Communication: Working with the gifted and talented

D. Sensory handicaps
    1. Definitions of visual impairment
      a.   Visually impaired. Any type of reduction in vision fits into this general classification.
      b.   Visually limited. When students have difficulty seeing under average conditions but adaptation (glasses) correct the condition, they are classified as sighted for educational purposes.
      c.   Legally blind. Legal blindness refers to those individuals with vision of 20/200 or less in the better eye (after correction).
    2. TIPS on Assessment: Working with the visually impaired
    3. Myths of the visually impaired
      a.   They are not born with greater auditory acuity, tactile sense, or musical talent. Superior performance may result from more constant use.
      b.   Visual problems do not adversely affect cognitive, language, motor, and social abilities.
    4. Hearing-impaired students possess the same potential for acquiring language as other children, but they lack linguistic input.
    5. Hearing impairment refers to any type of hearing loss that ranges in severity from mild to profound. There are two subdivisions of hearing impaired.
      a.   Deafness: Deafness defines a hearing disability so acute that an individual is prevented from processing linguistic information through audition with or without a hearing aid.
      b.   Hardness of hearing: These individuals have sufficient hearing potential that, with the use of a hearing aid, they can process linguistic information through audition.
    6. Eight percent, or over 17 million Americans, experience some form of hearing difficulty. Since most classrooms rely heavily on both spoken and written language, students with any type of hearing impairment remain at a distinct disadvantage in their learning.
    7. For the hearing impaired, there is controversy over what is the least restrictive placement. Placement in a regular classroom may require specialized support, such as interpreters.

E. Communication disorders
    1. "Speech or language impairment" is defined as a communication disorder, such as stuttering, impaired articulation, language impairment, or voice impairment that affects educational performance.
    2. Students with problems in sound, meaning, and/or grammar will experience communication disorders, which may be divided into two categories:
      a.   Speech disorders, such as misarticulation, which refers to difficulty with phonemes; apraxia, which refers to difficulty with commands to the muscles controlling speech; voice disorders, which are deviations of pitch, loudness, or quality; and fluency disorders, which usually take the form of stuttering.
      b.   Language disorders, which usually involve difficulty in learning the native language with respect to content, form, and usage, and possibly are present in those students with delayed language development.
    3. The possible causes of communication disorders range from neuropsychological elements that interfere with cognitive development and information-processing strategies to structural and physiological elements and environmental causes. These elements rarely act in isolation.

4. Watch for articulation delay or disorders; unusual things about a student's voice; smooth flow of speech; use of same type of speech with same meanings as most students; and use of speech to achieve goals in the same way as others.
5. Teachers can maximize interactions among students with communication disorders and peers, profile supports that allow all students to be successful, work with speech and language therapists, and encourage nondisabled classmates to talk to and play with students who have communication disorders.

F. Medical, physical and multiple disabilities
1. Students with medical disabilities are included under "orthopedic impairment" and "other health impairments" in the Federal guidelines. Orthopedic impairments include congenital disorders, disease, and impairments from other causes, and they may influence ability to learn. Other health impairments include heart conditions and many other diseases or conditions.
2. Children with physical disabilities have conditions that have been affected by the central nervous system or other body systems.
3. Children with orthopedic impairments have conditions that involve muscular, skeletal, or central nervous system features, and this affects their ability to move around and participate in academic and social activities.

G. Traumatic Brain Injury
1. This is defined as acquired injury to the brain caused by an external physical force, resulting in total or partial functional disability or psychosocial impairment, or both, that adversely affects the child's educational performance.
2. Traumatic brain injuries can range from mild to severe, and students may experience cognitive, physical, behavioral, and emotional difficulties that interfere with educational performance.
   a. Of special concern are problems with memory, learning new information, attention, and challenging behaviors. Students may have trouble mastering new skills or with "executive functions" needed for goal setting and attainment.

H. Autism
1. This means a developmental disability significantly affecting verbal and nonverbal communication and social interaction, generally evident before age three, that adversely affects a child's educational performance. It is relatively rare.
2. Early intervention procedures include teaching attention, compliance, motor imitation, communication, and social skills. A highly structured teaching environment and specific strategies to general the skills are needed.

I. Multiple disabilities
1. These students have more than one disability, or have a primary disability with secondary conditions.
2. "Full-service" schools offer a full range of medical, mental health, and social services. Teachers will be mainly concerned with ensuring that students are able to share fully in class activities without lowering expectations for them.

J. Emotional disturbances
1. Emotional disturbance includes any conditions in which one or more of the following characteristics are exhibited over a long period of time and to a marked degree, and that adversely affect educational performance.
   a. An inability to learn that cannot be explained by intellectual, sensory, or health factors
   b. An inability to build or maintain satisfactory interpersonal relationships with peers or teachers
   c. Inappropriate types of behavior or feelings under normal circumstances
   d. A general pervasive mood of unhappiness or depression
   e. A tendency to develop physical symptoms or fears associated with personal or school problems

K. Attention Deficit/Hyperactivity disorder
1. Research shows that ADHD occurs in approximately 3 to 5 percent of U. S. elementary school students and is three times more common in boys than girls.
2. The two core symptoms of ADHD are inattention and hyperactive-impulsive behavior (disinhibition).

3. ADHD seems to be caused by a variety of factors (neurological, emotional, dietary, and/or environmental) and can encompass a range of behaviors.
4. School can become a problem for these children because it may be the first time that they are required to demonstrate self-control and adjustment to a structured environment.
5. Medication is commonly used to treat children with ADHD. The major issue is that the drug must be carefully prescribed and monitored.
6. Suggestions to help these students:
   a. Keep your own emotions under control.
   b. Provide structure and feedback.
   c. Use feedback to improve their behavior.
   d. Help these students with their peer problems.
7. It is deceptively simple to classify a student's problem along a single dimension, but a student's behavior represents the interaction of many causal points. Although most educators believe that mainstreaming these students is positive, good guidelines for the best way to handle them in a regular class are still lacking.
8. Case Notes: Marsha Warren's class

L. Learning disabilities
1. Learning disabilities are a heterogeneous group of disorders manifested by significant difficulties in the acquisition and use of reading, writing, reasoning, or mathematical abilities. These disorders are intrinsic to the individual and presumed to be due to central nervous system dysfunction.
2. Aspects of the problem:
   a. Discrepancy. There is a difference between what these students should be able to do and what they actually are doing.
   b. Deficit. There is a task other students can do that an LD child can't do.
   c. Focus. The child's problem is centered on one or more of the basic psychological processes involved in using or understanding language.
   d. Exclusions. Learning disabilities are not the direct result of poor vision or hearing, disadvantage, or retardation, but these students still aren't learning.

M. Development and learning disabilities
1. An exclusion component now is used to identify as accurately as possible students with learning disabilities. This component means that the problems are not a result of mental retardation, visual or hearing impairment, motor handicaps, or environmental disadvantage.
2. TIPS on Time: Working with children with learning disabilities
3. The role of prior knowledge is critical to children with learning disabilities. Instruction should focus on where the student is now and appropriate methods that match a particular level of competence.

N. Mental retardation
1. The APA defines mental retardation as "a) significant limitations in general intellectual functioning; b) significant limitations in adaptive functioning, which exists concurrently; and c) onset of intellectual and adaptive limitations before the age of 22 years"
2. Current definitions of mental retardation consist of a multidimensional approach designed to broaden the traditional ideas of mental retardation, reduce or avoid the sole reliance on the use of IQ scores to assign a disability, and include an individual's level of support.
3. The level of support needed by an individual is typically determined by a multidisciplinary team.
4. Common problems of students with cognitive disabilities
   a. Remember that mentally retarded students have the same basic needs as the nonretarded and demonstrate considerable individual differences.
   b. Common problems include attention, cognitive processing, memory, transfer, and distractibility.

O. Exceptionality in infancy and toddlerhood
1. Two different traditions characterize the development of special children.
   a. The first views babies within a risk/protection dynamic, the interaction of which may predict the child's outcome. Risk factors can be due to biological or social factors or a combination of both.
   b. Young children, even during infancy, can be characterized as experiencing various disorders.

2. Many school districts now conduct systematic child screening activities at the preschool level.
3. Some feel screening needs to be done earlier than preschool.
   a. Many early risk factors predict the development of problems.
   b. The family context is important. If schools can identify potential problems in the family context, perhaps early interventions there can be helpful.

III. The assessment and classification of students
   A. Assessment is an information-gathering process central to decision making about exceptional children.
   B. Issues that school professionals take into account in the decision-making process include the following:
      1. Children as developing organisms
      2. Epidemiological considerations
      3. The abnormality and severity of the handicap
   C. The severity of a problem can be judged by four criteria: the degree of personal suffering that a student experiences, the social restriction involved, interference with development, and the effect on others.
   D. Most problems are too intricate to be explained by one cause and can respond only to a search for multiple causes. The diagnostic process is both complex and controversial, given the unreliability of the diagnostic and classification systems now available.
   E. Potential problems with labeling students
      1. Stereotyping: A student may be considered disabled in one situation but not another.
      2. Though labels are sometimes necessary, a rigid classification system can lead to indiscriminate exclusion from a regular classroom, to the label becoming a self-fulfilling prophecy.

IV. Mainstreaming and inclusion
   A. What is mainstreaming or inclusion?
      1. Mainstreaming means integrating children with disabilities and children who are gifted and talented into regular classrooms.
      2. Mainstreaming may be a mixed blessing for some exceptional children because insensitive classmates can make life miserable for them.
      3. A favorable but cautious attitude toward mainstreaming reflects an awareness of the dangers of pendulum swings in education.
      4. Case Notes: Marsha Warren's class
   B. Regular classroom support for exceptional students
      1. Mainstreaming means that children with disabilities may require additional classroom support.
      2. Almost 50 percent of schoolchildren experience problems, some of which require special help.
      3. Much of the responsibility rests with teachers.
      4. Professional activities you may find helpful in planning for exceptional children include
         a. Classroom visitation
         b. Teacher demonstrations
         c. Meetings, institutes, and conferences
         d. Professional libraries
         e. Curriculum and research
   C. More students are being maintained in the regular classroom through prereferral intervention.
      1. The regular classroom teacher's role is to provide services to the exceptional student at the prereferral stage, with the consultation support of various school professionals.
      2. There is modest research support for prereferral interventions. These programs can have a positive impact on special education services delivery practices, the abilities of teachers to work with students, teachers' attitudes toward special needs students, and student performance.
      3. There are various models of intervention, and many are including more parental involvement.
   D. Some results of mainstreaming
      1. Three meta-analyses showed small-to-moderate positive effects of inclusive education on the academic and social outcomes of exceptional children.

2. We must be cautious in interpreting the results of studies investigating differences between segregated and mainstreamed students, particularly with regard to
    a. the nature of the disability
    b. parental warmth, acceptance, and cooperation
    c. uncontrolled, multiple variables
3. General guidelines:
    a. Students should be capable of doing some work at grade level.
    b. Students should be capable of doing some work without requiring special materials, adaptive equipment, or extensive assistance from the regular classroom teacher.
    c. Students should be capable of "staying on task" in the regular classroom without as much help and attention as they would receive in the special classroom or resource room.
    d. Students should be capable of fitting into the routine of the regular classroom.
    e. Students should be able to function socially in the regular classroom and profit from the modeling or appropriate behavior of their classmates.
    f. The physical setting of the classroom should not interfere with the student's functioning.
    g. Scheduling should accommodate the students' various classes and should be kept flexible as students progress.
    h. The classroom teacher should have adequate support to serve the needs of all children placed in the classroom.
4. Current Issues and Perspectives: The Regular Education Initiative

V. Multicultural students and special education
A. Of growing concern to U. S. educators is the large number of multicultural students in special education classes.
    1. Difficulty in identifying students in need of services remains the culprit.
    2. You should prepare for involvement at two key points: helping to identify a student's needs by reporting on educational status, and working with the student and specialized personnel to implement the educational plan.
    3. Case Notes: Marsha Warren's class

VI. Technology and exceptional students
A. Definitions
    1. An assistive technology device is any item, piece of equipment, or product system used to increase, maintain, or improve functional capabilities of an individual with disabilities.
    2. An assistive technology service is any service that directly assists an individual with a disability in the selection, acquisition, or use of an assistive technology device.
B. The use of assistive technology devices and services must be done on a case-by-case basis and should be considered during the development of each student's IEP.
C. Advantages of assistive technology
    1. Lewis (1993) uses an ABC model to describe the benefits: technology can Augment abilities, and Bypass or Compensate for disabilities.
    2. Technology can improve academic performance, increase motivation, improve behavior, allow accomplishment of tasks previously considered impossible, increase feelings of self-worth, produce more positive perceptions by others, and empower disabled students.
D. Limitations of assistive technology
    1. Technology must be seen as an education tool rather than a cure-all. It must be used as part of an integrated and thoughtful educational program.
    2. It can be expensive.
    3. Disabled students can be resistant to changes and not want to give up their familiar ways of communicating.
E. Assistive technology for each category of exceptionality
    1. Problem-solving software, computer simulation programs, and connections to the Internet are useful for helping gifted and talented students move at their own pace and in directions of personal interest.
    2. Students with vision, hearing, or communication disorders can benefit from enhanced screens with large print, speech synthesizers, Braille output devices, and/or programs that provide guided practice with feedback on using language effectively.

3. Students with physical disabilities are helped by speech synthesizers, touch screens, or alternate input devices like switches or light pens.
4. Technology can be a motivational tool for students with behavior disorders.
5. Students with specific learning disabilities can use software that provides practice in number and letter recognition, more time to practice basic word and number skills, and multiple repetitions. Spell-checkers are also helpful for these students.
6. Several resources are available to help beginning teachers learn more about assistive technology, such as various organizations that publish information about it, computer companies, and the Internet.

VII. Case reflections

VIII. Chapter highlights

IX. What do you think? questions

X. Key terms

KEY TERMS

acceleration
at risk
attention-deficit/hyperactivity disorder   (ADHD)
behavior disorders
bilingual education
enrichment
exceptional
gifted
hard of hearing
hearing impairment

learning disabilities
least restrictive environment
legally blind
mainstreaming
mental retardation
neverstreaming
Regular Education Initiative (REI)
triad model
visually impaired
visually limited

GUIDED REVIEW

1.   Children considered to have a high probability of becoming handicapped are said to be

_____.

at risk

2.   Effective educational programs for at-risk students include intensive _____, tutors, and _____ instruction; cooperative learning programs and _____ models; frequent _____ of student progress; and many supportive materials. Ineffective strategies include _____ and pull-out programs.

resources, small-group, continuous-progress, assessment, retention

3.   The mainstreaming legislation requires that all handicapped children must be provided with a free, appropriate public education, regardless of the _____ of their handicap; must be included in general state and district _____ and with appropriate _____; must be fairly and accurately _____; must receive an education that matches individual _____; must be educated in the least _____, most normal educational environment possible; and must have their own and their parents' _____ protected throughout all stages.

severity, assessments, accommodations, evaluated, capacities and needs, restrictive, rights

4.   _____ means that students are to be removed from the regular classroom, home, and family as infrequently as possible.

Least restrictive environment

5.   When discussing students with exceptional needs, considering prevalence by three broad categories is useful. First, there are _____ categories, which typically include students with learning disabilities, gifted and talented children, and those with speech and language problems. The _____ category contains those with cognitive disabilities and those who are emotionally disturbed. _____ categories of exceptionality include students with hearing and visual problems, health and orthopedic handicaps, and multiple handicaps.

high-prevalence, moderate-prevalence, Low-prevalence

6.   The term "_____ children" means children identified as possessing demonstrated or potential abilities that give evidence of high-performance capabilities in areas such as intellectual, creative, specific academic, or leadership abilities, or in the performing and visual arts, and therefore requiring services or activities not ordinarily provided by the school.

gifted

7.   Schools frequently fail to _____ and challenge the gifted, and their talents are lost to themselves, the professions, and society.

identify

8.   Minority students are _____ in programs for the gifted, perhaps due to problems in identifying minority gifted students. Different techniques have been suggested to broaden the concept of giftedness in multicultural populations, including seeking _____, using _____ indicators, using _____ sources of data, and delaying decision making until all data are available.

underrepresented, nominations, behavioral, multiple

9.   A modification in the regular school program that permits a gifted student to complete the program in less time or at an earlier age than usual is called _____. Reactions to acceleration are _____, but recent reactions have turned more positive.

acceleration, mixed

10.   _____ is a term designating different learning experiences in the regular classroom. These techniques usually involve assigning _____, _____ the school's gifted together occasionally, providing _____, or employing a _____.

Enrichment, extra readings, grouping, special offerings, special teacher

11.   The chief advantage of enrichment is that it can provide _____, meaningful work for gifted youngsters while they remain with _____. The major disadvantage is the tendency to provide the gifted with _____ and call it enrichment.

challenging, their peers, busywork

12.   Special grouping implies _____ special classes, or even _____, and not the temporary groupings mentioned under enrichment. There is considerable controversy surrounding self-contained units for the gifted, and research is _____.

self-contained, special schools, inconclusive

13.   _____ refers to any type of reduction in vision.

Visual impairment

14.   _____ means having difficulty seeing under average conditions; however, adaptation (glasses) corrects the condition.

Visually limited

15.   _____ describes vision of 20/200 or less in the better eye (after correction).

Legal blindness

16.   The visually impaired are not born with greater _____ acuity, _____ sense, or musical talent. Superior performance may result from _____. Visual problems _____ cognitive, language, motor, and social abilities.

auditory, tactile, more constant use, do not adversely affect

17.   _____ refers to any type of hearing loss, ranging in severity from mild to profound. These students are at a disadvantage in their learning because most classrooms rely heavily on _____. Individuals who are _____ have a hearing disability so severe that they cannot process linguistic information through audition at all. Individuals who are _____ can process linguistic information through audition if they have the help of a hearing aid.

Hearing impairment, spoken and written language, deaf, hard of hearing

18.   Students with mild hearing loss often ____ well enough to go for several years in school without being ____. They ____ so that teachers do not notice the problem, but they suffer because they cannot work to their ____ .

adapt, identified, compensate, full potential

19.   Under P.L. 94-142, "speech or language impairment" is defined as a _____, such as stuttering, impaired articulation, language impairment, or voice impairment, that affects educational performance.

communication disorder

20.   There are two categories of communication disorders. The first is _____disorders, such as misarticulation, apraxia, voice disorders, and fluency disorders. The second is _____disorders, which usually involve difficulty in learning the native language. There are many possible causes of communication disorders, and the different causes rarely act _____.

speech, language, in isolation

21.   Teachers should try to provide supports that allow all students to be successful, work with speech and language _____, and encourage nondisabled classmates to _____ students who have communication disorders.

therapists, talk to and play with

22.   _____ include congenital disorders, disease, and impairments from other causes, and they may influence ability to learn. _____ health impairments include heart conditions and many other diseases or conditions. Children with _____ have conditions that have been affected by the central nervous system or other body systems. Children with orthopedic impairments have conditions that involve _____, skeletal, or _____ features, and affects their ability to move around and participate in academic and social activities.

Orthopedic impairments, Other, physical disabilities, muscular, central nervous system

23.   _____ is an acquired injury to the brain caused by an external physical force, resulting in _____ functional disability or psychosocial impairment, or both, that adversely affects the child's educational performance. They can range from mild to severe, and students may experience _____, physical, behavioral, and _____ difficulties that interfere with educational performance. Of special concern are problems with _____, learning _____, attention, and _____ behaviors. Students may have trouble mastering new skills or with "executive functions" needed for _____ and attainment.

Traumatic brain injury, total or partial, cognitive, emotional, memory, new information, challenging, goal setting

24. _____ means a developmental disability significantly affecting verbal and nonverbal communication and _____, generally evident before age three, that adversely affects a child's educational performance. It is relatively rare. Early intervention procedures include teaching _____, compliance, motor imitation, _____, and social skills. A highly _____ teaching environment and specific strategies to generalize the skills are needed.

Autism, social interaction, attention, communication, structured

25. Students with _____ have more than one disability, or have a primary disability with secondary conditions. _____ schools offer a full range of medical, mental health, and social services. Teachers will be mainly concerned with ensuring that students are able to _____ in class activities without lowering _____ for them.

multiple disabilities, "Full-service", share fully, expectations

26. _____ includes conditions with one or more of: an inability to _____ that cannot be explained by intellectual, sensory, or health factors; an inability to build or maintain satisfactory _____; inappropriate types of _____ under normal circumstances; a general pervasive mood of unhappiness or _____; and/or a tendency to develop physical symptoms or _____. These characteristics are shown to a marked degree and over a _____ period of time, and they adversely affect educational performance.

Emotional disturbance, learn, interpersonal relationships, behavior or feelings, depression, fears, long

27. A _____ is any condition in which environmental conflicts and personal disturbance persist and negatively affect academic performance.

behavior disorder

28. Attention-Deficit/Hyperactivity Disorder involves symptoms of _____ and of _____ behavior. It is caused by a _____ of factors and can encompass a range of behaviors. Methods used to help these students include _____, behavior _____, skills training, and special _____.

inattention, hyperactivity-impulsivity, variety, medication, modification, family support

29. When working with ADHD students, teachers should keep their _____ under control, provide _____, use _____ to improve students' behavior, and help ADHD students with their _____ problems.

emotions, structure, feedback, peer

30. _____ are a group of disorders manifested by significant difficulties in the acquisition and use of reading, writing, reasoning, or mathematical abilities. These disorders are intrinsic to the individual and presumed to be due to _____ dysfunction.

Learning disabilities, central nervous system

31.   Those who work with learning disabled students agree that there is a difference between what these students _____ and _____; these students show _____; their problems are centered on one or more basic _____ involving language; and learning disabilities are not the direct result of poor vision or hearing, disadvantage, or retardation, but these students still aren't learning.

should be able to do, what they are actually doing, deficits, psychological processes

32.   The _____ now is used to identify students with learning disabilities; this means that the problems are not a result of mental retardation, visual or hearing impairment, motor handicaps, or environmental disadvantage.

exclusion component

33.   The role of _____ is critical to children with learning disabilities. Instruction should focus on where the student is now and methods that _____ their level of competence. Have students with learning disabilities work with _____ who can guide their efforts and carefully _____ the environment for them.

prior knowledge, match, expert peers, structure

34.   The APA defines mental retardation as significant limitations in _____ and concurrently existing significant limitations in _____, with the onset of the limitations before the age of ____ years.

general intellectual functioning, adaptive functioning, 22

35.   Teachers should remember that mentally retarded students have the same _____ as the nonretarded and demonstrate considerable individual differences. These students face some common problems, in such areas as _____, cognitive _____, poor _____ for short-term events and information, _____ to new tasks, and _____.

basic needs, attention, processing, memory, transfer, distractibility

36.   Two different traditions characterize the development of special children. The first views babies within a _____, the interaction of which may predict the child's outcome. Risk factors can be due to _____ or _____ factors or a combination of both. The second says that young children, even during infancy, can be characterized as experiencing _____.

risk/protection dynamic, biological, social, various disorders

37.   Many school districts now conduct systematic child screening activities at the _____ level. Some feel screening needs to be done earlier than preschool because many early risk factors _____ the development of problems, and because schools might be able to _____ potential problems in the family context and implement _____.

preschool, predict, identify, early interventions

38. An information-gathering process central to decision making about exceptional children is called an _____.

assessment

39. When making decisions about exceptional students, school professionals take into account the fact that children are developing _____, _____ considerations, and the abnormality and _____ of the handicaps.

organisms, epidemiological, severity

40. The severity of a problem can be judged by four criteria: the degree of _____ that a student experiences, the social _____ involved, interference with _____, and the effect on _____.

personal suffering, restriction, development, others

41. Potential problems with labeling students include negative consequences of a rigid _____ and the possibility that the label will become a _____.

classification system, self-fulfilling prophecy

42. Integrating physically, mentally, and behaviorally handicapped or talented children into regular classes is called _____.

mainstreaming

43. The meaning of _____ ranges from the earlier concepts associated with the Regular Education Initiative to ideas of decentralization of _____, empowerment of teachers, reorganization of _____, and the total elimination of _____.

inclusion, power, teaching methods, special education

44. Including all children in regular education may be a _____ for some due to _____, lack of _____ for individual teachers in providing services for students with special needs, and lack of _____ to provide necessary special equipment.

mixed blessing, insensitive classmates, training, funds

45. Professional activities you may find helpful in planning for exceptional children include classroom _____, teacher _____, attendance at meetings and conferences, using professional _____, and examining curriculum and _____ pertaining to instruction of handicapped students.

visitation, demonstrations, libraries, research

46.   The regular classroom teacher's role is to provide services to the exceptional student at the _____ stage, with the _____ support of various school professionals. Prereferral interventions can have a positive impact on special education services _____ , the abilities of teachers to work with students, teachers' _____ toward special needs students, and student _____. Many newer models of intervention are including more _____ involvement.

prereferral, consultation, delivery practices, attitudes, performance, parental

47.   Three meta-analyses showed small-to-moderate _____ effects of inclusive education on the academic and social outcomes of exceptional children. We must be _____ in interpreting the results of studies investigating differences between segregated and mainstreamed students, particularly with regard to the _____; _____ warmth, acceptance, and cooperation; and _____, multiple variables.

positive, cautious, nature of the disability, parental, uncontrolled

48.   A growing concern to U.S. educators is the large number of _____ students in special education classes. Difficulty in _____ students in need of services continues to be a problem. _____ and occasional _____ problems are often the cause of their difficulties.

multicultural, identifying, Physical, emotional

49.   There are few linguistically and culturally appropriate _____ instruments for students who speak languages other than English or Spanish, and there is a limited understanding of many of these students' background _____.

assessment, cultures

50.   An _____ is any item, piece of equipment, or product system used to increase, maintain, or improve functional capabilities of individuals with disabilities. An _____ is any service that directly assists an individual with a disability in the selection, acquisition, or use of an assistive technology device. The use of assistive technology devices and services must be done on a _____ basis and should be considered during the development of each student's _____.

asssistive technology device, assistive technology service, case-by-case, IEP

51.   Lewis (1993) uses an ABC model to describe the benefits: Technology can _____ abilities, and _____ or _____ for disabilities. Technology can improve academic _____, increase _____, improve behavior, allow accomplishment of tasks previously considered _____, increase feelings of _____, produce more positive _____ by others, and _____ disabled students.

Augment, Bypass, Compensate, performance, motivation, impossible, self-worth, perceptions, empower

52.   Technology must be seen as an _____ rather than a cure-all. It must be used as part of an _____ educational program. It can be _____, and disabled students can be _____ to changes and not want to give up their familiar ways of communicating.

educational tool, integrated and thoughtful, expensive, resistant

53.   Problem-solving _____, computer _____ programs, and connections to the _____ are useful for helping gifted and talented students move at their own pace and in directions of personal interest.

software, simulation, Internet

54.   Students with vision, hearing, or communication disorders can benefit from _____ with large print, speech _____ , Braille output devices, and/or programs that provide guided practice with feedback on using _____ effectively.

enhanced screens, synthesizers, language

55.   Students with physical disabilities are helped by speech _____, _____ screens, or _____ like switches or light pens.

synthesizers, touch, alternate input devices

56.   Technology can be a _____ tool for students with behavior disorders. Students with specific learning disabilities can use software that provides practice in number and letter _____, more _____ to practice basic word and number skills, and multiple _____. Spell-checkers are also helpful for these students.

motivational, recognition, time, repetitions

57.   Assistive technology changes _____. Several resources are available, such as various _____ that publish information about it, _____ companies, and the Internet.

rapidly, organizations, computer

SUMMARIZE THE MAIN POINTS

This section of your study guide is designed to help you identify and understand the main points in each chapter. You've already reviewed the details using the Guided Review (above), and will consider the importance, relevance, and usefulness of the information in later sections. For now, focus on summarizing the main ideas.

For each major section in the chapter, summarize the main point and the evidence presented in the text to support and/or discuss it. If there are key terms presented in the section, define them. Some prompting questions are provided to help you structure your review.

The main sections of Chapter 5 are:

- Exceptional children in the classroom
- Children in need of special education
- Areas of exceptionality
- The assessment and classification of children
- Mainstreaming and inclusion
- Multicultural students and special education
- Technology and exceptional students

For each section, answer the following questions:

1. In two sentences or less, **summarize** what the **main point** of this section was.

2. Briefly **summarize the evidence** for and against each main point (a simple list of details they use to support each of their points is sufficient). If the authors discuss research studies to support the point, summarize the findings in one sentence. If the authors are presenting a logical argument to support the point (i.e., not citing data from research studies), briefly list the supporting points they made. Use the detailed chapter outline to help you identify the supporting points.

3. Briefly review the **definitions of any key terms** in each main section.

WHY SHOULD YOU CARE?

The purpose of this section of your study guide is to help you understand how and why the information in the chapter is relevant for you personally. You'll be asked to think more about the relevance and usefulness of the information in later sections of this study guide.

Look back at the work you did in summarizing the main points in the section above and answer the following questions:

1. For each section you summarized, why or how is the **main point** you identified **important to and/or relevant for teachers in general**? Try to limit your answer to only one or two sentences so you don't get bogged down in details, but focus on general usefulness.

2. Now think about the chapter as a whole. **Identify two specific events, contexts, or problems** for which the ideas presented in this chapter are relevant. Briefly discuss how they're relevant and how they could be useful.

3. Now **identify three concepts** from the chapter that **YOU find useful** in some way. Discuss how/why these concepts are useful, and specify how you will actually use them in your teaching and/or your daily life. (It's okay if there is some overlap between your answers for numbers 2 and 3.)

DISCUSSION QUESTIONS

The following "What do you think?"questions are printed in the text.

1. What are the guidelines for implementing least restrictive environment (LRE) placements? Consider a child in your classroom who is experiencing a severe behavior problem. Apply the criteria of LRE to this case.

2. Monitor mainstreamed students more carefully when they are in class. If so, you could try something like this (Bos & Vaughn, 1988):

   Student Helped (Name)

   <u>Date</u>   <u>Time</u>   <u>Comments</u>

   Carefully mark the date and time and use appropriate comments, such as these:
   -difficulty with long and short vowels
   -trouble with two-place multiplication

   You can use this technique with behavioral problems as well. Keep a close check on dates to determine if the time between incidents is improving.
   - What was the time of day?
   - Was it the same time each time the incident occurred?
   - What was the subject matter when the incident occurred?

   With these and other simple techniques, you can keep a close check on the progress of your students who are exceptional.

3. Suppose you were presenting an in-service on gifted and talented students to novice teachers. What suggestions would you offer to teachers working with such students in their classes?

4. Outline guidelines that you would use for working with students who are visually and hearing impaired and students who are physically or health impaired.

5. What can you do to help a student with attention-deficit/hyperactivity disorder?

6. Name myths and facts that you know about learning disabilities. Discuss a child that you know who may have a learning disability.

7. Identify types of mental retardation and describe characteristics of school-age children with each type. How would these characteristics influence your teaching strategies?

Additional discussion questions:

8. List and explain each of the highlights of the laws on education of students with special needs.

9. Summarize the major requirements of the mainstreaming legislation.

10. Outline guidelines for working with students who have communication disorders.

11. Suggest ways a teacher can effectively work with students who have Attention-Deficit/Hyperactivity Disorder.

12. What are learning disabilities? How would a parent or teacher identify the existence of a LD in their child/student? What teaching techniques would be helpful for a student with a LD?

13. What are some of the common problems of students with cognitive disabilities, and how can teachers help them?

14. What is the function of assessment for students with exceptionalities? What are the dangers?

15. How are gifted students identified?

16. What are mainstreaming and inclusion, and how do they differ? What are their purposes and their legal requirements? Do they work?

17. Why are multicultural students identified as needing special education so frequently? Why are they identified as gifted so rarely? What can be done to change these situations?

18. What is labeling? List two advantages and two disadvantages of labeling students.

19. Summarize the types of assistive technology that are useful to students with exceptional needs. What is available, and how can these technologies be helpful?

TAKE IT PERSONALLY!

The questions in this section are designed to help you personalize, integrate, and apply the information from the text. Personalization questions ask you to consider the personal relevance and usefulness of concepts, and consider how they might be useful in your life now and in the future. Integration questions ask you to pull together information from the text to evaluate it, summarize it or synthesize a recommendation on the basis of it, or express an opinion about it. Application questions ask you to think about how the concepts might be useful to address real problems or situations you may find yourself in. All three question types will help you consider the information at a deeper conceptual level, understand it more fully, and remember it.

1. What teaching strategies might help a mainstreamed handicapped student in the regular classroom? What concerns for, or prejudices against, mainstreamed students do you have?

2. Have you ever been in a class with a mainstreamed student? What do you think the effect of mainstreaming was, academically and socially, on the handicapped child? What effect did the mainstreamed student have on the rest of the class?

3. Are you gifted? Do you know someone who is gifted? How did/would you identify a gifted student? What programs have you or has the gifted person you know received? How could educational programs for gifted students be improved? Did you or the gifted person you know experience any special educational problems?

4. For each category of exceptionality discussed in the text, discuss what this exceptionality means, common problems these students might face in the classroom, and how you as a teacher will deal with students who have these exceptionalities. Give at least two concrete, specific suggestions for each category. How can assistive technology help these students?

5. Summarize the types of programs offered to gifted students. Identify the main differences between the types. In your opinion, which approach is best?

6. Develop a program for identifying and teaching gifted students. What will be included in your program, and why have you chosen to include these aspects?

7. What does it mean to have a communication disorder? How will you as a teacher work with students who have communication disorders in your classes?

8. Have you experienced inclusive teaching practices? How do they differ from less inclusive teaching practices? What aspects of inclusive teaching will you strive to use?

CASE IN POINT...

Remember to use the cases from the text as contexts for identifying examples of concepts from the text and as contexts for solving educational problems. Also remember to use a consistent framework (like the DUPE model or the CASE NOTES in the text) to structure your "Mini-Case Report." Review the "Case in Point..." section of Chapter 1 in this study guide for more details.

SOME CONCEPTS TO IDENTIFY FOR CHAPTER 5

at risk
attention-deficit/hyperactivity disorder (ADHD)
behavior disorders
bilingual education
inclusion
learning disabilities
least restrictive environment
mainstreaming
neverstreaming
strategies for educating gifted/talented students

Review Case #1 in your text about Marsha Warren. Use the following questions to prompt your thinking about this case.

1. Are the needs of gifted and talented students being met in Marsha's classroom? What instructional strategies and materials can be used to meet these needs?

2. Some of Marsha's students are showing poor academic performance and significant behavior problems. What specific steps can she take to appropriately identify the specific problems she faces, and then what changes could she make in her classroom environment (teaching strategies, management, and classroom setup) to improve the situation?

3. If some of the students in Marsha's class are determined to have special educational needs, what role should Marsha play in their instruction? What instructional techniques can she use to meet the needs of all her students?

END-OF-CASE WRAPUP

This chapter is the last on in the text dealing specifically with Marsha Warren's classroom. Take a moment to review your thoughts, "mini-case reports," and suggestions for Marsha. Jot down a brief summary of your suggestions for her, highlighting what you think are the main issues/problems she must address and the actions that you think would be most successful for her. Reflect on what you have learned about teaching and learning interactions by analyzing this case and which ideas you think will be most useful to you in your teaching career.

BIG IDEAS IN EDUCATIONAL PSYCHOLOGY

Thinking about the "big ideas" in educational psychology will help you organize and apply your newly acquired knowledge. Use the following steps to identify your own principles and strategies from the chapter and to relate them to the five main themes of the text (i.e., the "big ideas").

1. Review the TIPS from the text.

2. List some of the main concepts from the chapter. Use the work you did in prior sections of the study guide to help generate this list. Also look at the list of key terms from the chapter.

3. Select what you think are two or three of the most important concepts from your list.

4. For each concept you select, try to state it as a principle (use the TIPS format in the text and the example shown below as a guide for how to state principles).

5. Develop two or three specific teaching strategies that follow from each stated principle.

6. Relate your work to the five main themes from the text, identifying which theme(s) are relevant for each principle and strategy. This step will help you see how the information in each chapter contributes to improved teaching for each of these five critical aspects of instruction.

7. Think about and discuss with classmates how the principles and strategies you identify will help you improve your teaching for each theme you listed as relevant.

The five main themes from the text are:
ASSESSMENT, COMMUNICATION, LEARNING, MOTIVATION, AND TIME

Some example concepts, principles, and strategies for Chapter 5:

at risk
behavior disorders
bilingual education
exceptional
gifted/talented education
        (acceleration, enrichment)
hearing impairment
inclusion
learning disabilities

least restrictive environment
legally blind
mainstreaming
mental retardation
neverstreaming
Regular Education Initiative (REI)
triad model
visually impaired

Principle   *Early identification and treatment of children at risk for academic problems can have a strong positive effect on both academic and social outcomes. (ASSESSMENT, LEARNING, MOTIVATION)*

Strategy   Learn what is considered to be the "average" range of normative development for the ages you will teach so you can more easily identify at-risk children. (ASSESSMENT)

Strategy   Don't go it alone. If you suspect a developmental delay, LD, BD, etc., of any kind, talk to the student's parents and school personnel (e.g., school psychologist, nurse, reading specialist, speech/hearing specialist, etc.) to get help and guidance. (ASSESSMENT, COMMUNICATION)

SUGGESTED READINGS

Bloom, B. (1985). *Developing talent in young people.* New York: McGraw-Hill.

Brown, A., & Campione, J. (1986). Psychological theory and the study of learning disabilities. *American Psychologist, 41,* 1059-1068.

First, J. M., & Carrera, J. W. (Eds.). (1988). *New Voices. Immigrant students in U.S. public schools.* Boston: The National Coalition of Advocates for Students.

McDonnell, L. M., McLauglin, M. J., & Morison, P. (Eds.) (1997). *Educating one and all: Students with disabilities and standards-based reform.* Washington, D. C.: National Research Council.

Sroufe, L. A., & Rutter, M. (1984). The domain of developmental psychopathology. *Child Development, 55,* 17-29.

Witt, J. C., Elliott, S. N., Daly III, E. J., Gresham, R. M., & Dramer, J. J. (1998). *Assessment of at-risk and special needs children* (2nd ed.). Boston: McGraw-Hill.

PRACTICE TEST 1

1. Children who are considered to have a high probability of becoming handicapped are considered
   a. at risk.
   b. learning disabled.
   c. dysfunctional.
   d. disabled.

2. Nathan, a first-grader, has been identified as an at-risk student. His school is planning to place him in a pullout program. What does the literature indicate about such a program?
   a. It is a good way to help Nathan catch up with his peers academically.
   b. It is likely to accelerate Nathan's achievement.
   c. It is likely to negatively affect Nathan's self-esteem.
   d. It may keep Nathan from falling farther behind his peers.

3. P.L. 94-142, now called IDEA, provides services for handicapped students in the
   a. accelerated environment.
   b. enriched environment.
   c. least restrictive environment.
   d. most restrictive environment.

4. In order to be successfully mainstreamed, students
   a. should be capable of doing some grade-level work.
   b. do not necessarily have to follow the regular classroom routine.
   c. will require extensive assistance from the teacher or other students.
   d. should be held to a strict schedule that is convenient for the majority of the class.

5. Mainstreaming involves integrating _____ handicapped children into regular classes.
   a. physically and mentally
   b. mentally
   c. behaviorally and mentally
   d. physically, mentally, and behaviorally

6. Research on the efficacy of mainstreaming shows that the nature of the disability affects adjustment and peer acceptance in regular classes. A student with which disability is most likely to experience adjustment problems?
   a. vision impairment
   b. hearing impairment
   c. emotional problems
   d. learning disability

7. Which of the following categories of exceptionality is NOT a high-prevalence category?
   a. health and visual problems
   b. learning disabilities
   c. gifted and talented
   d. speech and language problems

8. Gifted and talented children are those who possess demonstrated or potential abilities that give evidence of high performance capabilities in _____ ability.
   a. intellectual
   b. creative
   c. leadership
   d. All of the answers are correct.

9. Garrett is a gifted minority student, but is not doing well in school. Which of the following is a likely explanation for Garrett's lack of achievement?
   a. He has been given academic work that is too difficult for him.
   b. He was identified as gifted too early in his academic career.
   c. His school puts too much emphasis on programs for the gifted.
   d. He has not been identified as gifted and so has not been placed in a gifted and talented program.

10. Charlyce was identified as a gifted and talented student and skipped an elementary grade. What is the name of this technique?
   a. special grouping
   b. enrichment
   c. acceleration
   d. neverstreaming

11. Individuals with vision of 20/200 or less after correction are considered
   a. legally blind.
   b. visually limited.
   c. legally impaired.
   d. visually impaired.

12. Emotional disorders are characterized by long-term and significant exhibition of any/all of the following EXCEPT
   a. throwing temper tantrums for inappropriate reasons.
   b. general feelings of depression of being unhappy.
   c. inability to learn due to subnormal intelligence levels.
   d. development of fears of school.

13. In Mrs. Gregg's class, there are two students with ADHD. Mrs. Gregg works to make sure these students know what is expected of them, provides frequent feedback to help them control their behavior, and is very patient with their behavior. She encourages them to work together, but not with the other students, so as to minimize frustration for them and the class. Which of the following suggestions might help Mrs. Gregg improve the education these ADHD students are receiving?
   a. Mrs. Gregg should try to maintain a greater control over her own frustration with these students.
   b. Mrs. Gregg should try to provide structure for these students.
   c. Mrs. Gregg should try to encourage more interaction between these students and the rest of the class.
   d. Mrs. Gregg should provide additional assignments for these students to help them practice the material being taught.

14. The exclusion component for students with learning disabilities means that the problems are not a result of
   a. visual or hearing impairment.
   b. mental retardation.
   c. environmental disadvantage.
   d. All of the answers are correct.

15. Why should preschool children be screened for the possibility of exceptionality?
   a. Early screening devices have become very accurate for diagnosing problems.
   b. Protective developmental factors can be eliminated.
   c. Early interventions can be implemented to reduce the effects of risk factors.
   d. Risk factors can be further encouraged.

16. Students with mental retardation typically show
    a. attentional problems.
    b. superior memory for specific types of information.
    c. good concentration skills.
    d. average organizational and classification skills.

17. Amber is a student with mental retardation. Which of the following problems is Amber likely to show?
    a. poor ability to use what she knows on new tasks.
    b. poor memory for things she has just been taught.
    c. a tendency to be distracted by irrelevant information.
    d. All of the above are likely.

18. Which of the following must be considered when judging the severity of a student's handicap?
    a. Whether the problem affects others with whom the student interacts.
    b. Whether the problem keeps the student from doing things he/she would like to do.
    c. Whether the problem keeps the students from functioning adequately in the classroom.
    d. All of the above must be considered.

19. Assistive technology devices and services must be
    a. made available to all handicapped students regardless of the type and severity of their handicap.
    b. reserved for only those with the most severe levels of disability due to cost restrictions.
    c. considered during each student's IEP development and decided upon individually for each student.
    d. paid for at least in part by the handicapped student's family.

PRACTICE TEST 2

1. Which of the following is NOT effective in working with at-risk students?
   a. first-grade prevention programs
   b. pullout programs
   c. cooperative learning programs
   d. frequent assessment of student progress

2. Monica is an at-risk first-grade student. Her parents and teachers are considering several options for her education. Which of the following would be a good educational strategy for Monica?
   a. a cooperative learning program
   b. a continuous progress mode
   c. a first-grade prevention program
   d. All of the above would be good strategies for Monica.

3. In special education, class sizes must be kept
   a. low.
   b. high.
   c. moderate.
   d. to a ratio of one teacher per one student.

4. Mainstreamed students
   a. do not need to function socially in the regular classroom.
   b. do not need to be able to stay on task on their own.
   c. should be able to fit into the routine of the regular classroom.
   d. are usually not able to fit into the physical setting of the classroom.

5. One requirement of mainstreaming is that each exceptional child must receive
   a. a regular education initiative.
   b. an exclusive component.
   c. an individualized educational plan.
   d. None of the answers is correct.

6. Results of mainstreaming studies must be interpreted with caution, particularly with regard to
   a. the nature of the disability.
   b. uncontrolled, multiple variables.
   c. parental warmth, acceptance, and cooperation.
   d. All of the answers are correct.

7. Anna stated emphatically, "Mainstreaming is a good thing. Research has shown that mainstreaming definitely improves performance, attitudes, and process outcomes for exceptional students. There really is no question that this is the best thing for exceptional students." Anna is
   a. correct in her conclusions.
   b. overstating the research data.
   c. incorrect in her conclusions.
   d. correct about the social effects, but not the academic effects of mainstreaming.

8. Which of the following categories of exceptionality is considered the low-prevalence category?
   a. gifted and talented
   b. learning disabilities
   c. emotionally disturbed
   d. hearing problems

9. Which of the following is TRUE regarding gifted and talented students?
   a. Minority students are overidentified as gifted and talented.
   b. Accurate identification of gifted and talented students remains a problem.
   c. Acceleration is recognized as the most effective way to meet the needs of gifted and talented students.
   d. Giftedness is defined by most to mean superior ability in language and mathematical skills.

10. Michelle is a minority student who is probably gifted. Which of the following can we expect about Michelle's school experiences?
    a. She is less likely to be identified as gifted than a non-minority child.
    b. She will probably be placed in an acceleration program for the gifted.
    c. She will probably experience negative effects from her gifted program on her social development.
    d. She will probably develop a very strong sense of self-esteem.

11. A teacher assigns extra reading to his gifted students in an attempt to challenge them. What is this technique called?
    a. enrichment
    b. special grouping
    c. acceleration
    d. neverstreaming

12. According to the text, what is one of the most realistic dangers that students with hearing impairments face?
    a. The danger of being diagnosed too early.
    b. The danger of being labeled as slow or difficult.
    c. The danger of being overloaded with linguistic input.
    d. The danger of being placed in a regular classroom too frequently.

13. Which communication disorder refers to difficulty with commands to the muscles controlling speech?
    a. apraxia
    b. language disorders
    c. speech disorders
    d. aphasia

14. Which of the following physical disabilities involves orthopedic impairment?
    a. cerebral palsy
    b. asthma
    c. epilepsy
    d. diabetes

15. Attention-Deficit/Hyperactivity Disorder (ADHD) seems to be caused by
    a. neurological factors.
    b. emotional factors.
    c. dietary factors.
    d. All of the answers are correct.

16. Most students with ADHD
    a. require heavy doses of strong medication.
    b. develop normally with a minimum of difficulties.
    c. are hyperactive/impulsive, but have few attentional problems.
    d. are girls.

17. Which of the following statements regarding learning disabilities is true?
    a. All LD students have perceptual problems.
    b. Hyperactivity is easily controlled by drugs.
    c. Two out of three LD students receive special instruction in math.
    d. All LD students are brain damaged.

18. When attempting to diagnose or classify a student's handicap, which of the following is true?
    a. The classification process is relatively straightforward as long as reliable classification guidelines are used.
    b. Labeling the problem may be needed to allow access to special services, but labeling carries some risks.
    c. Most problems have one predominant cause.
    d. Labels usually are good descriptors and convey reliable and accurate information about the problem.

19. Lewis' ABC model of assistive technology describes
    a. the range of assistive technology available for different disabilities.
    b. the ways in which technology can help handicapped students.
    c. guidelines for deciding which types of assistive technology to use for which handicaps.
    d. ways to reduce the costs associated with assistive technology.

ANSWER KEY

Practice Test 1

1. ANSWER: A, Factual; OBJECTIVE: 2; PAGE: 148
2. ANSWER: D, Applied; OBJECTIVE: 5; PAGE: 149
3. ANSWER: C, Factual; OBJECTIVE: 1; PAGE: 150
4. ANSWER: A, Factual; OBJECTIVE: 6; PAGE: 187
5. ANSWER: D, Factual; OBJECTIVE: 5; PAGE: 182
6. ANSWER: C, Factual; OBJECTIVE: 5; PAGE: 186
7. ANSWER: A, Conceptual; OBJECTIVE: 2; PAGE: 157
8. ANSWER: D, Factual; OBJECTIVE: 2; PAGE: 158
9. ANSWER: D, Applied; OBJECTIVE: 3; PAGE: 159
10. ANSWER: C, Conceptual; OBJECTIVE: 3; PAGE: 160
11. ANSWER: A, Factual; OBJECTIVE: 2; PAGE: 162
12. ANSWER: C, Factual; OBJECTIVE: 2; PAGE: 169
13. ANSWER: C, Applied; OBJECTIVE: 7; PAGE: 171-172
14. ANSWER: D, Factual; OBJECTIVE: 2; PAGE: 174
15. ANSWER: C, Conceptual; OBJECTIVE: 7; PAGE: 179
16. ANSWER: A, Factual; OBJECTIVE: 2; PAGE: 176-177
17. ANSWER: D, Applied; OBJECTIVE: 2; PAGE: 178-179
18. ANSWER: D, Factual; OBJECTIVE: 4; PAGE: 180
19. ANSWER: C, Factual; OBJECTIVE: 8; PAGE: 190

Practice Test 2

1.   ANSWER: B, Factual; OBJECTIVE: 7; PAGE: 149
2.   ANSWER: D, Applied; OBJECTIVE: 3; PAGE: 148-149
3.   ANSWER: A, Factual; OBJECTIVE: 7; PAGE: 154
4.   ANSWER: C, Factual; OBJECTIVE: 5; PAGE: 187
5.   ANSWER: C, Factual; OBJECTIVE: 1; PAGE: 150
6.   ANSWER: D, Conceptual; OBJECTIVE: 5; PAGE: 186-187
7.   ANSWER: B, Applied; OBJECTIVE: 5; PAGE: 186
8.   ANSWER: D, Factual; OBJECTIVE: 2; PAGE: 157
9.   ANSWER: B, Factual; OBJECTIVE: 2; PAGE: 158-160
10.   ANSWER: A, Applied; OBJECTIVE: 6; PAGE: 159
11.   ANSWER: A, Conceptual; OBJECTIVE: 3; PAGE: 160
12.   ANSWER: B, Factual; OBJECTIVE: 2; PAGE: 164
13.   ANSWER: A, Factual; OBJECTIVE: 2; PAGE: 165
14.   ANSWER: A, Factual; OBJECTIVE: 2; PAGE: 165-166
15.   ANSWER: D, Factual; OBJECTIVE: 2; PAGE: 171
16.   ANSWER: B, Factual; OBJECTIVE: 2; PAGE: 172
17.   ANSWER: C, Factual; OBJECTIVE: 7; PAGE: 175
18.   ANSWER: B, Conceptual; OBJECTIVE: 4; PAGE: 181-182
19.   ANSWER: B, Conceptual; OBJECTIVE: 8; PAGE: 191

Chapter 6   BEHAVIORAL PSYCHOLOGY AND LEARNING

LEARNING OBJECTIVES

After completing this chapter, you should be able to

1. Explain the basic concepts of classical conditioning.

2. Recognize how students may acquire fears through classical conditioning.

3. Describe Thorndike's major laws of learning and explain how these laws can be applied to the classroom.

4. Identify the major elements of operant conditioning.

5. Understand how the principles of reinforcement and punishment can be used in the classroom.

6. Distinguish between classical and operant conditioning.

7. Define Bandura's social cognitive learning and describe four important processes involved in observational learning.

8. Apply the principles of social cognitive theory (such as imitation and modeling) to your instruction techniques.

9. Define self-control and describe three components of self-control that can be used to teach students self-control.

10. Identify advantages and disadvantages of behaviorally based computer-assisted instruction.

CHAPTER HIGHLIGHTS

Classical Conditioning

- Ivan Pavlov's work has educational implications, especially with regard to generalization, discrimination, and extinction of behavior.
- Conditioning principles should make teachers aware of a need to use classroom stimuli sensitively.

Thorndike's Connectionism

- Edward Lee Thorndike was a powerful force in American psychology, and his ideas remain influential today, especially the Law of Effect.
- The Law of Effect influenced Skinner, and Thorndike's views of exercise and transfer are still applicable.

Operant Conditioning

- B. F. Skinner's interpretation of conditioning has become the most accepted and widely used form of behaviorism today. Its impact is felt in education, psychology, and business.
- Skinner's ideas on reinforcement have led to broad acceptance of programmed instruction and computers as effective teaching tools.
- His views of punishment have clarified its meaning and use.

Social Cognitive Learning

- Albert Bandura's stress on the impact of modeling has shown the potency and far-reaching effects of this type of learning.
- Observational learning attempts to include the influence of cognitive processes within a behavioral framework.
- The principles of observational learning emphasize the need for multicultural models that meet the needs of a variety of students.

Behavioral Theories and Teaching

- The principles of behaviorism are widely used in today's classrooms.
- Techniques for shaping behavior can be effectively used in the classroom, if thoroughly understood and carefully applied.

Behaviorism and the Future

- The future success of behaviorism demands clear adherence to its basic principles, while introducing compatible changes from related disciplines.

Technology and Behaviorism

- Programmed instruction consists of a set of instructional materials that students can use to teach themselves about a particular topic, skill, or content area.

DETAILED CHAPTER OUTLINE

I. Classical conditioning
    A. Pavlov's work
        1. Pavlov's studies of digestion in animals led to the discovery of the conditioned reflex.
        2. The sequence in classical conditioning is as follows:
            a. US (unconditioned stimulus) produces UR (unconditioned response).
            b. CS (conditioned stimulus) produces no response.
            c. CS "plus" US (conditioned stimulus "plus" unconditioned stimulus) produces UR (unconditioned response).
            d. CS (conditioned stimulus) produces CR (conditioned response).
    B. Features of classical conditioning
        1. Stimulus generalization refers to the process by which the conditioned response transfers to other stimuli that are similar to the original conditioned stimulus.

       a.   Once conditioning to any stimulus occurs, its effectiveness is not restricted to that stimulus.

       b.   As a stimulus becomes less similar to that originally used, its ability to produce a response lessens accordingly.

    2.   Discrimination refers to the process by which we learn not to respond to similar stimuli in an identical manner.

    3.   Extinction refers to the process by which conditioned responses are lost.

  C.   Case Notes: Mark Siegel's class

II.   Thorndike's connectionism

  A.   Thorndike believed that all learning is explained by connections (or bonds) that are formed between stimuli and responses. These connections occur mainly through trial and error.

  B.   The law of readiness is an important condition of learning, because satisfaction or frustration depends on an individual's state of readiness. When organisms are ready to form connections, to do so is satisfying and not to do so is annoying.

  C.   The law of exercise means that any connection is strengthened in proportion to the number of times it occurs and in proportion to the average vigor and duration of the connection. Conversely, when a connection is not made between a stimulus and a response for some time, the connection's strength decreases. There also must be a strengthening of the bond by reinforcement; that is, the law of effect also must operate.

  D.   The law of effect states that responses accompanied by satisfaction are more firmly connected with the situation; responses accompanied by discomfort have their connections weakened. The greater the satisfaction or discomfort is, the greater is the strengthening or weakening of the bond. In 1932, Thorndike revised the law to stress that the strengthening effect of reward is much greater than the weakening effect of punishment.

  E.   Thorndike's explanation of transfer is called identical elements, and states that learning can be applied to new situations only when there are identical elements in both situations.

III. Operant conditioning

  A.   Skinner's views

    1.   Skinner argued that the environment reacts to one's behavior and either reinforces or eliminates that behavior. The environment holds the key to understanding behavior.

    2.   For Skinner, behavior is a causal chain of three links:

       a.   An operation performed upon the organism from without

       b.   Some inner condition

       c.   A kind of behavior

    3.   Until his death in 1990, Skinner emphasized the importance of consequences of behavior and cautioned us about the limitation of a cognitive-oriented psychology.

  B.   Skinner and reinforcement

    1.   A reinforcer is a stimulus event that, if it occurs in the proper temporal relation with a response, tends to maintain or increase the strength of a response, a stimulus-response connection, or a stimulus-stimulus connection.

    2.   The principle of reinforcement refers to an increase in the frequency of a response when certain consequences immediately follow it. The consequences that follow behavior must be contingent upon the behavior.

    3.   Be sure to distinguish reward from reinforcement.

    4.   The Skinnerian model attempts to link reinforcement to response as follows: antecedents—response—reinforcement.

    5.   Case Notes: Mark Siegel's class

  C.   The nature of reinforcement

    1.   Control the reinforcers, control the behavior.

    2.   Positive reinforcement refers to events presented after a response has been performed whose appearance increases the behavior or activity they follow.

3. Negative reinforcement refers to events (aversive stimuli) removed after a response has been performed, whose removal also increases the behavior or activity they follow.
4. Types of reinforcers
    a. Primary reinforcers are those that affect behavior without the necessity of learning.
    b. Secondary reinforcers are those that acquire reinforcing power because they have been associated with primary reinforcers.
    c. Generalized reinforcers, a form of secondary reinforcers, are those that acquire reinforcing power because they have accompanied several primary reinforcers.
5. Schedules of reinforcement
    a. Interval reinforcement refers to a schedule whereby reinforcement occurs at definite established time intervals.
        (1) Fixed interval, in which a response results in reinforcement after a specific time
        (2) Variable interval, in which reinforcement again depends on time and a response, but the time between reinforcements varies
    b. A ratio schedule means that reinforcement occurs after a certain number of responses.
        (1) Fixed ratio, in which reinforcement depends on a definite number of responses
        (2) Variable ratio, in which the number of responses needed for reinforcement will vary from one reinforcement to the next
    c. Intermittent reinforcement.
4. Conclusions about Skinner's analysis of reinforcement schedules
    a. Continuous reinforcement produces a high level of response only as long as reinforcement persists.
    b. Intermittent reinforcement, although producing slower acquisition of responses, results in greater resistance to extinction.
    c. Ratio schedules can be used to generate a high level of responding, but fatigue may hinder performance.
    d. Interval schedules produce the most stable behavior.
5. Case Notes: Mark Siegel's class
D. Skinner and punishment
1. Punishment is "the presentation of an aversive event or the removal of a positive event following a response that decreases the frequency of that response" (Kazdin, 1989, p. 144).
    a. Something aversive (unpleasant) appears after a response.
    b. Something positive (pleasant) disappears after a response.
2. Punishment always is intended to decrease a certain type of behavior.
E. Categories of punishment
1. The presentation of aversive events
2. Withdrawal of positive consequences. The two major forms of withdrawal of positive consequences are time out from reinforcement and response cost.
    a. Time out from positive reinforcement refers to the removal of all positive reinforcers for some time period. It is often not effective because not all sources of reinforcement are removed.
    b. Response cost involves a loss of a positive reinforcer and, unlike time out, does not involve a period during which positive events are unavailable. Response cost most often involves a fine or penalty of some sort.
3. Aversiveness following some response. Requiring a person to do something that involves effort or work may reduce the response.
    a. Overcorrection involves a penalty for some inappropriate behavior with two procedures: restitution followed by positive practice
F. How punishment works
1. Schedule of punishment. Generally, punishment is more effective when it is delivered every time rather than intermittently.
2. Intensity of punishment. If punishment is to be considered, you should use mild forms.
3. Source of reinforcement. Punishment is usually enhanced when other sources of reinforcement that maintain the behavior are removed.

4. Timing of reinforcement. Punishment is usually more effective when it is delivered early in a sequence of behaviors that form a response group.
5. Delay of punishment. The longer the interval is between behavior and punishment, the less effective is the punishment. Punishment becomes more effective if students know exactly why you're punishing them.
6. Variation of punishment. Varying the punishment that follows a behavior can actually enhance the effects of the punishment.
7. Reinforcement of alternative behaviors. First, aversive events of relatively weak intensity can effectively suppress behavior if reinforcement also is provided for an alternative positive response. Second, punishment usually trains a person in what *not* to do rather than in what *to* do.

G. For the classroom
1. Skinner believed that schools should search for positive reinforcers that they now have at their disposal, then make them contingent upon desired behavior.
2. Teaching machines divide materials to be learned into small units and reinforce successful behaviors. These devices are mechanical, and they provide positive reinforcement. They also eliminate aversive stimuli.
   a. Advantages of teaching machines include these: reinforcement for the right answer is immediate, presentation of carefully controlled material is possible, and reinforcers can be made contingent upon completion of the program.
   b. Teaching machines enhance motivation, increase attention, and make education more efficient.
3. Reinforcement remains such a powerful tool in controlling behavior that teachers should constantly be aware of the consequences they provide.
4. The well-known Premack principle has valuable classroom implications. After noting a student's preferred activities, a teacher can then use them as positive reinforcers.
5. Aversive stimulation (punishment) may cause more problems than it solves.
6. Be alert to the timing of reinforcement.
7. A teacher should determine precisely what he or she wants students to learn, and then arrange the material so that they make as few mistakes as possible.

IV. Social cognitive learning
A. The information we process from observing other people, things, and events influences the way we act.
B. As a result of observing others, the observer may acquire new responses, existing responses may strengthen or weaken, and responses that were apparently forgotten may reappear.
C. An explanation of modeling
1. Modeling behavior may be described as one person's observation of another's behavior and acquiring of that behavior in representation form without simultaneously performing the responses. Four important processes seem to be involved in observational learning.
   a. Attention. An observer must attend to and recognize the distinctive features of the model's response.
   b. Retention. To reproduce the desired behavior, a student must symbolically retain the observed behavior.
   c. Motor reproduction processes. Bandura believes that symbolic coding produces internal models of the environment that guide the observer's future behavior.
   d. Motivational processes. Although an observer acquires and retains the ability to perform modeled behavior, there will be no overt performance unless conditions are favorable.
2. For Bandura, reinforcement acts on our students' motivation to behave, and not on the behavior itself.
3. Case Notes: Mark Siegel's class

4. Self-efficacy
    a. Feelings of competency, called self-efficacy, develop from information conveyed by four sources:
       (1) Enactive mastery experiences, or learning from first-hand experiences.
       (2) Vicarious experience
       (3) Verbal persuasion
       (4) Physiological and affective states
    b. Success raises our sense of self-efficacy, while failure diminishes it.
    c. A teacher's feedback to and instructional techniques with students can have a powerful effect on their feelings of competency.
    d. Observation of models who cope well can also produce beneficial results.
5. Case Notes: Mark Siegel's class

D. Multicultural models
    1. Introduce into the classroom outstanding representatives of a particular culture in order to reinforce the characteristics, abilities, and behaviors that members of that culture hold in esteem. This will contribute to greater intercultural understanding.
    2. When inviting models to the classroom, consider whether they have status, are competent, and are respected.
    3. TIPS on Learning: Using social cognitive theory in the classroom.
E. For the classroom
    1. Certain characteristics of models seem to relate positively to observational learning: those who have high status, competence, and power are more effective in prompting others to behave similarly than are models of lower standing.
    2. Estimates of self-efficacy affect choices of activities and situations and the quality of our behavior and persistence on difficult tasks.
    3. The schools offer an excellent opportunity for the development of self-efficacy. Materials and methods should be evaluated not only for academic skills and knowledge, but also for what they can accomplish in enhancing students' perceptions of themselves.
    4. Remember to consider the specific behaviors to be modeled, the kinds of reinforcements available, how you will inform them of the desired behaviors, and whether your lessons will improve your students' self-efficacy.

V. Behavioral theories and teaching
A. Techniques to increase behavior
    1. Consequences must be contingent upon appropriate behavior.
    2. Effective reinforcers
      a. Choose appropriate reinforcers. It is not always easy to identify positive reinforcers, since what one student reacts well to may antagonize another.
      b. Be aware of the manner in which you apply reinforcers.
      c. Consider the ages, interests, and needs of your students; know precisely the behavior you wish to strengthen; list potential reinforcers; use the Premack principle; vary the reinforcers; keep a record of the effectiveness of each reinforcer for each student.
    3. Secondary reinforcers can be grouped into three major categories.
      a. Social reinforcers can be verbal or nonverbal. They include expression, contact, proximity, privileges, and words.
      b. Activity reinforcers such as the Premack principle are high-frequency behaviors. As reinforcers, they are used following low-frequency behaviors.
      c. Generalized reinforcers are those associated with a variety of other reinforcers.

4. Reducing dependence on such reinforcers as points or tokens, or any other artificial reinforcer, is called thinning, which means that reinforcement is provided less frequently. Greater amounts of appropriate behavior must occur before reinforcement occurs.
    a. Benefits of thinning include a more constant rate of responding with appropriate behavior, a lessened anticipation of reinforcement, shift of control to typical classroom procedures, and maintenance of appropriate behavior over longer periods of time.
5. TIPS on Motivation: Don't rely on punishment

B. Techniques to decrease behavior
1. Don't fall into the trap of relying on punishment.
2. Alberto and Troutman (1986) offer a sequential hierarchy with four levels as a means of reducing inappropriate behavior. This hierarchy begins at Level I with the least restrictive and least aversive methods and gradually progresses to Level IV methods, which are more restrictive and aversive.
    a. Level I strategies are based on the idea of differential reinforcement; that is, they rely on reinforcement to decrease or completely eliminate some behavior.
    b. Level II strategies are intended to reduce misbehavior by withholding reinforcement. Be aware that students may show initial resistence to extinction, or occasional spontaneous recovery of the undesired behavior.
    c. Level III strategies involve the use of punishment techniques, from less to more severe. They include the use of time-out procedures and response cost.
        (1) To use response cost effectively be sure you actually withdraw the reinforcers when needed, know what reinforces individual students, be sure students understand clearly what constitutes misbehavior and its cost, make sure you can withdraw a reinforcer, and combine response cost with positive reinforcement for behavior.
        (2) Nonseclusionary time out refers to when the student remains in the classroom but is barred from normal reinforcement. Seclusionary time out is when the student is removed from an activity or from the classroom. It should be reserved for special situations and used with sensitivity and caution.
    d. Level IV strategies involve the use of aversive stimuli and are what is most frequently regarded as punishment.
    e. Current Issues and Perspectives: Alternatives to Punishment

C. Techniques to maintain behavior and facilitate generalization
1. Teach and hope.
2. Teach in the natural setting.
3. Teach sequentially.
4. Introduce students to natural maintaining contingencies.
5. Use indiscriminable contingencies.
6. Train students to generalize.
7. Program common stimuli.
8. Use sufficient exemplars.
9. Use multiple exemplars.
10. Conduct general case programming.
11. Teach loosely.
12. Mediate generalization.
13. TIPS on Communication: Communicate to help generalize behavior

D. Techniques of self-control
1. Self-control usually refers to those behaviors a person deliberately undertakes to achieve self-selected outcomes.
2. Help students acquire self-control by helping them understand precisely what behavior produced reinforcement in a given instance, helping them note the frequency of their positive behaviors, and involving them in the management of reinforcement.
3. TIPS on Time: Student managed learning

4. Teaching students self-control
   a. Self-assessment requires that students examine their own behavior or thinking and determine whether they have performed some behavior or thought process.
   b. Self-monitoring is a procedure in which students record their performance or keep a record of what they are doing.
   c. Self-reinforcement refers to students' giving themselves a reward following successful completion of the activity being monitored.
   d. Advantages of using self-control strategies are that they allow students to manage their own behavior in the absence of adults, help students develop responsibility for their own behavior, and help improve the chances that a given student's behavior will transfer to other settings.
5. Case Notes: Mark Siegel's class

VI. Behaviorism and the future
   A. TIPS on Assessment: Recording student behavior
   B. Applying behavior analysis to schooling
      1. Critics of behavioral techniques have noted that behavioral procedures often are ignored because they are applied to circumscribed or isolated problems in the schools.
      2. Greer developed the Comprehensive Application of Behavior Analysis to Schooling (CABAS), designed to apply behavior analysis to the school roles of students, teachers, and supervisors; it includes the following components.
         a. Application to students, which consists of collecting data for all instructional trials.
         b. Application to teachers, which includes instructing the teachers to use the skills and terminology of behavior analysis.
         c. Application to supervisors, who design the teacher modules and tutor the teachers to the point of mastery, maintain a log of their activities, and have to meet criteria for job performance themselves.
   C. Skinner's suggestions
      1. Be clear about what is to be taught.
      2. Teach first things first.
      3. Teach to individual differences.
      4. Program subject matter.
   D. Accomplishments of behaviorists
      1. Behavioral techniques have been successfully used with a wide range of students, from disabled to advanced students.
      2. Evidence exists that complex behaviors are as teachable with behavioral techniques as are simple topics.
      3. Behaviorism has made it clear to educators that the key to teaching complex skills is to distinguish, clearly and precisely, the critical features of the task.
      4. Behaviorists note that students experiencing difficulty may lack the basic prerequisite skills and advise dividing the learning task into its component parts.
   E. Lack of information about behavioral strategies, lack of the skills to implement them, and societal contingencies impede the use of behavioral techniques.

VII. Technology and behaviorism
   A. Programmed instruction
      1. Programmed instruction consists of a set of instructional materials that students can use to teach themselves about a particular topic, skill, or content area.
      2. Skinner argued that programming instruction would result in students learning twice as much in half the time. In one study, students went through the entire eighth- and ninth-grade curricula in one semester, with good results on tests of retention and problem-solving.

3. Skinner outlined several principles to consider in programmed instruction.
   a. Clearly define the final goal.
   b. Solve the problem of the first instance.
   c. Carefully and thoughtfully sequenced, instruction with careful definition of subgoals.
   d. Prevent incorrect responses.
   e. Provide immediate, nonthreatening, but clear feedback.
4. There are several types of programmed instruction.
   a. In linear programmed instruction, the sequencing of problems is the same regardless of whether the answers are correct, and no instruction is given to explain why an answer was wrong.
   b. In branching programs, students are sent to different parts of the program depending on the answer given. The different parts of the program provide instruction as to why the answer was wrong, additional instruction, and/or additional problems or examples.

B. Drill and practice
   1. The goal is to help students master the basic elements in a particular subject by providing practice after they have received an initial introduction to the skills from the teacher.
   2. There are many drill and practice programs available, and they can easily be incorporated into many teachers' existing teaching styles.
   3. They can also be used in cooperative groups.
   4. Lockard, Abrams, and Many (1994) described several levels of drill and practice programs.
      a. At the basic level, there are a fixed number of problems, and all students face the same tasks.
      b. Programs with an arbitrary mastery criterion allow students to move at their own pace through the problems.
      c. A more adaptive program could require students to reach mastery after relatively few responses increase the difficulty of the materials, or force students to switch the operations needed.
   5. Opponents of using computers for drill argue the programs are boring, all students receive the same content regardless of ability, programs may provide undesirable feedback, some teachers use them for primary instruction, it is an expensive waste of money, and they result in memorized knowledge only.
   6. Supporters argue that extra practice is provided where it is needed most, attention can be maintained during practice sessions, problems are usually the result of poorly designed programs, and unexpected bonuses like student interest in computers can result.
   7. Two summaries of the effectiveness of computer-assisted instruction showed that CAI students had achievement gains of about three months in a school year.
      a. One analysis showed that CAI was very effective when used for four weeks or less, but when continued for several months or longer, the effects were less robust. This raises the possibility of a novelty effect.
      b. One analysis highlighted the importance of the amount of teacher training received. The amount of training was related to academic achievement of students in the CAI groups, with short-term training actually being counterproductive.
   8. Conclusions about CAI
      a. The results will only be as good as the quality of the programs.
      b. Using CAI can help students master basic skills, particularly automatic recall of basic facts.
      c. Keep in mind the possible novelty effect.
      d. Teachers and administrators must both keep in mind the need for continuing support and training for teachers using CAI in their classrooms.

VIII. Case reflections
IX. Chapter highlights
X. What do you think? questions
XI. Key terms

KEY TERMS

activity reinforcers
classical conditioning
conditioned reflex
conditioned stimulus
connectionism
discrimination
extinction
fixed interval
fixed ratio
intermittent reinforcement
interval reinforcement
negative reinforcers
operant conditioning
overcorrection

Personalized System of Instruction (PSI)
positive reinforcers
Premack principle
punishment
ratio reinforcement
reinforcer
response cost
self-efficacy
social cognitive learning
stimulus generalization
time out
variable interval
variable ratio

GUIDED REVIEW

1.   Behaviorism applies to those who believe that any analysis of learning should focus on the observable _____ of our students. _____ attempt to include cognitive processes such as motivation and intention.

behavior, Neobehaviorists

2.   Pavlov's studies of digestion in animals led to the discovery of an important psychological discovery, the _____. For example, the anticipation of food caused the flow of saliva in his experimental dogs.

conditioned reflex

3.   A hungry dog was harnessed with a ticking metronome present (the _____). After a controlled interval, food (the _____) was placed in the dog's mouth. After several repetitions, saliva began to flow during the interval when the metronome was ticking, before any food appeared. Thus Pavlov had established a conditioned reflex, with the metronome acting as the _____ and salivation as the _____.

conditioned stimulus, unconditioned stimulus, conditioned stimulus, conditioned response

4.   The process by which the conditioned response transfers to other stimuli that are similar to the original conditioned stimulus is called _____.

stimulus generalization

5.   Once conditioning to any stimulus occurs, its effectiveness is _____ to that stimulus. As a stimulus becomes _____ to that originally used, its ability to produce a response lessens accordingly.

not restricted, less similar

6.   _____ refers to the process by which we learn not to respond to similar stimuli in an identical manner.

Discrimination

7.   The process by which conditioned responses are lost is called _____.

extinction

8.   Thorndike believed that all learning is explained by _____ that are formed between stimuli and responses.

connections

9.   According to Thorndike, satisfaction or frustration depends on an individual's state of _____. When organisms are ready to form connections, to do so is _____ and not to do so is _____.

readiness, satisfying, annoying

10. The Law of _____ states that any connection is strengthened in proportion to the number of times it occurs and in proportion to the average vigor and duration of the connection. Thorndike revised this law in 1930 after realizing that _____ alone was _____ for improvement, and that there must also be a strengthening of the bond by _____.

Exercise, practice, not enough, reinforcement

11. The Law of _____ states that responses accompanied by satisfaction are more firmly connected with the situation; responses accompanied by discomfort have their connections weakened.

Effect

12. The _____ theory states that learning can be applied to new situations only when the learner sees similar features in both situations.

identical elements

13. Skinner, in his explanation of operant conditioning, argued that the _____ reacts to our behavior and either reinforces or eliminates that behavior. Skinner emphasized the importance of _____ on behavior.

environment, consequences

14.   A _____ is a stimulus event that, if it occurs in the proper _____ relation with a response, tends to maintain or increase the strength of a response, a stimulus-response connection, or a stimulus-stimulus connection.

reinforcer, temporal

15.   The principle of reinforcement refers to an _____ in the frequency of a response when certain consequences immediately follow it.

increase

16.   Pavlov concentrated on conditioning stimuli, so his theory is called _____ conditioning. Skinner focused on responses, so his theory is called _____ conditioning.

Type S, Type R

17.   _____ refers to events (aversive stimuli) removed after a response has been performed, whose removal also increases the behavior or activity they follow.

Negative reinforcement

18.   Primary reinforcers are those that affect behavior without the necessity of _____. Secondary reinforcers are those that acquire reinforcing power because they have been associated with _____ reinforcers. _____ reinforcers, a form of secondary reinforcers, are those that acquire reinforcing power because they have accompanied several primary reinforcers.

learning, primary, Generalized

19.   Skinner identified two kinds of intermittent reinforcement: _____ and _____. _____ refers to a schedule whereby reinforcement occurs at definite established time intervals. A _____ occurs after a certain number of responses.

interval, ratio, Interval reinforcement, ratio reinforcement

20.   Continuous reinforcement produces a high level of response only as long as _____ persists. Intermittent reinforcement produces slower acquisition of responses, but the response is more likely to _____. Ratio schedules can be used to generate a high level of responding, but _____ may hinder performance. _____ schedules produce the most stable behavior.

reinforcement, continue, fatigue, Interval

21.   The presentation of an aversive event or the removal of a positive event following a response that decreases the frequency of that response is called _____.

punishment

22. _____ from positive reinforcement refers to the removal of all positive reinforcers for some time period. It is often not effective because not all sources of reinforcement are removed.

Time out

23. _____ involves a loss of a positive reinforcer and, unlike time out, does not involve a period during which positive events are unavailable. This technique most often involves a fine or penalty of some sort.

Response cost

24. A relatively new class of punishment techniques is based on _____ following some response. _____ involves a penalty for some inappropriate behavior with two procedures. First, restitution is involved, since the person corrects the effects of some negative action. Second, positive practice is included, and consists of repeatedly practicing an appropriate behavior.

work, Overcorrection

25. Generally, punishment is more effective when it is delivered _____. Punishment usually is enhanced when other _____ that maintain the behavior are removed and when it is delivered _____ in a sequence of behaviors that form a response group. More _____ punishments are not more effective.

every time, sources of reinforcement, early, intense

26. The longer the interval is between _____ and _____, the less effective the punishment is.

behavior, punishment

27. Aversive events of relatively weak intensity can suppress behavior effectively if reinforcement also is provided for an _____. Punishment usually trains a person in _____, rather than in _____.

alternative positive response, what not to do, what to do

28. _____ divide materials to be learned into small units and reinforce successful behaviors. These devices are mechanical, and they provide positive reinforcement.

Teaching machines

29. Teaching machines reinforce correct answers _____, they present carefully _____ material, and reinforcers can be made _____ upon completion of the program.

immediately, controlled, contingent

30.	The _____ principle is used when, after noting a student's preferred activities, the teacher then uses them as positive reinforcers.

Premack

31.	For Bandura, _____ means that the information we process from observing other people, things, and events influences the way we act.

social cognitive learning

32.	As a result of observing others, the observer may acquire _____, existing responses may _____, and responses that were apparently forgotten _____.

new responses, strengthen or weaken, may reappear

33.	Mere exposure to a model does not insure acquisition of behavior. An observer must _____ to and _____ the distinctive features of the model's response. The behavior will not be produced unless some kind of _____ occurred.

attend, recognize, reinforcement

34.	For Bandura, reinforcement acts on our students' _____ to behave, and not on the behavior itself.

motivation

35.	Bandura believes that _____ produces internal models of the environment that guide the observer's future behavior.

symbolic coding

36.	Feelings of competency, called self-efficacy, develop from information conveyed by four sources: enactive _____ experiences, _____ experiences, _____, and physiological _____. _____ raises our sense of self-efficacy, while _____ diminishes it.

mastery, vicarious, verbal persuasion, affective states, Success, failure

37.	A teacher's _____techniques are important for student's self-efficacy. When students are given _____, their performance improves, which affects their self-efficacy. Using _____ can also be effective for improving self-efficacy.

instructional, strategy training, models

38.   When inviting models to the classroom, consider whether they have _____, are _____, and are _____.

status, competent, respected

39.   Estimates of self-efficacy affect choices of _____ and situations, quality of our behavior, and _____ on difficult tasks. The schools offer an excellent opportunity for the development of self-efficacy. Materials and _____ should be evaluated not only for academic skills and knowledge, but also for what they can accomplish in enhancing students' _____.

activities, persistence, methods, perceptions of themselves

40.   When selecting reinforcers, remember to consider the _____, interests, and needs of your students; know precisely the _____ you wish to strengthen; _____ potential reinforcers; use the _____ principle; _____ the reinforcers; and keep a record of the _____ of each reinforcer for each student.

ages, behavior, list, Premack, vary, effectiveness

41.   Most teachers will use secondary reinforcers frequently. These can be grouped into three major categories. (1) _____, which typically include attention, can be verbal or nonverbal. (2) _____ reinforcers are high-frequency behaviors. As reinforcers, they are used following low-frequency behaviors. (3) _____ reinforcers are those associated with a variety of other reinforcers.

Social reinforcers, Activity, Generalized

42.   Reducing dependence on such reinforcers as points or tokens, or any other artificial reinforcer, is called _____; this means that reinforcement is provided less frequently.

thinning

43.   Alberto and Troutman (1986) offer a sequential hierarchy with four levels as a means of reducing inappropriate behavior. Level _____ strategies are designated as the preferred option because by using them, teachers employ positive techniques. They rely on reinforcement to decrease or completely eliminate some behavior. Level II strategies are intended to reduce misbehavior by withholding _____. Level III strategies involve the use of _____, from less to more severe. Level IV strategies involve the use of _____ and are what is most frequently regarded as punishment.

I, reinforcement, punishment techniques, aversive stimuli

44.   Level III strategies involve the use of _____ techniques, from less to more severe. The first suggested strategy is _____, which attempts to reduce behavior by removal of a reinforcer. _____ acts as punishment. Combining a _____ with response cost is an effective technique for classroom teachers.

punishment, response cost, Withdrawal of reinforcement, token reinforcement system

45.   In _____ time out, the student remains in the classroom, but is barred from normal reinforcement. In _____ time out, the student is removed from an activity or the actual classroom.

nonseclusionary, seclusionary

46.   Techniques to maintain behavior and facilitate generalization include teach and _____, teach in the _____ setting, teach _____, introduce students to natural maintaining _____, use _____ contingencies, train students to generalize, program _____ stimuli, use _____ and multiple exemplars, conduct general case programming, teach loosely, and _____ generalization.

hope, natural, sequentially, contingencies, indiscriminable, common, sufficient, mediate

47.   _____ refers to those behaviors a person deliberately undertakes to achieve self-selected outcomes.

Self-control

48.   _____ requires that students examine their own behavior or thinking and determine whether they have performed some behavior or thought process.

Self-assessment

49.   _____ is a procedure in which students record their performance or keep a record of what they are doing.

Self-monitoring

50.   _____ refers to students' giving themselves a reward following successful completion of the activity being monitored.

Self-reinforcement

51.   Advantages of using self-control strategies are that they allow students to _____ their own behavior, help students develop _____ for their own behavior, and help improve the chances that a given student's behavior will _____ to other settings.

manage, responsibility, transfer

52.   Greer developed the Comprehensive Application of Behavior Analysis to Schooling (CABAS), designed to apply _____ to the school roles of students, teachers, and supervisors. It includes such behavioral components as direct _____, a _____ system of instruction, _____ instruction, and an organizational behavior management component for supervision and administration.

behavior analysis, instruction, personalized, programmed

53.	When applying behaviorism to education, Skinner suggested that teachers be _____ about what is to be taught, teach _____, teach to _____, and _____ subject matter.

clear, first things first, individual differences, program

54.	Behavioral techniques have been successfully used with a _____ of students, from disabled to advanced students. Evidence exists that _____ behaviors are as teachable with behavioral techniques as are simple topics. Behaviorism has made it clear to educators that the key to teaching complex skills is to distinguish, clearly and precisely, the _____ of the task. Behaviorists note that students experiencing difficulty may lack the _____ and advise dividing the learning task into its _____.

wide range, complex, critical features, basic prerequisite skills, component parts

55.	_____ consists of a set of instructional materials that students can use to teach themselves about a particular topic, skill, or content area. Instruction is designed to progress in _____ toward a well-defined final goal, and sequenced so that students can give _____ responses the majority of the time, thereby allowing frequent use of _____.

Programmed instruction, small steps, correct, positive reinforcement

56.	Skinner felt that programmed instruction would result in teaching "what is now taught in American schools in half the _____ with half the _____." To improve teaching and learning, he argued that teachers must clearly _____ the final goal; solve the problem of the _____; carefully and thoughtfully _____ instruction and define subgoals; prevent _____ responses; and provide immediate, nonthreatening, but clear _____.

time, effort, define, first instance, sequence, incorrect, feedback

57.	An earlier, more traditional type of programmed instruction is called _____ programmed instruction. The sequence of problems is the _____ regardless of whether the answers are correct or not, and _____ is given to explain why the answer the student provided was wrong, to avoid reinforcing mistakes.

linear, same, no instruction

58.	A more recent type of programmed instruction is the _____ program, which incorporates aspects of a _____ approach to instruction. If an answer is incorrect, the student is sent to a _____ of the program to receive instruction as to why the response was incorrect, additional instruction in the correct answer, and/or additional problems or examples dealing with the same concept.

branching, cognitive, different part

59.	_____ programs help students master the basic elements in mathematics, reading, spelling, and other subjects _____ they already have received initial instruction in them.

Drill and practice, after

60.   At the basic level of drill and practice programs, a program may offer students a _____ to solve; only after successful completion can they move on to a higher level. The next level contains an arbitrary _____ level. Finally, more _____ programs adjust the difficulty of the materials in some way.

fixed number of problems, mastery criterion, adaptive

61.   Opponents of using computers for drill argue that programs are _____; all students receive the same _____; programs may provide undesirable _____; programs sometimes are used for _____; the use of computers is an expensive _____; it results in _____ knowledge only.

boring, content, feedback, primary instruction, waste of money, memorized

62.   Proponents of using computers for drill argue that extra _____ is provided where needed most; _____ can be maintained during practice sessions; problems that exist are usually the result of poor _____; and unexpected bonuses can often result.

practice, attention, program design

63.   Two recent meta-analyses indicated that students using CAI showed achievement gains of approximately _____ over students taught without CAI. When treatments were continued for several months or longer, the effects were _____. _____ was related significantly to academic achievement of students in the CAI treatment groups, but short-term training (less than 10 hours) was actually _____.

3 months, less robust, Teacher training, counterproductive

64.   Research indicates that the results of CAI will only be as good as the _____ of the programs, and that using CAI can help students master _____, particularly automatic recall of basic facts. Teachers should keep in mind the possible _____ effect, and both teachers and administrators must keep in mind the need for continuing _____ for teachers using CAI in their classrooms.

quality, basic skills, novelty, support and training

SUMMARIZE THE MAIN POINTS

This section of your study guide is designed to help you identify and understand the main points in each chapter. You've already reviewed the details using the Guided Review (above), and will consider the importance, relevance, and usefulness of the information in later sections. For now, focus on summarizing the main ideas.

For each major section in the chapter, summarize the main point and the evidence presented in the text to support and/or discuss it. If there are key terms presented in the section, define them. Some prompting questions are provided to help you structure your review.

The main sections of Chapter 6 are:

- Classical conditioning
- Thorndike's connectionism
- Operant conditioning
- Social cognitive learning
- Behavioral theories and teaching
- Behaviorism and the future

For each section, answer the following questions:

1. In two sentences or less, **summarize** what the **main point** of this section was.

2. Briefly **summarize the evidence** for and against each main point (a simple list of details they use to support each of their points is sufficient). If the authors discuss research studies to support the point, summarize the findings in one sentence. If the authors are presenting a logical argument to support the point (i.e., not citing data from research studies), briefly list the supporting points they made. Use the detailed chapter outline to help you identify the supporting points.

3. Briefly review the **definitions of any key terms** in each main section.

WHY SHOULD YOU CARE?

The purpose of this section of your study guide is to help you understand how and why the information in the chapter is relevant for you personally. You'll be asked to think more about the relevance and usefulness of the information in later sections of this study guide.

Look back at the work you did in summarizing the main points in the section above and answer the following questions:

1. For each section you summarized, why or how is the **main point** you identified **important to and/or relevant for teachers in general**? Try to limit your answer to only one or two sentences so you don't get bogged down in details, but focus on general usefulness.

2. Now think about the chapter as a whole. **Identify two specific events, contexts, or problems** for which the ideas presented in this chapter are relevant. Briefly discuss how they're relevant and how they could be useful.

3. Now **identify three concepts** from the chapter that **YOU find useful** in some way. Discuss how/why these concepts are useful, and specify how you will actually use them in your teaching and/or your daily life. (It's okay if there is some overlap between your answers for numbers 2 and 3.)

DISCUSSION QUESTIONS

The following "What do you think?" questions are printed in the text.

1. Develop an example of classical conditioning in the classroom. Identify the sequence in classical conditioning, including naming the US, UR, CS, and CR.

2. Provide an example of a primary, a secondary, and a generalized reinforcer. Apply the three types of reinforcers to a student who is learning math.

3. Describe how schedules of reinforcement affect the rate and strength of responses for a child who is disruptive in your classroom.

4. How could the Premack principle be implemented in a classroom with a child who is not paying attention in your class?

5. What processes are involved in observational learning? Develop a teaching strategy that uses these processes.

Additional discussion questions:

6. Provide five examples of classical conditioning in the classroom. Identify the sequence in classical conditioning, including naming the US, UR, CS, and CR.

7. Identify the main similarities and differences between classical conditioning, operant conditioning, and social learning theory.

8. Provide one example each of primary, secondary, and generalized reinforcers.

9. Describe how schedules of reinforcement affect the rate and strength of a response.

10. How could the Premack principle be implemented in the classroom with a child who is not paying attention in class?

11. What processes are involved in observational learning?

12. Define and give examples of generalization and discrimination.

13. List and explain Thorndike's laws.

14. Discuss punishment. Define it and give details as to how and when it should and should not be used. What are some alternatives to punishment? What are some of the possible effects of it, both positive and negative?

15. Describe time out and response cost. How and when should they be used?

16. Define self-efficacy. List and give examples of the four sources for self-efficacy.

17. What role does student self-control play in their learning and school performance? How can teachers help students develop self-control?

TAKE IT PERSONALLY!

The questions in this section are designed to help you personalize, integrate, and apply the information from the text. Personalization questions ask you to consider the personal relevance and usefulness of concepts, and consider how they might be useful in your life now and in the future. Integration questions ask you to pull together information from the text to evaluate it, summarize it, synthesize a recommendation on the basis of it, or express an opinion about it. Application questions ask you to think about how the concepts might be useful to address real problems or situations you may find yourself in. All three question types will help you consider the information at a deeper conceptual level, understand it more fully, and remember it.

1. Identify an example of classical conditioning in your life. Identify the elements (US, UR, NS, CS, CR).

2. Give two examples of how you could use classical conditioning in your classroom. What roles do generalization and discrimination play in your examples?

3. How can you use Thorndike's theory of identical elements when teaching? Is this concept useful to you as a student?

4. Identify an example of operant conditioning in your life. Identify whether it is positive or negative reinforcement, aversive stimulus, or removal punishment. Identify the antecedents, the behavior itself, and the consequences.

5. Identify a real behavior (your own or that of someone you know) that you would like to see change. Describe in detail how you would go about changing it using operant conditioning. How effective do you think your plan will be?

6. Identify one example each of primary, secondary, and generalized reinforcers in your life. Are these effective in changing or maintaining your behavior?

7. Identify an example of social cognitive learning in your life. Identify a specific person who has served as a model to you. Why was that person an effective model?

8. Give an example of how you could use social cognitive learning theory in the classroom. How will you deal with the four elements necessary for learning to take place?

9. Discuss ways you can increase your students' self-efficacy.

10. How can you use self-assessment, self-monitoring, and self-reinforcement to change your own behavior? How can you use it to increase your students' self-control?

11. Will you use computer-assisted instruction (CAI) in the classes you teach? Why or why not?

CASE IN POINT...

Remember to use the cases from the text as contexts for identifying examples of concepts from the text and as contexts for solving educational problems. Also remember to use a consistent framework (like the DUPE model or the CASE NOTES in the text) to structure your "Mini-Case Report." Review the "Case in Point..." section of Chapter 1 in this study guide for more details.

SUGGESTED CONCEPTS TO IDENTIFY FOR CHAPTER 6

activity reinforcers
classical conditioning
conditioned reflex
conditioned stimulus
extinction
intermittent reinforcement
negative reinforcers
operant conditioning
overcorrection
Personalized System of Instruction (PSI)
positive reinforcers
Premack principle
punishment
reinforcer
response cost
self-efficacy
social cognitive learning
time out

In this section of the text, you were introduced to Mark Siegel, a fourth-grade teacher (Case #2). Review Case #2 in your text and use the following questions to prompt your thinking about this case.

1. How would B. F. Skinner describe the problems that Mark is having with Karim? What would Skinner suggest as solutions?

2. What kinds of reinforcers could Mark try to help improve Karim's classroom performance? Could applied behavior analysis be helpful?

3. How could Mark use social cognitive learning theory to understand and address the problems he and Karim are having?

BIG IDEAS IN EDUCATIONAL PSYCHOLOGY

Thinking about the "big ideas" in educational psychology will help you organize and apply your newly acquired knowledge. Use the following steps to identify your own principles and strategies from the chapter and to relate them to the five main themes of the text (i.e., the "big ideas").

1. Review the TIPS from the text.

2. List some of the main concepts from the chapter. Use the work you did in prior sections of the study guide to help generate this list. Also look at the list of key terms from the chapter.

3. Select what you think are two or three of the most important concepts from your list.

4. For each concept you select, try to state it as a principle (use the TIPS format in the text and the example shown below as a guide for how to state principles).

5. Develop two or three specific teaching strategies that follow from each stated principle.

6. Relate your work to the five main themes from the text, identifying which theme(s) are relevant for each principle and strategy. This step will help you see how the information in each chapter contributes to improved teaching for each of these five critical aspects of instruction.

7. Think about and discuss with classmates how the principles and strategies you identify will help you improve your teaching for each theme you listed as relevant.

The five main themes from the text are:
ASSESSMENT, COMMUNICATION, LEARNING, MOTIVATION, AND TIME

Some example concepts, principles, and strategies for Chapter 6:

classical conditioning	reinforcer
discrimination	response cost
extinction	self-efficacy
operant conditioning	social cognitive learning
Personalized System of Instruction (PSI)	stimulus generalization
Premack principle	time out
punishment	

Principle   Classical conditioning (specifically, stimulus generalization) can explain the emotional reactions some students have to certain classroom situations. (ASSESSMENT, LEARNING, MOTIVATION)

Strategy   Reduce the generalization of negative responses (e.g., anxiety and fear) students may have learned to some classroom situations by making your classroom less similar to the original, anxiety-producing situation. Try soft, relaxing music, soft lighting, etc. to help students learn new associations of comfortable concentration with tests, projects, and individual work. (ASSESSMENT, LEARNING, MOTIVATION)

Strategy   Help students generalize their knowledge and skills to other contexts both in and out of the classroom by making the stimuli in the original learning more similar to the contexts and problems students will encounter outside the classroom. Use realistic problem situations in math and science, use real-life examples of relevance and importance to students whenever possible. (LEARNING, MOTIVATION)

SUGGESTED READINGS

Alberto, P., & Troutman, A. (1986). *Applied behavior analysis.* Columbus, OH: Merrill.

Bandura, A. (1986). *Social foundations of thought and action.* Englewood Cliffs, NJ: Prentice Hall.

Kazdin, A. (1989). *Behavior modification in applied settings* (4th ed.). Pacific Grove, CA: Brooks/Cole.

Skinner, B. F. (1953). *Science and human behavior.* New York: Macmillan.

Skinner, B. F. (1990). *Skinner's keynote address: Lifetime scientific contributions remarks.* Washington, DC: American Psychological Association. Videocassette.

PRACTICE TEST 1

1. When a puff of air blows into your eye, it automatically elicits an eye blink. The eye blink is a(n)
   a. conditioned stimulus.
   b. unconditioned stimulus.
   c. conditioned response.
   d. unconditioned response.

2. When Tommy's mother told him the iron was hot and he shouldn't touch it, he also learned to stay away from the stove, oven, and hot water in the bathtub. What is Tommy's learning process called?
   a. extinction
   b. operant conditioning
   c. stimulus generalization
   d. stimulus discrimination

3. Sam feeds his dogs canned dog food. The dogs run to the kitchen whenever they hear the can opener, sit down, and excitedly wag their tails. One day Sam turned on the electric mixer and the dogs came flying into the kitchen. This is an example of
   a. secondary reinforcement.
   b. aversive stimulus.
   c. generalization.
   d. discrimination.

4. Who held that learning depends on an individual's state of readiness?
   a. Pavlov
   b. Bandura
   c. Skinner
   d. Thorndike

5. Which type of reinforcer typically includes verbal or nonverbal attention?
   a. social
   b. activity
   c. generalized
   d. primary

6. What type of reinforcement schedule depends on a definite number of responses?
   a. fixed ratio
   b. fixed interval
   c. variable ratio
   d. variable interval

7. The presentation of an aversive event or the removal of a positive event following a response that decreases the frequency of that response is called
   a. negative reinforcement.
   b. positive reinforcement.
   c. extinction.
   d. punishment.

8. Generally, punishment is most effective when it is delivered
   a. every time.
   b. every other time.
   c. intermittently.
   d. over a long period of time.

9. Dana punished her son whenever he hit his brother. She was consistent, delivered the punishment immediately after the behavior, was firm but used mild forms of punishment, and intervened early in the sequence of behaviors leading up to the misbehavior. Her son still hit, though. What could Dana be doing wrong?
   a. She is forgetting to explain fully why she is punishing her son.
   b. She is forgetting to reinforce her son for a positive alternative behavior.
   c. She is not using a harsh enough punishment.
   d. She is not allowing enough time between the behavior and the punishment.

10. A teacher becomes aware that some of her students dislike having to work independently on math problems. She tells them that after completing their problems, they can engage in a group activity. This illustrates
    a. response cost.
    b. thinning.
    c. seclusionary time out.
    d. the Premack principle.

11. Skinner believed that educators should
    a. teach general concepts rather than focus on specific steps.
    b. teach classes of students together rather than focusing on individuals.
    c. not try to be too specific about what to teach, since part of learning is figuring out what is important.
    d. program the content of subjects.

12. Which of the following is NOT one of the four important processes involved in observational learning?
    a. attention
    b. retention
    c. reinforcement
    d. motivation

13. Vicarious experience leads to self-efficacy by the fact that by watching "similar others" perform,
    a. there is mere exposure to a model.
    b. we persuade ourselves that we can probably do it too.
    c. there is increased motivation.
    d. we attend to the distinctive features of the model's response.

14. A teacher asked students to keep a record of how much time they spend doing homework daily, and they found that their study time increased. What is this procedure called?
    a. self-assessment
    b. self-monitoring
    c. self-enhancement
    d. self-reinforcement

15. Students in Maria's second-grade class are allowed to play a game following completion of a class assignment. This exemplifies which type of reinforcer?
    a. primary
    b. secondary
    c. generalized
    d. negative

16. Computer-assisted instruction is
    a. generally effective in producing achievement gains.
    b. generally ineffective in producing achievement gains.
    c. more effective the longer students work on it.
    d. more effective when teachers have short-term rather than long-term training.

17. The use of technology to present material that progresses in small steps toward a well-defined final goal and is sequenced so that students can answer correctly the majority of the time is called
    a. applied behavior analysis.
    b. computer-tailored instruction.
    c. drill and practice.
    d. programmed instruction.

18. In an effort to increase positive interactions and helping one another in the classroom, a teacher invited a local football hero to assist students with a project on friendship. Which of the following is this teacher using to increase helping behavior?
    a. positive reinforcement
    b. modeling
    c. self-efficacy training
    d. response cost strategies

19. Which of the following is true regarding classical conditioning and operant conditioning?
a. Classical conditioning explains the development of new behaviors.
b. Operant conditioning explains associations between reflexes and other existing behaviors.
c. Classical conditioning emphasizes the environment's response to a behavior.
d. Operant conditioning links reinforcement to responses.

PRACTICE TEST 2

1. When a puff of air blows into your eye, it automatically elicits an eye-blink reflex. The puff of air is considered a(n)
a. unconditioned stimulus.
b. unconditioned response.
c. conditioned stimulus.
d. conditioned response.

2. Students who have been through a disaster may be anxious in school following the event. A teacher could help them to make their concern realistic by assuring them of school safety precautions against disaster. How is classical conditioning being used in this classroom?
a. By transferring a conditioned response to other stimuli that are similar to the original conditioned stimulus.
b. By learning not to respond to similar stimuli in an identical manner.
c. By losing conditioned responses through extinction.
d. None of the answers is correct.

3. Ted feeds his cats canned cat food. The cats run to the kitchen whenever they hear the can opener and start meowing loudly. One day Ted turned on the electric mixer and the cats yawned, stretched, and left the room. This is an example of
a. secondary reinforcement.
b. aversive stimulus.
c. generalization.
d. discrimination.

4. Thorndike's theory of identical elements states that learning can be applied to new situations only when the
a. learner sees similar features in both situations.
b. learner sees dissimilar features in both situations.
c. learner responds to similar stimuli in an identical manner.
d. learner responds to dissimilar stimuli in an identical manner.

5. When a teacher asks for student responses at different times throughout the hour, this is an example of what type of reinforcement schedule?
a. fixed ratio
b. fixed interval
c. variable ratio
d. variable interval

6. When Kent was tardy three days in a row, he lost his recess privileges for a week. What type of punishment was used?
a. time out
b. response cost
c. presentation of aversive events
d. consequences based on effort

7. The longer the interval is between behavior and punishment,
a. the more effective is the punishment.
b. the less effective is the punishment.
c. the more harsh the punishment should be.
d. the more lenient the punishment should be.

8. Jamie's dad took away the pencil she had been using to draw on the walls. When she picked up a crayon and started drawing on her drawing pad, her father praised her. What is Jamie's father doing?
   a. Combining punishment with reinforcement for an alternative, positive behavior.
   b. Inadvertently reinforcing the very behavior he wishes to get rid of.
   c. Harming Jamie's self-esteem by punishing her for drawing on the wall.
   d. Using time out to change Jamie's behavior.

9. If a teacher decides that a certain behavior is critical, he or she should reinforce it
   a. immediately.
   b. every other time.
   c. only after the behavior has been maintained.
   d. None of the answers is correct.

10. If a student appeared disinterested during math class, what would Skinner conclude?
    a. The student was unmotivated.
    b. The student had a learning disability.
    c. Something was done to the student that led to this behavior.
    d. None of the answers is correct.

11. In Skinner's opinion, part of what is wrong with American education is that
    a. it is too behavioristic in orientation.
    b. educators attempt to reach a final goal too slowly.
    c. educators are unclear about what is to be taught.
    d. there is too great a reliance on technology and teaching machines.

12. How does Bandura define social cognitive learning?
    a. The environment reacts to our behavior and either reinforces or eliminates that behavior.
    b. We process information in a fashion similar to that of a computer.
    c. The information we process is stored in long-term memory, and retrieved to our working memory for social cognition processes.
    d. The information we process from observing other people, things, and events influences the way we act.

13. A teacher shows her students how to prepare a microscope slide; this results in their improved performance. This will also influence their
    a. self-awareness.
    b. self-concept.
    c. self-control.
    d. self-efficacy.

14. When Greg threw his book on the floor to disrupt the class, his teacher told him to put his head on his desk for five minutes. What is this procedure called?
    a. response cost
    b. negative reinforcement
    c. nonseclusionary time out
    d. seclusionary time out

15. Teachers help students accept responsibility for their own behavior by teaching them to exercise
    a. self-efficacy.
    b. self-awareness.
    c. self-control.
    d. self-esteem.

16. The principle of operant conditioning is that _____ is key to understanding behavior.
    a. intelligence
    b. motivation
    c. the environment
    d. aptitude

17. Andre holds down a second part-time job to help pay for groceries and rent. His paycheck is considered to be a
    a. primary reinforcer.
    b. secondary reinforcer.
    c. generalized reinforcer.
    d. All of the answers are correct.

18. According to Ryan's 1991 study, teachers using CAI in their classrooms need
    a. powerful computer systems to run newer and more useful types of CAI.
    b. to work with students for six months before they can expect to see any positive changes.
    c. less than ten hours of training in the system and related instructional procedures.
    d. more than ten hours of training in the system and related instructional procedures.

19. Programmed instruction in which the sequence of problems does not change regardless of whether students' answers are correct or incorrect is called
    a. branching.
    b. linear.
    c. prompted.
    d. drill and practice.

20. Pavlov's theory is known as Type S conditioning because it
    a. focuses on conditioned stimuli.
    b. focuses on the responses that are elicited by stimuli.
    c. links reinforcement to responses.
    d. explains the development of new student responses.

ANSWER KEY

Practice Test 1

1. ANSWER: D, Applied; OBJECTIVE: 1; PAGE: 203
2. ANSWER: C, Applied; OBJECTIVE: 2; PAGE: 205
3. ANSWER: C, Applied; OBJECTIVE: 2; PAGE: 205
4. ANSWER: D, Factual; OBJECTIVE: 4; PAGE: 206
5. ANSWER: A, Factual; OBJECTIVE: 6; PAGE: 212
6. ANSWER: A, Factual; OBJECTIVE: 7; PAGE: 212
7. ANSWER: D, Factual; OBJECTIVE: 8; PAGE: 214
8. ANSWER: A, Factual; OBJECTIVE: 10; PAGE: 216
9. ANSWER: B, Applied; OBJECTIVE: 10; PAGE: 217
10. ANSWER: D, Conceptual; OBJECTIVE: 11; PAGE: 218
11. ANSWER: D, Factual; OBJECTIVE: 11; PAGE: 238
12. ANSWER: C, Factual; OBJECTIVE: 13; PAGE: 221-222
13. ANSWER: B, Factual; OBJECTIVE: 15; PAGE: 222
14. ANSWER: B, Applied; OBJECTIVE: 17; PAGE: 235
15. ANSWER: B, Applied; OBJECTIVE: 6; PAGE: 211
16. ANSWER: A, Factual; OBJECTIVE: 7; PAGE: 242
17. ANSWER: D, Factual; OBJECTIVE: 9; PAGE: 239
18. ANSWER: B, Applied; OBJECTIVE: 8; PAGE: 224
19. ANSWER: D, Conceptual; OBJECTIVE: 6; PAGE: 209-210

Practice Test 2

1. ANSWER: A, Applied; OBJECTIVE: 1; PAGE: 203
2. ANSWER: C, Applied; OBJECTIVE: 2; PAGE: 206
3. ANSWER: D, Applied; OBJECTIVE: 2; PAGE: 205
4. ANSWER: A, Factual; OBJECTIVE: 4; PAGE: 207
5. ANSWER: D, Applied; OBJECTIVE: 7; PAGE: 213
6. ANSWER: B, Applied; OBJECTIVE: 8; PAGE: 215, 229
7. ANSWER: B, Factual; OBJECTIVE: 10; PAGE: 216
8. ANSWER: A, Applied; OBJECTIVE: 10; PAGE: 217, 229
9. ANSWER: A, Factual; OBJECTIVE: 11; PAGE: 216
10. ANSWER: C, Conceptual; OBJECTIVE: 11; PAGE: 217
11. ANSWER: C, Factual; OBJECTIVE: 11; PAGE: 218, 240
12. ANSWER: D, Factual; OBJECTIVE: 13; PAGE: 219
13. ANSWER: D, Applied; OBJECTIVE: 15; PAGE: 223
14. ANSWER: C, Applied; OBJECTIVE: 16; PAGE: 231
15. ANSWER: C, Factual; OBJECTIVE: 17; PAGE: 234
16. ANSWER: C, Factual; OBJECTIVE: 5; PAGE: 208
17. ANSWER: C, Applied; OBJECTIVE: 6; PAGE: 211
18. ANSWER: D, Factual; OBJECTIVE: 7; PAGE: 242
19. ANSWER: B, Factual; OBJECTIVE: 9; PAGE: 240
20. ANSWER: A, Factual; OBJECTIVE: 6; PAGE: 210

Chapter 7   COGNITIVE PSYCHOLOGY AND THE CONSTRUCTION OF KNOWLEDGE

LEARNING OBJECTIVES

After completing this chapter, you should be able to

1. Define cognitive psychology and identify typical topics researched by cognitive psychologists.

2. Understand the key role that representation plays in learning.

3. Define schema and describe ways they are relevant to classroom teaching.

4. Describe, compare and contrast the major cognitive approaches to learning.

5. Help students construct meaning from classroom material.

6. Discuss issues regarding the relationship between the brain and thinking.

7. Discuss the information processing approach to cognition.

8. Recognize elements of instruction that affect student memory.

9. Define metacognition and discuss its importance for teaching and learning.

CHAPTER HIGHLIGHTS

The meaning of cognitive psychology

- The concept of representation is basic to an understanding of cognitive psychology. We attend, perceive, and reason, and these cognitive activities affect our behavior.

The emergence of cognitive psychology

- Cognitive psychology has a long and rich tradition, with its roots in many disciplines. Among modern cognitive psychologists, Jerome Bruner has been particularly influential. Bruner's studies on perception and thought have been landmarks in modern cognitive psychology.

Major approaches to learning with a cognitive psychology orientation

- Cognitive constructivism holds that people actively construct their own knowledge. Such knowledge is constructed through the process of adapting to events and ideas one experiences.
- The construction of knowledge is significantly influenced by one's environment and the symbols and materials one uses.

- Teachers who use a constructivist approach act as facilitators of knowledge and skill acquisition, as a guide or resource person whose purpose is to structure the learning environment. Thus, learning can be very individualized and personalized for each student, taking into account one's prior knowledge, interests, and cognitive level and skills.

The Brain and thinking

- Cognitive psychologists have been interested in mind-brain relationships and the functioning of the brain.
- Pattern detection and pattern matching is an inherent function of the human brain. Knowledge of pattern matching is relevant to some instructional methods and has been part of a development movement referred to as brain-based learning.

Information processing and the acquisition of knowledge

- Representation, which is at the heart of information processing, is the manner in which information is recorded or expressed.
- No matter how data are represented, the information remains the same; this is called the content of representation.
- The different ways that information can be expressed are called the representational codes; these codes may be either mental or verbal.
- Perceiving is an active process demanding our involvement with the objects, events, and people in our environment.
- The active process of perception helps us to receive information from our environment.
- Helping students structure, or organize, their environments aids their perceptual processes, thus furthering learning.
- The better students categorize (form classes and put information in these categories), the more efficient learners they become.
- Studies of memory have long fascinated cognitive psychologists because of memory's critical role in thought and decision making.

Cognition across cultures

- Researchers have noted there are cognitive differences across cultures. One area in particular where differences have been noted is in the process of classifying information or objects.
- Because culture is perceived to make a difference in how some students learn, the concept of contextualized instruction emerged among cognitive psychologists. In this approach, a student's personal experiences in a particular culture are used to introduce new material.

DETAILED CHAPTER OUTLINE

I.   The meaning of cognitive psychology
    A. Cognitive psychology is the study of the structures and components for processing information
        1. Gardner (1985) identified five features of cognitive science:
            a. representations
            b. computers
            c. deemphasis on affect, context, culture, and history
            d. belief in interdisciplinary studies
            e. rootedness in classical philosophical problems
    B. Central to cognitive psychology is a belief in mental representation; in other words, external events can be coded so that they become retrievable in an internal form.
        1. The internal form is not a direct copy of the external stimulus, but can be significantly altered and affected by prior knowledge, beliefs, and experiences.
        2. Our thought processes are not an accumulation of stimulus-response connections; cognition intervenes and distinctly colors our reactions.
    C. Most cognitive scientists have been strongly influenced by the computer.
        1. Humans, like computers, can be viewed as "symbol manipulation devices" that code external information into internal representations, manipulate or store these internal representations in some way, then produce some output.
        2. The computer is a valuable research tool in information processing, and often has been used as a model to describe thinking from the cognitive perspective.
    D. Cognitive psychology has become a potent force in the classroom.
        1. If you can aid your students in organizing and processing information, you will help them to become more competent and to improve their learning.
        2. Today we are much more aware of the important effects of students' prior knowledge and memory strategies on learning.
        3. We also face cognitive limitations: Our students can simultaneously manipulate only a certain number of symbols, with limits on the speed at which they can manipulate them.
        4. Students are taught or invent strategies to overcome these obstacles, such as organizing material, rehearsing data over and over, and devising schemes to help solve problems.
    E. Current Issues and Perspectives: Does a computer provide a reasonable model of human cognition?

II.   The emergence of cognitive psychology
    A. The influence of the Gestaltists
        1. The early Gestaltists were convinced that behaviorism could not account for the full range of human behavior, so they launched a determined attack against early behaviorism.
        2. Max Wertheimer, the founder of the Gestaltist movement, discovered the phi phenomenon: When two lights are turned on and off at a definite rate, one receives the impression that a single light is moving back and forth. This cannot be explained by stimulus-response theory, and indicates that humans add something to the incoming sensory data to form their perception of movement.
        3. One of the lasting legacies of Gestalt theory has been its principles of perceptual organization.
    B. Bartlett and the schema
        1. Schemata of events are mental frameworks that modify incoming data so that they "fit" the person's experiences and perceptions.
        2. Students try to fit something new into an existing cognitive framework: the schema.
        3. Schemata are the basis of memory and result from our previous experiences, which are organized in an individual manner. Organization is at the heart of the schema concept, and is important at three levels:
            a. organization that already exists in one's long-term memory
            b. organization that can be perceived or generated within the material to be learned

  c. organization that links the first two levels, allowing integration of old and new knowledge

  4. Memory is believed to be more a reconstruction of past events than a literal recalling of them.

C. The role of schema in contemporary cognitive psychology

  1. A schema is a unit of organized knowledge about events, situations, or objects that guides informational input and retrieval.

  2. A schema may be quite specific or quite general.

  3. Scientists accept the notion of schemata because of the realization that we do not approach any topic totally devoid of knowledge; we have both prior knowledge and present expectations. We possess schemata that shape how we encode and "feel about" incoming material.

  4. Research on schema use during reading indicates that there is a need to provide poor readers with a clear structure of what they are reading.

D. Schema and problem solving in the classroom

  1. Use schemata to help students decrease their feelings of frustration when faced with challenging situations.

   a. Teach students about the basic types of problems in a given subject.

   b. Make sure they master the fundamental data.

   c. Ensure they are familiar with the necessary steps to solve a problem.

E. CASE NOTES: Mark Siegel's class

III. Major approaches to learning with a cognitive psychology orientation

A. Meaningful learning

  1. David Ausubel made two basic distinctions: between reception and discovery learning, and between rote and meaningful learning.

  2. Reception learning and discovery learning pose two different tasks for students.

   a. In reception learning, the potentially meaningful material becomes meaningful as students internalize it. Reception learning need not be rote; it can be meaningful.

   b. In discovery learning, students must discover what is to be learned, and then rearrange it to integrate the material with existing cognitive structures.

  3. Meaningful learning is the acquisition of new meanings, or the process by which students turn potentially meaningful material into actual meaningfulness.

   a. Meaningful learning occurs when the material to be learned is related to what students already know.

  4. An advance organizer is an abstract, general overview of new information to be learned that occurs in advance of the actual reading.

   a. This introductory material is intended to help students ready their cognitive structures to incorporate potentially meaningful material.

   b. Advance organizers are presented before introducing the new material and at a slightly higher level of abstraction.

  5. To help students acquire meaning, Ausubel suggests you identify relevant anchoring ideas that your students already possess. Advance organizers are effective when they utilize the anchoring ideas already present in the students' cognitive structures because this helps reduce students' dependence on rote memorization.

  6. The principal function of advance organizers is to bridge the gap between what your students already know and what they need to know before they can successfully learn new material.

  7. Recent research indicates that advance organizers have a consistent, moderate, and positive effect on learning. However, learning variables such as a student's cognitive structures and general state of developmental readiness must be taken into consideration.

B. TIPS on learning: Using schema to enhance student's comprehension and memory

C. Discovery learning

  1. In 1956, Bruner, Jacqueline Goodnow, and George Austin published *A study of thinking,* which analyzed categorizing.

   a. The authors believed that this study explained why humans are not overwhelmed by environmental complexity.

      b.   The authors showed that subjects actively participate in the classification process, rather than being simple reactors to whatever stimuli were presented to them.

      c.   The authors stated that three types of concepts exist:
          (1)   conjunctive concepts, which rely on the joint presence of several attributes;
          (2)   disjunctive concepts, in which classification can be based on any one of its attributes; and
          (3)   relational concepts, which are formed by the relationship that exists among defining attributes.

      d.   The authors concluded that categorizing implies more than merely recognizing instances. Rules are learned and then applied to new situations.

      e.   Bruner's work on discovery learning, along with Piaget and Vygotsky, led to constructivism, a current approach in cognitive psychology.

D. Constructivism

   1.   Cognitive constructivism holds that people actively construct their own knowledge, and that reality is determined by the experiences of the knower, rather than existing as an objective truth.

   2.   The roots of constructivism began with the early philosophers Piaget, Vygotsky, Bruner, Gardner, Goodman, and others.

   3.   Main ideas of cognitive constructivism

      a.   We cannot know an objective reality.

      b.   Knowledge is subjective.

      c.   The knowledge of two people is "taken-as-shared" to the extent that their constructions seem to function in the same way in given situations. Many of the unspoken cultural rules that govern social interactions are "taken-as-shared" knowledge.

      d.   Knowledge is constructed through the process of adapting to the events and ideas one experiences.
          (1)   Experiencing cognitive conflict leads people to try to resolve the conflict, thus engaging in reflective abstraction about the conflict. Existing knowledge structures are reorganized and new knowledge structures are constructed.
          (2)   One good way to create cognitive conflict is to engage students in discussion, or discourse. Discourse can create cognitive conflict and influence how this conflict is resolved, and so the new knowledge is constructed.
          (3)   The particular "community of discourse" one regularly engages with influences the kinds of cognitive constructions that are seen as acceptable within that group.

      e.   The construction of knowledge is significantly influenced by one's environment and by the symbols and materials one uses or has ready access to.
          (1)   Environment refers to physical environment, social contacts, and larger cultural environment.
          (2)   The symbols and materials used become the "tools to think with" and affect how one perceives, interprets, and functions in the environment.
          (3)   Different materials give rise to different interpretations and thus to different cognitive constructions of the things one experiences.
          (4)   One's culture also affects what you actually perceive from the physical surroundings.
          (5)   The groups with whom you regularly interact affect the kinds of constructions and solutions developed, the kinds of problems seen as socially acceptable to think about, and they provide a vocabulary with which to think.

      f.   "Readiness to learn" has a different meaning for cognitive constructivists.
          (1)   A person is ready to learn about a concept when the cognitive constructions are able to incorporate some aspect of that concept, even though the knowledge constructed may not be "correct," according to some outsider's criterion.
          (2)   Students' existing cognitive constructions will lead each student to focus on and learn about different aspects of the same materials.

E. Applying cognitive constructivism in the classroom
   1. There are important differences between a teaching approach based on cognitive constructivism and a more traditional teaching approach.
      a. A constructivist teacher is a facilitator of knowledge and skill acquisition, a guide or resource person whose purpose is to structure the learning environment to help each student construct his/her own understandings.
      b. Learning is individualized and personalized for each student.
      c. The teacher relinquishes some control over what and how a student learns, and cannot prepare a single lecture or set of learning experiences for an entire class.
      d. The students are more active and self-directive.
      e. Assessment of learning is often more informal and takes place more often.

   2. Brooks and Brooks (1993) offer five guidelines:
      a. Pose problems of emerging relevance to students. Create cognitive conflict by presenting interesting and complex problems, allow students plenty of time to come to a deeper level of understanding, and continually watch for each student's understanding of the concepts.
      b. Structure learning around primary concepts.
      c. Seek and value students' points of view.
      d. Adapt curriculum to address students' current understandings.
      e. Assess student learning in the context of teaching. Move beyond simple right or wrong answers and continually assess students' learning, using the information to adjust instruction.
         (1) Use nonjudgemental feedback techniques (such as questions, plausible contradictions, and requests for examples) to help students evaluate their own work. Teachers gain more information and students learn self-assessment skills.
   3. Case Notes: Mark Siegel's Class

IV. The brain and thinking
   A. The relationship of brain and mind
      1. Until recently, extreme positions have been the rule when it comes to discussing the brain-mind relationship.
      2. Luria's work
         a. Russian neuropsychologist Alexander Luria proposed a neurological view, which holds that intellectual activity begins with analyzing the conditions of a task and then identifying its most important elements.
         b. Luria traces the thinking process through four stages.
            (1) Motivation of a person to solve a problem for which there is no ready solution
            (2) Restraint of impulsive responses
            (3) Selection of what seems to be the most satisfactory alternative and creation of a general plan
            (4) Putting into action the methods and operations of the proposed solution
         c. Neuropsychological deficits differentiate specific aspects of the brain-mind relationship. Luria noted that lesions in different parts of the brain cause different types of intellectual disturbances.
   B. Lateralization
      1. We tend to think of the brain as a single unit, but actually it consists of two halves: the cerebral hemispheres. The two halves are connected by a bundle of nerve fibers called the corpus callosum.
      2. Differences between the two hemispheres, called functional asymmetry, offer insight to your brain's organization.
      3. There is general agreement today that although there may be some rationale for the distinction between left and right hemispheric dominance, both hemispheres are involved in all activities.

4. Much of our knowledge of cerebral lateralization has resulted from studying individuals with brain damage.
   a. Damage to the left hemisphere typically results in speech difficulties, while right hemisphere damage causes perceptual and attentional disorders.
   b. Psychologists place importance in the right hemisphere's control of visual and spatial activities, as well as on the left hemisphere's language emphasis.
5. Classroom-relevant implications from lateralization literature include these:
   a. Data clearly suggest functional asymmetry in hemisphere use at various ages and between the two sexes.
   b. Gender differences exist in certain abilities, such as verbal and spatial skills. Females generally seem superior in anything relating to language, while males excel in spatial tasks, but the differences tell us nothing about why they exist. Though these results should be considered, they should not be the basis for curriculum construction or different instructional techniques.
   c. Research to date remains vague as to how much involvement of either hemisphere is present in the activities of the other—how much one interferes with the other. Human activity, especially learning, entails the commitment of both hemispheres.
   d. One way of integrating current knowledge of lateralization into the curriculum is to become aware of your reliance on verbal directions. Try also to present material graphically, in visual form, and encourage students to express their understanding of a topic in a creative manner.
C. Pattern matching
   1. Pattern detection and matching seem to be inherent functions of the brain. It is present even in infants, utilizes both specific elements and relationships between elements, is aided by negative clues, uses clues in a probabilistic manner, and depends on one's experience. The patterns are continually changing to meet the demands of new experiences.
   2. You can help students improve their classroom performance by presenting information in a way that helps their brains extract patterns, using such methods as integrated instruction, thematic teaching, and whole language.
D. Biological basis of learning
   1. Humans demonstrate plasticity (flexibility or resiliency) in their mental functioning.
   2. Hyden discovered that, in animals, during and after learning both brain cells and their synapses show an increase in protein production. He believed a "wave of protein synthesis" pervades the brain at learning; that is, system changes occur in brain cell protein during learning. Calcium production also increases. Stimuli cause electrical changes in the nervous system that induce production of specific proteins in the brain.
   3. Developmental changes also occur in brain structures: size, number of connections, and changes in such brain support systems as the glial cells. The growth of intellectual capacity in students appears to match the brain's anatomical and biochemical changes.

V. The importance of information processing
   A. Information processing encompasses such topics as attention, perception, thinking, memory, and problem-solving strategies.
   B. The meaning of representation
      1. Representation, or the manner in which information is recorded or expressed, lies at the very heart of information processing.
      2. The information represented is the content of the representation, while the different ways that the information can be expressed is called the representational code.
      3. We appear to use two types of codes for representing information.
         a. Mental imagery is a visually based representation of continuously varying information. It is abstract (i.e., not a "picture in your head"), responds to mental operations, and can be distorted by one's general knowledge.
         b. Verbal processing is a representational code that does not resemble in any way what it represents. Language is one example.

c. Though most people use both codes, individuals typically prefer one over the other. If a teacher can determine which code a student prefers, they can use instructional methods that match preferred codes whenever possible.

C. The role of perception in learning
   1. Our ability to recognize the familiar and to realize what we do not know is called perception. Perceiving something means that you recall past experiences with the stimulus, you experience meaning, and you have certain expectations about the stimulus.
   2. Humans do not respond to elements in the environment on an item-by-item basis, but organize the relevant stimuli and ignore the irrelevant, creating a figure-ground relationship.
   3. Explanation of the perceptual process
      a. Perception gives meaning to the discrete, meaningless stimuli that initially aroused awareness.
      b. The meaning given to the stimulus depends on the manner in which you pattern it.
      c. How you structure stimuli determines the quality of the percept and the concept.
      d. Teachers should use materials that form a meaningful pattern for students.
   4. For the classroom
      a. Almost from birth, students react to patterns of stimuli as they perceive them at the moment. Learning, maturation, emotions, needs, and values are all intertwined in perception.
      b. When shown a stimulus pattern, students proceed from a gross reaction to a discriminated response, though even newborn infants not only see but also have preferences for certain patterns.
      c. Visual attention focuses earlier on patterns than on color differences, suggesting that there are definite properties in the visual world of the infant. This suggests that perceptual training should begin early in life, since children show an early readiness for perception.
      d. Perceptual learning allows students to make finer and finer discriminations, and thus allows them to make more and more fine-grained analysis of stimuli.
      e. Many of the skills that a child must master in school, such as reading, require accurate discriminations and competence in detecting the unchanging nature of stimulus patterns in spite of possible surface changes. Teacher knowledge of the perceptual process aids both the construction of suitable curriculum materials and the nature of instruction.
      f. Teachers can capitalize on their students' tendency to group, i.e., their cognitive tendencies to organize and structure. Students' past experiences should be used to form cognitive schemata to be used in mastering new materials, solving problems, and looking at subjects more creatively.

D. Categorizing information to better understand it
   1. Forming categories
      a. Categorizing reduces the complexity of the environment.
      b. Categorizing permits us to identify the objects of the world.
      c. Categorizing allows humans to reduce their need of constant learning.
      d. Categorizing provides direction for instrumental activity.
      e. Categorizing encourages the ordering and relating of classes.
   2. Recent research
      a. The classic theory of classification holds that a category consists of certain definite criteria. If an object possesses these criteria, it belongs to that category.
      b. Not all categories possess a neat, defining set of criteria. Some are better identified by the actions they signify. These and other difficulties caused Rosch to propose a "prototype" theory, which says that categorization is based on similarity to a common standard form of the category under consideration, i.e., the prototype.

3. For the classroom
   a. Teachers consistently give examples, compare the concept to other categories that do not include it, appeal to information in a child's natural world, and do not depend solely on artificial criteria.
   b. The quality of a student's concepts is the best measure of probable success in learning because meaning is basic to learning.
4. Concepts order the environment, add depth to perceptual relationships, clarify thinking, facilitate the entire learning process, and aid memory.
5. TIPS on Communicating: Teaching new concepts and making connections among ideas

E. Memory at work
   1. One analysis of memory makes a distinction between episodic and semantic memory.
      a. Episodic memory is recall of personal experiences within a specific context or period of time. It is autobiographical and provides an individual with a personal history.
      b. Semantic memory is the memory necessary for the use of language, a kind of dictionary without reference to personal experiences that represents one's general knowledge.
   2. Atkinson and Shiffrin proposed a three-store system of memory. The stores are structurally distinct because they hold information differently, for varying times, and for different purposes, and lose information differently.
      a. The sensory register holds input in almost the same form as the sensory image. Information is lost in less than a second, either through spontaneous decay or through the entry of new data.
      b. The short-term store entails conscious processes. Input comes from both the sensory register and the long-term store. It is of limited capacity, but information can be held indefinitely if attention remains constant. The longer information remains in the short-term store, the more likely it is to be transmitted to the long-term store.
      c. The long-term store holds both conscious and unconscious data. Data can be stored indefinitely, but still may be lost.
   3. Craik and Lockhart advocated a levels-of-processing analysis of memory, which focuses on the depth of processing.
      a. Data are processed by various operations called perceptual-conceptual analysis, which reflect an individual's attention. If material is deemed worthy of long-term recall, it is analyzed differently from material judged as relatively unimportant.
      b. Whether a stimulus is processed at a shallow level or at a deeper level depends on the nature of the stimulus, the time available for processing; and the subject's own motivation, goals, and knowledge base.
      c. The initial processing of a stimulus determines the length of time students remember it and which aspects are remembered.

F. Recognition, Recall, and Forgetting
   1. Based on research, speculation, and common sense, the following generalizations about memory are possible:
      a. similarity of material can cause interference
      b. personally meaningful material aids recall
      c. time on task helps student to remember
      d. rehearsal is an important memory strategy
      e. mnemonic strategies can help students remember
   2. A distinction should be made between storage and retrieval.
      a. Storage implies "putting information into" memory, which occurs as a result of attending, encoding, and using memory strategies.
      b. Retrieval implies recognizing, recalling, and reconstructing what was previously "put into" memory.

3. Recognition means comparing a present, incoming representation with a representation already stored in memory. There are three major elements involved in recognition:
   a. Similarity
   b. Prior experience
   c. Expectation and context
4. Recall goes beyond recognition because the individual is not given a "copy" of the representation. Any retrieval cue is minimal; consequently, students must generate their own cues in their search for the necessary information.
5. Forgetting is a normal process and here does not refer to an abnormal loss of memory occasioned by aging, shock, or brain injury. Theorists have proposed several explanations for forgetting:
   a. Disuse or fading: the trace decay hypothesis
   b. Motivated forgetting, or repressed forgetting
   c. Forgetting because of interference
   d. Forgetting because of extinction and reorganization
6. There are some specific measures you can adopt to aid your students' storage and retrieval.
   a. Repeatedly urge students to remember and encourage student self-activity through overlearning.
   b. Encourage comprehension, not mere mastery of facts. Strategies for increasing comprehension include summarization, imagery, story grammar, prior knowledge activation, self-questioning, and question-answer.
   c. Provide distributed rather than massed practice and insure that overlearning occurs.
   d. Conduct periodic review.
   e. Reduce interference.
   f. Encourage both convergent and divergent thinking.
   g. Reminiscence refers to a gain in retention after a rest period. It may be due either to fatigue during original learning and retention periods or to faulty test procedures.
   h. Students learn the beginning and end of any memory task much more easily than the middle elements, probably due to interference. To help students with the difficult middle section, furnish some organization or structure to which they can relate it.
   i. Learning meaningful material to mastery lessens students' susceptibility to interference.
G. Metacognition
   1. Metacognitive knowledge refers to our knowledge and beliefs about cognitive matters gained from experience and that we have stored in our long-term memory. We acquire metacognitive knowledge about people, tasks, and strategies.
      a. A distinction is made between cognitive strategies and metacognitive strategies. Over time, students learn which strategies are best suited for success on particular tasks.
      b. By teaching students how to attack a problem, you can do much to improve their achievement.
   2. Metacognitive experiences are either cognitive or affective experiences that relate to cognitive activities.

VI. Cognition across cultures
   A. Cole and Scribner state that our modes of responding to stimuli are not "experience-free." Rather, our reactions depend on our past histories of dealing with similar stimuli.
   B. Culture influences how people think, relate, and learn. Consequently, we can too frequently misperceive and misunderstand our students' behavior when we interpret it solely from our own cultural perspective.
   C. Students who come from different racial, ethnic, or socioeconomic backgrounds than their teacher and the school administrators may have values, goals, and interests that are highly acceptable to their families and communities, but not to the school community. Consequently, educators may not be able to accept behavior that the students and their parents find completely appropriate.

D. Contextualized instruction means that a student's personal experiences in a particular culture are used to introduce new material, and materials that reflect the students' cultural community are used.

E. Mental life can be viewed as consisting of two quite different methods of functioning:
1. The logical, abstract, scientific thinking
2. Narrative thinking, a much more personal kind of thinking that concentrates on people and the causes of their behavior.

VII. Helping you remember: An integrated summary

VIII. Case reflections

IX. Chapter highlights

X. What do you think? questions

XI. Key terms

KEY TERMS

advance organizers
cerebral lateralization
constructivism
contextualized instruction
discovery learning
episodic memory
forgetting
information processing
levels of processing
long-term store
meaningful learning
mental image
mental representation
metacognition
metacognitive experiences

metacognitive knowledge
negative transfer
perception
plasticity
positive transfer
reception learning
recognition
reminiscence
retrieval
schema (pl. schemata)
semantic memory
sensory register
short-term store
storage
verbal processing

GUIDED REVIEW

1.   Cognitive psychology is the study of the structures and components for _____. Central to cognitive psychology is a belief in _____; in other words, external events can be coded so that they become retrievable in an internal form. Most cognitive scientists have been strongly influenced by the _____.

processing information, mental representations, computer

2.   Gardner (1985) identified five features of cognitive science: _____; computers; deemphasis on affect, _____, culture, and history; belief in _____ studies; and rootedness in classical _____ problems.

representations, context, interdisciplinary, philosophical

3.   Our thought processes are not an accumulation of _____ connections; _____ intervenes and distinctly colors our reactions.

stimulus-response, cognition

4.   Classroom implications of cognitive theory include the importance of _____ and processing information, the influence of students' _____ on present learning, the significance of memory _____ for student learning, the understanding that we also face cognitive _____, and the notion that students can be taught or _____ strategies to overcome these obstacles.

organizing, prior knowledge, strategies, limitations, invent

5.   The early Gestaltists were firmly convinced that behaviorism could not account for the full range of human behavior. Consequently, they launched a determined and effective attack against early _____.

behaviorism

6.   _____ of events are mental frameworks that modify incoming data so that they "fit" the person's experiences and perceptions.

Schemata

7.   Schemata are the basis of memory and result from our _____, which we organize in an individual manner.

previous experiences

8.   Organization is at the heart of the _____ concept. There are three levels: organization that _____ in one's long-term memory, organization that can be perceived or _____ within the material to be learned, and organization that links the first two levels, allowing _____ of old and new knowledge.

schema, already exists, generated, integration

9.   Memory is believed to be more a _____ of past events than a literal recalling of them.

reconstruction

10.   A schema is a unit of _____ about events, situations, or objects that _____ informational input and retrieval. It may be specific or _____. Schemata shape how we encode and _____ incoming material.

organized knowledge, guides, general, feel about

11.   Use schemata to help students decrease their feelings of _____ when faced with challenging situations, teach students about the _____ of problems in a given subject, make sure they master the _____, and ensure they are familiar with the necessary _____ to solve a problem.

frustration, basic types, fundamental data, steps

12.   Reception learning and discovery learning pose two different tasks for students. In _____ learning, the potentially meaningful material becomes meaningful as students internalize it. In _____ learning, however, students must discover what is to be learned and then rearrange it to integrate the material with existing cognitive structures.

reception, discovery

13.   Ausubel has long been an outspoken advocate of meaningful learning, which he defines as the _____ of new _____, or the process by which students turn _____ material into actual meaningfulness. Meaningful learning occurs when the material to be learned is _____ to what students already know.

acquisition, meanings, potentially meaningful, related

14.   The _____ is an abstract, general overview of new information to be learned that occurs in advance of the actual reading. This introductory material is intended to help students ready their _____ for incorporating potentially meaningful material. Advance organizers are effective when they utilize the _____ already present in the students' cognitive structures because this helps reduce students' dependence on rote memorization.

advance organizer, cognitive structures, anchoring ideas

15.   Research indicates that advance organizers have a consistent, _____, and _____ effect on learning. Variables such as a student's cognitive structures and general state of _____ must be considered.

moderate, positive, developmental readiness

16.   Bruner and his colleagues analyzed categorizing and believe it explains why humans are not overwhelmed by environmental complexity. The authors state that three types of concepts exist. (1) _____ concepts rely upon the joint presence of several attributes. These attributes are abstracted from many individual experiences with the object, thing, or event. (2) _____ concepts are composed of concepts, any one of whose attributes may be used in classification. That is, one or another of the attributes enable(s) an object to be placed in a particular category. (3) _____ concepts are formed by the relationships that exist among defining attributes.

Conjunctive, Disjunctive, Relational

17.   Cognitive constructivism holds that people _____ their own knowledge, and that reality is determined by the experiences of the knower, rather than existing as an _____.

actively construct, objective truth

18.   According to constructivism, we _____ an objective reality, knowledge is _____, and the knowledge of two people is "taken-as-shared" to the extent that their constructions seem to _____ in given situations. These three ideas describe _____ from a constructivist view.

cannot know, subjective, function in the same way, what knowledge is

19.   According to constructivism, knowledge is constructed through the process of _____ to the events and ideas one experiences. _____ is encountered and resolved, which leads to changes in the person's cognitive constructions.

adapting, Cognitive conflict

20.   Discourse can _____ cognitive conflict and influence how this conflict is _____, and so the new knowledge that is constructed.

create, resolved

21.   The construction of knowledge is influenced by one's _____ and by the _____ and materials one uses or has ready access to. Different materials give rise to different _____ and thus to different cognitive constructions. Culture also affects what we actually _____ about the physical surroundings.

environment, symbols, interpretations, perceive

22.   The _____ with whom you regularly interact affect the kinds of constructions and _____ developed, the kinds of problems seen as _____ to think about, and they provide a _____ with which to think.

discourse groups, solutions, socially acceptable, vocabulary

23.   For cognitive constructivists, a person is ready to learn about a concept when the cognitive constructions are able to _____ of that concept, even though the knowledge constructed may not be "correct" according to some outsider's criterion.

incorporate some aspect

24.   One of the biggest differences among constructivists is in how much emphasis is placed on the role of _____ versus the role of the _____ in developing constructions. _____ emphases the contexts of development, while Piaget emphasizes the individual's _____ of conflicts.

culture and contexts, individual, Situated cognition, reflective abstraction

25.   A constructivist teacher is a _____ of knowledge and skill acquisition whose purpose is to _____ the learning environment to help each student construct their own understandings. Learning is _____ for each student. The teacher relinquishes some _____ over what and how a student learns, while students are more active and _____. _____ of learning is often more informal and frequent.

facilitator, structure, individualized, control, self-directive, Assessment

26.   Brooks and Brooks (1993) offer several guidelines for teaching from a constructivist perspective: Pose problems of _____ to students; structure learning around _____; seek and value students' points of _____; adapt curriculum to address students' _____; assess student learning in the _____ of teaching; use _____ techniques to help students evaluate their own work.

emerging relevance, primary concepts, view, current understandings, context, nonjudgmental feedback

27.   Alexander Luria proposed a _____ view of the thinking process.

neurological

28.   According to Luria, the thinking process involves _____ to solve a problem for which there is no ready solution, then restraint of _____, _____ of what seems to be the most satisfactory alternative, the creation of a _____, and finally, putting into _____ the methods and operations of the proposed solution.

motivation, impulsive responses, selection, general plan, action

29.   The brain consists of two halves, called _____. The two halves are connected by a bundle of nerve fibers called the _____. The left hemisphere controls the _____ side of the body, while the right hemisphere controls the _____ side of the body.

cerebral hemispheres, corpus callosum, right, left

30.   Differences between the two hemispheres, called _____ , offer insight to your brain's organization.

functional asymmetry

31.   Much of our knowledge of cerebral lateralization has resulted from _____ patients.

brain-damaged

32.   Females generally seem superior in anything relating to _____, while males excel in _____ tasks.

language, spatial

33.   One way of integrating current knowledge of lateralization into the curriculum is to become aware of your reliance on _____. Try also to present material in _____ and encourage students to express their understanding of a topic in a creative manner.

verbal directions, visual form

34.   _____ seems to be an inherent function of the brain. It is present even in infants, utilizes both specific elements and _____ between elements, is aided by _____ clues, uses clues in a probabilistic manner, and depends on one's _____.

Pattern detection, relationships, negative, experience

35.   Human beings show amazing resiliency, which is the meaning of _____.

plasticity

36.   Hyden discovered that during and after learning, both brain cells and their synapses show an increase in _____ production. _____ production also increases. There are also changes in the size and number of connections, and changes in brain support systems such as the glial cells.

protein, Calcium

37.   The manner in which information is recorded or expressed is a _____ of that information.

representation

38.   This common represented information is called the _____ of the representation; the different ways that the information can be expressed is called the _____. We appear to use two types of codes for representing information: _____ and _____.

content, representational code, mental imagery, verbal processing

39.   Mental _____ is a visually based representation of continuously varying information. It is _____, responds to _____, and can be _____ by one's general knowledge. _____ is a representational code that does not resemble in any way what it represents.

imagery, abstract, mental operations, distorted, Verbal processing

40.   _____ is giving meaning to the discrete, meaningless stimuli that initially aroused awareness.

Perception

41.   Our ability to recognize the familiar and to realize what we do not know is _____. Perceiving something means that you _____ past experiences with the stimulus, you experience _____, and you have certain _____ about the stimulus.

perception, recall, meaning, expectations

42.   Perceptual learning allows students to make finer and finer _____, and thus allows them to make more and more _____ analysis of stimuli.

discriminations, fine-grained

43.   Teachers can capitalize on their students' tendencies to _____ and structure by remembering that people tend to group by _____ and that objects that are similar form _____.

organize, familiar objects, natural groups

44.   Categorizing reduces the _____ of the environment, permits us to _____ the objects of the world, allows humans to reduce their need for _____ learning, provides direction for instrumental activity, and encourages the _____ and relating of classes.

complexity, identify, constant, ordering

45.   The classic theory of _____ holds that a category consists of certain definite criteria. If an object possesses these criteria, it belongs to that category; if it lacks the defining criteria, it must be a member of another category. But every category does not seem to possess a neat, defining set of criteria. A _____ does not contain clearly defined critical attributes, but a common standard form.

classification, prototype

46. _____ is recall of personal experiences within a specific context or period of time. _____ is the memory necessary for the use of language, a kind of dictionary without reference to our personal experiences that represents our general knowledge.

Episodic memory, Semantic memory

47. Atkinson and Shiffrin (1968) proposed a three-store system. These three stores are structurally distinct because they hold information differently, for varying times, and for different purposes. The _____ holds input in almost the same form as the sensory image. The _____ is seen as our working memory, which entails conscious processes. The _____ holds both conscious and unconscious data.

sensory register, short-term store, long-term store

48. Several cognitivists advocate levels of processing analysis, which focuses on the _____. Data are processed by various operations called _____, which reflect an individual's _____. The initial processing of a stimulus determines the length of time students _____ it and which aspects are remembered.

depth of processing, perceptual-conceptual analyses, attention, remember

49. _____ implies "putting information into" memory, which occurs as a result of attending, encoding, and the use of memory strategies. _____ implies recognizing, recalling, and reconstructing what we previously have "put in."

Storage, Retrieval

50. _____ means that we compare a present, incoming representation with a representation already stored in memory.

Recognition

51. There are three major elements involved in recognition: _____, _____, and _____.

similarity, prior experience, expectation and context

52. _____ goes beyond recognition because the individual is not given a "copy" of the representation. Any retrieval cue is minimal; consequently, students must generate their own cues in their search for the necessary information.

Recall

53.   Forgetting is a _____ process and here does not refer to an abnormal loss of memory occasioned by aging, shock, or brain injury. Theorists have proposed several explanations. Forgetting as _____ means that once it is learned, students will forget an item unless they use it. _____ forgetting occurs when a person has had experiences that he or she tries to forget because of the unpleasantness, fear, or anxiety associated with them. Forgetting because of _____ happens because new learning interferes with past learning. Forgetting because of _____ occurs because of disuse and a lack of reinforcement. When forced to recall, one applies newly acquired experiences and undoubtedly reshapes the original response, so that it may or may not suit the original stimulus.

normal, disuse or fading, Motivated, interference, extinction and reorganization

54.   To aid your students' storage and retrieval, repeatedly urge students to _____, aim for _____ and not mere mastery of facts, provide _____ rather than _____ practice, insure that _____ occurs, conduct periodic _____, and reduce _____.

remember, comprehension, distributed, massed, overlearning, reviews, interference

55.   _____ transfer is when something a person learns at one time hinders later learning or performance. _____ transfer is when something a person learns in one situation helps learning or performance in another situation.

Negative, Positive

56.   _____ refers to the phenomenon that after rest, memory seems to improve. It may be because _____ developed during the original learning but improved after rest, or because the initial test of retention _____ performance on the later test.

Reminiscence, fatigue, helped

57.   The _____ of items in a list to be memorized affects memory for the items. Students learn items at the _____ and _____ of any memory task more easily that they do the _____ items.

position, beginning, end, middle

58.   _____ is the ability to think about thinking.

Metacognition

59.   _____ refers to our knowledge and beliefs about cognitive matters gained from experience and that we have stored in our long-term memory.

Metacognitive knowledge

60.   _____ are either cognitive or affective experiences that relate to cognitive activities. They are most likely to occur when careful _____ of your cognitive efforts is required.

Metacognitive experiences, conscious monitoring

61. Cole and Scribner state that our modes of responding to stimuli are not _____, but our reactions depend on our past histories of dealing with similar stimuli. We can too frequently misperceive and misunderstand our students' behavior when we interpret it solely from our own _____.

experience-free, cultural perspective

62. _____ instruction means that a student's personal experiences in a particular culture are used to introduce new material.

Contextualized

63. Mental life can be viewed as consisting of either the logical, abstract manner of _____ or _____ thinking, a much more personal kind of thinking that concentrates on people and the causes of their behavior.

scientific thinking, narrative

SUMMARIZE THE MAIN POINTS

This section of your study guide is designed to help you identify and understand the main points in each chapter. You've already reviewed the details using the Guided Review (above), and will consider the importance, relevance, and usefulness of the information in later sections. For now, focus on summarizing the main ideas.

For each major section in the chapter, summarize the main point and the evidence presented in the text to support and/or discuss it. If there are key terms presented in the section, define them. Some prompting questions are provided to help you structure your review.

The main sections of Chapter 7 are:

- The meaning of cognitive psychology
- The emergence of cognitive psychology
- Major approaches to learning with a cognitive psychology orientation
- The brain and thinking
- Information processing and the acquisition of knowledge
- Cognition across cultures
- Helping you remember: An integrated summary

For each section, answer the following questions:

1. In two sentences or less, **summarize** what the **main point** of this section was.

2. Briefly **summarize the evidence** for and against each main point (a simple list of details they use to support each of their points is sufficient). If the authors discuss research studies to support the point, summarize the findings in one sentence. If the authors are presenting a logical argument to support the point (i.e., not citing data from research studies), briefly list the supporting points they made. Use the detailed chapter outline to help you identify the supporting points.

3. Briefly review the **definitions of any key terms** in each main section.

WHY SHOULD YOU CARE?

The purpose of this section of your study guide is to help you understand how and why the information in the chapter is relevant for you personally. You'll be asked to think more about the relevance and usefulness of the information in later sections of this study guide.

Look back at the work you did in summarizing the main points in the section above and answer the following questions:

1. For each section you summarized, why or how is the **main point** you identified **important to and/or relevant for teachers in general**? Try to limit your answer to only one or two sentences so you don't get bogged down in details, but focus on general usefulness.

2. Now think about the chapter as a whole. **Identify two specific events, contexts, or problems** for which the ideas presented in this chapter are relevant. Briefly discuss how they're relevant and how they could be useful.

3. Now **identify three concepts** from the chapter that **YOU find useful** in some way. Discuss how/why these concepts are useful, and specify how you will actually use them in your teaching and/or your daily life. (It's okay if there is some overlap between your answers for numbers 2 and 3.)

DISCUSSION QUESTIONS

The following "What do you think?" questions are printed in the text.

1. Now that you have read about behavioral theories of learning and cognitive theories of learning, which one do you think best explains classroom learning? Which aspects of these different perspectives of learning really makes them different?

2. If you want to teach somebody a new concept, what do you think are the most important steps in the instructional process? List at least three things you would do to increase the likelihood that a student would learn the concept.

3. Think about how you learn best. Does a constructivist approach to learning characterize your activities as a learner? If not, why not?

4. Think about how your memory works. This is part of metamemory. Do you often intentionally think about how you are going to remember something? Does it help you to plan ways to remember information? How can you get students to think about their memory abilities?

Additional discussion questions:

5. Compare and contrast behavioral and traditional cognitive theories of learning and cognition.

6. Define meaningful learning and discovery learning and describe the differences between them. Give examples of each.

7. Discuss how a teacher can facilitate information processing in the classroom by using the techniques of mental imagery and verbal processing for representing information.

8. Why is it important to help students learn to categorize information? How can teachers help students learn to categorize?

9. Distinguish between the multistore model of memory and the perceptual-conceptual analysis of memory.

10. Identify four explanations for why forgetting occurs.

11. List and explain three ways a teacher can help students store information. Then list and explain three ways a teacher can help students retrieve information.

12. Explain how and why mental representations and computers are important in cognitive psychology.

13. How are the Gestaltists and Bartlett relevant to today's cognitive psychology?

14. What is reconstructive memory and what implications does it have for the classroom?

15. Describe how culture affects cognition.

16. What biological changes occur when you learn?

17. How is knowledge of perception useful to teachers?

18. Summarize the main aspects of constructivism. List four ways you would use a constructivist approach in your teaching.

TAKE IT PERSONALLY!

The questions in this section are designed to help you personalize, integrate, and apply the information from the text. Personalization questions ask you to consider the personal relevance and usefulness of concepts, and consider how they might be useful in your life now and in the future. Integration questions ask you to pull together information from the text to evaluate it, summarize it, synthesize a recommendation on the basis of it, or express an opinion about it. Application questions ask you to think about how the concepts might be useful to address real problems or situations you may find yourself in. All three question types will help you consider the information at a deeper conceptual level, understand it more fully, and remember it.

1. Describe your theory of learning. Is it more similar to a behaviorist or a cognitive perspective?

2. Identify an example of a schema in your life. How could you use schemata to enhance your learning and your teaching?

3. Summarize Ausubel's and Bruner's theories and identify the major similarities and differences between the two. For each theory, give two specific examples of how it could be used in teaching.

4. Identify examples of advance organizers in this course. What effect are these organizers supposed to have on your learning? What effect do they actually have?

5. Define discovery learning. Have you had any experience with this approach to instruction? If so, evaluate the experience and analyze whether, how, and why it worked for you. How could this approach to instruction be used in this course?

6. What is cerebral lateralization? How will knowledge of this concept help you as a teacher?

7.	How is pattern matching relevant for teachers?

8.	Describe information processing. Identify an example of how you could use information processing concepts in your teaching.

9.	Identify an example of mental imagery and verbal processing in this course. Give specific examples of how each of these modes of representation could be useful to you in your learning in this course.

10.	Identify an example of perceptual learning. Has this type of learning contributed to your ability to solve problems or learn? How?

11.	Describe your own theory of memory. Compare and contrast it with those described in the text.

12.	What is metacognition and why should teachers care about it? How can you go about fostering your students' metacognitive abilities?

13.	Will you use a constructivist approach in your teaching? Why or why not? If so, what aspects will you use?

CASE IN POINT...

Remember to use the cases from the text as contexts for identifying examples of concepts from the text and as contexts for solving educational problems. Also remember to use a consistent framework (like the DUPE model or the CASE NOTES in the text) to structure your "Mini-Case Report." Review the "Case in Point..." section of Chapter 1 in this study guide for more details.

SUGGESTED CONCEPTS TO IDENTIFY FOR CHAPTER 7

advance organizers	nonjudgemental feedback
constructivism	perception
contextualized instruction	recognition
discovery learning	retrieval
episodic memory	schema (pl. schemata)
forgetting	semantic memory
levels of processing	sensory register
long-term memory	short-term memory
meaningful learning	verbal processing
metacognition	

Review Case #2 about Mark Siegel in your text and use the following questions to prompt your thinking about this case.

1. Could Mark use the information on schemas, metacognition, and levels of processing to help Karim improve his reading comprehension? How might these ideas be helpful?

2. Could knowledge of cognitive psychology, especially of constructivism and of discovery learning, help Mark deal with Karim? How?

BIG IDEAS IN EDUCATIONAL PSYCHOLOGY

Thinking about the "big ideas" in educational psychology will help you organize and apply your newly acquired knowledge. Use the following steps to identify your own principles and strategies from the chapter and to relate them to the five main themes of the text (i.e., the "big ideas").

1. Review the TIPS from the text.

2. List some of the main concepts from the chapter. Use the work you did in prior sections of the study guide to help generate this list. Also look at the list of key terms from the chapter.

3. Select what you think are two or three of the most important concepts from your list.

4. For each concept you select, try to state it as a principle (use the TIPS format in the text and the example shown below as a guide for how to state principles).

5. Develop two or three specific teaching strategies that follow from each stated principle.

6. Relate your work to the five main themes from the text, identifying which theme(s) are relevant for each principle and strategy. This step will help you see how the information in each chapter contributes to improved teaching for each of these five critical aspects of instruction.

7. Think about and discuss with classmates how the principles and strategies you identify will help you improve your teaching for each theme you listed as relevant.

The five main themes from the text are:
ASSESSMENT, COMMUNICATION, LEARNING, MOTIVATION, AND TIME

Some example concepts, principles, and strategies for Chapter 7:

advance organizers
cerebral lateralization
cognitive conflict
constructivism
contextualized instruction
discovery learning
forgetting
information processing
levels of processing
meaningful learning
mental image

mental representation
metacognition
nonjudgemental feedback
perception
plasticity
reception learning
retrieval
schema (pl. schemata)
semantic vs. episodic memory
stores model of memory

Principle   Each person constructs his or her own knowledge based on their personal experiences, physiologies, and environments. (ASSESSMENT, COMMUNICATION, LEARNING, MOTIVATION)

Strategy   To better assess how students are understanding the content you are teaching, ask them to externalize it in some way. Restatements, demonstrations, and performance assessments of many kinds require that students show in detail how they are thinking about and using the information. (ASSESSMENT, COMMUNICATION, LEARNING)

Strategy   Make your classroom a "culture of inquiry" or a "problem-solving zone" to encourage thoughtful, reflective, and high-quality thinking. Encourage students to develop discourse groups that encourage, value, and reward intellectual curiosity and activity by letting them work together on interesting, complex projects, addressing realistic problems, etc. (COMMUNICATION, LEARNING, MOTIVATION)

SUGGESTED READINGS

Anderson, J. R. (1990). *Cognitive psychology and its implications. (III).* New York: W. H. Freeman.

Aylward, G. P. (1997). *Infant and early childhood neuropsychology.* New York: Plenum Press.

Best, J. B. (1994). *Cognitive psychology.* St. Paul, MN: West.

Brooks, J. G., & Brooks, M. G. (1993). *In Search of Understanding: The Case for Constructivist Classrooms.* Alexandria, VA: Association for Supervision and Curriculum Development.

Bruner, J. (1983). *In search of mind.* New York: Harper and Row.

Fosnot, C. T. (1996). Constructivism: A Psychological theory of learning. In C. T. Fosnot (Ed.), *Constructivism: Theory, Perspectives, and Practice.* New York: Teachers College Press.

Gardner, H. (1986). *The mind's new science.* New York: Basic.

Glover, J. A., Ronning, R. R., & Bruning, R. H. (1990). *Cognitive psychology for teachers.* New York: Macmillan.

Lave, J. (1988). *Cognition into practice.* Cambridge: Cambridge University Press.

Miller, B. (1956). The magical number seven, plus or minus two. *Psychological Review, 63,* 81-97.

Reese, H. W., & Frazen, M. D. (1997). *Biological and neuropsychological mechanisms.* Mahwah, NJ: Erlbaum.

Rogoff, B. (1990). *Apprenticeship in thinking: Cognitive development in social context.* New York: Oxford University Press.

Rumelhart, D. E., McClelland, J. L., & the PDP Research Group. (1986). *Parallel distributed processing: Explorations in the microstructure of cognition: Vol. 1. Foundations.* Cambridge, MA: MIT Press.

Tharp, R. G., & Gallimore, R. (1988). *Rousing minds to life: Teaching, learning, and schooling in social context.* Cambridge, MA: Cambridge University Press.

PRACTICE TEST 1

1. The different ways that information can be expressed is called the
   a. content of the representation.
   b. context of the representation.
   c. representational code.
   d. All of the answers are correct.

2. Discussion of activities of the mind is
   a. the central issue in cognitive theory, while not permitted in behavioral learning theory.
   b. the central issue in behavioral learning theory, while not permitted in cognitive theory.
   c. the central issue in both cognitive and behavioral learning theories.
   d. not permitted in either cognitive or behavioral learning theories.

3. Mental frameworks that modify incoming data so that they "fit" the person's experiences and perceptions are called
   a. relational concepts.
   b. schemata.
   c. anchoring ideas.
   d. advance organizers.

4. Schemata involve organization
   a. of information in one's long-term memory.
   b. within the materials to be learned.
   c. linking information in long-term memory and the materials to be learned.
   d. all of the answers are correct.

5. How could a teacher facilitate meaningful learning in a class discussion on *Moby Dick*?
   a. By using a representational code.
   b. By relating the story's themes to the schemata recommended by an expert.
   c. By providing a general overview of new information to be learned in advance of the actual reading.
   d. By introducing conjunctive concepts.

6. In health education class, a teacher illustrates the sequence of pregnancy, labor, and birth before explaining the process in more detail. This illustrates the use of
   a. schema.
   b. advance organizers.
   c. relational concepts.
   d. mental images.

7. Which of Bruner's concepts relies upon the joint presence of several attributes?
   a. conjunctive
   b. disjunctive
   c. relational
   d. All of the answers are correct.

8. According to the text, most teachers expect that their students will function cognitively in a verbal analytical manner. Which of the following groups does not "fit" these school expectations, performing better on spatial tasks?
   a. Japanese-Americans
   b. Chinese-Americans
   c. Native-Americans
   d. None of the answers is correct.

9. What gives meaning to the discrete, meaningless stimuli that initially aroused awareness?
   a. perception
   b. memory
   c. knowledge base
   d. experience

10. Although football and water polo are both sports, most people would probably state that football is a more typical example of a sport; it is a
    a. conjunctive concept.
    b. "fit."
    c. schema.
    d. prototype.

11. David knows that Abraham Lincoln was the sixteenth president of the United States. This illustrates his
    a. short-term memory.
    b. sensory memory.
    c. episodic memory.
    d. semantic memory.

12. When we compare a present, incoming representation with a representation already stored in memory, we are using
    a. recall.
    b. recognition.
    c. context.
    d. a representational code.

13. Which explanation of forgetting has been referred to as the trace decay hypothesis?
    a. motivated forgetting
    b. forgetting because of interference
    c. forgetting as disuse or fading
    d. forgetting because of extinction and reorganization

14. To facilitate students' storage and retrieval, the aim of instruction should be
    a. mastery of facts.
    b. sequential information.
    c. comprehension.
    d. metacognitive knowledge.

15. Our knowledge and beliefs about cognitive matters gained from experience and which we have stored in our long-term memory is called
    a. fit.
    b. schema.
    c. metacognitive experiences.
    d. metacognitive knowledge.

16. Alexander Luria's view of the brain-mind relationship is based on
    a. psychoanalysis.
    b. neuropsychology.
    c. motivation theory.
    d. expectancy-value theory.

17. After Bill's auto accident, he suffered a loss of memory for several months, after which he regained his memory. What does this illustrate?
    a. plasticity
    b. hemispheric specialization
    c. pattern matching
    d. lateralization

18. Pattern detection
    a. is an inherent function of the brain.
    b. starts developing after about 3 years of age.
    c. is hindered by negative cues.
    d. leads to the development of patterns that remain stable across time and situations.

19. Females generally are superior in _____ ,whereas males tend to excel in_____.
    a. language; spatial tasks
    b. spatial tasks; language
    c. motor skills; processing skills
    d. processing skills; motor skills

20. Discourse is important for cognitive constructivism because it
    a. allows students to practice expressing their views to others.
    b. can signal the need to change one's current cognitive constructions.
    c. eliminates differences in the ways that different communities of discourse resolve cognitive conflicts.
    d. decreases the effect of one's social environment on how cognitive conflict is resolved.

PRACTICE TEST 2

1. Which of the following statements regarding images is true?
    a. Images are linked to a "picture" of the object.
    b. Images often stay the same because of our past knowledge.
    c. Images represent static information.
    d. Images possess the capability of responding to certain mental operations.

2. What is the basis of memory and results from our previous experiences?
    a. schemata
    b. perception
    c. anchoring ideas
    d. mental images

3. One of the central, defining characteristics of a schema is
    a. self-regulation.
    b. organization.
    c. self-efficacy.
    d. metacognition.

4. An abstract, general overview of new information to be learned that occurs in advance of the actual reading is called
    a. levels of representation.
    b. schema.
    c. advance organizers.
    d. relational concepts.

5. Which of Bruner's concepts are composed of concepts, any one of which may be used in classification?
    a. conjunctive
    b. disjunctive
    c. relational
    d. All of the answers are correct.

6. A student's personal experiences in a particular culture can be used to introduce new material. This is called
    a. relational concepts.
    b. discovery learning.
    c. metacognitive experience.
    d. contextualized instruction.

7. Students are asked to interview a person about their career, and then present a speech to the class on what they learned. This task is an example of
    a. rote learning.
    b. discovery learning.
    c. reception learning.
    d. meaningless learning.

8. To perceive something means to
    a. not be able to recall any experiences you have had with it.
    b. have little idea of what it means.
    c. like it.
    d. have expectations about it.

9. When teaching a concept, teachers should
    a. use artificial examples.
    b. compare the concept to other categories that are not the same.
    c. use few examples so students will not become confused.
    d. avoid referring to students' prior knowledge of the concept, because the prior knowledge could be incorrect.

10. Which part of the multistore model is seen as our working memory?
    a. sensory register
    b. short-term store
    c. long-term store
    d. All of the answers are correct.

11. When you are not given a "copy" of the representation, you are being asked to
    a. recall.
    b. recognize.
    c. forget.
    d. represent.

12. When a person has had experiences that he or she tries to forget because of the anxiety associated with them, the forgetting is called
    a. motivated forgetting.
    b. forgetting because of interference.
    c. forgetting as disuse, or fading.
    d. forgetting because of extinction and reorganization.

13. One strategy for increasing comprehension is to create a representation of the central idea. What is the name of this strategy?
    a. summarization
    b. question-answer
    c. story grammar
    d. reduction of interference

14. Cognitive or affective experiences that relate to cognitive activities are called
    a. levels of representation.
    b. perception.
    c. levels of processing analysis.
    d. metacognitive experiences.

15. According to Luria, the thinking process begins when a person is
    a. motivated.
    b. curious.
    c. challenged.
    d. given freedom.

16. Studies of brain cell changes during learning indicate that
    a. a student's approach to learning is psychologically, but not neurologically, based.
    b. production of calcium decreases temporarily.
    c. production of brain cell protein increases.
    d. there is little relation between changes in brain cells and changes in intellectual capacity.

17. Helping students identify patterns
    a. can help students make sense of what they are learning.
    b. is difficult, since pattern matching does not come naturally to most students.
    c. interferes with students' abilities to consider relations among the concepts they are learning.
    d. is useful because it increases students' metacognitive monitoring skills.

18. Since results of lateralization research have become known, criticism has been directed at the schools for teaching
    a. to both hemispheres equally.
    b. without regard to hemispheres.
    c. to the left hemisphere.
    d. to the right hemisphere.

19. Which of the following illustrates a cognitive approach to teaching and learning?
    a. A teacher is more interested in the specific answer a student gives than in how the student arrives at the answer.
    b. A teacher does not think it is important to understand what students already know about a topic.
    c. A teacher spends time directly teaching strategies for improving students' memory skills.
    d. None of the above illustrates a cognitive approach.

20. Which of the following is true of
    constructivism?
    a. Different individuals typically
       understand a given set of information
       in the same way.
    b. Two people's constructions are hardly
       ever similar enough to say they both
       understand something in a similar
       way.
    c. Knowledge is objective.
    d. All a person's knowledge is interpreted
       with respect to what the person
       already knows.

ANSWER KEY

Practice Test 1

1.   ANSWER: C, Factual; OBJECTIVE: 2; PAGE: 270
2.   ANSWER: A, Factual; OBJECTIVE: 1; PAGE: 246
3.   ANSWER: B, Factual; OBJECTIVE: 3; PAGE: 250
4.   ANSWER: D, Factual; OBJECTIVE: 3; PAGE: 251
5.   ANSWER: B, Conceptual; OBJECTIVE: 5; PAGE: 254
6.   ANSWER: B, Applied; OBJECTIVE: 5; PAGE: 253
7.   ANSWER: A, Factual; OBJECTIVE: 4; PAGE: 255
8.   ANSWER: C, Factual; OBJECTIVE: 8; PAGE: 288
9.   ANSWER: A, Factual; OBJECTIVE: 7; PAGE: 273
10. ANSWER: D, Applied; OBJECTIVE: 4; PAGE: 278
11. ANSWER: D, Applied; OBJECTIVE: 8; PAGE: 280
12. ANSWER: B, Factual; OBJECTIVE: 8; PAGE: 282
13. ANSWER: C, Factual; OBJECTIVE: 8; PAGE: 283
14. ANSWER: C, Factual; OBJECTIVE: 7; PAGE: 284
15. ANSWER: D, Factual; OBJECTIVE: 9; PAGE: 286
16. ANSWER: B, Factual; OBJECTIVE: 6; PAGE: 267
17. ANSWER: A, Applied; OBJECTIVE: 6; PAGE: 270
18. ANSWER: A, Factual; OBJECTIVE: 6; PAGE: 269
19. ANSWER: A, Factual; OBJECTIVE: 6; PAGE: 268
20. ANSWER: B, Factual; OBJECTIVE: 4; PAGE: 258

Practice Test 2

1. ANSWER: D, Factual; OBJECTIVE: 2; PAGE: 272
2. ANSWER: A, Factual; OBJECTIVE: 3; PAGE: 251
3. ANSWER: B, Factual; OBJECTIVE: 3; PAGE: 251
4. ANSWER: C, Factual; OBJECTIVE: 4; PAGE: 253
5. ANSWER: B, Factual; OBJECTIVE: 4; PAGE: 255
6. ANSWER: D, Factual; OBJECTIVE: 5; PAGE: 288
7. ANSWER: B, Applied; OBJECTIVE: 5; PAGE: 253, 255
8. ANSWER: D, Factual; OBJECTIVE: 7; PAGE: 273
9. ANSWER: B, Factual; OBJECTIVE: 4; PAGE: 278
10. ANSWER: B, Factual; OBJECTIVE: 7; PAGE: 280
11. ANSWER: A, Factual; OBJECTIVE: 8; PAGE: 282
12. ANSWER: A, Factual; OBJECTIVE: 8; PAGE: 283
13. ANSWER: A, Factual; OBJECTIVE: 5; PAGE: 284
14. ANSWER: D, Factual; OBJECTIVE: 9; PAGE: 287
15. ANSWER: A, Factual; OBJECTIVE: 6; PAGE: 267
16. ANSWER: C, Factual; OBJECTIVE: 6; PAGE: 270
17. ANSWER: A, Factual; OBJECTIVE: 6; PAGE: 270
18. ANSWER: C, Factual; OBJECTIVE: 6; PAGE: 269
19. ANSWER: C, Applied; OBJECTIVE: 1; PAGE: 247
20. ANSWER: D, Factual; OBJECTIVE: 4; PAGE: 257

Chapter 8   THINKING SKILLS AND PROBLEM-SOLVING STRATEGIES

LEARNING OBJECTIVES

After completing this chapter, you should be able to

1.   Define cognitive style and discuss its educational implications.

2.   Compare and contrast Bloom's, Costa's, PIFs', and the CoRT models of thinking skills.

3.   Discuss the use of questioning to improve thinking skills.

4.   Teach students the basics of the DUPE problem-solving model.

5.   Identify the weaknesses in your students' problem-solving skills.

6.   Define creativity and identify characteristics of creative people.

7.   Identify strategies to help students remember information.

8.   Identify factors that influence transfer of learning and strategies for helping students transfer their learning.

CHAPTER HIGHLIGHTS

Thinking

- The need for thinking and problem-solving skills dominates our lives.
- Cognitive or learning style refers to preferences in learning and studying.
- Knowing your cognitive style and that of your students improves both teaching and learning.

Thinking Skills: An Analysis

- Bloom's Taxonomy of Educational Objectives is intended to specify desirable cognitive objectives in behavioral terms, to suggest means of evaluating the attainment of these goals, and to aid in curriculum construction.
- Costa's Thinking Skills program is based upon knowledge of how the brain works, humans' awareness of their own thinking, and the acquiring of knowledge. He urged that an information-processing model should be the basis for teaching, learning, and curriculum construction.
- Several thinking skills programs have been designed to help students.

Problem Solving

- Good problem solvers have identifiable characteristics.
- Though some students are probably better than others at solving problems, the problem-solving ability of all students can be improved.
- Difficulty in solving problems can come from simple mistakes, such as failing to use all of the clues present in the problem.
- Some students are reluctant, for a variety of reasons, to attack problems.

The DUPE Model

- D   *Determining* the nature of a problem heps you to identify the "givens" of a problem and then decide what actions can be performed on them, that is, to "bridge the gap between where one is and where one wants to go."
- U   *Understanding* the nature of a problem means identifying the nature of the problem and also representing it.
- P   *Planning* means to represent a problem and cast its information in either symbolic (internal) or graphic (external) form.
- E   *Evaluation* of a problem solving plan can occur at two stages: after the plan is devised (is it adequate?) and after the solution is proposed (did it work?).
- When a solution proves elusive, a new and creative approach is often called for.
- Memory plays a crucial role in problem solving.

Transferring Strategies and Skills

- Transfer refers to the ability to use past experiences to help understand new challenging situations.
- Several factors influence transfer.
- A major goal of instruction should be to teach for transfer.

DETAILED CHAPTER OUTLINE

I. Thinking
    A. Thinking plus problem-solving strategies produce competence.
    B. Ann Brown noted that thinking means knowing when you know, knowing what you know, knowing what you need to know, and knowing when to acquire new knowledge.
    C. Cognitive style
        1. Style is a strategy used consistently across a wide variety of tasks.
        2. Cognitive styles are those involved in thinking and problem solving, while learning styles point to preferences in learning and studying.
        3. Classroom implications
            a. The mastery style learner absorbs information concretely, processes it sequentially, and judges its value by its clarity and practicality.
            b. The understanding style learner focuses on ideas and abstractions and learns by a process of questioning and reasoning.
            c. The self-expressive style learner depends more on feelings and emotions to form new ideas and products, and judges the value of learning products by their originality and aesthetics.
            d. The interpersonal style learner is more social by nature and tends to learn better in groups and judges learning by its potential use in helping others.

e. Goodness of fit refers to the attempt to match students' learning preferences with teaching methods.

f. Don't confuse style with ability; otherwise, you're apt to teach and assess students in ways that benefit those with certain styles of thinking and learning, but put other students at a disadvantage.

4. Case Notes: Mark Siegel's class

5. Analyzing your personal style

    a. A *grouper* prefers as wide a grasp of a subject as possible, likes to learn general principles, prefers unstructured situations, and begins by studying general concepts and the total situation before commencing more detailed analysis.

    b. A *stringer* prefers systematic, methodical analysis leading to mastery of details, likes to acquire specifics first then more general concepts, likes to acquire knowledge sequentially and gradually, and prefers to learn information directly related to the task at hand.

II. Thinking skills: an analysis

  A. The Bloom taxonomy

    1. The main purpose of the taxonomy is to provide a classification of the goals of our educational system.

    2. The taxonomy consists of three major sections: the cognitive, affective, and psychomotor domains.

    3. The cognitive taxonomy is divided into six major classes.

      a. Knowledge—recall of specific facts

      b. Comprehension—understanding what is communicated

      c. Application—generalization and use of abstract information in concrete situations

      d. Analysis—breakdown of a problem into subparts and detection of relationships among the parts

      e. Synthesis—putting together parts to form a whole

      f. Evaluation—using criteria to make judgments

    4. Case Notes: Mark Siegel's class

    5. Do not focus merely on questions about facts. Stretch your students' thinking abilities by asking questions that require application, analysis, synthesis, and evaluation.

    6. Using questions to improve thinking skills

      a. Using questions is a specific example of how teachers can help students to improve their thinking skills.

      b. Good questions cause your students to pay attention, process information, organize their ideas, and compose an answer.

      c. Three issues seem critical to efforts to frame thoughtful questions.

        (1) How to ask questions. Phrase them clearly and concisely; ask what, where, when, who, how, and why; use appropriate language; ask only one question at a time; and pay attention to the level of thought required for an answer.

          (a) Questions can be convergent (requiring a right answer) or divergent (requiring students to expand, explore, and be creative).

        (2) Obtaining good answers. Give students enough time to answer and give all students an equal chance to respond.

        (3) Following-up student responses. You should clarify, expand, and synthesize when you can; never let an incorrect answer stand.

  B. Costa and thinking skills

    1. Costa favors direct instruction of thinking skills.

    2. Costa suggested a four-level hierarchy of thinking skills.

      a. Level I: The discrete level of thinking. Involves individual skills prerequisite to more complex thinking.

      b. Level II: Strategies of thinking. Involves the combination of individual, discrete skills to formulate strategies.

      c.   Level III: Creative thinking. Requires the use of strategies to create new thought patterns and innovative solutions.

      d.   Level IV: The cognitive spirit. Requires students' willingness, disposition, inclination, and commitment to think.

  3. Four categories of teacher behaviors are effective in facilitating thinking skills:

      a.   Questioning. Questions containing higher-order thinking will require students to use higher-order thinking skills to answer them. Questions can activate each part of Costa's model.

      b.   Structuring, or how teachers control the classroom environment. Good structure comes from instructional clarity, structuring time and energy, and carefully organizing your interactions with students.

      c.   Responding. Teacher responses are closed (criticism and praise) or open (silence, accepting, clarifying, and facilitating).

      d.   Modeling. Demonstrate good thinking skills and enthusiasm by your own behavior.

  4. Case Notes: Mark Siegel's class

C. Thinking skills programs

  1. Practical Intelligence for School

      a.   The PIFS program is based on Sternberg's triarchic model of intelligence and Gardner's multiple intelligences model.

      b.   Gardner's theory expresses the domains in which intelligence manifests itself, whereas Sternberg's componential subtheory identifies the mental processes involved in these domains. The contextual subtheory defines the practical ways the processes are applied, and the experiential subtheory deals with the transfer of skills to new situations.

  2. The CoRT thinking program

      a.   deBono linked his theory of thinking skills to a neurological and information processing base, and argued for the direct teaching of thinking skills to students.

      b.   The CoRT program has several objectives.

         (1)   The program should be simple and practical.

         (2)   The program should apply to a wide range of ages.

         (3)   The thinking skills taught should be those required in real life.

         (4)   The program should be independent of any detailed knowledge base.

         (5)   Students should be able to transfer the thinking skills they acquire to all of life's situations.

  3. TIPS: Helping students with their thinking skills

III. Problem solving

A. Characteristics of good problem solvers:

  1. Positive attitude

  2. Concern for accuracy

  3. Habit of breaking the problem into parts

  4. Avoidance of guessing

  5. Metacognition is the ability to think about thinking; knowing something, thinking about what we can do with this knowledge, and developing strategies to solve the problems we face.

B. What is a problem?

  1. A problem is a significant discrepancy between the actual behavior and the desired behavior.

  2. Problem solving requires that we understand the meaning of the gap or discrepancy, and then construct ways of bridging the gap.

      a.   Internal representation (try to solve it in your head).

      b.   External representation, or use paper and pencil and sketch a proposed solution.

      c.   Whatever works for you is right, that is, it matches your learning style.

C. Improving problem-solving skills

  1. Individual differences in problem-solving ability exist. Regardless of how you react to problems, it is possible to improve your ability to solve them.

2. Although efforts to incorporate problem-solving activities and content within the curriculum are increasing, the situation still needs to be improved.
3. What kinds of mistakes do your students make?
    a. failure to use all relevant facts of a problem
    b. failure to adopt systematic, step-by-step procedures
    c. failure to perceive vital relationships in the problem
    d. frequent use of sloppy techniques in acquiring information and using one's reasoning processes
4. Retreating from problems. It's easier to ignore or avoid problems that demand effort to solve, especially for students who constantly experience frustration in school. They may transfer this attitude to other problems outside of school.
5. Categories of excuses for poorer problem solving:
    a. I just wasn't born smart.
    b. I have a terrible memory.
    c. I was never good at that.
6. It is difficult to help anyone break away from customary attitudes toward and beliefs about problem solving, but creative thinking leads to changes in both attitudes and approach.
7. Case Notes: Mark Siegel's class

IV. The DUPE model
 A. DUPE is an acronym you can pass on to your students, one that they should be able to remember easily and that they can transfer to any problem.
    1. D—*Define* the nature of the problem.
    2. U—*Understand* the nature of the problem.
    3. P—*Plan* your solution. Select appropriate strategies.
    4. E—*Evaluate* your plan for its suitability and success.
 B. Defining the nature of a problem
    1. Before students can determine the nature of a problem, they must realize that one exists.
        a. Teach students that when things aren't working as well as they should, or when a technique that worked before doesn't work now, they have a problem.
        b. Teach students to look carefully at the problem itself and identify the givens (the facts that are provided).
        c. A well-defined problem is one in which the steps to solution are specified clearly in the problem's statement. An ill-defined problem is one in which the givens are much more vague and the steps to solution more elusive.
    2. Defining the problem
        a. This means identifying exactly what is causing the difficulty.
        b. Brighter problem solvers spend relatively more time up front figuring out what to do and less time doing it, while less bright problem solvers spend less time figuring out what to do and more time doing it because they really haven't defined the problem.
 C. Understanding the nature of the problem
    1. Understanding the nature of a problem implies that we can both define and represent it.
    2. The knowledge base
        a. Much that passes for cleverness or innate quickness of mind actually depends on specialized knowledge.
        b. The acquisition of knowledge in itself is not enough; what is also critical is the availability of knowledge when needed.
    3. Problem representation
        a. The first and most basic step in problem solving is to represent the information in either symbolic or diagrammatic form.
            (1) Symbolic form casts the problem's information in words, letters, or numbers.
            (2) Diagrammatic form expresses the information by some collection of lines, dots, or angles.
        b. Representation may be either internal or external.

c. There are several reasons for using external representation:
   (1) It focuses on the most important concepts.
   (2) It helps the individual to see relationships among the givens.
   (3) Representing intermediate steps aids memory.
   (4) It is hard to visualize some givens in detail.
d. Internal representation entails the addition and elimination of details from the original and the interpretation of information.
e. The manner in which we represent a problem determines the ease or difficulty with which we will solve it, if at all.

D. Planning the solution
1. Planning the solution involves two critical aspects:
   a. the need to be familiar with the core concepts required for solution
   b. the need to apply certain general strategies that seem appropriate
2. Helping you plan. Hayes (1989) suggested four learning strategies:
   a. Using the structuring strategy, one searches for relations in the learning material; it is a method for discovering structures.
   b. Using the context strategy, one searches for relations within the material to be learned. This differs from the structuring strategy because the relations may be between the learning material and what we already know.
   c. Instantiation means to furnish an example.
   d. Multiple coding represents the information—the givens in our problem—in more than one way: verbally or through mental imagery.

E. Evaluating the solution
1. In examining a plan and solution, two aspects of evaluation seem especially pertinent:
   a. Stop here and evaluate the plan.
   b. If the first evaluative phase indicated the plan is sound, then you should activate your plan. After you have worked through the plan, a second evaluative phase is needed, in which you must decide whether you need a new solution or are totally satisfied with the solution that you have achieved.

F. The creative student
1. Creativity means generating novel and appropriate ideas.
2. Creativity is an essential element in human nature.
3. All of use engage in two types of thinking.
   a. Convergent thinking is directed toward finding correct solutions.
   b. Divergent thinking searches for novel ideas and products.
4. Characteristics of creative children
   a. They learn the strategies needed to solve the problems they inevitably encounter.
   b. They don't quit, they persevere.
   c. They are sensitive to problems.
   d. They are more fluent than others; that is, they generate large numbers of ideas.
   e. They propose novel ideas that are also useful.
   f. They demonstrate considerable flexibility of mind, looking for new combinations or new ways of attacking a problem.
   g. They reorganize the elements
5. TIPS on learning and memory: Helping in the search for creativity

G. The role of memory
1. The appropriateness of the memory strategy depends on the level of material involved and the conditions under which the information must be remembered.
2. Retrieval aids
   a. Often we have something in memory (we have stored it) but we can't get at it (we can't retrieve it).
   b. Cues
      (1) The most effective cues are those that we generate ourselves.

      (2)   A particularly effective cue is the use of acronyms and acrostics. An acronym is a word consisting of the letters of a series of words (e.g., DUPE). There is a two-fold value to acronyms: the compression of several facts into a smaller number, and the cues it provides for remembering large amounts of data.

      (3)   In an acrostic, a sentence or phrase is devised using words whose first letters are the cues for certain information.

    c.   Imagery refers to visualizing objects or events.

    d.   The method of loci utilizes a series of familiar visual images and links each image to the object to be retained. It is a way of formulating personal retrieval cues.

    e.   To elaborate is to add information to what you are trying to learn so that the material becomes more personally meaningful.

      (1)   Elaboration strategies improve recall because they increase the depth of processing and facilitate storage of new information with related information that is well known to the learner.

  3. Two warnings about retention and recall strategies: They should not be so complex and cumbersome that they require more effort to remember than the content; and students (and teachers) should adopt techniques that are best suited to them.

  4. Current Issues and Perspectives: Thinking, problem solving, and technology

V. Transferring strategies and skills

  A. Transfer of learning refers to attempts to understand how learning one topic influences later learning.

    1. Transfer may be positive, such as when learning one topic helps you to learn another. It may also be negative, however, such as when learning one topic hinders the learning of another.

  B. Influences on transfer

    1. Task similarity exercises a strong influence on transfer.

    2. The degree of original learning is an important element in transfer.

    3. Personal variables such as intelligence, motivation, and past experiences are important, but uncontrollable, influences on transfer.

  C. Teaching for transfer

    1. Teach to overlearning.

    2. Be certain that the material you teach is well organized.

    3. Use advance organizers, if possible.

    4. Emphasize the similarity between classroom work and the transfer situation.

    5. Specify what is important in the task.

    6. Try to understand how students perceive the possibility of transfer.

VI.   Case reflections

VII.   Chapter highlights

VIII. What do you think? questions

IX.   Key terms

KEY TERMS

cognitive research trust (CoRT)
cognitive style
convergent questions
cues
divergent questions
DUPE
elaboration
external representation
grouper
imagery
instantiation
internal representation
learning style

metacognition
method of loci
multiple coding
multiple intelligences
retrieving
storing
stringer
structuring
style
thinking skills
transfer of learning
triarchic model of intelligence

GUIDED REVIEW

1. _____ plus problem solving strategies produce _____. Ann Brown noted that thinking means knowing _____ you know, knowing _____ you know, knowing what you _____ know, and knowing when to _____ new knowledge.

Thinking, competence, when, what, need to, acquire

2. _____ is a strategy used consistently across a wide variety of tasks. Cognitive styles are those involved in thinking and _____, while _____ point to preferences in learning and studying.

Cognitive style, problem solving, learning styles

3. The _____ style learner absorbs information concretely, processes it sequentially, and judges its value by its clarity and practicality. The _____ style learner focuses on ideas and abstractions and learns by a process of questioning and reasoning. The _____ style learner depends more on feelings and emotions to form new ideas and products, and judges the value of learning products by their originality and aesthetics. The _____ style learner is more social by nature, tends to learn better in groups, and judges learning by its potential use in helping others. _____ refers to the attempt to match students' learning preferences with teaching methods.

mastery, understanding, self-expressive, interpersonal, Goodness of fit

4. Don't confuse _____, otherwise you're apt to teach and assess students in ways that benefit those with certain styles of thinking and learning, but put other students at a _____.

style with ability, disadvantage

5.   A _____ prefers a wide a grasp of a subject, likes to learn _____ principles, prefers _____ situations, and begins by studying general concepts and the total situation before commencing more detailed analysis. A _____ prefers systematic, methodical _____ leading to mastery of details; likes to acquire _____ first, then more general concepts; likes to acquire knowledge _____ and gradually; and prefers to learn information directly related to the task at hand.

grouper, general, unstructured, stringer, analysis, specifics, sequentially

6.   The main purpose of Bloom's taxonomy is to provide a classification of the goals of our _____. The taxonomy consists of three major sections: the _____, the _____, and the _____ domains.

educational system, cognitive, affective, psychomotor

7.   Bloom's cognitive taxonomy includes six categories. Recall of specific facts refers to _____. Understanding what is communicated refers to _____. _____ is the generalization and use of abstract information in concrete situations. _____ is the breakdown of a problem into subparts and the detection of relationships among the parts. Putting together parts to form a whole defines _____. _____ involves using criteria to make judgements.

knowledge, comprehension, Application, Analysis, synthesis, Evaluation

8.   Do not focus merely on questions about _____. Stretch your students' thinking abilities by asking questions that require _____, analysis, synthesis, and _____.

facts, application, evaluation

9.   Good questions cause your students to pay _____, process information, _____ their ideas, and _____ an answer.

attention, organize, compose

10.   Phrase questions _____; ask what, where, when, who, how, and why; use appropriate _____; ask _____ question at a time; and pay attention to the level of _____ required for an answer.

clearly and concisely, language, one, thought

11.   Questions can be _____ (requiring a right answer) or _____ (requiring students to expand, explore, and be creative).

convergent, divergent

12.   To get good answers to your questions, give students _____ to answer and give all students an equal _____.

enough time, chance to respond

13.   You should always _____ student responses and clarify, expand, and _____ when you can; never let an _____ stand.

follow up, synthesize, incorrect answer

14.   Costa takes a firm stand in favor of _____ instruction of thinking skills. He suggests a four-level hierarchy of thinking skills that should be helpful in teaching, curriculum construction, and development of instructional materials. _____—involves individual skills prerequisite to more complex thinking. _____—involves the combination of individual, discrete skills to formulate strategies. _____—requires the use of strategies to create new thought patterns and innovative solutions. _____—requires students' willingness, disposition, inclination, and commitment to think.

direct, Level I—the discrete level of thinking, Level II—strategies of thinking, Level III—creative thinking, Level IV—the cognitive spirit

15.   Costa believes that certain teacher behaviors can be quite effective in fostering thinking skills. Four categories of behavior seem particularly relevant: _____, _____, _____, and _____.

questioning, structuring, responding, modeling

16.   The Practical Intelligence for School program is an outgrowth of the combination of Sternberg's _____ model of intelligence and Gardner's _____ model. Gardner's theory expresses the _____ in which intelligence manifests itself, while Sternberg's theory identifies the _____ involved in these domains.

triarchic, multiple intelligences, domains, mental processes

17.   The main goal of deBono's Cognitive Research Trust (CoRT) is to teach _____ skills. The objectives of the CoRT program are to develop a thinking skills programs that is _____, applies to a _____ of ages, teaches the skills required in _____, is independent of any detailed _____, and from which students can _____ the thinking skills they acquire to all of life's situations.

problem-solving and thinking, simple and practical, wide range, real life, knowledge base, transfer

18.   Categories that describe the "good problem solver" have been identified. Good problem solvers believe that they can _____ problems by careful, persistent analysis. The good problem solver has a concern for _____. Good problem solvers consistently try to break problems into _____. Poor problem solvers tend to jump at the _____ answer that comes to mind.

solve, accuracy, parts, first

19.   A problem occurs when there is a significant discrepancy between the _____ behavior and the _____ behavior.

actual, desired

20.   There are two primary ways of bridging the gap between a problem and answer: using an _____ (try to solve it in your head) or an _____, or using paper and pencil to sketch a proposed solution. Whatever works for you is right, that is, it matches your _____.

internal representation, external representation, learning style.

21.   Students can improve their problem-solving skills by attending more closely to the _____ of problems, better understanding their own _____, and using the _____ they make to improve their skills.

nature, thinking processes, mistakes

22.   When solving problems, people often fail to use all _____ of a problem, fail to adopt _____ procedures, fail to _____ vital relationships in the problem, and use _____ techniques in acquiring information and in reasoning.

relevant facts, systematic, perceive, sloppy

23.   Several excuses for not solving problems exist. The excuse that "I just wasn't born smart" retains its popularity because it shifts responsibility for failure from the _____ to some _____. Another misleading belief has to do with having a poor _____. The third belief is that the student has always been _____ at a given task.

individual, genetic blueprint, memory, poor

24.   _____ must be the initial step in problem solving because identifying _____ determines what _____ to use.

Attending, details, strategy

25.   The DUPE model has been proposed to help people solve a wide variety of problems. The meaning of each letter is as follows. D: _____ the nature of the problem. U: _____ the nature of the problem. P: _____ your solution. E: _____ your plan; this entails examining the plan itself in an attempt to determine its suitability, and then deciding how successful the solution is. This acronym is meant to convey this message: Don't let yourself be _____.

Define, Understand, Plan, Evaluate, deceived

26.   Before students can determine the nature of a problem they must realize that one _____. Teach students to look carefully at the problem itself and identify the _____ (the facts that are given). A _____ problem is one in which the steps to solution are specified clearly in the problem's statement. An _____ problem is one in which the givens are much more vague and the steps to solution more elusive.

exists, givens, well-defined, ill-defined

27.   Brighter problem solvers spend relatively _____ time up front figuring out what to do and _____ time doing it, while less-bright problem solvers spend _____ time figuring out what to do and _____ time doing it because they really haven't _____ the problem.

more, less, less, more, defined

28.   Understanding the nature of a problem implies that you can both _____ and _____ it. You must have a sufficient _____ to recognize the givens and adequate _____ that permit you to represent the problem.

define, represent, amount of knowledge, problem-solving skills

29.   Much that passes for cleverness or innate quickness of mind actually depends on _____. The acquisition of knowledge in itself is not enough; what is also critical is the _____ of knowledge when needed.

specialized knowledge, availability

30.   Representation may be either _____ or _____.

internal, external

31.   Using an external representation when solving problems helps one _____ on the most important concepts, see _____ among the givens, represent _____ to aid memory, and _____ the givens.

focus, relationships, intermediate steps, visualize

32.   Internal representation entails the _____ and _____ of details from the original problem and the _____ of information. We often impose _____ on ourselves when we face problems. If you are having difficulty solving a problem, change your _____.

addition, elimination, interpretation, limits, representation

33.   Planning the solution involves the need to be familiar with the _____ required for solution and the need to apply the _____ that seem appropriate.

core concepts, strategies

34.   The _____ strategy can be helpful if the goal and givens are clearly stated. _____ is another general strategy that aids solution when the goal is obvious but the means to achieve it require additional planning.

working backward, Means-end analysis

35.   Hayes identified several learning strategies. The _____ strategy is intended to have you search for relations in the learning material. In the _____ strategy, you are urged to search for relations between new material and material that is already known. _____ means to furnish an example. _____ looks at whether you can represent the information—the givens in the problem—in more than one way: verbally or through mental imagery.

structuring, context, Instantiation, Multiple coding

36.   In examining your plan and solution, you first must realize the necessity to stop and _____ the plan. If this first evaluative phase indicates the plan is sound, activate your plan. Then, a second evaluative phase is needed, in which you must decide whether you are _____. If not, you must continue the search process and not let _____ halt your progress.

evaluate, satisfied, frustration

37.   _____ means generating novel and appropriate ideas. All of us engage in two types of thinking: _____ thinking is directed toward finding correct solutions, while _____ thinking searches for novel ideas and products.

Creativity, Convergent, divergent

38.   Creative children learn the _____ needed to solve the problems they inevitably encounter, don't _____, are sensitive to _____, generate large numbers of _____, propose novel ideas that are also _____, demonstrate _____ of mind, and reorganize the _____.

strategies, quit, problems, ideas, useful, flexibility, elements

39.   Often we have something in memory (we have _____ it) but we can't get at it (we can't _____ it).

stored, retrieve

40.   The most effective cues for triggering memory are those we _____ ourselves. A particularly effective cue is the use of _____, or words consisting of the initial letters of a series of words, such as DUPE. Another is the use of the _____: making up a sentence or phrase with words whose first letters are the cues for certain information.

generate, acronyms, acrostic

41.   _____ refers to visualizing objects or events.

Imagery

42.   The _____ uses familiar locations to utilize a series of familiar visual images and link each image to the object to be retained.

method of loci

43.   To _____ is to add information to what you are trying to learn, so that the material becomes more personally meaningful. These strategies improve recall because they increase the _____ and facilitate _____ of new information with related information that is well known to the learner.

elaborate, depth of processing, storage

44.   Elaboration strategies should not be so _____ that they require more effort to remember than the content. You and your students also should be sure to adopt techniques that are _____ to you.

complex, best suited

45.   Transfer of learning refers to attempts to understand how learning one topic influences _____.

later learning

46.   Task _____ exercises a strong influence on transfer. The degree of _____ learning is an important element in transfer. Personal variables such as intelligence, motivation, and past experiences, although difficult-to-_____, are important influences on transfer.

similarity, original, control

47.   To help make your students aware of the value of transfer, teach to _____, be certain that the material you teach is _____, use _____ if possible, emphasize the _____ between classroom work and the transfer situation, specify what is _____ in the task, and try to understand how students _____ the possibility of transfer.

overlearning, well organized, advance organizers, similarity, important, perceive

SUMMARIZE THE MAIN POINTS

This section of your study guide is designed to help you identify and understand the main points in each chapter. You've already reviewed the details using the Guided Review (above), and will consider the importance, relevance, and usefulness of the information in later sections. For now, focus on summarizing the main ideas.

For each major section in the chapter, summarize the main point and the evidence presented in the text to support and/or discuss it. If there are key terms presented in the section, define them. Some prompting questions are provided to help you structure your review.

The main sections of Chapter 8 are:

- Thinking
- Thinking skills: An analysis
- Problem solving
- The DUPE model
- Transferring strategies and skills

For each section, answer the following questions:

1. In two sentences or less, **summarize** what the **main point** of this section was.

2. Briefly **summarize the evidence** for and against each main point (a simple list of details they use to support each of their points is sufficient). If the authors discuss research studies to support the point, summarize the findings in one sentence. If the authors are presenting a logical argument to support the point (i.e., not citing data from research studies), briefly list the supporting points they made. Use the detailed chapter outline to help you identify the supporting points.

3. Briefly review the **definitions of any key terms** in each main section.

WHY SHOULD YOU CARE?

The purpose of this section of your study guide is to help you understand how and why the information in the chapter is relevant for you personally. You'll be asked to think more about the relevance and usefulness of the information in later sections of this study guide.

Look back at the work you did in summarizing the main points in the section above and answer the following questions:

1. For each section you summarized, why or how is the **main point** you identified **important to and/or relevant for teachers in general**? Try to limit your answer to only one or two sentences so you don't get bogged down in details, but focus on general usefulness.

2. Now think about the chapter as a whole. **Identify two specific events, contexts, or problems** for which the ideas presented in this chapter are relevant. Briefly discuss how they're relevant and how they could be useful.

3. Now **identify three concepts** from the chapter that **YOU find useful** in some way. Discuss how/why these concepts are useful, and specify how you will actually use them in your teaching and/or your daily life. (It's okay if there is some overlap between your answers for numbers 2 and 3.)

DISCUSSION QUESTIONS

The following "What do you think?" questions are printed in the text.

1. How important is it for teachers to recognize the learning styles of their students? Why?

2. What are some of the common sources of error you experience when trying to solve a problem?

3. How would you go about helping your students acquire the characteristics of a "good problem solver?"

4. How would you foster creative behavior in a young student?

Additional discussion questions:

5. List, explain, and give an example from your experience of the common sources of error in problem solving.

6. What are "working backward" and "means-ends analysis?" How can these be helpful in solving problems?

7. Define internal representation and external representation, and explain why they are important for successful problem solving.

8. What are four learning strategies that are helpful in planning problem solutions? Identify a classroom problem a teacher might encounter and discuss how the teacher could use each strategy in planning a solution for the problem.

9. Define cues, imagery, and the method of loci and explain how each is helpful in retrieving information.

10. Describe, compare, and contrast Costa's, PIFS, and CoRT thinking skills programs. What are their goals, methods, assumptions, and results? Would you use them? Why?

11. Define cognitive style. List the four types of cognitive style discussed in the text and give three characteristics of each.

12. Summarize how and why technology can help improve thinking and problem-solving skills.

TAKE IT PERSONALLY!

The questions in this section are designed to help you personalize, integrate, and apply the information from the text. Personalization questions ask you to consider the personal relevance and usefulness of concepts, and consider how they might be useful in your life now and in the future. Integration questions ask you to pull together information from the text to evaluate it, summarize it or synthesize a recommendation on the basis of it, or express an opinion about it. Application questions ask you to think about how the concepts might be useful to address real problems or situations you may find yourself in. All three question types will help you consider the information at a deeper conceptual level, understand it more fully, and remember it.

1. Identify a problem. Create an external representation of it. Describe your internal representation of it. Do the internal and external representations differ? What advantages and disadvantages do each type of representation have for this problem?

2. Use Bloom's taxonomy of cognitive objectives to evaluate the level of your own thought and your own questions in this course. How could more of the higher-level questions be incorporated, and how might this be useful for your personal understanding and use of the material?

3. Develop a thinking skills program. What is included, and why? How will it be taught? How will its effects be evaluated? How is your program similar to and different from those described in the text?

4. Evaluate your own problem-solving skills. Do you make any of the common errors or believe any of the common myths about problem solving? What are your strengths and weaknesses when solving problems? Do you show any of the characteristics of a better or poorer problem solver? Give specific ideas for how you could improve your problem solving.

5. Identify a real problem you have. Use the DUPE model to address this problem:
   D—Identify the problem elements, whether the problem is well- or ill-defined;
   U—Identify the category of the problem, its knowledge base requirements, and how you are representing it, and discuss other ways you could represent it.
   P—Discuss what strategies you are considering and why, whether others are possible, and the role that memory plays in your problem.
   E—Evaluate whether you have addressed all aspects of the problem. Consider whether your proposed strategy is reasonable, then evaluate whether it worked. Is creativity of the solution a factor, and if so, how could you increase the creativity of your solution or solution strategy?

6. What is problem representation and why is it important in problem solving? How can you teach your students to represent problems more effectively?

7. Define imagery, discuss why it is important to teachers, and describe how it can be used in the classroom.

8. Explain how a teacher could help students use elaboration after reading the class novel, *Huckleberry Finn*. How would this be helpful for students?

9. Are you creative? How do you know? Do you show any of the common characteristics of creative people? Is it important for teachers to be concerned about creativity? How can you help your students become more creative?

10. What is transfer? Give four specific suggestions for how you can foster transfer in your students.

11. Identify characteristics of a "good problem solver" and explain how a teacher can help students acquire these characteristics.

12. Suppose that a teacher observes in her classroom that students are not turning in homework assignments on time. Explain how the DUPE model can help the teacher solve the problem.

13. Identify the six major categories of Bloom's cognitive taxonomy and implement these categories into the following example. Suppose a teacher discusses the poem *Stopping by the Woods on a Snowy Evening* by Robert Frost. How could the teacher teach and test his or her students on each of the six categories? Show how Bloom's cognitive domain can be used to foster thinking skills by providing an example of exam questions that address the higher levels of the taxonomy.

14. List and explain three ways that Bloom's ideas can be used by teachers to foster higher-order thinking.

15. Suppose a teacher is teaching a science unit on the planets. How can the teacher facilitate transfer of learning?

16. What kinds of questions will you ask as a teacher? How could you use questions to help improve your students' thinking skills?

17. Summarize Costa's model for teaching thinking skills, including his four levels of thinking skills and his four categories of teacher behaviors. Then identify which aspects of this model you will likely use in your teaching.

CASE IN POINT...

Remember to use the cases from the text as contexts for identifying examples of concepts from the text and as contexts for solving educational problems. Also remember to use a consistent framework (like the DUPE model or the CASE NOTES in the text) to structure your "Mini-Case Report." Review the "Case in Point..." section of Chapter 1 in this study guide for more details.

SUGGESTED CONCEPTS TO IDENTIFY FOR CHAPTER 8

cognitive style
convergent questions
divergent questions
DUPE model of problem solving
elaboration
external representation
internal representation
learning style
metacognition
multiple intelligences
thinking skills
transfer of learning
triarchic theory of intelligence

Review Case #2 about Mark Siegel in your text and use the following questions to prompt your thinking about this case.

1. How well is Mark engaging Karim in meaningful problem solving? Might it be helpful if Mark tried using a more problem-solving focus in his instruction with Karim, perhaps using the DUPE model?

2. How could Mark use the information on the thinking skills programs discussed in your text to get Karim more interested in his schoolwork? Are Karim's critical thinking skills being addressed in his classroom experiences?

3. What kinds of questioning techniques could Mark try to help Karim master the content in the classroom and improve Karim's metacognitive skills?

4. How might the information on memory strategies presented in the text be helpful?

BIG IDEAS IN EDUCATIONAL PSYCHOLOGY

Thinking about the "big ideas" in educational psychology will help you organize and apply your newly acquired knowledge. Use the following steps to identify your own principles and strategies from the chapter and to relate them to the five main themes of the text (i.e., the "big ideas").

1. Review the TIPS from the text.

2. List some of the main concepts from the chapter. Use the work you did in prior sections of the study guide to help generate this list. Also look at the list of key terms from the chapter.

3. Select what you think are two or three of the most important concepts from your list.

4. For each concept you select, try to state it as a principle (use the TIPS format in the text and the example shown below as a guide for how to state principles).

5. Develop two or three specific teaching strategies that follow from each stated principle.

6. Relate your work to the five main themes from the text, identifying which theme(s) are relevant for each principle and strategy. This step will help you see how the information in each chapter contributes to improved teaching for each of these five critical aspects of instruction.

7. Think about and discuss with classmates how the principles and strategies you identify will help you improve your teaching for each theme you listed as relevant.

The five main themes from the text are:
ASSESSMENT, COMMUNICATION, LEARNING, MOTIVATION, AND TIME

Some example concepts, principles, and strategies for Chapter 8:

Bloom's taxonomy	problem representation (internal, external)
cognitive style	questions (convergent, divergent)
elaboration	metacognition
imagery	multiple intelligences
incidental learning	thinking skills
learning style	transfer of learning

Principle	Questioning is an effective teaching technique that can help students learn to attend to information, process information at a meaningful level, and think more carefully about information. (ASSESSMENT, COMMUNICATION, LEARNING, MOTIVATION)
Strategy	Become familiar with and use one of the taxonomies of thinking skills (e.g., Bloom's taxonomy of cognitive skills, Costa's model of critical thinking skills) to structure your questioning of students. Using a system like these helps ensure that your questions during instruction and on assessments vary in the levels and types of thinking required of students. (ASSESSMENT, LEARNING, MOTIVATION)
Strategy	Vary the types of questions you ask (convergent vs. divergent; what, where, when, who, how, why questions) to teach students that different questions require different knowledge and levels of thinking. (COMMUNICATION, LEARNING)
Strategy	Encourage students to question each other and themselves through the use of "question journals," in which they note questions they have and/or further information they'd like to know about a topic, or question and answer sessions when students can work in pairs or groups to help address one another's questions. (LEARNING, MOTIVATION)

SUGGESTED READINGS

Bransford, J., & Stein, B. (1984). *The ideal problem solver*. New York: Freeman.

Costa, A. (Ed.). (1985). *Developing minds*. Alexandria, VA: ASCD.

Gardner, H. (1983). *Frames of mind*. New York: Basic.

Gardner, H., & Hatch, T. (1990). Multiple intelligences go to school: Educational implications of the theory of multiple intelligences. *Educational Researcher, 18*(8), 4-10.

Hayes, J. (1989). *The complete problem solver*. Philadelphia: The Franklin Institute Press.

Jones, B. F., Pierce, J., & Hunter, B. (1988/1989). Teaching students to construct graphic representations. *Educational Leadership, 46*(4), 20-25.

Lewis, A., & Smith, D. (1993). Defining higher order thinking. *Theory into Practice, 32*(3), 131-137.

Lewis, D., & Greene, J. (1982). *Thinking better*. New York: Pauson, Wade.

Sternberg, R. (1988). *The triarchic mind: A new theory of human intelligence*. New York: Viking.

PRACTICE TEST 1

1. If you are asked to recall the sixteenth president of the United States, this exemplifies which of Bloom's categories?
   a. synthesis
   b. analysis
   c. knowledge
   d. application

2. After the students finished reading a poem, the teacher asked the students questions about how the poem was relevant for their own lives and what kinds of feelings it stimulated. This teacher
   a. is asking good questions.
   b. is asking lower level questions.
   c. needs to learn to ask questions that require students to analyze, synthesize, and evaluate information.
   d. is asking convergent questions.

3. Which of Costa's levels of thinking requires the use of strategies to create new thought patterns and innovative solutions?
   a. the discrete level of thinking
   b. strategies of thinking
   c. creative thinking
   d. the cognitive spirit

4. The Practical Intelligence for School program was developed by
   a. Bloom.
   b. Costa.
   c. deBono.
   d. Sternberg and Gardner.

5. The objectives of the CoRT program include this:
   a. the program should target specific, narrow age ranges.
   b. a detailed knowledge base is an important part of the instruction.
   c. the program should be simple and practical.
   d. the thinking skills taught will be powerful, but probably useful in only a few contexts.

6. Most errors in problem solving are due to
   a. lack of information about the problem.
   b. inattention to the problem.
   c. poor memory capacity.
   d. overinterpretation of the problem.

7. Which of the following is an example of the method of loci?
   a. Using the word DUPE to remember the steps in solving problems.
   b. Visualizing a mental picture of a woman named Polly running through a field of flowers to remember the definition of "pollination."
   c. Saying the words in a grocery list over and over again until you have found all the times.
   d. Linking the items on a grocery list with different places in your house, then taking a mental walk through the house to remember the items.

8. Which of the following is a characteristic of good problem solvers?
   a. They generate more ideas than poor problem solvers.
   b. They have better memories in general than poor problem solvers.
   c. They spend relatively more time defining the problem than solving it.
   d. They spend relatively less time defining the problem than solving it.

9. What does the U in the DUPE model represent?
   a. Uncover the proper analysis.
   b. Understand the nature of the problem.
   c. Utilize resources for problem solving.
   d. Understand the terminology used.

10. What is the major focus in solving an ill-defined problem?
    a. representation of the problem
    b. achieving insight
    c. the sequence of steps needed
    d. proposing a solution and then proving or disproving it

11. The facts that are presented in a problem are called the
    a. givens.
    b. goals.
    c. elements.
    d. operations.

12. Mary is asked to solve a word problem involving use of mathematics. She uses paper and pencil to solve the problem. This is an example of
    a. cueing strategies
    b. elaboration strategies
    c. internal representation
    d. external representation

13. When Jack and Sam got lost hiking in Wyoming and were trying to figure out how to get back to the camp, Jack told Sam about how he had been lost on a trail when he was hiking in Appalachia. What strategy was Jack using to help him find the way back to the camp?
    a. instantiation
    b. inferencing
    c. context
    d. monitoring

14. "Every good boy does fine" helps recall the lines of a G clef. This illustrates a(n)
    a. acrostic.
    b. acronym.
    c. method of loci.
    d. elaboration.

15. Learning to make the same response to new but similar stimuli usually produces
    a. temporary transfer.
    b. reflexive transfer.
    c. positive transfer.
    d. negative transfer.

16. Which of the following is true about cognitive style?
    a. Cognitive style describes how students prefer to learn and think.
    b. A student's cognitive style has little effect on what that student learns.
    c. A student's cognitive style has little effect on how that student learns.
    d. Cognitive style is a good indicator of cognitive ability.

17. Which of the following is NOT a characteristic of creative people?
    a. They keep trying even after failing on their first attempts to solve a problem.
    b. They generate fewer but better ideas than other people.
    c. They notice problems more than other people.
    d. They search for new approaches to solve problems.

PRACTICE TEST 2

1. This question was given to students in a social studies class: "What were three main causes and three main effects of the stock market crash of 1929?" Which level of Bloom's taxonomy is this an example of?
   a. analysis
   b. application
   c. synthesis
   d. evaluation

2. In science class, Ellen teaches her students the steps of the scientific method, then quizzes them on how well they can remember the steps in the correct order. Ellen is asking which type of questions?
   a. synthesis
   b. evaluation
   c. convergent
   d. divergent

3. Which of Costa's levels of thinking requires students' willingness, disposition, inclination, and commitment to think?
   a. the discrete level of thinking
   b. strategies of thinking
   c. creative thinking
   d. the cognitive spirit

4. In the PIFS program, Gardner's theory provides which of the following parts of the program?
   a. Information on the mental processes to be taught.
   b. Information on the domains of intelligence.
   c. Information on how to combine the domains of intelligence with specific mental processes.
   d. Information on specific memory strategies to be taught.

5. Micky is not a very good problem solver. He is observant and never guesses at the meaning of any terms or aspects of the problem, but he often finds that he has forgotten to do part of the problem or has offered a solution too hastily. Which common error in problem solving is Micky making?
   a. Failure to observe and use all the relevant facts.
   b. Failure to adopt a systematic, step-by-step procedure.
   c. Failure to perceive vital relationships in the problem.
   d. Use of sloppy techniques in acquiring information.

6. A teacher teaches her students to more carefully consider the instructions in a problem-solving task. Which characteristic of good problem solvers is she trying to improve?
   a. problem memory
   b. positive problem solving attitude
   c. problem definition
   d. specialized knowledge base

7. The DUPE model was designed to facilitate
   a. memory.
   b. problem solving.
   c. plasticity.
   d. intelligence.

8. The need to be familiar with the core concepts required for solution and the need to know strategies that seem appropriate are two critical aspects of which part of the DUPE model?
   a. Planning the solution.
   b. Understanding the nature of the problem.
   c. Determining the nature of the problem.
   d. Evaluating the plan.

9. When solving a problem, Brigid often tries to figure out how the different parts of the problem relate to each other and to other information that she knows. Which of Hayes' learning strategies is Brigid using?
   a. the structuring strategy
   b. the context strategy
   c. the instantiation strategy
   d. the multiple coding strategy

10. What type of representation involves adding and eliminating details from the original and interpreting information?
   a. structured
   b. operational
   c. internal
   d. external

11. Every problem has which of the following?
   a. good definition
   b. givens
   c. a clear goal
   d. one best answer

12. Which of the following involves using what we already know to help make sense of what we are trying to learn?
   a. acronym
   b. acrostic
   c. elaboration
   d. imagery

13. Which of the following would be the most effective for helping Alison retrieve information from memory?
   a. working backward to figure out the information
   b. a cue that experts agree is useful
   c. a cue that Alison made up for herself
   d. an acronym that her teacher made up

14. Manny is persistent and flexible in his thinking, comes up with a lot of useful and new ideas, and often tries to reshuffle the parts of a problem to see if he can think of different ways to look at it. Manny is likely to be
   a. gifted.
   b. high in creativity.
   c. low in creativity.
   d. a poor problem solver.

15. Jane is thoroughly familiar with conversational Spanish. When she visited Spain, she had little difficulty conversing with the people. This illustrates which influence on transfer?
   a. task similarity
   b. personal variables
   c. degree of original learning
   d. degree of motivation

16. Marta values ideas and information on the basis of how useful they are for practical purposes. She prefers concrete learning situations and has trouble when discussions focus on higher-level abstract concepts, emotions, or involve cooperative group work. Marta is most likely a/an
   a. mastery style learner.
   b. understanding style learner.
   c. self-expressive style learner.
   d. interpersonal style learner.

ANSWER KEY

Practice Test 1

1.   ANSWER: C, Applied; OBJECTIVE: 2; PAGE: 297-298
2.   ANSWER: A, Applied; OBJECTIVE: 3; PAGE: 298
3.   ANSWER: C, Factual; OBJECTIVE: 2; PAGE: 303
4.   ANSWER: D, Factual; OBJECTIVE: 2; PAGE: 304
5.   ANSWER: C, Factual; OBJECTIVE: 2; PAGE: 305
6.   ANSWER: B, Factual; OBJECTIVE: 5; PAGE: 308
7.   ANSWER: D, Applied; OBJECTIVE: 7; PAGE: 325
8.   ANSWER: C, Factual; OBJECTIVE: 5; PAGE: 313
9.   ANSWER: B, Factual; OBJECTIVE: 4; PAGE: 313
10. ANSWER: B, Factual; OBJECTIVE: 4; PAGE: 312
11. ANSWER: A, Factual; OBJECTIVE: 4; PAGE: 312
12. ANSWER: D, Applied; OBJECTIVE: 5; PAGE: 314
13. ANSWER: A, Applied, OBJECTIVE: 5; PAGE: 317
14. ANSWER: A, Factual; OBJECTIVE: 5; PAGE: 324
15. ANSWER: C, Factual; OBJECTIVE: 8; PAGE: 327
16. ANSWER: A, Conceptual; OBJECTIVE: 1; PAGE: 294-295
17. ANSWER: B, Factual; OBJECTIVE: 6; PAGE: 320

Practice Test 2

1.   ANSWER: A, Applied; OBJECTIVE: 2; PAGE: 297
2.   ANSWER: C, Applied; OBJECTIVE: 3; PAGE: 300
3.   ANSWER: D, Factual; OBJECTIVE: 2; PAGE: 303
4.   ANSWER: B, Factual; OBJECTIVE: 2; PAGE: 304
5.   ANSWER: B, Applied; OBJECTIVE: 5; PAGE: 309
6.   ANSWER: C, Applied; OBJECTIVE: 5; PAGE: 313
7.   ANSWER: B, Factual; OBJECTIVE: 4; PAGE: 311
8.   ANSWER: A, Factual; OBJECTIVE: 4; PAGE: 316-317
9.   ANSWER: A, Applied; OBJECTIVE: 4; PAGE: 317
10. ANSWER: C, Factual; OBJECTIVE: 4; PAGE: 315
11. ANSWER: B, Conceptual; OBJECTIVE: 5; PAGE: 312
12. ANSWER: C, Factual; OBJECTIVE: 7; PAGE: 325
13. ANSWER: C, Applied; OBJECTIVE: 5; PAGE: 323
14. ANSWER: B, Applied; OBJECTIVE: 6; PAGE: 320-321
15. ANSWER: A, Applied; OBJECTIVE: 8; PAGE: 327
16. ANSWER: A, Applied; OBJECTIVE: 1; PAGE: 295

Chapter 9   MOTIVATION AND STUDENT LEARNING

LEARNING OBJECTIVES

After completing this chapter, you should be able to

1.   Define motivation and describe the role motivation plays in learning.

2.   Identify causes of motivation and provide theoretical explanations of how these causes might actually work in the lives of students.

3.   Make suggestions about what affects students' motives and can influence student behavior in the classroom.

4.   List several educational implications of motivation theories and outline strategies that have the potential to improve both teaching and self-directed learning.

5.   Contrast intrinsic and extrinsic motivation.

CHAPTER HIGHLIGHTS

Motivation: Meaning and Myths

*   Motivation arouses, sustains, and integrates behavior.
*   Several myths have grown up around motivation that can obscure its actual meaning and cause classroom difficulty.
*   Recognizing the distinction between intrinsic and extrinsic motivation can help you to devise techniques that improve learning in your classes.

Theories of Motivation: Explanations of Motivated Students

*   Of the various attempts to explain motivation, Abraham Maslow's needs hierarchy has had a lasting impact due to the appeal of its theoretical and practical implications.
*   Bruner posited that educators use discovery learning as a means of stimulating students' interest in learning. One of Bruner's basic assumptions underlying discovery learning is that individuals behave according to their perceptions of their environment; that is, students see meaning in knowledge, skills, and attitudes when they themselves discover it.
*   Students search for the causes of their behaviors just as teachers do. To explain this phenomenon, Weiner has been a leader in the development of attribution theory. Knowing whether students attribute their behaviors to ability, effort, task difficulty, or luck can help you to improve their self-concepts by realistically examining their abilities in light of the tasks, thus furthering learning.
*   Skinner has long believed that the proper use of schedules of reinforcement (see chapter 7) can improve motivation and, in general, enhance classroom performance.
*   According to Bandura, the teacher's performance in the classroom can be a powerful model for the students to imitate. Once you recognize desirable behavior in your students, act swiftly to reinforce that behavior.

- Among the most potent influences on motivation are anxiety, attitudes, curiosity, and locus of control.
- Anxiety, either situational or trait, affects classroom performance either positively or negatively. Increasing anxiety lessens performance as task complexity increases.
- A positive attitude toward school and learning increases achievement. Be particularly concerned with not only your students' attitudes toward you and the subjects you are teaching, but also their attitudes about themselves.
- All of your students possess a certain degree of curiosity that, if capitalized upon, can lead to richer and more insightful learning. Structured but relaxed classroom conditions that allow for an acceptance of students' ideas can encourage the creative use of curiosity.
- The locus of control concept can be useful in improving the achievement of your pupils, especially the "externals." By carefully providing reinforcement for selected behaviors, you not only improve their learning, but also help them to develop more positive self-concepts.
- Repeated criticism and failure can produce learned helplessness, a form of behavior that causes pupils to give up, just refusing to try. If you encounter such students, your first task will be to persuade them to make an effort so that you can begin to reinforce them for trying.
- Cooperative learning has been found to motivate student learning through group goal structures and rewards for group successes. The most effective methods for cooperative groups emphasize group goals and individual responsibility.
- Technology, in particular computers in the classroom, have been found to have a positive impact on students' motivation to learn. Four reasons for this have been identified: novelty, individualized level of material, opportunities to receive help in privacy, and high-interest material.

Educational Implications of Motivational Theories and Research

- Considering various stages of learning—the beginning, the middle, and the end—leads to the direct application of motivational theory and research in the classroom, for both you and your students.

DETAILED CHAPTER OUTLINE

I. Motivation: meaning and myths
  A. Motivation is defined as an internal state that arouses us to action, pushes us in particular directions, and keeps us engaged in certain activities.
  B. Motivation affects learning and performance in at least four ways:
    a. It increases an individual's energy and activity level.
    b. It directs an individual toward certain goals.
    c. It promotes initiation of certain activities and persistence in those activities.
    d. It affects the learning strategies and cognitive processes an individual employs.
  C. What are the myths about motivation?
    1. Failure is a good motivator.
    2. Teachers motivate students.
    3. Threats increase motivation.
  D. Intrinsic and extrinsic motivation
    1. Intrinsic motivation means that students themselves want to learn in order to achieve specific objectives. This is an ideal state that can result in considerable learning and a minimum of discipline problems.
    2. Extrinsic motivation refers to the use of rewards and inducements external to students.
    3. The intrinsic-extrinsic dichotomy is a false one. It is more accurate to say that students are primarily intrinsically or primarily extrinsically motivated to learn.

4. A feeling of one's own competence is a strong motivating force. Not only will students feel they can do it, but they want to do it.
5. If you match tasks to students' abilities, having students imagine successful performance will produce more effective behavior, which then will aid motivation for the next task.
6. If motivation is faulty, learning will suffer. Attention is limited; behavior is not directed at objectives; discipline may become a problem.
7. Motivation arouses, sustains, directs, and integrates a person's behavior.

E. Case Notes: Mark Siegel's class

II. Theories of motivation: Explanations of motivated students
A. Maslow's needs hierarchy and its application in the classroom
1. Maslow's most famous concept is self-actualization, which means that we use our abilities to the limit of our potentialities. Self-actualization is a growth concept; students move toward this goal as they satisfy their basic needs.
2. Growth toward self-actualization requires the satisfaction of a hierarchy of needs. There are five basic needs in Maslow's theory.
   a. *Physiological needs*, such as hunger and sleep, are dominant and are the basis of motivation. Unless they are satisfied, everything else recedes.
   b. *Safety needs* represent the importance of security, protection, stability, and freedom from fear and anxiety, as well as the need for structure and limits.
   c. *Love and belongingness needs* are our needs for family and friends.
   d. *Esteem needs* encompass the reactions of others to us as individuals and our opinions of ourselves.
   e. *The need for self-actualization* refers to that tendency, in spite of the satisfaction of lower needs, to feel restless unless we are doing what we think we are capable of doing.
3. Case Notes: Mark Siegel's class
4. For the classroom
   a. A deficit in any one need category will affect student performance.
   b. Students—and all of us—need to feel that they are worthy of respect from both themselves and others, a respect that is based on actual achievement.
   c. Unless students believe that they are doing all that they could be doing, they will be plagued by feelings of restlessness and even discontent.
5. TIPS on Learning: Making learning activities enjoyable for students
B. Bruner and discovery learning
1. Bruner believed that there is some ideal level of arousal between apathy and wild excitement, since passivity causes boredom, while intense activity leaves little time for reflection and generalization.
2. Encouraging discovery causes students to organize material to determine regularities and relationships and also to avoid the passivity that blinds them to the use of the information learned. Students learn to manipulate their environments more actively and achieve considerable gratification from personally coping with problems.
3. The goal of discovery learning is to have students use their information in solving problems in many different circumstances. Bruner said that individuals behave according to their perceptions of their environment. Students see meaning in knowledge, skills, and attitudes when they themselves discover it.
4. Case Notes: Mark Siegel's class
5. For Bruner, information is most helpful when it is at the learner's level and encourages self-activity and intrinsic motivation. Present ideas at students' level, so that they achieve a sense of discovery.
C. Weiner and attributions about success or failures
1. Attribution theory rests on three basic assumptions.
   a. First, people want to know the causes of their own behavior and that of others, particularly behavior that is important to them.

b. Second, attribution theory assumes that we do not randomly assign causes to our behavior. Rather, there is a logical explanation for the causes to which we attribute our behavior.

c. Third, the causes that we assign to our behavior influence subsequent behavior.

2. Weiner holds that when achievement is aroused, we attribute our performance to one of four elements: ability, effort, task difficulty, or luck.

    a. Ability: Students' assumptions about their abilities usually are based upon past experiences. Students who consistently question their own abilities pose a serious challenge for educators since their history of failure and feelings of incompetence undercut motivation and learning.

    b. Effort: Students judge their efforts by how well they did on a particular task. Success increases effort; effort produces more success.

    c. Luck: If there is no tangible link between behavior and goal attainment, the tendency is to attribute success to luck.

    d. Task difficulty: Is judged by the performance of others on the task. If many succeed, the task is perceived as easy, and vice versa.

3. Applying the model

    a. Weiner (1990) stated that there is a relationship between a student's attributions, the stability of the attribution, its resistance to extinction, and expectancy of future goal attainment. Consequently, in achievement-related situations, students experience both cognitive and emotional reactions.

    b. Case Notes: Mark Siegel's class

    c. Some motivation is learned, but the relationship between learning and motivation is bidirectional: New learning depends upon motivation.

D. Skinner and the use of reinforcers to increase motivation

1. According to Skinner, behavior is shaped and maintained by its consequences. Thus, the consequences of previous behavior influence students.

2. According to Skinner, motivated behavior results from the consequences of similar previous behavior.

3. For the classroom

    a. Skinner believed that teachers can improve their control over the classroom through the appropriate use of positive reinforcement schedules.

    b. Telling students they don't know something is not highly motivating, so Skinner suggested you cover small amounts of material that you can immediately and positively reinforce.

    c. Case Notes: Mark Siegel's class

    d. Use of reinforcement in the classroom has drawn a number of criticisms, some legitimate and others that indicate a misunderstanding of behavior modification techniques.

        (1) Reinforcement is bribery. But the appropriate use of reinforcement in schools is designed to facilitate attainment of desired educational objectives.

        (2) Reinforcement develops dependence on concrete, external rewards for appropriate behavior. But behavior modification does not necessarily involve material reinforcers, and reinforcement is often used only after more traditional methods of changing behavior have failed.

        (3) It is legitimate to be concerned when extrinsic reinforcement is used to change a behavior that is already motivated by intrinsic reinforcement. This may undermine the intrinsically reinforcing value of that behavior.

    e. Reinforcement methods are best used with students who exhibit high anxiety about learning, poor motivation, or a history of academic failures. Age is not the best indicator of who will benefit from extrinsic reinforcements; rather, success in achieving the desired behaviors is the best indicator.

4. TIPS on Motivation: When faced with an unmotivated student

E. Bandura and the development of self-efficacy
   1. Students who come to school are all able, and often willing, to imitate. Students' behavior can be significantly affected by observing their teachers and classmates, and observing models may cue the appearance of apparently forgotten responses.
   2. To obtain information about the self, students use four sources of information.
      a. Performance accomplishments. Human beings acquire personal and effective information from what we do.
      b. Vicarious experience. If "similar others" can perform a task successfully, students usually feel more optimistic when they begin. The opposite is also true.
      c. Verbal persuasion. Students can be led, through persuasion, into believing that they can overcome any difficulties and improve their performance.
      d. Emotional arousal. Stressful situations constitute a source of personal information.
   3. Classroom implications
      a. Students' successful imitation of what they see and hear in the classroom is partially influenced by how the teacher—the model—responds to them.
      b. Students must attend if they are going to imitate, they must remember what they have imitated if they are to reproduce it in the future, and their imitation behavior must have been reinforced for them to remember and use later.
      c. There is a two-way influence. Students attend to and imitate a teacher, and the teacher then attends to and reinforces the students.
      d. Students can mentally rehearse what they view to escape the limitations of direct imitation and form new patterns of modeled behavior.
   4. Case Notes: Mark Siegel's class

III. What affects students' motivation?
   A. Anxiety
      1. Within the classroom setting, there are numerous sources of anxiety for students.
      2. Anxiety will affect student performance.
      3. The Yerkes-Dodson law states that ideal motivation for learning decreases in intensity with increasing task difficulty. Increasing intensity improves performance only to a certain level, and then continued intensity results in a deteriorating performance.
      4. Anxiety is an unpleasant sensation that is usually experienced as feelings of apprehension and general irritability accompanied by restlessness, fatigue, and various somatic symptoms. It may appear at any time, be confined to one situation, or generalize widely.
      5. Test anxiety
         a. Test anxiety describes the behavior and emotions of students who find preparing for and taking tests stressful.
         b. The main characteristics of text anxiety include the test situation is seen as difficult, challenging, and threatening; students see themselves as ineffective in handling the task; students focus on undesirable consequences of persona inadequacy; self-deprecatory preoccupations are strong and interfere with the activity; and students expect and anticipate failure and loss of regard by others.
         c. Text anxiety first appears in children at an early age and persists well into high school.
         d. Hembree (1988) concluded the following about test anxiety:
            (1) Test anxiety and academic performance are significantly and inversely related at grade three and above.
            (2) It occurs in students from all sociocultural groups.
            (3) Females show more test anxiety than males, but are more likely to admit it and seek help.
            (4) Average students experience higher levels of test anxiety than higher- and lower-ability students.
            (5) High-test-anxious students do better when they have low-stress instructions, memory supports, performance incentives, and minimal classroom distractions.
            (6) Worry components are stronger than emotional components.

(7) Test anxiety is directly related to fears of negative evaluation, dislike of tests, cognitive self-preoccupation, and less effective study skills.

(8) High-test-anxious students have lower self-esteem than low-test-anxious students.

(9) High-test-anxious students spend more time attending to task-irrelevant behaviors.

B. Curiosity and interest

  1. What is curiosity?

    a. Explanations have focused on the external (something in the pupil's environment is attractive), or the internal (human beings need stimulation). Current interpretations include both.

    b. Curiosity is a cognitively based emotion that occurs when a student recognizes a discrepancy or conflict between what he or she believes to be true about the world and what turns out to actually be true.

    c. Students feel curious about events they can neither make sense of nor explain fully, and it occurs when they encounter unexpected, novel, and unpredictable objects.

    d. Piaget said cognitive conflicts (the unexpected) produce disequilibrium (confusion, wonderment), which then stimulates an emotional desire or curiosity to resolve the conflict. This leads to assimilation or accommodation.

  2. For the classroom

    a. A relaxed atmosphere, freedom to explore, and an acceptance of the unusual all inspire curiosity.

    b. Let your students see your enthusiasm for a subject.

    c. Depending upon a student's level of sophistication, stimulate cognitive conflicts: cause some apparent confusion, but simultaneously provide clues to the solution.

    d. When possible, allow students to select topics they are curious about.

    e. Model curious, inquiring behavior.

  3. Interest is an enduring characteristic expressed by a relationship between a person and a particular activity or object, while curiosity is more fleeting.

  4. To facilitate the development of interest, a teacher should:

    a. Invite students to participate in meaningful projects with connections to the outside world.

    b. Provide activities that involve students' needs, and provide developmentally appropriate challenges

    c. Allow students to have a major role in evaluating their own work and monitoring progress.

    d. Facilitate the integration and use of knowledge.

    e. Help students learn to work cooperatively with others.

  5. Case Notes: Mark Siegel's class

C. Locus of control

  1. If students believe they have little control over the consequences of their actions, they are said to have an external locus of control; if they believe they can control what happens to them, they are thought to have an internal locus of control.

  2. There is a positive relationship between externality and the use of extrinsic forms of motivation.

  3. In general, as students become more mature and as they experience more success, their attributions about control become more internal.

  4. Locus of control can change under certain conditions, especially with experiences that change the relationship between what a student does and its outcome.

  5. Dacey (1989) review of locus of control studies suggests:

    a. Teachers tend to attribute more negative characteristics to external students than internals, and externals describe teachers more negatively than internals do.

    b. Externals perform better when they receive specific comments about teachers' expectations.

    c. Internals are more effective in recognizing and using available information.

    d. Externals do less well in competitive situations than internals, perhaps due to their higher levels of anxiety.

6. For the classroom
    a. First, present students with realistic challenges; this implies that you must know the students so that you can determine what is realistic for them.
    b. Carefully reward their accomplishments, or at least their efforts. Reinforcement must be based on actual accomplishment. Also, reinforce their effort; be specific in noting that you realize that they have taken responsibility.
    c. Use any initial successes, and attempt to foster a habit of trying and taking responsibility for one's actions.
D. Learned helplessness
    1. Learned helplessness means that after repeated failure, students become frustrated and simply will not try.
    2. Students who experience nothing but failure and abuse at home and school have little chance of obtaining positive reinforcement for their behavior.
    3. Dweck traced discernible patterns of behavior in helpless versus mastery-oriented children.
        a. When helpless students failed, they tended to dwell on the cause of their lack of success. They underestimate their number of successes and overestimate their number of failures. When they do have successes, they report they don't expect them to continue.
        b. When mastery-oriented students fail, they focus on finding a solution to why they failed.
    4. Training to help students overcome learned helplessness teaches them to attribute their failures to a lack of effort rather than lack of ability.
        a. Students are taught to see that lack of motivation and effort (things they can control) are the primary determinants of failure, rather than lack of ability (something they can not control).
        b. It does not appear that simply increasing the number of successes will significantly influence helpless students' outlook on learning.
        c. Help students to assess their failures realistically and focus on increasing their effort to achieve success and overcome feelings of helplessness.
    5. Three components of learned helplessness have pertinence for the classroom:
        a. Failure to initiate action means that students who have experienced learned helplessness tend not to try to learn new material.
        b. Failure to learn means that even when new directions are given to these students, they still learn nothing from them.
        c. Emotional problems like frustration, depression, and incompetence seem to accompany learned helplessness.
E. Self-efficacy and its role in motivation
    1. Bandura defined self-efficacy as people's beliefs in their own capabilities to exert control over aspects of their lives. They are the product of one's own performances, vicarious experiences, verbal persuasion from others, and emotional arousal.
    2. Even when students have encountered prior difficulties, their belief that they are capable of succeeding can override the negative effects of prior performances and produce motivated behaviors.
    3. In self-efficacy theory, efficacy expectations are differentiated from outcome expectations.
        a. An outcome expectation represents a person's estimate that a given behavior will lead to a certain outcome.
        b. An efficacy expectation means that individuals believe that they can perform the behavior or behaviors required to produce certain outcomes.
        c. Outcome and efficacy expectations are differentiated because students can believe that certain behaviors will produce an outcome, but may not believe that they can execute the behaviors that will produce the outcome.
    4. Individuals may possess low perceptions of efficacy in one skill domain and high perceptions of efficacy in other skill domains.

5. Self-perceptions of efficacy often vary as a function of setting.
6. Perceived self-efficacy affects a student's functioning by influencing an individual's choice of activities, effort expenditure, and persistence in the face of difficulties.
7. TIPS on Motivation: Facilitate learners' sense of competence

F. Classroom environments
1. Students' efforts at academic help-seeking vary according to the characteristics of the student and the social-interactional conditions in the classroom.
    a. The stronger the belief that help-seeking is beneficial and the weaker the belief that it has associated costs, the greater the students' expressed likelihood of seeking help.
    b. The greater the student's perceived competence, the less strongly the student feels there is a cost associated with seeking help.
    c. Newman (1990) describes a vulnerability hypothesis of help-seeking. Students with low self-esteem or efficacy have a greater need than those with high self-esteem to avoid situations in which they feel threatened by an admission of failure, and are therefore less likely to seek help.
2. Case Notes: Mark Siegel's class
3. Graham and Barker (1990) found that when teachers help students, it can be interpreted as indicating that the student lacks ability. Unsolicited teacher assistance signals low ability to students. This view appears to emerge with the advent of schooling, but isn't present in four- and five-year-olds.
4. Alderman's link model stressed that students need to see a link between what they do and a given learning outcome.
    a. Link 1: Proximal goals. To be effective, goals should be specific, attainable, and proximal.
    b. Link 2: Learning strategies. Students are asked to identify an effective learning strategy that will help them to accomplish their goals.
    c. Link 3: Successful experience. Students measure their success using the proximal goal as the criterion. Teachers create opportunities for students to work on their goals and foster effective learning conditions.
    d. Link 4: Attributions for success. Students are encouraged to attribute their success to their personal efforts or abilities.
    e. When failure does occur, students' attributions for it are important determinants of their future expectations for success.
5. TIPS on Communication: The importance of setting and monitoring goals

G. Motivation and multicultural students
1. One of the major contributions teachers can make to the successful integration and accomplishments of multicultural students is to provide an understanding, supportive environment.
2. Suggestions:
    a. Help students establish goals early in life.
    b. Make an effort to recognize the need for racial pride and awareness of distinct learning styles.
    c. Try to foster a sense of self-control, and cultivate academic motivation as much as possible.
    d. Language can be a serious obstacle to acceptance for many students.
    e. Make sure these students experience immediate success by assigning tasks within their capabilities and rewarding them for successful performance.
    f. Individualize instruction by sequencing and pacing the programs as correctly as possible for individual children.
    g. Consider using a classwide peer tutoring program or cooperative learning groups.
3. Current Issues and Perspectives: Will a multicultural curriculum better motivate minority children?

H. Cooperative learning
   1. Cooperative learning is a set of instructional methods in which students are encouraged or required to work together on academic tasks, to help one another learn.
   2. Increases in students' achievement depend on the conditions of cooperative learning, which have important motivational consequences.
      a. Group effort. The cooperative groups must have a group goal that is meaningful to them.
      b. Individual accountability. The group's success must emerge from the individual learning of all group members.
   3. Cooperative learning involves two aspects of classroom organization: task structure and reward structure.
   4. Johnson and Johnson (1987) discussed goal structures, or the way that students relate to each other as they pursue similar goals.
      a. Cooperative, in which students work together to achieve a goal.
      b. Competitive, in which students work against each other while pursuing a a goal.
      c. Individualistic, in which students' activities are unrelated to each other as they work toward a goal.
   5. Slavin (1987) proposed that
      a. Students should work in small, mixed-ability groups of four members: one higher, two average, and one lower achiever.
      b. Students in each group are responsible for the material taught under regular classroom conditions, but also for helping other group members learn and achieve a group goal.
      c. One technique is the Student Teams-Achievement Division (or STAD), in which the teacher initially presents a lesson, students attempt to master the material in their groups, students take individual tests without help from one another, then teachers compute a team score. The focus is on improvement rather than outright scores.
   6. Slavin warned that simply putting students together will not produce learning gains or motivation. When group goals and individual responsibility are incorporated, achievement effects are consistently positive. Positive effects also have been found on self-esteem, intergroup relations, acceptance of academically handicapped students, and attitudes toward school.
   7. Case Notes: Mark Siegel's class
I. Computer technology
   1. The common belief is that if the material is programmed, then students will be more interested, spend more time on the material, and learning will be enhanced.
   2. Most studies assessing student attitudes report positive changes when technology is used, and these results hold for varying ages. Advantages students cite include computer have infinite patience, never get tired, never forgot to correct or praise them, were impartial to ethnicity, and were great motivators. Negative attitudes and fears were shown more often by teachers than by students.
   3. Some researchers raise the possibility of a novelty effect. Recent work on attitudes toward computers is mixed, showing novelty effects in some dimensions of attitudes but not in others.
   4. Motivation created by technology-based instruction is probably not caused by only novelty because:
      a. Software is becoming increasingly better at providing students with their own, individual optimal level of excitement.
      b. Software is often designed to allow students to ask for and receive help in private, which helps preserve a student's sense of esteem and capability and reduces embarrassment.
      c. There is a wide range of characteristics and contexts in which learning can occur.
      d. Educational technology provides access to different kinds and levels of information than a typical teacher can.

IV. Educational implications of motivation
  A. The beginning of learning
     1. There are two key motivational processes involved at this stage: attitudes and needs.

        a.   Attitudes. Given the three classes of attitudes—cognitive, affective, and behavioral—you must identify what exactly is causing a student's negative attitude. Once you locate the problem, then you can direct your efforts precisely toward its solution.

        b.   Needs. Students behave to satisfy their needs, and the need that is most predominant at any moment will be a student's primary concern.

B. During the learning

    1. The key motivational processes involved during the middle stage of learning are stimulation and affect.

        a.   Stimulation

           (1)   One of the most effective means of ensuring that students find a lesson stimulating is to involve their need for achievement.

           (2)   deCharms asserted that motivation is tightly linked to students' identification of the origin of their actions. "Origins" are those who feel that they control their own fates. "Pawns" feel that they are at the mercy of everyone and everything.

           (3)   To enhance the motivation of teachers, the first step is to have them focus on their own motives. Some of the same techniques used to do this work well with students.

        b.   Affect. Different emotions are associated with different attributions for success and failure.

C. When learning ends

    1. The key motivational processes involved during the last stage of learning are competence and reinforcement.

        a.   You can help your students achieve competence by making sure that they have the skills necessary to attain desired goals. Feelings of competence reduce fear and anxiety and increase the effort expended.

        b.   Reinforce immediately, with small rather than large amounts; reinforce small improvements in learning and motivation.

V. Current wisdom: Balance the internal and external motivation methods

  A. Four conclusions about motivation

    1. Students differ in how they are motivated and in what motivates them.

    2. Differences in motivation can lead to important differences in learning.

    3. No single theory of motivation adequately informs educators how to motivate students.

    4. Over the course of development, students generally become more in control of and responsible for actions that influence their level of motivation.

  B. Current theories and research on motivation support the use of both external and internal motivational strategies for most learners.

  C. Teachers control many aspects of instruction that can directly influence students' motivation to learn.

  D. Brophy (1987) argued that no motivational strategies will succeed if certain preconditions are not met.

    1. The classroom conditions must be supportive, warm, and encouraging.

    2. Teachers must know and understand their pupils and set appropriate challenges.

    3. Worthwhile, meaningful objectives that are clearly understood by the class can be powerful motivators.

    4. Motivational strategies should be moderate and monitored.

    5. Teachers must adjust these preconditions according to the developmental level of their students.

  E. The more you know about your students as individuals and the more you know about motivation, the more effective your teaching will be and the more your students will learn.

VI.   Case reflections

VII. Chapter highlights

VIII. What do you think? questions

IX.   Key terms

KEY TERMS

attribution
cooperative learning
curiosity
discovery learning
efficacy expectations
external locus of control
extrinsic motivation
interest
internal locus of control
intrinsic motivation

learned helplessness
locus of control
hierarchy of needs
modeling
outcomes expectation
reinforcement
self-actualization
self-efficacy
test anxiety
Yerkes-Dodson law

GUIDED REVIEW

1. _____ is defined as an internal state that arouses us to action, pushes us in particular directions, and keeps us engaged in certain activities.

Motivation

2. Motivation affects learning and performance because it increases _____ levels, directs an individual toward certain _____, promotes _____ of certain activities and _____ in those activities, and affects the learning _____ and cognitive processes an individual employs.

energy and activity, goals, initiation, persistence, strategies

3. There are some common myths about motivation, including the beliefs that _____ is a good motivator; _____ motivate students; and that _____ increase motivation.

failure, teachers, threats

4. _____ motivation means that students themselves want to learn in order to achieve a specific objective. Since rewards and inducements are external to a student, they are characterized as _____ motivation.

Intrinsic, extrinsic

5. If motivation is faulty, learning will suffer. _____ is limited; _____ is not directed at objectives; and _____ may become a problem.

Attention, behavior, discipline

6. One of Maslow's most famous concepts is that of _____; this means that human beings use our abilities to the limit of our potentialities.

self-actualization

7.   There are five basic needs in Maslow's theory: _____, _____, _____, _____, and
_____.

physiological, safety, love and belonging, esteem, self-actualization

8.   According to Maslow, a _____ in any one need category will affect student performance.
Everyone needs to feel that we are worthy of respect that is based on _____.

deficit, actual achievement

9.   _____ learning results in students' learning to manipulate their environments more actively and
achieve gratification from personally coping with problems.

Discovery

10.   The goal of _____ learning is to have students use their information in solving problems in many
different circumstances. Bruner said that individuals behave according to their _____ of their
environment. Students see _____ in knowledge, skills, and attitudes when they themselves discover it.

discovery, perceptions, meaning

11.   _____ is valuable if it comes when learners compare their results with what they attempt to
achieve. Learners use feedback according to their _____ state. Information is _____ useful when
learners are highly anxious or focus on only one aspect of a problem too closely.

Knowledge of results, internal, least

12.   Attribution theory rests on three basic assumptions. First, people want to know the _____ of
their own behavior and that of others. Second, attribution theory assumes that we do not _____ assign
causes to our behavior. There is a _____ explanation for the causes to which we attribute our behavior.
Third, the causes that we assign to our behavior influence_____.

causes, randomly, logical, subsequent behavior

13.   Attribution theory relates to the need for achievement. Weiner believes that when achievement is
aroused, we tend to attribute our performance to one of four elements: _____, _____, _____, or
_____.

ability, effort, task difficulty, luck

14.   Students' assumptions about their abilities are usually based upon _____. Students judge their
_____ by how well they did on particular tasks. Task difficulty usually is judged by the _____ on the
task. If there is no tangible link between behavior and goal attainment, the tendency is to attribute
success to _____.

past experiences, efforts, performance of others, luck

15. Weiner (1990) stated that there is a relationship between a student's _____, the _____ of the attribution, its resistance to _____, and _____ of future goal attainment. Consequently, in achievement-related situations, students experience both cognitive and emotional reactions.

attributions, stability, extinction, expectancy

16. Some motivation is learned, but the relationship between learning and motivation is _____: New learning depends upon motivation.

bidirectional

17. According to Skinner, behavior is shaped and maintained by its _____.

consequences

18. According to Skinner, motivated behavior results from consequences of _____ behavior.

similar previous

19. According to Skinner, teachers can improve their control over the classroom by the appropriate use of _____ schedules. Telling students they _____ something is not highly motivating. Instead, Skinner suggested covering _____ amounts of material that you can immediately and positively _____.

positive reinforcement, don't know, small, reinforce

20. There are several criticisms of the use of reinforcement, including the ideas that reinforcement is _____; it develops _____ on concrete, external rewards for appropriate behavior; and, when used to change a behavior that is already motivated by intrinsic reinforcement, it may _____ the intrinsically reinforcing value of that behavior.

bribery, dependence, undermine

21. Reinforcement methods are best used with students who exhibit high _____, poor _____, or a history of academic _____. _____ is not the best indicator of who will benefit from extrinsic reinforcements; rather, _____ in achieving the desired behaviors is the best indicator.

anxiety about learning, motivation, failures, Age, success

22. Bandura believes that self-knowledge is gained from information conveyed by either personal or _____ experiences. There are four major sources of information available to students: _____, _____, _____, and _____.

socially mediated, performance accomplishments, vicarious experience, verbal persuasion, emotional arousal

23.   Students must _____ if they are going to imitate; they must _____ what they have imitated if they are to reproduce it in the future; and their imitation behavior must have been _____ for them to remember and later use it.

attend, remember, reinforced

24.   Extremely intense motivation that produces high anxiety has a _____ effect on performance. Moderate motivation seems to be the desirable state for learning complex tasks. This is the _____, which states that ideal motivation for learning decreases in intensity with increasing task difficulty.

negative, Yerkes-Dodson law

25.   _____ is a feeling of apprehension and general irritability accompanied by restlessness, fatigue, and various somatic symptoms like headaches and stomachaches. It may _____ from one subject or teacher to another.

Anxiety, generalize

26.   _____ describes the behavior and emotions of students who find preparing for and taking tests stressful. _____ and _____ students exhibit more test anxiety, and test anxiety is directly related to fears of _____, dislike of tests, cognitive _____, and less effective _____. Test-anxious students have _____ self-esteem and spend more time attending to task-irrelevant behaviors.

Test anxiety, Females, average, negative evaluations, self-preoccupation, study skills, lower

27.   _____ is a cognitively based emotion that occurs when a student recognizes a discrepancy or _____ between what he or she believes to be true about the world and what turns out to actually be true. Piaget said cognitive conflicts produce _____, which then stimulates an emotional desire or curiosity to resolve the conflict. This leads to _____ or _____.

Curiosity, conflict, disequilibrium, assimilation, accommodation

28.   To encourage curiosity, the teacher's _____ for a subject should be discernible to students. Stimulate _____ that cause some apparent confusion but simultaneously provide clues to the solution. When possible, allow students to _____ topics they are curious about. _____ curious, inquiring behavior.

enthusiasm, cognitive conflicts, select, Model

29.   _____ is an enduring characteristic expressed by a relationship between a person and a particular activity or object, To encourage the development of interest, teachers should use _____ for students, provide activities that involve students' needs, provide developmentally appropriate _____, have students _____ their own work and _____ their progress, facilitate the integration and use of knowledge, and use _____ learning strategies.

Interest, meaningful projects, challenges, evaluate, monitor, cooperative

30.   A student who believes he or she has little control over the consequences of his or her actions is said to have an _____ locus of control; a student who believes he or she can control what happens to him or her is thought to have an _____ locus of control.

external, internal

31.   Locus of control can _____ under certain conditions, especially with experiences that change the relationship between _____ and _____.

change, what a student does, its outcome

32.   Dacey's (1989) review of locus of control studies suggests: Teachers tend to attribute more _____ characteristics to external students than internals, and externals describe teachers more _____ than internals do; externals perform better when they receive specific comments about teachers' _____; internals are more effective in recognizing and using _____; and externals do less well in _____ situations than internals, perhaps due to their higher levels of anxiety.

negative, negatively, expectations, available information, competitive

33.   A condition called _____ occurs when, after repeated failure, students become frustrated and simply will not try.

learned helplessness

34.   To help students develop an internal locus of control present _____ challenges; carefully reward their _____, or at least their efforts; base reinforcement on _____ accomplishment; reinforce _____; and use initial successes and foster a habit of trying and taking _____ for one's actions.

realistic, accomplishments, actual, effort, responsibility

35.   When helpless students failed in Dweck's study, they tended to dwell on the _____ of their _____ success. They _____ their number of successes and _____ their number of failures. When they did have successes, they reported they _____ them to continue. When mastery-oriented students failed, they focused on finding a _____ to why they failed.

cause, lack of, underestimated, overestimated, didn't expect, solution

36.   Three components of learned helplessness are relevant for the classroom: Failure to _____ means that students who have experienced learned helplessness tend not to try to learn new material; failure to _____ means that even when new directions are given to these students, they still learn nothing from them; and _____ like frustration, depression, and incompetence seem to accompany learned helplessness.

initiate action, learn, emotional problems

37. _____ refers to individuals' beliefs in their capabilities to exert control over aspects of their lives.

Self-efficacy

38. An _____ expectation represents a person's estimate that a given behavior will lead to a certain outcome. An _____ expectation means that individuals believe that they can perform the behavior or behaviors required to produce certain outcomes. Perceived self-efficacy affects a student's functioning by influencing an individual's choice of _____, effort _____, and _____ in the face of difficulties.

outcome, efficacy, activities, expenditure, persistence

39. The stronger the belief is that help-seeking is _____ and the weaker the belief is that it has associated _____, the greater is the student's expressed likelihood of seeking help. The greater the student's perceived _____ is, the less strong the belief is that there are costs associated with seeking help. Unfortunately, those most in need of help may be those most _____ to seek help. Unsolicited teacher assistance often signals _____ to students.

beneficial, costs, competence, reluctant, low ability

40. The link model stresses that students need to see a link between what they do and a given _____. It involves instruction in proximal _____ and learning _____; _____ experience; and attribution of their successes to _____ or _____.

learning outcome, goals, strategies, successful, effort, abilities

41. Teachers should provide an understanding, supportive environment for multicultural students. Help students establish _____ early in life; recognize the need for _____ and be aware of distinct learning _____; foster a sense of _____ and academic motivation; recognize that _____ can be a serious obstacle to acceptance for many students; make sure students experience immediate _____; _____ instruction; and use peer tutoring or _____ learning groups.

goals, racial pride, styles, self-control, language, success, individualize, cooperative

42. _____ is a set of instructional methods in which students are encouraged or required to work together on academic tasks.

Cooperative learning

43. Two conditions must be met if cooperative learning is to be effective. First, the cooperating groups must have a _____ that is meaningful to them. Second, the group's success must emerge from the individual learning of _____ group members.

group goal, all

44.   Johnson and Johnson (1987) discussed three goal structures, or the way that student relate to each other as they pursue similar goals. A _____ goal structure is one in which students work together to achieve a goal; in a _____ goal structure, students work against each other while pursuing a a goal; and in an _____ goal structure, students' activities are unrelated to each other as they work toward a goal.

cooperative, competitive, individualistic

45.   Slavin (1987) proposed that students work in small, mixed-ability groups of four members with one _____, two _____, and one _____ achiever. Students in each group are responsible for the material taught under regular classroom conditions, but also for _____ other group members learn and achieve a _____. _____ technique is the Student Teams-Achievement Division (or STAD), in which the teacher initially presents a lesson, students attempt to _____ the material in their groups, student take _____ tests, then teachers compute a team score. The focus is on _____.

higher, average, lower, helping, group goal, Teacher, master, individual, improvement

46.   Slavin warned that simply _____ would not produce learning gains. When group goals and individual responsibility are incorporated, achievement effects are consistently _____. Positive effects also have been found on self-esteem, _____ relations, _____ of academically handicapped students, and attitudes toward _____.

putting students together, positive, intergroup, acceptance, school

47.   Most studies assessing student attitudes report _____ changes when technology is used, and these results hold for varying ages. Advantages students cite include computers have infinite _____, never get _____, never forgot to correct or _____ them, were _____ to ethnicity, and were great _____. Negative attitudes and fears were shown more often by _____ than by _____.

positive, patience, tired, praise, impartial, motivators, teachers, students

48.   Some researchers raise the possibility of a _____ effect of technology. Recent work on attitudes toward computers is _____, showing this effect in some dimensions of attitudes but not in others. The existence and degree of this effect is probably related to _____ used in the classroom

novelty, mixed, how technology is used

49.   Motivation created by technology-based instruction is probably not caused by only novelty because software is becoming better at providing students with their own, individual optimal level of _____; software is often designed to allow students to ask for and receive _____ in private; there is a wide range of _____ and _____ in which learning can occur; and educational technology provides access to different kinds and levels of _____ than a typical teacher can.

excitement, help, characteristics, contexts, information

50.   The two key motivational processes involved at the beginning of the learning stage are _____ and _____.

attitudes, needs

51.   The key motivational processes involved during the middle stage of learning are _____ and _____.

stimulation, affect

52.   _____ are those who feel that they control their own fate. _____ feel that they are at the mercy of everyone and everything.

Origins, Pawns

53.   The key motivational processes involved during the last stage of learning are _____ and _____.

competence, reinforcement

54.   Brophy (1987) argued that no motivational strategies will succeed if certain preconditions are not met. The classroom conditions must be _____; teachers must know and _____ their pupils and set worthwhile, meaningful _____ that are clearly understood by the class; and motivational strategies should be moderate and _____.

supportive, understand, objectives, monitored

SUMMARIZE THE MAIN POINTS

This section of your study guide is designed to help you identify and understand the main points in each chapter. You've already reviewed the details using the Guided Review (above), and will consider the importance, relevance, and usefulness of the information in later sections. For now, focus on summarizing the main ideas.

For each major section in the chapter, summarize the main point and the evidence presented in the text to support and/or discuss it. If there are key terms presented in the section, define them. Some prompting questions are provided to help you structure your review.

The main sections of Chapter 9 are:

- Motivation: Meaning and myths
- Theories of motivation: Explanations of motivated students
- What affects students' motivation?
- Educational implications of motivational theories and research
- Current wisdom: Balance the internal and external motivation methods

For each section, answer the following questions:

1. In two sentences or less, **summarize** what the **main point** of this section was.

2. Briefly **summarize the evidence** for and against each main point (a simple list of details they use to support each of their points is sufficient). If the authors discuss research studies to support the point, summarize the findings in one sentence. If the authors are presenting a logical argument to support the point (i.e., not citing data from research studies), briefly list the supporting points they made. Use the detailed chapter outline to help you identify the supporting points.

3. Briefly review the **definitions of any key terms** in each main section.

WHY SHOULD YOU CARE?

The purpose of this section of your study guide is to help you understand how and why the information in the chapter is relevant for you personally. You'll be asked to think more about the relevance and usefulness of the information in later sections of this study guide.

Look back at the work you did in summarizing the main points in the section above and answer the following questions:

1. For each section you summarized, why or how is the **main point** you identified **important to and/or relevant for teachers in general**? Try to limit your answer to only one or two sentences so you don't get bogged down in details, but focus on general usefulness.

2. Now think about the chapter as a whole. **Identify two specific events, contexts, or problems** for which the ideas presented in this chapter are relevant. Briefly discuss how they're relevant and how they could be useful.

3. Now **identify three concepts** from the chapter that **YOU find useful** in some way. Discuss how/why these concepts are useful, and specify how you will actually use them in your teaching and/or your daily life. (It's okay if there is some overlap between your answers for numbers 2 and 3.)

DISCUSSION QUESTIONS

The following "What do you think?" questions are printed in the text.

1. Which of the myths of motivation do you believe? How has this belief affected your learning?

2. What motivational strategies do you use to get yourself to invest more time and energy in studying?

3. Distinguish between intrinsic and extrinsic motivation. Which form best characterizes your motivation for success in school?

4. Define the Yerkes-Dodson law. How does this apply to your learning in this course?

5. Describe cooperative, competitive, and individualistic goal structures. Which goal structure do you work best under?

Additional discussion questions:

6. Define internal and external motivation. Give an example of how both have been used in your educational experiences.

7. Describe each of the levels in Maslow's hierarchy of needs. Explain how an unmet need in any one category will affect student learning.

8. List and explain the basic assumptions of attribution theory. What are the effects on motivation when a student attributes success to ability? To effort? To task difficulty? To luck?

9. How does observation of a model affect students' behavior and motivation? Explain and give an example of each of the four elements that a teacher must keep in mind to make effective use of modeling.

10. What is curiosity and why is it important for teachers? How does curiosity differ from interest?

11. Define and give an example of Bruner's discovery learning. Describe how discovery learning can increase students' motivation for learning.

12. Describe how Skinner would go about increasing students' motivation to learn.

13. Describe Alderman's LINK model and discuss how it can be useful for motivating students.

14. Which students are most likely and which least likely to seek a teacher's help when they don't understand something, and why? How can you help students learn to seek help when they need it?

TAKE IT PERSONALLY!

The questions in this section are designed to help you personalize, integrate, and apply the information from the text. Personalization questions ask you to consider the personal relevance and usefulness of concepts, and consider how they might be useful in your life now and in the future. Integration questions ask you to pull together information from the text to evaluate it, summarize it or synthesize a recommendation on the basis of it, or express an opinion about it. Application questions ask you to think about how the concepts might be useful to address real problems or situations you may find yourself in. All three question types will help you consider the information at a deeper conceptual level, understand it more fully, and remember it.

1. How do you define motivation? What tasks and activities are you motivated to pursue? What are the common characteristics of these tasks and activities? What elements (e.g., self-efficacy, goals, emotions, etc.) are important in your definition of motivation?

2. Does the Yerkes-Dodson law describe your learning and motivation? How well? If it does not describe you, identify the points of difference and discuss the reasons for the differences.

3. Think about someone you know who seems to have an internal locus of control, and describe that person's characteristics. Now describe a person you know who seems to have an external locus of control. How do the two differ? What motivational strategies would be most effective with each person, and how do these strategies differ?

4. What are self-efficacy, efficacy expectations, and outcome expectations? How are these concepts important for teachers?

5. Summarize the research on test anxiety. What causes it, and how can you deal with it as a teacher?

6. Are you more intrinsically or extrinsically motivated? Does the specific task or situation affect whether you're intrinsically or extrinsically motivated?

7. What causes motivation? Describe your theory, then compare and contrast it with those in the text.

8. In general, to what do you attribute success? Failure? What implications do these attributions have for your motivation?

9. What is learned helplessness, and why is it important for teachers? How can you avoid it or remediate it in the classroom? Have you ever experienced a sense of learned helplessness?

10. Give several specific examples of how you can use modeling to increase your students' motivation.

11. Describe cooperative learning. What are its goals, critical aspects, and outcomes? Reflect on any cooperative learning experiences you have had. Did these experiences include the two critical aspects of cooperative learning? How could cooperative learning be used effectively for this course?

12. What strategies can you use to increase and maintain motivation in your multicultural students?

13. Does educational technology affect your motivation to learn? Why or why not?

CASE IN POINT...

Remember to use the cases from the text as contexts for identifying examples of concepts from the text and as contexts for solving educational problems. Also remember to use a consistent framework (like the DUPE model or the CASE NOTES in the text) to structure your "Mini-Case Report." Review the "Case in Point..." section of Chapter 1 in this study guide for more details.

SUGGESTED CONCEPTS TO IDENTIFY FOR CHAPTER 9

> attribution theory
> cooperative learning
> curiosity
> discovery learning
> extrinsic vs. intrinsic motivation
> interest
> learned helplessness
> locus of control
> Maslow's hierarchy of needs
> modeling
> self-efficacy
> test anxiety
> Yerkes-Dodson law

Review Case #2 about Mark Siegel and use the following questions to prompt your thinking about this case.

1. Mark is obviously having problems fostering Karim's motivation. What theory of motivation does Mark seem to be working from? Would a different theoretical orientation be more helpful?

2. Would knowledge of Maslow's theory (involving a hierarchy of needs) be helpful as Mark tries to foster Karim's motivation? How?

3. Could the text concepts of curiosity and interest, locus of control and attributions, and discovery learning be helpful to Mark? How?

END-OF-CASE WRAPUP

This chapter is the last on in the text dealing specifically with Mark Siegel and Karim. Take a moment to review your thoughts, "mini-case reports," and suggestions for Mark. Jot down a brief summary of your suggestions for him, highlighting what you think are the main issues/problems he and Karim must address and the actions that you think would be most successful for them. Reflect on what you have learned about teaching and learning interactions by analyzing this case and which ideas you think will be most useful to you in your teaching career.

Also think about the content covered in Section 1 of the text dealing with the development of students. Take a moment to consider whether and how any of this information might be helpful to Mark and Karim, then make a brief list of the relevant concepts.

Finally, take a moment to review Case #1 about Marsha Warren. Would any of the information covered in the second section of the text be useful for Marsha? Make a brief list of which concepts from Section 2 might be helpful to Marsha.

BIG IDEAS IN EDUCATIONAL PSYCHOLOGY

Thinking about the "big ideas" in educational psychology will help you organize and apply your newly acquired knowledge. Use the following steps to identify your own principles and strategies from the chapter and to relate them to the five main themes of the text (i.e., the "big ideas").

1. Review the TIPS from the text.

2. List some of the main concepts from the chapter. Use the work you did in prior sections of the study guide to help generate this list. Also look at the list of key terms from the chapter.

3. Select what you think are two or three of the most important concepts from your list.

4. For each concept you select, try to state it as a principle (use the TIPS format in the text and the example shown below as a guide for how to state principles).

5. Develop two or three specific teaching strategies that follow from each stated principle.

6. Relate your work to the five main themes from the text, identifying which theme(s) are relevant for each principle and strategy. This step will help you see how the information in each chapter contributes to improved teaching for each of these five critical aspects of instruction.

7. Think about and discuss with classmates how the principles and strategies you identify will help you improve your teaching for each theme you listed as relevant.

The five main themes from the text are:
ASSESSMENT, COMMUNICATION, LEARNING, MOTIVATION, AND TIME

Some example concepts, principles, and strategies for Chapter 9:

attribution theory	learned helplessness
cooperative learning	modeling
curiosity	outcomes expectation
discovery learning	reinforcement
efficacy expectation	self-actualization
locus of control (internal, external)	self-efficacy
extrinsic vs. intrinsic motivation	test anxiety
interest	Yerkes-Dodson law

Principle   *Motivation is a crucial element in successful academic performance. Without adequate levels of motivation, students will not achieve the levels of learning they are capable of. (LEARNING, MOTIVATION)*

Strategy   Foster intrinsic motivation whenever possible by promoting cognitive disequilibrium; that is, take advantage of the human tendency to be curious about events they don't completely understand. Use riddles, games, and issues that students perceive as directly relevant to their own lives. (LEARNING, MOTIVATION)

Strategy   Use/present tasks that are challenging but achievable by students, given some help and guidance, and that are reasonably realistic. (LEARNING, MOTIVATION)

SUGGESTED READINGS

deCharms, R. (1976). *Enhancing motivation: Change in the classroom.* New York: Irvington.

Dienstbier, R. (Ed.). (1990). *Nebraska Symposium on motivation: Perspectives on motivation.* Lincoln, NE: University of Nebraska Press.

Ford, M. (1992). *Motivating humans: Goals, emotions, and personal agency beliefs.* Newbury Park, CA: Sage.

Reeve, J. (1996). *Motivating others: Nurturing inner motivational resources.* Allyn & Bacon: Boston.

Stipek, D. (1998). *Motivation to learn: From theory to practice* (3rd ed.). Allyn & Bacon: Boston.

PRACTICE TEST 1

1. Motivation
   a. is a belief that one is capable of successful performance.
   b. consists of one's emotional reactions to failure.
   c. arouses, sustains, directs, and integrates behavior.
   d. is the belief that one is in control of outcomes.

2. Andrew's classroom is supportive and encouraging. He understands his students' needs and tries to set meaningful objectives, and he monitors the difficulty and effort levels of his students. It sounds like Andrew's class
   a. has the preconditions necessary for good levels of motivation.
   b. does not have the preconditions necessary for good levels of motivation.
   c. is based on a behavioristic explanation of motivation.
   d. is based on a cognitive explanation of motivation.

3. A student interested in American poetry brings a poem to class because she wants to learn what metaphors are in the poem. How would her motivation be described?
   a. instructional
   b. directed
   c. intrinsic
   d. extrinsic

4. Jason's teacher was concerned about him because he appeared lethargic and showed poor concentration every morning in class. When she found out he never ate breakfast because of his family background of poverty, she knew that Jason's learning potential was lowered due to his
   a. safety needs.
   b. esteem needs.
   c. self-actualization needs.
   d. physiological needs.

5. According to Bruner, discovery learning helps students
   a. develop high levels of the need to achieve.
   b. be active learners and achieve meaningful insights in learning.
   c. obtain favorable judgments from others.
   d. differentiate between ability and effort as the causes for successful academic performance.

6. Students' assumptions about their abilities usually are based on
   a. no tangible link between behavior and goal attainment.
   b. the performance of others on the task.
   c. past experiences.
   d. how well they did on a particular task.

7. Who held that motivated behavior results from the consequences of similar previous behavior?
   a. Skinner
   b. Bandura
   c. Bruner
   d. Maslow

8. Performance accomplishments, vicarious experience, verbal persuasion, and emotional arousal are sources of information for
   a. self-efficacy.
   b. self-awareness.
   c. self-actualization.
   d. self-knowledge.

9. To encourage curiosity, teachers should
   a. maintain a neutral attitude toward subject areas so that students are not intimidated.
   b. avoid cognitive conflicts in teaching so that students do not feel uncomfortable.
   c. always select topics and assign them to students to avoid confusion.
   d. None of the answers is correct.

10. Ideal motivation for learning decreases in intensity with increasing task difficulty. This is called the
    a. motivation coefficient.
    b. Yerkes-Dodson law.
    c. personal investment theory.
    d. task coefficient.

11. Jay believes that he will never go to college because of his disadvantaged family background. Which kind of locus of control does Jay seem to have?
    a. internal
    b. external
    c. historical
    d. regimental

12. Mitch repeatedly has failed spelling and grammar exams. After repeated failure, he becomes frustrated and will no longer study for such exams. What is this condition called?
    a. external locus of control
    b. internal locus of control
    c. situational anxiety
    d. learned helplessness

13. Individuals' beliefs in their capabilities to exert control over aspects of their lives is referred to as
    a. self-efficacy.
    b. self-knowledge.
    c. natural incentives.
    d. learned helplessness.

14. Anna, a tenth-grader, believes that asking questions is a good way to learn. She has good self-esteem and is confident in her own abilities. When she needs help, Anna is likely to
    a. be reluctant to ask her teachers.
    b. feel comfortable about asking her teachers for assistance.
    c. believe that there is a high cost for seeking help from her teachers.
    d. believe that seeking help signals lower ability.

15. According to Alderman's link model, students must see a link between
    a. intrinsic and extrinsic motivation.
    b. what they do and a given learning outcome.
    c. what they learn and how well they do in life.
    d. what they learn and what they are tested on.

16. An instructional method in which students are encouraged to help one another with their conversational Spanish is an example of
    a. cooperative learning.
    b. discovery learning.
    c. vicarious experience.
    d. need achievement.

17. Which of the following is a good idea for teachers working with multicultural students?
    a. Establish goals after students have had time to be exposed to several years of curricula.
    b. Assign tasks that are harder for them to help them strive for success.
    c. Teach at a level appropriate for the whole class to keep students from falling behind or working ahead.
    d. Foster self-control.

18. What are the key motivational processes involved during the middle stage of learning?
    a. attitudes and needs
    b. intelligence and insight
    c. stimulation and affect
    d. competence and reinforcement

19. The "novelty effect" is important for teachers to understand because
    a. it explains why technology-based instructional strategies may become less motivating for students over time.
    b. it explains why most students have negative attitudes toward technology.
    c. it can be used to help monitor over time students' motivation for technology-based teaching strategies.
    d. it explains why moderately difficult tasks are more motivating than either very easy or very difficult tasks.

PRACTICE TEST 2

1. Which of the following statements regarding motivation is true?
    a. Teachers motivate students.
    b. Threats increase motivation.
    c. Failure is poor motivation.
    d. Learning is more important than motivation.

2. Amanda's classroom is fairly competitive. Her teacher is often quick to criticize and sets goals that are very difficult to attain. The students are sometimes unclear as to what is expected, and reluctant to offer their opinions. It is likely that motivational strategies
    a. would be successful in this classroom.
    b. would not be successful in this classroom.
    c. are not needed in this classroom.
    d. are humanistically based in this classroom.

3. Hannah's teacher gives her a Barney sticker for every math story problem she solves correctly. Hannah's teacher is using
    a. extrinsic motivation.
    b. cooperative learning techniques.
    c. intrinsic motivation.
    d. discovery learning.

4. Which needs of Maslow's hierarchy refer to our need for family and friends?
    a. safety
    b. esteem
    c. self-actualization
    d. love and belongingness

5. Who proposed discovery learning?
    a. McClelland
    b. Bandura
    c. Bruner
    d. Maslow

6. Ability, effort, task difficulty, and luck are all elements of
    a. self-efficacy theory.
    b. social cognitive theory.
    c. need achievement theory.
    d. attribution theory.

7. According to Skinner, behavior is shaped and maintained by
    a. intelligence.
    b. its consequences.
    c. self-knowledge.
    d. motivation.

8. According to Bandura's social cognitive theory, which of the following concepts are important in explaining how motivation is created and maintained?
    a. need satisfaction
    b. ability, effort, luck, and task difficulty
    c. modeling, observation, and imitation
    d. schedules of reinforcement

9. Paulo is a very enthusiastic teacher. He gets visibly interested in and excited about the topics he teaches, and poses interesting and challenging questions for his students to consider. Sometimes they get a bit confused, but they always are interested in resolving the questions. The students are allowed to work on projects of their own choosing. It sounds like Paulo does a good job of
   a. encouraging curiosity in his students.
   b. encouraging good memorization techniques in his students.
   c. fostering an internal locus of control in his students.
   d. alleviating test anxiety in his students.

10. Jane's class is about to engage in learning a complex task. What is the ideal state for her students?
    a. low motivation
    b. moderate motivation
    c. high motivation
    d. no motivation

11. When does an individual's locus of control change?
    a. When the person perceives that his or her actions were instrumental in achieving success.
    b. When the person's success results from a teacher's manipulation of his or her work.
    c. When the person understands the uses of control.
    d. When the person has an identifiable goal.

12. Which of the following is NOT a component of learned helplessness?
    a. failure to understand task requirements
    b. failure to compete
    c. failure to learn
    d. failure to initiate action

13. The belief that one can perform the behavior(s) required to produce certain outcomes is a(n)
    a. locus of control.
    b. incentive.
    c. outcome expectation.
    d. efficacy expectation.

14. Graham and Barker (1990) found that students believed that when a teacher assists a student without being asked to, it signals that the student being helped is
    a. higher in ability.
    b. more likely to be successful in the future.
    c. lower in ability.
    d. a good person to work with on assignments.

15. After noticing that Joel was having difficulty solving a problem, the teacher asked, "What did you do when you tried to solve the problems?" As a result, Joel reread the problem, realized he had missed some relevant information, and was then able to solve the problem. Joel's teachers helped him with which component of Alderman's Link model?
    a. proximal goals
    b. learning strategies
    c. successful experience
    d. attributions for success

16. Cooperative learning involves which two aspects of classroom organization?
    a. motivation and anticipation
    b. task structure and reward structure
    c. motivation and cooperation
    d. task structure and interpersonal structure

17. Which of the following is a good idea for teachers working with multicultural students?
    a. Help them establish goals early in life.
    b. Help them experience immediate success.
    c. Recognize differences in learning styles.
    d. All of the answers are correct.

18. What key motivational processes are involved at the beginning of learning?
    a. attitudes and needs
    b. competence and reinforcement
    c. stimulation and affect
    d. intelligence and insight

19. Why do students seem to find computer software motivating?
    a. It limits the amount of information students have access to and so makes it easier to find information.
    b. It allows students to ask for and receive help in private.
    c. It keeps the level of learning excitement very high for all students.
    d. It ensures that all students learn the same information at the same pace.

ANSWER KEY

Practice Test 1

1. ANSWER: C, Factual; OBJECTIVE: 1; PAGE: 334
2. ANSWER: A, Applied; OBJECTIVE: 1; PAGE: 367
3. ANSWER: C, Applied; OBJECTIVE: 5; PAGE: 333
4. ANSWER: D, Applied; OBJECTIVE: 2; PAGE: 335
5. ANSWER: B, Conceptual; OBJECTIVE: 2; PAGE: 338
6. ANSWER: C, Factual; OBJECTIVE: 2; PAGE: 339
7. ANSWER: A, Factual; OBJECTIVE: 2; PAGE: 341
8. ANSWER: D, Factual; OBJECTIVE: 2; PAGE: 343
9. ANSWER: D, Factual; OBJECTIVE: 3; PAGE: 348
10. ANSWER: B, Factual; OBJECTIVE: 3; PAGE: 345
11. ANSWER: B, Applied; OBJECTIVE: 3; PAGE: 350
12. ANSWER: D, Applied; OBJECTIVE: 3; PAGE: 351
13. ANSWER: A, Factual; OBJECTIVE: 3; PAGE: 352
14. ANSWER: B, Applied; OBJECTIVE: 3; PAGE: 354-355
15. ANSWER: B, Factual; OBJECTIVE: 4; PAGE: 355
16. ANSWER: A, Conceptual; OBJECTIVE: 4; PAGE: 359
17. ANSWER: D, Factual; OBJECTIVE: 4; PAGE: 357
18. ANSWER: C, Factual, OBJECTIVE: 4; PAGE: 364
19. ANSWER: A, Conceptual, OBJECTIVE: 4; PAGE: 362

Practice Test 2

1.   ANSWER: C, Factual; OBJECTIVE: 1; PAGE: 332-333
2.   ANSWER: B, Applied; OBJECTIVE: 1; PAGE: 367
3.   ANSWER: A, Applied; OBJECTIVE: 5; PAGE: 333
4.   ANSWER: D, Factual; OBJECTIVE: 2; PAGE: 335
5.   ANSWER: C, Factual; OBJECTIVE: 2; PAGE: 338
6.   ANSWER: D, Factual; OBJECTIVE: 2; PAGE: 339
7.   ANSWER: B, Factual; OBJECTIVE: 2; PAGE: 341
8.   ANSWER: C, Conceptual; OBJECTIVE: 2; PAGE: 343-344
9.   ANSWER: A, Applied; OBJECTIVE: 3; PAGE: 348
10.   ANSWER: B, Conceptual; OBJECTIVE: 3; PAGE: 345
11.   ANSWER: A, Factual; OBJECTIVE: 3; PAGE: 350
12.   ANSWER: A, Conceptual; OBJECTIVE: 3; PAGE: 351
13.   ANSWER: D, Factual; OBJECTIVE: 3; PAGE: 352
14.   ANSWER: C, Factual; OBJECTIVE: 3; PAGE: 355
15.   ANSWER: B, Applied; OBJECTIVE: 4; PAGE: 356
16.   ANSWER: B, Factual; OBJECTIVE: 4; PAGE: 359
17.   ANSWER: D, Factual; OBJECTIVE: 4; PAGE: 357
18.   ANSWER: A, Factual; OBJECTIVE: 4; PAGE: 363
19.   ANSWER: B, Factual; OBJECTIVE: 4; PAGE: 363

Chapter 10 CLASSROOM MANAGEMENT: CREATING EFFECTIVE LEARNING ENVIRONMENTS

LEARNING OBJECTIVES

After completing this chapter, you should be able to

1. Describe characteristics of proactive classroom management.

2. Describe the significance of time in mastery of classroom material.

3. Match developmental tasks with appropriate management techniques.

4. Identify rules that are needed for a smoothly functioning classroom.

5. Use methods that maintain productive classroom control.

CHAPTER HIGHLIGHTS

Management Concerns in the Classroom

- Your students' learning depends on the orderly routine that you establish in the classroom. Remember that "orderly" does not imply an atmosphere of quiet terror. It means an atmosphere in which all students (and teachers) know exactly what is expected of them.
- Organizing your classroom in a way that satisfies you and that your students understand is the first step in providing effective teaching and learning.
- John Carroll's ideas on the use of time have had a significant impact on the way that teachers structure their classrooms. His basic thesis is that students will learn to the extent that time (that is, time on task) is available for learning.
- The developmental characteristics of your students affect the management techniques you use and influence your decision about the age group you would like to teach.

Life in the Classroom

- Students' attitudes toward school seem to be a mixture of happiness and unhappiness. The causes of these mixed feelings seem to be rooted in the conditions of the individual classrooms, that is, how you manage your work.
- Student engagement (what students are doing at any time) is related to your activity. Student engagement seems to be highest when teachers lead small groups and lowest during student presentations.
- Teachers in "higher-achieving schools" spend more time in actual teaching and in academic interactions with their students than do teachers in "lower achieving schools."
- As you decide how to organize your classroom, what to teach, and how to teach it, remember that you must adapt your techniques—both instructional and organizational—to the needs of your students.

Managing the Classroom

- The rules you establish for organizing your classroom are critical, since they establish the conduct that you think is important. Unless your students' behavior conforms to these rules, learning will be negatively affected.
- Good managers make their basic rules known on the first day of class and combine the teaching of the rules with a demonstration of the signals they would use for various activities.
- Good managers use as few initial rules as possible and then introduce others as needed. They also occasionally remind their students of these rules and act immediately when they see rule violations. Such action usually prevents minor difficulties from becoming major problems.
- By understanding the developmental characteristics of the students you are teaching, you can anticipate many of the sources of potential problems and formulate rules that will help you to prevent them.

Methods of Control

- You and you alone can determine what is misbehavior, since individual differences apply to teachers as well as to students. What one teacher may judge to be misbehavior, another may ignore.
- Among teacher behaviors that contribute to the successful management of their classrooms are withitness, overlapping, transition smoothness, and group alertness.
- Behavior modification, as a means of classroom control, relies on changing the classroom environment and the manner in which students interact with the environment to influence students' behavior.
- Understanding the causes of a student's misbehavior requires that teachers realize that their students' behavior has a purpose. Consequently, if teachers can identify the goal that a particular behavior is intended to achieve, they can correct problem behavior.
- Most teachers are eclectic in the manner in which they manage their classes, selecting and choosing from all of the techniques discussed in this chapter as the need arises.

DETAILED CHAPTER OUTLINE

I.   Management concerns in the classroom
   A. Classroom management is the use of rules and procedures to maintain order so that learning may result. Organizing the classroom is the first step in effective classroom management.
   B. Preventing classroom problems
      1. Schools are adopting a preventative approach as well as school-wide behavior management systems.
      2. A comprehensive classroom management program includes reactive responding to problems and proactive planning of productive behavior.
      3. Proactive classroom management has three characteristics that distinguish it from other management techniques.
         a. It is preventive rather than reactive.
         b. It integrates methods that facilitate appropriate student behavior with procedures that promote achievement, using effective classroom instructional techniques.
         c. It emphasizes the group dimensions of classroom management.
      4. Maintaining sufficient order requires that you have students enter the classroom and move to their seats with no disruption, have the materials they need, understand what they are to do, have engaged time, and leave the classroom in an orderly fashion.

5. Although learning is served by an instructional function, order is served by a managerial function.
6. TIPS on Time: Proactive classroom management

C. Time and teachers: The Carroll model
1. The primary job of the educational psychologist is to develop and apply knowledge concerning why students succeed or fail in their learning at school, and to assist in the prevention and remediation of learning difficulties.
2. Carroll stated that a learner will succeed in learning a task to the extent that the needed time is spent for that student to learn the task.
3. Carroll uses two categories to analyze time.
   a. The determinants of time needed for learning. There are three important aspects in this category:
      (1) Aptitude, which refers to the amount of time any student will need to learn a task
      (2) Ability to understand instruction, which refers to the effects of general intelligence and verbal ability
      (3) Quality of instruction, which refers to a teacher's ability to present appropriate material in an interesting manner
   b. Time spent in learning. Carroll focused on two important features of this category:
      (1) Time allowed for learning, which refers to the opportunity that individual schools allow for learning.
      (2) Perseverance, which refers to the amount of time students are willing to spend in learning.
   c. Aptitude and ability to understand instruction reside within the student and teachers have little control over them. Tile allowed for learning and quality of instruction are under the teachers' control. Perseverance reflects both student and classroom characteristics.
4. When Carroll's model is linked to an effectively managed classroom, we can draw three conclusions.
   a. Learning rarely emerges from chaos.
   b. A disorganized classroom substantially reduces time for learning.
   c. The quality of instruction is tightly bound to efficiency of classroom management.

D. Case Notes: Melissa Williams class
E. Developmental tasks and classroom management
1. The developmental changes students experience will require teachers of different grade levels to adopt different types of management techniques.
2. Preschool experiences are more protective and caring than educational, with children interacting with one or two teachers, perhaps an equal number of aides, and several peers. Socialization and communication needs are paramount and are shaped by adults with an important, often unarticulated goal: desirable socialization and individuation.
3. The elementary school classroom is more of a true social unit, with more intense interactions between teacher and student and among peers. Teachers, as authority figures, establish the climate of the classroom and the kind of relationships permitted. Peer-group relationships stress friendship, belongingness, and status.
4. In high school, the entire school, rather than a particular classroom, becomes the social context. Heterosexual relationships take on importance, and social behavior becomes the standard of acceptance. Extracurricular activities now play a greater and more significant part in adolescent life.
5. Management techniques change with age/grade level, with management usually more of an issue during the upper elementary and lower high school years.

F. Management and control of problem students
1. When working with students with a behavioral problem, try to answer the following questions:
   a. What do you see as the core of each of these problems?
   b. How would this problem affect the rest of the class?
   c. How would you handle each of these problems?
   d. Do you need help in working with this student?

II. Life in the classroom
  A. Management is an essential function of all organizations for goal attainment, which involves three basic functions:
    1. Planning, by which objectives and procedures are selected
    2. Communication, by which information is transferred
    3. Control, by which performance is matched to plans
  B. When you close the classroom door
    1. Philip Jackson, in his *Life in Classrooms* (1968), noted that although schools are places where skills are acquired, tests are given, and amusing and maddening things happen, they are also places where young people come together, make friends, learn, and engage in all sorts of routine activities.
    2. Jackson discusses three features of classroom life not typically mentioned: crowds, praise, and power.
    3. Jackson (1968) stated that students' attitudes toward school are complicated. Summarizing data from previous studies, he found considerable negative feelings among basically satisfied students. One way of interpreting the data is to suggest that most students do not feel too strongly about their classroom experience, one way or the other.
  C. Classroom activities
    1. Activities are relatively short blocks of classroom time (about 10 to 20 minutes) during which students are arranged and taught in a particular way.
    2. Berliner (1983) identified 11 activities that consistently appeared in K-6 classrooms: Reading circle, seatwork, one-way presentation, two-way presentation, use of media, silent reading, construction, games, play, transitions, and housekeeping.
    3. Doyle estimated that a teacher's involvement during a class consists mainly of actual instruction, organizing students, dealing with deviant behavior, and handling individual problems and social tasks.
    4. Laslett and Smith (1984) identified four "rules" that should help in classroom organization.
      a. Get them in. Lessons should start on time, and teacher attention should not be diverted by routines that should have been attended to earlier.
      b. Get them out. Consider what would be the ideal method for concluding the lesson and dismissing the class.
      c. Get on with it. Focus on the content, manner, and organization.
      d. Get on with them. Classroom disruptions are infrequent when positive interactions characterize the teacher-student interactions.
  D. The QAIT model
    1. Slavin (1987d) proposed an instructional model focusing on the alterable elements of Carroll's model. Called QAIT, the model encompasses the following four components: quality of instruction, appropriate levels of instruction, incentive, and time.
      a. Quality of instruction depends on both the curriculum and the lesson presentation. Instruction must make sense to students, which requires that teachers:
        (1) Present information in an orderly, systematic fashion.
        (2) Provide smooth transitions to new topics.
        (3) Use vivid images and concrete examples.
        (4) Ensure necessary repetition and reinforcement.
      b. Appropriate levels of instruction implies that you know that your students are ready to learn new material. Slavin (1987) identifies the following methods fro matching students to content level as most common:
        (1) Ability groups (elementary schools), in which students remain in heterogeneous classes most of the day but are grouped for certain subjects, such as reading and mathematics, can be effective.
        (2) Group-based mastery learning does not require permanent ability groups; students regroup after each skill is taught.
        (3) Individualized instruction provides for accommodation and can be effective if coupled with personalized contact with an instructor and some group work.

       (4)   Slavin separated the results of work on grouping practices into two categories.
- (a) Within-class groupings. Evidence for the value of mastery learning is inconclusive, while analyses of cooperative learning methods show consistent gains in student achievement if properly managed.
- (b) Between-class groupings. These have little effect on student achievement, although acceleration possibly may benefit some gifted students.
- c. Incentive refers to the degree of student motivation.
- d. Time refers to sufficient time for learning to occur.
2. These four elements of QAIT share one critical characteristic: each element must be adequate if instruction is to be effective.
3. Case Notes: Melissa Williams' class
4. TIPS on Motivation: Reducing behavior problems

E. Classroom contexts
1. Recitation refers to calling on individual students who give answers publicly before the rest of the class, usually for a brief time.
   - a. Recitation has several purposes: review, introducing new material, checking assigned work, practice, and comprehension. Consequently, the purpose of the recitation dictates the type of question and opportunity for participation.
   - b. Because recitation involves use of questions, questions asked must sustain the attention of the entire class.
   - c. Suggestions for recitation:
     - (1) Ask your question of the entire class.
     - (2) Wait for the answer.
2. Two types of seatwork are used most commonly.
   - a. First is supervised study, during which all students are assigned independent work and the teacher moves around the room, monitoring each student's work.
   - b. Second is independent work, when the teacher is busy with another group and does not monitor each student's work.
   - c. Suggestions to guide seatwork:
     - (1) Spend sufficient time explaining, discussing, and even practicing before your students begin work on their own.
     - (2) Practice should immediately precede the seatwork.
     - (3) The exercises assigned to your students should flow directly from your explanations and the practice.
     - (4) Guide your students through the first few exercises.
     - (5) Establish a set routine that your students should follow any time they do seatwork.

III. Managing the classroom
A. Rule setting and classroom procedures
1. Emmer et al. (1980) stated that good managers in elementary school classrooms
   - a. made known their rules and procedures on the first day of class and quite deliberately integrated them into a system, which they taught.
   - b. had rules that were explicit, concrete, and functional.
   - c. gave examples of the signals they would use for various activities.
   - d. did not initially overburden their students with rules.
   - e. periodically reminded their students of the rules.
2. Secondary school teachers also clearly and unmistakably stated the desired behaviors for their classes, gave precise indications of the expected work standards in their classes, and acted immediately to check disruptive behavior.
3. The main difference between the elementary and secondary "good managers" was that the secondary school instructors spent less time teaching and rehearsing the rules and procedures.
4. Remember to decide on as few important rules as necessary, make rules absolutely clear to all, enforce rules for all, and avoid playing favorites.

B. Rules and classroom activities
   1. Medland and Vitale (1984) suggested the following five steps to help teachers to formulate meaningful rules for their many classroom activities:
      a. Define the class activity.
      b. Determine social behaviors necessary for activities.
      c. Determine which activities need a list of rules.
      d. Make a set of rules for the selected activities.
      e. Formulate a set of general activity rules.
   2. Successful teachers set their rules at the beginning of the school year, even though their students previously have learned those general rules that apply to school behavior.
   3. Be ready to cope with rule violations.
   4. TIPS on Communication
C. Management and control
   1. Developmental issues noteworthy in considering students' problems:
      a. Some behaviors that characterize maladjustment are relatively common in childhood.
      b. As students develop and undergo rapid changes, problem behaviors wax and wane at different ages.
      c. As a result of rapid changes across development, a problem of one type may be replaced by another problem at a later age.
   2. The teacher's role (shared with parents) in helping students to master developmental crises is vital, because the manner in which they meet these difficulties shapes the way they will face future dilemmas.
   3. Eighty-five percent of students proceed normally, perhaps causing teachers some anxiety with temporary maladaptive behavior.
D. Aggression in the classroom
   1. It may be helpful to consider aggression developmentally, so that you can identify those classroom situations that could trigger an outburst. There seem to be clear developmental changes in aggression, and there are clear sex differences, with boys generally being much more aggressive.
   2. In dealing with most cases of aggression, try these suggestions:
      a. Stop trouble before it starts.
      b. Use signal interference.
      c. Avoid the tribal dance, which usually involves a dare.
      d. Watch for hidden effects. Though a student may do what you want, there are usually side effects, such as feelings of hostility and isolation.
      e. Recognize your own aggression.
      f. Evaluate your classroom procedures.
E. Searching for the causes of classroom problems
   1. Once you see that a problem exists, the next step is to identify what is causing it.
      a. Is your room arrangement causing any problems?
      b. Are your rules and procedures clear?
      c. Are you managing student work carefully?
      d. Are you satisfied with the consequences of appropriate and inappropriate behavior?
      e. Are you detecting misbehavior in its early stages?
      f. Is your teaching effective?

IV. Methods of control
   A. Misbehavior in the classroom
      1. The key to understanding misbehavior is to be alert to what students do while in the classroom.
      2. You must be aware of any change in your behavior when different students demonstrate the same behavior.
      3. Intervening frequently to check misbehavior characterizes the least effective teachers and is a clear signal that something is wrong.

B. Maintaining classroom control
  1. The ripple effect occurs when the effects of behavior correction are not confined to one student, but spread to other class members.
  2. Desists consist of a teacher's actions to stop misbehavior (e.g., clarity, firmness, intensity, focus, and student treatment). Kounin found, surprisingly, no relationship between these qualities of a teacher's desists and success in handling deviant behavior.
  3. Kounin found that some teachers' behaviors did correlate highly with managerial success.
    a. Withitness. Teachers know and understand what is happening in their classrooms.
    b. Overlapping. Some teachers had no difficulty in attending to two issues simultaneously.
    c. Transition smoothness. Some teachers had no trouble in handling activity and movement in their classes. They avoided jerkiness and slowdowns.
    d. Group alertness. Program for "learning-related" variety. Ask yourself: Am I an interesting teacher?
  4. Positive group alerting cues include such behaviors as creating suspense before calling on a student and consistently calling on different students.
  5. Negative group alerting cues are given when teachers engage in behaviors such as concentrating on only one student, designating a student to answer before asking the question, or having youngsters recite in a predetermined sequence.
C. Using behavior modification
  1. More teachers report using management techniques to control inappropriate social than inappropriate academic behavior.
  2. Teachers use verbal management techniques more than those based on concrete consequences.
  3. Behaviorism's basic assumptions are that both adaptive and maladaptive behavior are learned, and that the best way to treat problems is to structure a student's classroom environment so that you can reinforce desirable behavior.
  4. Definition of terms
    a. Behavior influence occurs whenever one person exercises some control over another.
    b. Behavior modification is a deliberate attempt to apply certain principles derived from experimental research to enhance human functioning. These techniques are designed to better a student's self-control by improving skills, abilities, and independence.
      (1) One basic rule guides the total process: people are influenced by the consequences of their behavior.
      (2) A critical assumption is that the current environment controls behavior more directly than an individual's early experience, internal conflicts, or personality structure.
    c. Behavior therapy usually refers to a one-on-one client-therapist relationship.
  5. The critical dimensions of applied behavioral techniques:
    a. Positive reinforcement. Positive reinforcement is any event following a response that increases the possibility of recurrence of that response.
    b. Token economy. Students receive tokens when they exhibit desirable behavior, collect the tokens, attain an accepted number, and can exchange them for something desirable.
    c. Shaping. You first determine the successive steps in the desired behavior and teach them separately, reinforcing each until students master it. The students then move to the next phase, where the procedure is repeated. Finally, they acquire the total behavior by these progressive approximations.
    d. Contingency contracting. A teacher and student decide on a behavioral goal and on what the student will receive when he or she attains the goal.
    e. Aversive control. Students maintain some undesirable behavior because the consequences are reinforcing. To eliminate the behavior, a teacher might apply an aversive stimulus. The removal of positive reinforcement is another example of aversive control.
    f. Overcorrection. Overcorrection combines both restitution and positive practice.

6. Behavior modification and the causes of behavior
   a. Applied behavior analysis involves a "systematic performance-based, self-evaluative method of studying and changing socially important behavior" (Sulzer-Azaroff & Mayer, 1991). The environment is emphasized as the cause of behavior.
   b. Behavior therapists say teachers should concentrate on student behavior and not on its causes, because teachers are not trained to explore the special circumstances that influence behavior, and even if teachers can identify the cause of maladaptive behavior they frequently can do little about it.
   c. Steps in any behavior management program:
      (1) Identify the problem.
      (2) Refine the target behavior.
      (3) Assess the baseline rate.
      (4) Identify the reinforcer and the contingency.
      (5) Begin the program.
      (6) Modify the program when necessary.
      (7) Fade out the program.
      (8) Ensure generalization.
   7. TIPS on Assessment: Functional analysis
D. Cognition and behavior change
   1. Social discipline and goal seeking
      a. Dreikurs et al. (1971) raised several provocative issues about discipline, and their discussion of goals is especially pertinent here.
      b. Their basic premise states that behavior is purposive and that correcting goals is possible, while correcting deficiencies is impossible.
      c. The following assumptions are associated with Dreikurs' social discipline model:
         (1) Students are social beings and desire to belong to a social group.
         (2) Students are decision makers.
         (3) All behavior is purposeful and directed toward social goals.
         (4) Students see reality as they perceive it to be.
         (5) A student is a whole being who cannot be understood by isolated characteristics.
         (6) A student's misbehavior results from faulty reasoning on how to achieve social recognition (Wolfgang & Glickman, 1986, p. 190).
      d. Self-discipline comes from freedom with responsibility, while only forced discipline comes from force, power, and fear.
   2. Mutual respect in the classroom
      a. Dreikurs and his colleagues state that teachers and students need inner freedom, which results from cooperating with each other, accepting responsibility for behavior, speaking truthfully respecting each other, and agreeing on common behavioral rules.
      b. Some practical suggestions:
         (1) Do not nag or scold.
         (2) Do not ask a student to promise anything.
         (3) Do not reward good behavior.
         (4) Avoid double standards.
         (5) Avoid threats and intimidation.
         (6) Try to understand the purpose of misbehavior.
         (7) Establish a relationship based on trust and mutual respect.
         (8) Emphasize the positive.
E. Packaged discipline programs
   1. These programs are designed to give teachers and administrators comprehensive procedures to address various discipline issues.
   2. Several interesting trends emerged in an analysis of five discipline programs.
      a. Most embraced a behavioral perspective.
      b. None included any data regarding the program integrity or its effectiveness.
      c. The authors did not emphasize environmental or instructional prescriptions.

      d.   Generally, the programs did not include orientation and procedural guidelines for training individuals in the system.

      e.   None provided specific guidelines for how it would be implemented and maintained in a school-wide system of discipline.

  F.   Current Issues and Perspectives: Do discipline programs promote ethical behavior?

V.   Don't cause any problems yourself
  A.   Your initial reaction might be to place all responsibility for discipline problems on students, but some responsibility may rest with the teacher. Ask the following questions:
     1.   Are you unfair?
     2.   Are you inconsistent?
     3.   Are you boring?
     4.   Have you established routine?
     5.   Do you know your subject?
     6.   Can you control your temper?
     7.   Have you considered how you should best respond?
  B.   Case Notes: Melissa Williams' class
  C.   Teacher-parent collaboration
     1.   There is a considerable amount of research to support the successful outcomes that occur with students when parents are involved in academic and behavioral programs.
     2.   One illustration of how parent involvement can make a difference is a project by Sheridan, Kratochwill, and Elliott (1990). In the study, two forms of consultation with teachers were implemented for the purpose of establishing an intervention program for students demonstrating social withdrawal. There were direct benefits to the students in the intervention when it was implemented by the teacher, but the program had greater impact when both the teacher and the parent were involved.
     3.   Similar programs have been established by teachers who make contact with parents in the hope of improving behavior in school. Many of these programs involve home-based reinforcement delivered by the parent or programs that involve a combination of a school-home note system with back-up contingencies administered by the parent.
     4.   Guidelines for implementing a school-home note system include plan a parent-teacher conference, define the problem behaviors, set small goals, design the note, establish responsibilities for everyone involved, collect baseline information, establish the reward system and how consequences will be delivered, implement the program, and fade out the note system.
  D.   Case Notes: Melissa Williams' class
  E.   You are not alone
     1.   Ways to make the task of classroom management easier:
       a.   Read more about classroom management techniques.
       b.   Take courses that focus on classroom management techniques.
       c.   Use your time in practice teaching to sharpen your classroom management skills.
       d.   Participate in preservice and inservice experiences that focus on developing successful classroom management skills.
       e.   Discuss a student's problem with the parents when possible.
       f.   Consult other professionals who will be able to offer you advice on solving specific discipline problems and suggest ways to improve your classroom management tactics.
     2. Case Notes: Melissa Williams' class

VI.   Case reflections
VII.   Chapter highlights
VIII.   What do you think? questions
IX.   Key terms

KEY TERMS AND CONCEPTS

aversive control
behavior influence
behavior modification
behavior therapy
contingency contracting
control theory
desists
engaged time
group alertness
overcorrection

overlapping
proactive classroom management
QAIT
ripple effect
shaping
social discipline
token economy
transition smoothness
withitness

GUIDED REVIEW

1. _____ is the use of rules and procedures to maintain order so that learning may result. _____ the classroom is the first step in effective classroom management.

Classroom management, Organizing

2. A comprehensive classroom management program includes reactive responding to problems and proactive planning for productive behavior. This later strategy has been labeled _____.

proactive classroom management

3. Proactive classroom management is _____ rather than reactive, integrates methods that facilitate appropriate student _____ with procedures that promote _____, uses effective classroom _____ techniques, and emphasizes the _____ of classroom management.

preventive, behavior, achievement, instructional, group dimensions

4. _____ is not the time allotted to any class; it is the time during which students are actively involved in their work.

Engaged time

5. Although learning is served by an _____ function, order is served by a _____ function.

instructional, managerial

6.   Carroll stated that a learner will succeed in learning a task to the extent that the needed time is spent for that student to learn the task. Carroll uses two categories to analyze time. The first is determinants of time needed for learning. There are three important aspects in this category: _____, which refers to the amount of time any student will need to learn a task; ability to understand _____, which refers to the effects of general intelligence and verbal ability; and _____ of instruction, which refers to a teacher's ability to present appropriate material in an interesting manner. The second category includes time spent in learning. Carroll focused on two important features of this category: the time allowed for _____, which refers to the opportunity that individual schools allow for learning; and _____, which refers to the amount of time students are willing to spend in learning.

aptitude, instruction, quality, learning, perseverance

7.   Aptitude and ability to understand instruction reside _____ and teachers have _____ over them. _____ allowed for learning and quality of _____ are under the teachers' control. _____ reflects both student and classroom characteristics.

within the student, little control, Time, instruction, Perseverance

8.   When Carroll's model is linked to an effectively managed classroom, we can draw three conclusions: Learning rarely emerges from _____, a disorganized classroom substantially reduces _____, and the quality of instruction is tightly bound to the _____ of classroom management.

chaos, time for learning, efficiency

9.   Assuming that schools are different social contexts at preschool, elementary, and secondary levels, Minuchin and Shapiro (1983) stated that they are organized differently, children perceive them differently, and different aspects of social behavior appear to meet students' changing needs. At the _____ level, the school is more protective and caring than educational, with children interacting with one or two teachers, perhaps an equal number of aides, and several peers. The _____ becomes more of a true social unit, with more intense interactions between teacher and student and among peers. At the _____ level, the entire school, rather than a particular classroom, becomes the social context.

preschool, elementary school classroom, high school

10.   Management techniques change with _____ level, with management usually more of an issue during the _____ and _____ high school years.

age/grade, upper elementary, lower

11.   When managing classrooms, it is useful to know something about the kinds of students who will be exhibiting _____. Any one student may have _____ particular behavior problem.

problem behaviors, more than one

12.   Management is an essential function of all organizations for goal attainment, which involves three basic functions: _____, by which objectives and procedures are selected; _____, by which information is transferred; and _____, by which performance is matched to plans.

planning, communication, control

13. Jackson discusses three features of classroom life not typically mentioned: _____ (learning to live with others), _____ (experiencing the pain of failure and the joy of success), and _____ (with respect to the teacher's authority).

crowds, praise, power

14. Jackson (1968) stated that students' attitudes toward school are _____. He found considerable _____ feelings among basically satisfied students. Most students do not feel too _____ about their classroom experience, one way or the other.

complicated, negative, strongly

15. Berliner (1983) identified eleven activities that consistently appeared in K-6 classrooms: _____ circle, seatwork, _____ presentation, two-way _____, use of _____, silent _____, _____, games, _____, transitions, and housekeeping.

reading, one-way, presentation, media, reading, construction, play

16. Doyle estimated that a teacher's involvement during a class consists mainly of actual _____, _____ students, dealing with _____, and handling individual problems and _____ tasks.

instruction, organizing, deviant behavior, social

17. Laslett and Smith (1984) identified four "rules" that should help in classroom organization. _____ means that lessons should start on time and teachers should not be distracted by routines that should have been attended to earlier. _____ means consider what would be the ideal method for concluding the lesson and dismissing the class. _____ means focus on the content, manner, and organization. _____ means that classroom disruptions are infrequent when positive interactions characterize the teacher-student interactions.

Get them in, Get them out, Get on with it, Get on with them

18. Slavin proposed an instructional model focused on the alterable elements of Carroll's model. Called _____, the model encompasses the following four components: quality of instruction, appropriate levels of instruction, incentive, and time. Each element must be _____ if instruction is to be effective.

QAIT, adequate

19. Quality of instruction depends on both the _____ and the _____.

curriculum, lesson presentation

20. Appropriate levels of instruction implies that you know that your students are _____ to learn new material. Slavin identified the following methods as most common. _____ (elementary schools), in which students remain in heterogeneous classes most of the day but are grouped for certain subjects such as reading and mathematics, can be effective. _____ does not require permanent ability groups: Students regroup after each skill is taught.

ready, Ability groups, Group-based mastery learning

21. _____ provides for accommodation and can be effective if coupled with personalized contact with an instructor and some group work.

Individualized instruction

22. Slavin separated the results of work on grouping practices into two categories. In within-class groupings, the evidence for the value of mastery learning is _____, while analyses of _____ learning methods show consistent gains in student achievement if properly managed. _____ seem to have little effect on student achievement, although acceleration possibly may benefit some gifted students.

inconclusive, cooperative, Between-class groupings

23. _____ refers to the degree of student motivation.

Incentive

24. Time refers to sufficient time for _____ to occur.

learning

25. _____ involves calling on individual students who give answers publicly before the rest of the class, usually for a brief time. When using recitation, ask your question of the _____ and _____ for the answer.

Recitation, entire class, wait

26. Two types of seatwork commonly are used. During _____, all students are assigned independent work and the teacher moves around the room, monitoring each student's work. _____ occurs when the teacher is busy with another group and does not monitor each student's work. When using seatwork, spend _____ explaining, discussing, and practicing before your students begin work on their own; see that _____ immediately precedes the seatwork; make sure the exercises assigned _____ from your instruction; and _____ your students through the first few exercises.

supervised study, Independent work, sufficient time, practicing, flow directly, guide

27. Teachers designated as "good managers" made known their _____ on the first day of class but quite deliberately integrated them into a system, which they taught. These teachers had rules that were _____, _____, and _____. They gave examples of the _____ they would use, did not _____ their students with rules, and periodically _____ their students of the rules.

rules and procedures, explicit, concrete, functional, signals, overburden, reminded

28. The main difference between the elementary and secondary "good managers" was that the secondary school instructors spent _____ time teaching and rehearsing the rules and procedures.

less

29. To formulate meaningful rules for class activities, _____ each activity, determine _____ necessary for activities, determine which activities need a _____, make a set of rules for the selected activities, and formulate a set of _____.

define, social behaviors, list of rules, general activity rules

30. Some of the behaviors that characterize maladjustment are relatively _____ in childhood. Problem behaviors _____ at different ages, and a problem of one type may be replaced by another problem at a later age.

common, wax and wane

31. There seem to be clear _____ changes in aggression, and there are clear sex differences, with _____ generally being much more aggressive.

developmental, boys

32. In dealing with most cases of aggression, try to _____ before it starts, use _____, avoid the _____, watch for _____ effects, recognize your own _____, and evaluate your _____.

stop trouble, signal interference, tribal dance, hidden, aggression, classroom procedures

33. The _____ means that punishment is not confined to one student; its effects spread to other class members. _____ are a teacher's actions to stop misbehavior.

ripple effect, Desists

34. _____ means that teachers know and understand what is occurring in their classrooms.

Withitness

35. _____ is the ability to handle two events simultaneously.

Overlapping

36. _____ means the ease with which some teachers handle activity and movement in their classes.

Transition smoothness

37. A _____ occurs when a teacher's behavior slows an activity's movement. Kounin identified two kinds: _____, when a teacher spends excessive time beyond that needed for student understanding on a topic; and _____, when a teacher has individual students do something it would be better to have the group do.

slowdown, overdwelling, fragmentation

38. _____ refers to programming for "learning-related" variety. To minimize misbehavior, remember to _____ of your students while one is responding, keep on the _____, call on students _____, and keep interest high by _____ to a question.

Group alertness, watch all, move, randomly, leading up

39. Kounin observed teacher behaviors that he designated as _____, such as creating suspense before calling on a student, and consistently calling on different students. _____ had teachers concentrating on only one student, designating a student to answer before asking the question, or having youngsters recite in a predetermined sequence.

positive group alerting cues, Negative group alerting cues

40. Behaviorism's basic assumptions are that both adaptive and maladaptive behavior are _____, and that the best means for treating problems is to structure a student's classroom environment so that you can _____ desirable behavior.

learned, reinforce

41. _____ occurs whenever one person exercises some control over another. _____ is a deliberate attempt to apply certain principles derived from experimental research to enhance human functioning.

Behavior influence, Behavior modification

42. _____ applies to a one-to-one client-therapist relationship.

Behavior therapy

43. _____ is defined as any event following a response that increases the possibility of recurrence of that response.

Positive reinforcement

44. _____ have been used widely in managing groups. For example, students, patients, and other group members receive tokens when they exhibit desirable behavior, collect them, and when they attain an accepted number, exchange them for something pleasurable.

Token economies

45. _____ occurs when you first determine the successive steps in the desired behavior and teach them separately, reinforcing each until students master it. The students then move to the next phase, where the procedure is repeated. Finally, they acquire the total behavior by these progressive approximations.

Shaping

46. _____ happens when a teacher and student decide on a behavioral goal and on what the student will receive when he or she attains the goal.

Contingency contracting

47. _____ occurs when students maintain some undesirable behavior because the consequences are reinforcing. To eliminate the behavior, a teacher might apply an aversive stimulus.

Aversive control

48. Overcorrection combines both _____ and _____.

restitution, positive practice

49. _____ involves a systematic, performance-based, self-evaluative method of studying and changing socially important behavior. The _____ is emphasized as the cause of behavior.

Applied behavior analysis, environment

50. Behavior therapists say teachers should concentrate on student behavior and not on _____, because teachers are not trained to explore the special circumstances that influence behavior, and even if teachers can identify the cause of maladaptive behavior, they frequently can _____.

its causes, do little about it

51. The steps in any behavior management program are these: _____ the problem, define the _____, assess the _____, identify the _____ and contingency, begin the program, _____ the program when necessary, _____ the program, and ensure _____.

identify, target behavior, baseline rate, reinforcer, modify, fade out, generalization

52.   Dreikurs and colleagues have raised several provocative issues about discipline. Their basic premise states that behavior is _____ and that correcting goals is possible, while correcting deficiencies is fantasy.

purposive

53.   Dreikurs' social discipline model assumes that students are _____ and desire to belong to a social group, students are _____, all behavior is _____ and directed toward social goals, students see _____ as they perceive it to be, a student is a _____ who cannot be understood by isolated characteristics, and a student's misbehavior results from _____ on how to achieve social recognition.

social beings, decision makers, purposeful, reality, whole being, faulty reasoning

54.   Self-discipline comes from _____, while _____ comes from force, power, and fear.

freedom with responsibility, forced discipline

55.   Dreikur suggested that when managing students' behavior, teachers should not _____, scold, ask a student to _____, or _____ good behavior. Teachers should avoid double standards, _____, and _____. They should try to understand the _____ of misbehavior, establish a relationship based on _____ and mutual _____, and emphasize the _____.

nag, promise anything, reward, threats, intimidation, purpose, trust, respect, positive

56.   _____ are designed to give teachers and administrators comprehensive procedures to address various discipline issues. In an analysis of five discipline programs, most of the programs embraced a _____ perspective, none included any data regarding the program _____ or its _____, and environmental or instructional _____ were not emphasized. Generally, the programs did not include _____ for training individuals in the system or specific guidelines for how the program would be implemented and maintained in a school-wide system of discipline.

Packaged discipline programs, behavioral, integrity, effectiveness, prescriptions, orientation and procedural guidelines

57.   When analyzing discipline problems, teachers must consider whether they are being _____, _____, and _____, and whether they are controlling their _____. They also must consider whether they have established _____ and know their _____.

fair, consistent, interesting, tempers, routine, subjects

58.   There is a considerable amount of research to support the successful outcomes that occur with students when _____ are involved in academic and behavioral programs.

parents

59.   In one study with two forms of consultation with teachers, there were direct benefits to the students in the intervention when it was implemented by the _____, but the program had greater impact when both the _____ and the _____ were involved.

teacher, teacher, parent

60.   Guidelines for implementing a school-home note system include plan a parent-teacher _____, _____ the problem behaviors, set small _____, design the note, establish _____ for everyone involved, collect _____ information, establish the _____ and how _____ will be delivered, implement the program, and _____ the note system.

conference, define, goals, responsibilities, baseline, reward system, consequences, fade out

61.   To make the task of classroom management easier, _____ about classroom management techniques, take relevant _____, use your time in _____ to sharpen your classroom management skills, participate in preservice and inservice experiences that focus on developing successful _____, discuss a student's problem with the _____ when possible, and consult other _____ for help and advice.

read, courses, practice teaching, classroom management, parents, professionals

SUMMARIZE THE MAIN POINTS

This section of your study guide is designed to help you identify and understand the main points in each chapter. You've already reviewed the details using the Guided Review (above), and will consider the importance, relevance, and usefulness of the information in later sections. For now, focus on summarizing the main ideas.

For each major section in the chapter, summarize the main point and the evidence presented in the text to support and/or discuss it. If there are key terms presented in the section, define them. Some prompting questions are provided to help you structure your review.

The main sections of Chapter 10 are:

- Management concerns in the classroom
- Life in the classroom
- Managing the classroom
- Methods of control
- Don't cause any problems yourself

For each section, answer the following questions:

1. In two sentences or less, **summarize** what the **main point** of this section was.

2. Briefly **summarize the evidence** for and against each main point (a simple list of details they use to support each of their points is sufficient). If the authors discuss research studies to support the point, summarize the findings in one sentence. If the authors are presenting a logical argument to support the point (i.e., not citing data from research studies), briefly list the supporting points they made. Use the detailed chapter outline to help you identify the supporting points.

3. Briefly review the **definitions of any key terms** in each main section.

WHY SHOULD YOU CARE?

The purpose of this section of your study guide is to help you understand how and why the information in the chapter is relevant for you personally. You'll be asked to think more about the relevance and usefulness of the information in later sections of this study guide.

Look back at the work you did in summarizing the main points in the section above and answer the following questions:

1. For each section you summarized, why or how is the **main point** you identified **important to and/or relevant for teachers in general**? Try to limit your answer to only one or two sentences so you don't get bogged down in details, but focus on general usefulness.

2. Now think about the chapter as a whole. **Identify two specific events, contexts, or problems** for which the ideas presented in this chapter are relevant. Briefly discuss how they're relevant and how they could be useful.

3. Now **identify three concepts** from the chapter that **YOU find useful** in some way. Discuss how/why these concepts are useful, and specify how you will actually use them in your teaching and/or your daily life. (It's okay if there is some overlap between your answers for numbers 2 and 3.)

DISCUSSION QUESTIONS

The following "What do you think?" questions are printed in the text.

1. What age group would you like to teach? The developmental characteristics that affect teacher management techniques will influence your decision. Do you hold the desirable qualities of teacher management for your desired grade level?

2. Describe the four components of the QAIT model. Apply the model to a problem that you will face in the classroom.

3. What effective teacher behaviors did Kounin identify regarding maintaining classroom control? How could you use these procedures in your classroom?

4. Provide examples of how you could use the following behavioral techniques in the classroom: token economy, shaping, contingency contracting, aversive control, and overcorrection.

5. Suppose seventh-grader Dale is late for school almost every day. Identify steps of a behavior management program that you could use to solve this problem.

Additional discussion questions:

6. What are some of the major physical, cognitive, social, and personal-emotional developmental tasks of early childhood, middle childhood, and adolescence?

7. How should teachers go about setting rules and classroom procedures? List some guidelines that teachers can follow.

8. What effective teacher behaviors did Kounin identify regarding maintaining classroom control? List them and give an example of each.

9. List and explain the eight steps in a behavior management program.

10. What do "good" classroom managers do differently from "poorer" classroom managers?

11. List and explain five ways to deal with aggression in the classroom.

12. Define the following terms: token economy, shaping, contingency contracting, aversive control, and overcorrection.

13. List and define the three most common grouping practices. List one advantage and one disadvantage of each.

TAKE IT PERSONALLY!

The questions in this section are designed to help you personalize, integrate, and apply the information from the text. Personalization questions ask you to consider the personal relevance and usefulness of concepts, and consider how they might be useful in your life now and in the future. Integration questions ask you to pull together information from the text to evaluate it, summarize it or synthesize a recommendation on the basis of it, or express an opinion about it. Application questions ask you to think about how the concepts might be useful to address real problems or situations you may find yourself in. All three question types will help you consider the information at a deeper conceptual level, understand it more fully, and remember it.

1. Describe the Carroll model. How can you use this model to improve the way time is used in your current class? In your future classrooms?

2. Choose a grade level. Describe a proactive management system for a class at this level. What elements are involved, and how would the system be taught and maintained?

3. How can you increase the engaged time of your students? How could your engaged time be increased in this course?

4. Read the category of problem behaviors presented in table 10.3. Answer the questions presented in the text about these behaviors: What do you see as the core of each of these problems? How would this problem affect the rest of the class? How would you handle each of these problems? Would you need help in working with this student?

5. Choose a topic. Design a lesson using both recitation and seatwork, and using Laslett and Smith's four "rules."

6. Choose a grade level. What rules and classroom procedures do you think are important at this level? How will you involve students in rule setting, and how will you ensure that students understand and follow these rules and procedures?

7. Identify a real classroom problem you have witnessed or experienced. Analyze the problem, identifying its nature, its cause, and strategies for dealing with it. Is the problem related to management? If so, how will management change alleviate the problem? Is it necessary for you to be able to pinpoint the cause of the problem? Why or why not?

8. Identify a real classroom problem. Outline a behavior management program to address the problem. Then use Drieker's social discipline model to address the same problem. What are the roles of the teacher, student, and parents in each plan? Which do you prefer, and why?

9. Think of how you will manage your future classrooms. Evaluate whether you'll likely be causing problems yourself. Do any of your current teachers cause problems in their classrooms? If so, describe how this information from this chapter could be used to improve the situation.

CASE IN POINT...

Remember to use the cases from the text as contexts for identifying examples of concepts from the text and as contexts for solving educational problems. Also remember to use a consistent framework (like the DUPE model or the CASE NOTES in the text) to structure your "Mini-Case Report." Review the "Case in Point..." section of Chapter 1 in this study guide for more details.

SUGGESTED CONCEPTS TO IDENTIFY FOR CHAPTER 10

- aversive control
- behavior modification
- classroom activities
- contingency contracting
- control theory
- desists
- engaged time
- group alertness
- overcorrection
- overlapping
- proactive classroom management
- ripple effect
- setting classroom rules
- shaping
- social discipline
- transition smoothness
- withitness

In this section of the text, you were introduced to Melissa Williams, a first-year middle school teacher (Case #3). Review Case #3 in your text and use the following questions to prompt your thinking about this case.

1. How well does Melissa seem to manage her students? Would use of a different classroom management style be helpful?

2. How could Melissa become more proactive in her classroom management?

3. Is Melissa herself the cause of any of the management and behavior problems she is facing?

BIG IDEAS IN EDUCATIONAL PSYCHOLOGY

Thinking about the "big ideas" in educational psychology will help you organize and apply your newly acquired knowledge. Use the following steps to identify your own principles and strategies from the chapter and to relate them to the five main themes of the text (i.e., the "big ideas").

1. Review the TIPS from the text.

2. List some of the main concepts from the chapter. Use the work you did in prior sections of the study guide to help generate this list. Also look at the list of key terms from the chapter.

3. Select what you think are two or three of the most important concepts from your list.

4. For each concept you select, try to state it as a principle (use the TIPS format in the text and the example shown below as a guide for how to state principles).

5. Develop two or three specific teaching strategies that follow from each stated principle.

6. Relate your work to the five main themes from the text, identifying which theme(s) are relevant for each principle and strategy. This step will help you see how the information in each chapter contributes to improved teaching for each of these five critical aspects of instruction.

7. Think about and discuss with classmates how the principles and strategies you identify will help you improve your teaching for each theme you listed as relevant.

The five main themes from the text are:
ASSESSMENT, COMMUNICATION, LEARNING, MOTIVATION, AND TIME

Some example concepts, principles, and strategies for Chapter 10:

behavior modification	ripple effect
contingency contracting	setting classroom rules
control theory	shaping
engaged time	social discipline
proactive classroom management	

Principle   *Behavior modification is a tool for addressing behavior problems in the classroom. (ASSESSMENT, COMMUNICATION, LEARNING, MOTIVATION, TIME)*
Strategy   Clearly identify and define the problem behavior(s). Don't depend on just your intuitions about the problem and what's causing it—set up a simple system for observing the student(s) or class to identify what the problem is, when it is most likely to occur, and that precedes and/or follows the problem's occurrence. (ASSESSMENT)
Strategy   Tell the student(s) about the program details, including what behavior(s) are expected and the contingencies. Be consistent in following through with the contingencies. (COMMUNICATION, MOTIVATION, TIME)
Strategy   Reassess periodically, using the simple observational system you used earlier. (ASSESSMENT)

SUGGESTED READINGS

Emmer, E., Evertson, C., Sanford, J., Clements, B., & Worsham, M. (1984). *Classroom management for elementary teachers.* Englewood Cliffs, NJ: Prentice-Hall.

Emmer, E., Evertson, C., Sanford, J., Clements, B., & Worsham, M. (1994). *Classroom management for secondary teachers.* Boston: Allyn and Bacon.

Glasser, W. (1986). *Control theory in the classroom.* New York: Harper and Row.

Jackson, P. (1968). *Life in classrooms.* New York: Holt, Rinehart, and Winston.

Sulzer-Azaroff, B., & Mayer, G. R. (1991). *Behavior analysis for lasting change.* Fort Worth: Holt, Rinehart, and Winston.

PRACTICE TEST 1

1. Which of the following DOES NOT characterize proactive classroom management?
   a. It is preventive.
   b. It emphasizes group dimensions of classroom management.
   c. It integrates methods that facilitate appropriate student behavior with procedures that promote achievement.
   d. It uses contingency contracting.

2. John's teacher observed that he needed additional time working on his project in science class because it caused him some difficulty. The teacher was observing John's
   a. perseverance.
   b. time management.
   c. ability to understand instruction.
   d. aptitude.

3. At what grade level does the entire school become the social context?
   a. lower elementary school
   b. upper elementary school
   c. junior high school
   d. high school

4. A school psychologist observes a child who has repeated temper tantrums and is uncooperative in class. The child's parents say he is disobedient and has been destructive. The child may have
   a. conduct disorder.
   b. attention problems.
   c. socialized aggression.
   d. motor overactivity.

5. What is the basic unit of classroom organization?
   a. classroom activities
   b. classroom procedures
   c. developmental tasks
   d. classroom rules

6. Which "rule" of classroom organization focuses on the content, manner, and organization of the lesson itself?
   a. Get them in.
   b. Get them out.
   c. Get on with it.
   d. Get on with them.

7. In the QAIT model, quality of instruction depends on
   a. the ripple effect.
   b. influence techniques.
   c. contingency contracting.
   d. the curriculum and lesson presentation.

8. Review, introducing new material, checking assigned work, practice, and comprehension are the purposes of
   a. supervised study.
   b. independent work.
   c. recitation.
   d. group-based mastery learning.

9. Which of the following methods is effective in making known classroom rules and procedures?
   a. Explain all rules to students on the first day of class.
   b. Explain basic rules to students on the first day of class and then gradually introduce more as they are needed.
   c. Explain rules and procedures only as needed.
   d. None of the answers is correct.

10. A teacher notices that Sarah and Emma are passing notes in class. The teacher coughs and gives them her special "evil-eye" look. Sarah and Emma stop passing notes. This teacher has used
    a. slowdown.
    b. overlapping.
    c. signal interference.
    d. avoidance of the tribal dance.

11. Overdwelling and fragmentation are two kinds of
    a. slowdowns.
    b. overlapping.
    c. group alertness cues.
    d. transition smoothness.

12. Presentation or removal of an event after a response that decreases the frequency of the response defines
    a. reinforcement.
    b. punishment.
    c. extinction.
    d. discrimination training.

13. A school psychologist observes the number of disruptive behaviors a student engages in before implementing behavior

management. What is the psychologist assessing?
   a. the baseline rate
   b. interest boosting
   c. aversive control
   d. proximity control

14. In the ABC model of behavior modification, what does the "A" represent?
    a. actions
    b. antecedents
    c. attitude
    d. appropriateness

15. Dreikurs' social discipline model assumes that behavior is
    a. random.
    b. intermittent.
    c. purposeful.
    d. controlled.

16. Packaged discipline programs
    a. are designed to provide school professionals with comprehensive procedures for managing student behavior.
    b. are designed to provide instruction to both teachers and parents in discipline techniques.
    c. reduce discipline problems by fostering students' study skills.
    d. usually are based on a cognitive perspective.

17. The one classroom management issue that students probably react most strongly to is
    a. unfairness.
    b. disrespect.
    c. boredom.
    d. lack of an established routine.

PRACTICE TEST 2

1. Classroom management that is preventive rather than reactive is called
   a. proximity control.
   b. aversive control.
   c. proactive.
   d. shaping.

2. A teacher observes the amount of time her students are willing to spend in a class debate on politics. She is observing their
   a. perseverance.
   b. aptitude.
   c. time management skills.
   d. ability to understand instruction.

3. What aspect(s) of social behavior meet(s) preschoolers' needs?
   a. status
   b. socialization and communication
   c. friendship and belongingness
   d. esteem

4. A withdrawn youngster will not talk to others, and seems sad and confused, staring blankly. She most likely has
   a. attention problems.
   b. conduct disorder.
   c. anxious-depressed withdrawal.
   d. schizoid-unresponsive pathology.

5. About 51% of a teacher's involvement during a class consists of
   a. actual instruction.
   b. organizing students.
   c. dealing with deviant behavior.
   d. handling individual problems and social tasks.

6. Which "rule" of classroom organization is concerned with positive teacher-student interactions?
   a. Get them in.
   b. Get them out.
   c. Get on with it.
   d. Get on with them.

7. Which of the following methods does not require permanent ability groups, but rather allows students to regroup after each skill is taught?
   a. ability group
   b. group-based mastery learning
   c. individualized instruction
   d. supervised study

8. In Renee's class, there are several reading groups. While Renee is reading a poem, her teacher is working with another group and does not monitor Renee's work. Renee is engaged in
   a. interest boosting.
   b. supervised study.
   c. planful ignoring.
   d. independent work.

9. A teacher decides what she wants her students to accomplish during a classroom activity and how they should go about it. She is
   a. defining the class activity.
   b. determining the social behaviors necessary for activities.
   c. making a set of rules for the selected activity.
   d. determining if the activity needs a list of rules.

10. Aggressive behavior of 1-year-olds most likely is caused by
    a. frustration.
    b. hostility toward others.
    c. possession of an object.
    d. insecurity.

11. In a mathematics class, students are divided into several groups. While the teacher is instructing one group, two classmates in another group begin disrupting the class. The teacher tells them to stop talking and continue with their worksheet, while simultaneously instructing the group. What is this effective teacher behavior called?
    a. overlapping
    b. withitness
    c. transition smoothness
    d. group alertness

12. What is behavior therapy?
    a. an occurrence in which one person exercises some control over another
    b. a one-to-one client-therapist relationship
    c. a deliberate attempt to apply certain principles derived from experimental research to enhance human functioning
    d. None of the answers is correct.

13. A teacher and a student decide that the student will work toward achieving the goal of reading ten units. They agree that when the student reaches this goal, he will be rewarded by choosing a classroom activity. What does this agreement illustrate?
    a. aversive control
    b. overcorrection
    c. contingency contracting
    d. token economy

14. Tony was late for school. When he sat at his desk, his classmates teased him. Tony ignored them. What is the "C" in the ABC model for this example?
    a. Tony was late.
    b. Tony's classmates teased him.
    c. Tony sat at his desk.
    d. Tony ignored his classmates.

15. Which of the following is a suggestion of Dreikurs' for instilling mutual respect in the classroom?
    a. Ask a student to promise to uphold rules.
    b. Reward good behavior.
    c. Emphasize the positive.
    d. Scold students for inappropriate behavior.

16. According to the Chard, Smith, and Sugai (1992) review, packaged discipline programs
    a. have been shown to be very effective in reducing classroom discipline problems.
    b. usually include detailed and comprehensive guidelines for training people in the discipline system.
    c. usually are based on a behavioral perspective of learning.
    d. usually include detailed information on how to implement and maintain the program.

17. One of the best safeguards against discipline problems is to make sure students know what to do, when to do it, and where to do it. This refers to
    a. fairness in classroom procedures.
    b. respectfulness in classroom procedures.
    c. establishing a routine in classroom procedures.
    d. teacher knowledge of the content.

ANSWER KEY

Practice Test 1

1. ANSWER: D, Factual; OBJECTIVE: 1; PAGE: 378
2. ANSWER: D, Applied; OBJECTIVE: 2; PAGE: 379
3. ANSWER: D, Factual; OBJECTIVE: 3; PAGE: 380-381
4. ANSWER: A, Applied; OBJECTIVE: 3; PAGE: 383
5. ANSWER: A, Factual; OBJECTIVE: 3; PAGE: 385
6. ANSWER: C, Factual; OBJECTIVE: 4; PAGE: 386
7. ANSWER: D, Factual; OBJECTIVE: 3; PAGE: 387
8. ANSWER: C, Factual; OBJECTIVE: 3; PAGE: 389
9. ANSWER: B, Conceptual; OBJECTIVE: 4; PAGE: 391
10. ANSWER: C, Applied; OBJECTIVE: 5; PAGE: 395
11. ANSWER: A, Factual; OBJECTIVE: 5; PAGE: 399
12. ANSWER: B, Factual; OBJECTIVE: 5; PAGE: 402
13. ANSWER: A, Applied; OBJECTIVE: 5; PAGE: 403
14. ANSWER: B, Factual; OBJECTIVE: 5; PAGE: 404
15. ANSWER: C, Factual; OBJECTIVE: 5; PAGE: 404
16. ANSWER: A, Factual; OBJECTIVE: 5; PAGE: 406
17. ANSWER: A, Factual; OBJECTIVE: 5; PAGE: 411

Practice Test 2

1. ANSWER: C, Factual; OBJECTIVE: 1; PAGE: 378
2. ANSWER: A, Conceptual; OBJECTIVE: 2; PAGE: 379
3. ANSWER: B, Factual; OBJECTIVE: 3; PAGE: 380
4. ANSWER: D, Applied; OBJECTIVE: 3; PAGE: 383
5. ANSWER: A, Factual; OBJECTIVE: 3; PAGE: 386
6. ANSWER: D, Factual; OBJECTIVE: 4; PAGE: 387
7. ANSWER: B, Factual; OBJECTIVE: 3; PAGE: 388
8. ANSWER: D, Applied; OBJECTIVE: 3; PAGE: 390
9. ANSWER: B, Applied; OBJECTIVE: 4; PAGE: 392
10. ANSWER: C, Conceptual; OBJECTIVE: 4; PAGE: 395
11. ANSWER: A, Applied; OBJECTIVE: 5; PAGE: 398
12. ANSWER: B, Factual; OBJECTIVE: 5; PAGE: 400
13. ANSWER: C, Conceptual; OBJECTIVE: 5; PAGE: 401
14. ANSWER: D, Applied; OBJECTIVE: 5; PAGE: 404
15. ANSWER: C, Conceptual; OBJECTIVE: 5; PAGE: 406
16. ANSWER: C, Factual; OBJECTIVE: 5; PAGE: 410
17. ANSWER: C, Factual; OBJECTIVE: 5; PAGE: 411

Chapter 11

ASSESSMENT OF STUDENTS' LEARNING USING TEACHER-CONSTRUCTED METHODS

LEARNING OBJECTIVES

After completing this chapter, you should be able to

1. Define assessment, teacher-constructed tests, measurement, and grading, and name four assumptions of assessment.

2. Assess the role of testing in a class.

3. Define and discuss the importance of validity and reliability.

4. Plan for tests that serve specific purposes.

5. Evaluate how successfully students attained desired objectives.

6. Evaluate instructional effectiveness by the results of an assessment program.

7. Discuss the use of performance and portfolio assessment methods to guide instruction and document students' learning.

8. Discuss teachers' roles and responsibilities for student assessment.

CHAPTER HIGHLIGHTS

Assessment: Terminology, Assumptions, and Purposes

- Assessment refers to the process of gathering pertinent information to help make decisions about students.
- Testing is one means of obtaining evidence about a student's learning or behavior.
- Measurement means to place a number on a student's performance.
- Grading is the assignment of a symbol to a student's performance.
- Careful analysis of testing results aids educators in improving instruction, revising curricula, guiding students to realistic decisions, judging the appropriateness of subject matter, and assessing the conditions of learning.
- Educators today are sensitive to the needs of multicultural students in taking tests. In giving tests to these students, teachers should be aware of students' test-taking skills, such as language comprehension, that could influence the test results.
- All forms of assessment contain error, which implies that we must assess students frequently and with a variety of methods.
- Assessment techniques should help you to determine if your objectives have been met.
- If objectives remain unmet, then you must search for the cause and attempt to discover whether it lies in the student(s), the material, or your methods.
- The evidence provided by assessment enables teachers and administrators to present appropriate materials that serve the needs of their students.

Methods and Technical Issues in the Assessment of Students

- Assessing classroom performance typically entails four methods: pencil-and-paper tests, oral questions, performance tests, and standardized tests.
- Teacher-constructed tests usually consist of essay questions or multiple-choice items.
- There are two general categories of standardized tests: aptitude and achievement.
- A norm-referenced test enables you to compare a student with a representative group.
- A criterion-referenced test enables you to determine if a student has achieved competence at one level before moving on to a new, higher level of content.
- Validity refers to a test's meaningfulness, that is, its ability to measure what it is supposed to measure.
- Reliability refers to a test's consistency, which can be affected by an individual's characteristics and by the design of the test.

Planning a Teacher-Constructed Test

- Test items should reflect the objectives of the subject or unit.
- Think about the test, take time to construct relevant items. Avoid the habit of hastily throwing a few questions together. This isn't fair to you, given the amount of time you have spent teaching, and it certainly isn't fair to your students, who deserve a thoughtful assessment of their achievements.
- Next you must decide what kind of test best serves your purpose, essay or objective, both of which have strengths and weaknesses. Consider carefully which type of test is better suited to obtain the information needed to evaluate students' achievement.
- Writing essay questions is more difficult than it initially appears. Clarity, level, and a necessary degree of objectivity are required.
- Scoring the answers to essay questions requires a clear understanding of the major points in the answer. Try to ensure that you do not know which student's paper you're marking. Also read all answers to one question rather than reading all of a student's answers at one time.
- Objective tests sample a wide range of material, and if carefully formulated, can also assess comprehension as well as knowledge.
- Be sure your students are ready for an objective test: Are there any mechanics they should be familiar with? Do they have a strategy for taking the test? What clues does the item furnish? What are the rules for guessing?

Performance and Portfolio Assessment Methods

- Advances in behavioral assessment and the school restructuring movement have led to the development of two new assessment approaches: curriculum-based assessment and authentic assessment.
- Behavioral assessment emphasizes observational techniques to characterize a student's overt behavior or performance.
- Behavioral assessment assumes that a student's behavior may be merely a sample of his/her behavior. Therefore, repeated assessments over time and in different situations is typical of a behavioral approach to assessment.
- Authentic assessment is a collection of assessment techniques (i.e., portfolios, performances, exhibitions) and interpretative tools (i.e., profiles and self-ratings) that are designed to link teaching and assessment.
- Authentic assessment focuses on authentic classroom performances rather than typical multiple-choice or essay pencil-and-paper tests. The integration of real world skills is stressed.
- Authentic assessment places a heavy emphasis on teacher judgements of student performance.

- If you assign work, mark it and return it as soon as possible with appropriate remarks.
- When you grade students (that is, judging their work over a period of time), be sure that your grade represents their work, not their behavior.
- One of the main reasons for reporting, if not the main reason, is to strengthen the association between home and school.
- Test-wiseness refers to familiarity with test-taking procedures that students can learn that will help them perform better on most tests. These include finding out what will be covered and the type of item format to be used, being physically prepared to take the test to ensure optimal alertness, reading instructions carefully, outlining an answer before responding to essay questions, and reading all parts of multiple-choice items before selecting the best answer.
- Professional organizations that represent teachers and educational assessment specialists in this country have established standards for teacher competence in assessment. Such competencies are considered an essential part of effective instruction.

DETAILED CHAPTER OUTLINE

I. Assessment: Terminology, assumptions, and purposes
   A. Terms
      1. Assessment means the process of gathering information about a student's abilities or behavior for the purpose of making decisions about the student.
      2. Testing is a procedure through which evidence is obtained about a student's learning or behavior. It is a sample of behavior.
      3. To measure means to quantify or place a number on a student's performance.
      4. Grading is the assignment of a symbol to a student's performance. It is not assessment, but is often an interpretation of the assessment process.
   B. Assumptions
      1. Tests are samples of behavior and serve as aids to decision making. They do not reveal everything a student does or does not know.
      2. A primary reason to conduct an assessment is to improve instructional activities for a student.
      3. The person conducting the assessment is properly trained. A poor test or the misuse of a well-constructed test can significantly damage the teaching-learning process.
      4. All forms of assessment contain error.
   C. Uses and users of classroom assessment information
      1. Research suggests that teachers spend as much as one-third of their time involved in some type of assessment.
      2. The purpose of one's assessment must be clear, for it influences assessment activities and the interpretation of any results.
      3. Teachers have three main purposes for assessing students.
         a. to form specific decisions about a student or a group of students.
         b. to guide their own instructional planning and subsequent activities with students.
         c. to control student behavior.
      4. Teachers can also use assessment activities and results to inform students about teacher expectations.
      5. Teachers can use tests and the assessment of students to facilitate classroom management.
      6. Assessments provide teachers with valuable feedback about how successful they have been in achieving their instructional objectives, and help them plan future instruction.
      7. Students are also decision makers and use classroom assessment information to influence many of their decisions.

8. The assessment activities and decisions of teachers affect parents as well as students, and provide information about the school's performance.
   D. Multicultural students and testing
   1. Tests often frighten students or cause them anxiety, particularly for those students who find the classroom a different cultural experience.
   2. Help students be adequately prepared for and feel comfortable when taking tests by providing information about why the test is being given, when it is being given, what material will be tested, what kind of items will be used, and making sure that language is not a barrier.
   3. As more and more multicultural students take classroom tests, you want them to do well and not be limited by the mechanics of the test.
   E. Integrating learning and assessment
   1. Good tests are a valuable and powerful tool that not only assess student progress, but also provide a means of examining teaching efforts.
   2. Case Notes: Melissa Williams' class
   3. Testing assesses students' learning and also has a guidance function.
      a. The results will portray the specific type of remedial work required, or the kind of advanced material that would be most suitable; they also further diagnosis of learning difficulties.
      b. If a class has failed to attain objectives, teachers search for the cause. There are three immediate possibilities: the student, the difficulty of the material, or your methods.
   4. Testing helps teachers and administrators in their search for appropriate subject matter.
   5. Tests provide information about the conditions of learning.
   F. Teachers and testing
   1. Teachers frequently feel that testing is an added burden that interferes with real teaching and learning.
   2. If teachers avoid, or merely tolerate, testing, it is impossible to judge materials, objectives, and teaching effectiveness without resorting to guessing. Poorly made and questionably interpreted tests can cause lasting damage.
   3. Teachers are frequently careless in the construction of tests and interpretation of test results because
      a. they may be confident about their judgment of students.
      b. a good test is extremely difficult and time-consuming to construct.
      c. the dependability of the score may be questionable due to classroom conditions, home conditions, or specific events.

II. Methods and technical issues in the assessment of students
   A. Educators have used four primary methods for assessing students' classroom performances: paper-and-pencil tests, oral questions, performance tests, and standardized tests.
   B. Teacher-constructed tests
   1. The multiple-choice, pencil-and-paper test is the most frequently used kind of test; other types of tests, such as true/false, essay, and performance tests are also popular with teachers.
   2. What to test
      a. For teachers, the question of what to test implies that the test must measure what was taught.
      b. Tests will be reliable and valid to the same degree that test constructors are successful in relating test items to what was taught.
      c. The test itself may fail to assess a student's learning because it does not adequately sample the appropriate material.
      d. Teachers occasionally stress certain aspects of a subject and then test other sections, which is obviously unfair to students.
      e. Teachers should also be alert to other issues, such as the type of test items (essay vs. multiple choice) and the type of behavior required (problem solving, creativity, etc.).

f.   Determining what to measure and deciding how to measure it are genuine concerns for teachers. Avoid absolute standards, do not postpone constructing a test until the last minute, and be aware of the trivial and ambiguous.

3.   Validity
a.   Validity is the extent to which a test measures what it is supposed to measure.
b.   There are three major kinds of validity: content validity, criterion-related validity, and construct validity.
    (1)   A test has content validity (face validity) if it adequately samples behavior that has been the goal of instruction. It usually is established when subject-matter experts agree that the content covered is representative of the tested domain of knowledge.
    (2)   A test has criterion-related validity if its results parallel some other external criteria.
    (3)   A test has construct validity when the particular knowledge domain or behavior purported to be measured is actually measured.
c.   Case Notes: Melissa Williams' class
d.   Evidence for the validity of a test or assessment instrument takes two forms: how the test or assessment instrument "behaves" given the content covered, and the effects of using the test or assessment instrument.
e.   Airasian (1994) noted these key aspects of validity:
    (1)   Validity is concerned with the general question, "To what extent will this assessment information help me make an appropriate decision?"
    (2)   Validity refers to the decisions that are made from assessment information, not the assessment approach or test itself.
    (3)   Validity is a matter of degree.

4.   Reliability
a.   A test is reliable to the extent that a student's scores are nearly the same in repeated measurements.
b.   A valid test must be reliable, but a reliable test need not be valid. In other words, reliability is a necessary but not sufficient condition for validity.
c.   The reliability of a test is often operationalized by the computing of a correlation statistic between scores.
d.   Unless a test is reasonably consistent on different occasions or with different samples of the same behavior, we can have very little confidence in its results.
e.   Student characteristics affecting a test's reliability include guessing, test anxiety, and practice in answering items like those on the test.
f.   Characteristics of the test that can influence reliability include its length (longer tests are generally more reliable), the homogeneity or similarity of items (more homogeneous tests are usually more reliable), and the time needed to take the test (speeded tests are typically more reliable than unbound tests).
g.   Keep in mind the following points about reliability.
    (1)   Reliability refers to the stability or consistency of assessment information, not the appropriateness of the assessment information collected.
    (2)   Reliability is a matter of degree.
    (3)   Reliability is a necessary, but not sufficient, condition for validity.

III. Planning a teacher-constructed test
A.   Nitko (1983) summarized the importance of developing skill in test construction.
    1.   Developing a test helps you identify more precisely those behaviors important for students to learn.
    2.   As you develop a test, your perspective on both teacher and learning broadens.
    3.   As you gain skill in constructing tests, you usually become more critical of published testing material.
    4.   A carefully constructed test furnishes fair and objective information for the evaluation of students.
B.   Test planning and objectives

1. The first step in planning the test is to review the objectives of the unit or subject.
2. As you plan your test, be guided by several considerations:
   a. Know the purpose of your test.
   b. Know what type of item will best serve your purposes.
   c. Devote time to preparing relevant items.

C. Selecting test items
   1. Objective test items
      a. Supply items require students to give answers.
      b. Selection items require students to choose from among several alternatives. Selection items are more highly structured and restrict the types of responses students can make.
   2. Essay questions
      a. The extended response type furnishes students with complete freedom to make any kind of response they choose.
      b. The restricted response type asks for specific information, thus somewhat restricting students' responses.

D. Writing essay tests
   1. General considerations that may be helpful:
      a. Determine the level of thought you want the students to use.
      b. Phrase your questions so that they demand some novelty in students' responses.
      c. Write essay questions that clearly and unambiguously define the students' task.
      d. Be certain that your question specifies the behavior you want.
   2. TIPS on Assessment: Writing essay test questions
   3. Suggestions for scoring essay tests
      a. Decide what major points must be in an answer for full credit.
      b. Read all answers to one question; do not read all the answers on a single student's test.
      c. Do not associate a name with a test because your previous knowledge and feelings about a student could possibly bias your scoring.
      d. Remember that essays are a good means of obtaining more than factual material from students, but scoring can be unreliable unless you're careful.

E. Writing objective tests
   1. Objective tests' range of coverage in a relatively brief period and objectivity of their scoring make them an attractive tool, though you must consider the time and care that go into the construction of the items.
   2. One of the major criticisms is its apparent emphasis on fragmented, factual knowledge.
   3. Objective items fall into two general categories: supply type (free response, simple recall, completion) and selection type (alternative response, multiple-choice, matching).
   4. Suggestions for writing supply items
      a. Don't be fancy or ambiguous with the wording of items.
      b. Avoid writing verbatim from a text.
      c. Avoid giving clues.
   5. Suggestions for writing selection items
      a. In true/false items you are asking students to judge the correctness of a statement. Avoid opinion statements since students are unsure if it is your opinion.
      b. TIPS on Assessment: Writing true/false test items.
      c. The multiple choice item presents students with a question or incomplete statement and several possible responses, one of which is correct. It is thought to be the best of the objective items.
      d. TIPS on Assessment: Writing multiple-choice items
      e. The matching item usually utilizes two columns, each item in the first column to be matched with an item in the second.
      f. When writing matching items, remember to keep the instructions simple, clear, and precise; include more than the required number of responses; keep homogeneous material in both columns; and keep the list of responses fairly short.

F. Current Issues and Perspectives: Subjectivity in the assessment of students' achievement

IV. Performance and portfolio assessment methods
   A. These methods are curriculum-relevant and require students to apply their knowledge, emphasize observation techniques to characterize students' overt behavior, and are useful in linking assessment results to interventions.
      1. The learner must demonstrate she can apply her knowledge and skills by actually doing or creating something that is valued and purposeful.
      2. The performance is observed by judges (the teacher).
      3. The judges use preestablished criteria to score the performance, which in turn provides the learner with feedback. The criteria are based on a set of performance standards developed by experts in the field, and they increase the likelihood that the scores will be consistent.
      4. The scores are used to determine how well the learner does in comparison to others.
   B. Performance assessment is defined as testing methods that require students to create an answer or product that demonstrates their knowledge or skills, and can take many forms. It is seen as an important supplement to other types of assessment.
      1. Common features involve:
         a. students' construction rather than selection of a response
         b. direct observation of student behavior on tasks resembling those commonly required for functioning in the world outside of schools.
         c. illumination of students' learning and thinking processes along with their answers.
         d. the use of predetermined scoring criteria to score the performance and provide feedback.
   C. The term "performance" emphasizes a student's active generation of a response and highlights that the response is observable. "Authentic" refers to the nature of the task and context in which an assessment occurs.
      1. The authenticity dimension of assessment has become a very salient issue because most educators assume that the more realistic or authentic a task is, the more interesting and motivating it is to students, and it is important for educators espousing an outcomes-oriented approach to education to focus assessments on skills and conditions like those to which they wish to generalize their educational efforts.
   D. Portfolio assessment is an approach to documenting students' skills and competencies by assembling previously completed work samples and other permanent products produced by the student.
   E. The relationship among performance, authenticity, and the classroom curriculum in educational assessment tasks
      1. Three key dimensions that educators want to manipulate in their assessments of students' achievement are student response, nature of the task, and relevance to instruction.
      2. Assessment tasks can be characterized as varying in the degree to which they are performance in nature, authentic, and aligned with curriculum outcomes.
      3. What is new about current approaches to performance assessment is the use of this form of assessment in core curricular areas, the use of scoring criteria or rubrics, and the encouragement of students to conduct self-assessments.
      4. These new forms of performance assessment influence students' performances by selecting assessment tasks that are clearly aligned with what has been taught, sharing the scoring criteria for the assessment task with students prior to working on the task, providing students clear statement of standards and/or models of good performance, encouraging students to complete self-assessments of their performances, and interpreting students' performances by comparing them with consensus standards.
   F. Examples of classroom performance assessments and guidelines for use
      1. There are not published sets or kits of performance assessment tasks, nor should there be. The power of alternative assessments lies in their ability to be constructed by individual teachers so they correspond to specific instruction and provide information to learners and teachers about the learners' accomplishment of important competencies.
      2. Performance spelling was designed to increase students' use of spelling words to communicate and to advance their writing skills.

     a. This approach is individualized, encourages active parent involvement in selecting works and studying, has public scoring criteria, and has scoring and progress monitoring systems that students manage.

     b. The spelling tests focus on accuracy, usage, punctuation, and legibility of writing.

     c. Students progress from writing 10 separate sentences to writing a paragraph with 5 words they pick and another paragraph with 5 words selected by the teacher, to using all 10 words in a thematically focused paragraph.

     d. Students in this program on average correctly spell more words and more difficult words, and write much more on a weekly basis.

     e. This assessment is connected to the curriculum and is authentic, uses pre-established scoring criteria, and teachers can use the results to plan the next week's instructional focus.

     f. Analytic approach to scoring is where a skill area is broken down into parts.

  3. Oral classroom presentation

     a. The first step is to have a clear instructional purpose and vision of the desired outcomes of the assessment.

     b. Then you need to identify the subcomponents of the outcome and describe them in objective terms so they can be observed by two or more people.

     c. An evaluator must decide which dimensions to use to evaluate each component, such as frequency and quality.

     d. It is possible to break a task down into many specific behaviors, but there is a point at which the list becomes too long and cumbersome. A balance must be established between specificity and practicality of the scoring criteria.

G. General guidelines for developing performance criteria

  1. TIPS on Communication: Developing performance criteria

  2. Written communication scoring guide. This example covers five characteristics of writing and uses a 5-point quality scale with descriptions to anchor some of the rating points.

  3. Case Notes: Melissa Williams' class

H. Scoring, interpreting, and reporting results of performance assessments

  1. Stiggins (1994) said there are three critical issues in developing scoring criteria: the level of detail needed in assessment results, the manner in which results will be recorded, and who will do the observing and evaluating.

  2. Rating scales that characterize performances or products on a continuum of frequency or quality allow scorers to record their observations of a skill or dimension and at the same time indicate their judgement of the quality.

  3. A less informative approach is to use a checklist, which simply records whether the skill is observed and doesn't rate the quality of it.

  4. An anecdotal record involved writing some detailed descriptions of the performance or product. This allows for richer portraits of the achievement but requires more time. This is a good adjunct method to the others and should be encouraged when the purpose is to provide students feedback about a set of skills needed in subsequent learning activities.

  5. The interpretation of any performance or project involves subjective judgements.

  6. TIPS on Assessment: Enhancing the objectivity of results

  7. It is especially important to use other raters to monitor scoring so that bias or inaccurate judgements is discovered.

  8. Learners appear to benefit from scoring his or her own work because they internalize the characteristics of good work, gain a more personal sense of their strengths and weaknesses, and get an opportunity to review and reflect on their work.

I. Portfolio assessment

  1. A portfolio is a revealing collection of a student's work that a teacher and/or a student judges to be important evidence of the student's learning.

  2. A portfolio serves the two purposes of documentation and evaluation.

  3. TIPS on Assessment: Implementing a portfolio

4. Portfolios are flexible assessment tools that are being used in many subjects and with students of all ability levels. It encourages students to recognize their successes, seek opportunities to fill in gaps in skills, and connect what they do in school to the world of work.
5. Case Notes: Melissa Williams' class
6. Exhibitions are one of the most frequently discussed components of an authentic assessment system. They require integration of a broad range of competencies and ever-increasing student initiative and responsibility.
7. A profile is an evaluation scheme that provides meaningful feedback about academic and behavioral strengths and weaknesses. Meaningful profiles are developed by expert teachers and provide clearly articulated criteria that allow reliable judgements.
8. A final common component of a performance-oriented assessment system is student self-assessment. In an authentic assessment system, learning outcomes are made explicit, and students are encouraged to review and analyze their performances, portfolios, and other activities that provide feedback about their learning.

V. Using test data and teachers' roles and responsibilities for student assessment
   A. Marking
      1. Marking refers to your assessment of a test or an oral or written report.
      2. How to improve your marking technique:
         a. Be sure to mark any work you assign.
         b. Return work promptly or as soon as possible.
         c. If possible, personally comment on the test.
         d. Be specific in your comments.
         e. Mark the student's work, not the student.
         f. Avoid sarcasm and belittling remarks.
         g. Decide whether to have students repeat their work and correct errors.
      3. Page concluded that when secondary school teachers write truthful but encouraging remarks on student papers, they have a measurable and potent effect on students so that learning improves.
   B. Grading
      1. Grading refers to your evaluation of tests, reports, and essays.
      2. Grades represent competence in most secondary schools, while elementary school grades often represent some combination of competence, effort, and general attitude.
      3. The more variables included in a grade, the less effective it is as an indication of achievement. Grades will represent true achievement to the extent that they reflect objectives and satisfactory test construction.
   C. Reporting
      1. Reporting refers to the manner in which you communicate results to children and parents.
      2. Other than informing parents and students of progress, a reporting system should bring together parents and teachers so that they can combine efforts to encourage and help children.
      3. TIPS on Communication: Grading and reporting achievement
   D. Research on teachers' judgments of students' achievement
      1. Hoge and Coladarci (1994) reviewed research examining the match between teacher-based assessments of student achievement levels and objective measures of student learning.
      2. They found generally "high levels of agreement between teachers' judgmental measures and the standardized achievement test scores."
      3. Demaray and Elliott (1998) found that teachers were good (79% accurate) at predicting the achievement of students, both for students with high and below average ability.
      4. These studies indicate that teachers, in general, can provide valid performance judgements of their students.
   E. Helping students take tests
      1. Test-wiseness refers to teaching students how to take all kinds of tests.

2. Don't confuse test-wiseness with coaching, which means preparing students to take a specific test.
3. To help students improve their test-taking skills, suggest that they:
   a. Find out what the test is like beforehand.
   b. Decide how to study for the test, then study with intensity.
   c. Make sure they are physically prepared to take the test.
   d. When taking essay tests, before writing an answer, students should take time to formulate or outline their answer. After completing the answer, they should reread what they have written, making corrections in spelling and minor additions to the text.
   e. When taking multiple-choice tests, student should remember to read the instructions carefully and complete identifying information; read all the possible answers before selecting an answer; answer the items they are sure about first, then go back to those they are doubtful about; eliminate any response they know is wrong, then use clues like wording or contradictions to eliminate other false responses; and remember that true/false items with terms like "always" or "never" are usually false and those items that are lengthy are usually true.
F. Teachers' roles and responsibilities for student assessment
   1. Teachers should understand a variety of assessment tools, and should be capable of using several different techniques to describe students' learning and to communicate with students, parents, and others about such learning.
   2. Seven standards for teacher competence in student assessment are that teachers should be skilled in:
      a. choosing assessment methods.
      b. developing assessment methods.
      c. administering, scoring, and interpreting the results of assessments.
      d. using assessment results.
      e. developing valid pupil grading procedures.
      f. communicating assessment results.
      g. recognizing unethical, illegal, and otherwise inappropriate assessment methods and uses of assessment information.
   3. Assessment activities prior to instruction involve clarifying and articulating the performance outcomes expected, understanding students' motivations, creating connections between in and out of school interests and contexts, and planning instruction that is aligned with what will be tested.
   4. Assessment-related activities occurring during instruction involve monitoring student progress, identifying gains and difficulties, adjusting instruction, giving, specific praise and feedback, and judging the extent that students have attained instructional outcomes.
   5. Assessment-related activities occurring after instruction involve communicating strengths and weaknesses based on assessment results, recording and reporting assessment results, analyzing assessment information before and during instruction to understand student progress and inform instructional planning, and evaluating the effectiveness of instruction and curriculum materials.
   6. Case Notes: Melissa Williams' class

VI. A comparative summary of teacher-constructed assessment methods

VII. Case Reflections

VIII. Chapter Highlights

IX. What do you think? questions

X. Key terms

KEY TERMS

achievement tests
assessment
authentic/performance assessment
construct validity
content validity
criterion-referenced tests
criterion-related validity
essay test
evaluation
exhibitions
extended response
grading
marking

measurement
multiple-choice items
performance test
portfolio assessment
reliability
reporting
restricted response
standardized tests
supply items
teacher-constructed tests
test-wiseness
validity

GUIDED REVIEW

1. _____ is the process of gathering information about a student's abilities or behavior for the purpose of making decisions about the student.

Assessment

2. _____ is a procedure used to obtain evidence about a student's learning or behavior. It is a _____ of behavior.

Testing, sample

3. To _____ means to quantify or place a number on a student's performance.

measure

4. _____ is the assignment of a symbol to a student's performance.

Grading

5. Four important assumptions about testing are that tests are only _____ of behavior and do not reveal everything a student does or does not know; a primary reason to conduct an assessment is to improve _____; the person conducting the assessment is properly _____; and all forms of assessment contain _____.

samples, instructional activities, trained, error

6.   The purpose of one's assessment must be _____. Teachers assess students to make specific _____, to guide their instructional _____ and classroom activities, and to _____ student behavior. Assessments affect _____ as well as students, and provide information about the school's performance.

clear, decisions, planning, control, parents

7.   Tests often frighten students or cause them _____, particularly for those students who find the classroom a different _____. _____, reading, learning _____, and behavior all may be different and influence test performance.

anxiety, cultural experience, Language, expectations

8.   Help students be adequately prepared for and feel comfortable when taking tests by providing information about _____ the test is being given, _____ it is being given, what _____ will be tested, what _____ will be used, and making sure that _____ is not a barrier.

why, when, material, kind of items, language

9.   Testing has a _____ function. The results will portray the specific type of _____ work required or the kind of advanced material that would be most suitable, and also further diagnosis of _____.

guidance, remedial, learning difficulties

10.   Teachers are frequently _____ in the construction of tests and interpretation of test results because they may be confident about their _____ of students and because a good test is extremely _____ and _____ to construct.

careless, judgment, difficult, time-consuming

11.   Educators have used four primary methods for assessing students' classroom performances: _____ tests, _____ questions, _____ tests, and _____ tests.

paper-and-pencil, oral, performance, standardized

12.   _____ are tests that are administered under a uniform set of conditions. They are usually _____ published and based on a large _____ sample.

Standardized tests, commercially, normative

13.   Individuals who construct tests are challenged by _____ to assess, _____ to assess it, and whether they measure it in a _____ and _____ manner. The question of what to test implies that the test must measure _____. When determining what to measure and how to measure it, avoid _____ standards. Often teachers postpone constructing a test until the last moment; the test is then often _____ to sample student's attainment of objectives. Be aware of the trivial and _____ when constructing tests.

what, how, reliable, valid, what was taught, absolute, inadequate, ambiguous

14. _____ is the extent to which a test measures what it is supposed to measure. A test has _____ if it adequately samples behavior that has been the goal of instruction. A test has _____ if its results parallel some other, external, criteria. A test has _____ when the particular knowledge domain or behavior purported to be measured is actually measured.

Validity, content validity, criterion-related validity, construct validity

15. Evidence for the validity of a test or assessment instrument takes two forms: how the test or assessment instrument _____ given the content covered, and the _____ of using the test or assessment instrument.

"behaves", effects

16. Airasian (1994) noted that validity is concerned with the general question, "To what extent will this assessment information help me make an _____?" Validity refers to the _____ that are made from assessment information, not the assessment approach or test itself, and validity is a matter of _____.

appropriate decision, decisions, degree

17. A test is _____ to the extent that a student's scores are nearly the same in repeated measurements. The reliability of a test is often characterized by a _____ between scores.

reliable, correlation statistic

18. Some _____ always exists in any test. As _____ increase, the _____ of a test decreases.

error, errors in measurement, reliability

19. A valid test must be _____, but a reliable test need not be _____. In other words, reliability is a _____ condition for validity.

reliable, valid, necessary but not sufficient

20. Characteristics of the test that can influence _____ include its length, the homogeneity or similarity of items, and the time required to take the test. Student characteristics affecting a test's reliability include _____, test _____, and _____ in answering items like those on the test.

reliability, guessing, anxiety, practice

21. Keep in mind that reliability refers to the _____ or _____ of assessment information, not the appropriateness of the assessment information collected; that reliability is a matter of _____; and that reliability is a _____, but not sufficient, condition for validity.

stability, consistency, degree, necessary

22.   The first step in planning the test is to review the _____ of the unit or subject. When planning a test, teachers should know the _____ of the test, know what _____ will best serve the purpose, and devote _____ to preparing relevant items.

objectives, purpose, type of item, time

23.   Objective test items are usually separated into two classes: _____, which require students to give answers, and _____, which require students to choose from among several alternatives.

supply items, selection items

24.   Essay questions are divided into two types. The _____ type furnishes students with complete freedom to make any kind of response they choose. The _____ type asks for specific information, thus restricting students' responses somewhat.

extended response, restricted response

25.   When writing essay tests, determine the _____ desired, phrase questions so they demand _____ in the responses, write questions that clearly and unambiguously define the students' _____, and be certain that your question specifies the _____ you want.

level of thought, novelty, task, behavior

26.   When scoring essay tests, decide on the _____, read _____ to one question before going on to the next question, and do not associate a _____ with a test.

required major points, all answers, name

27.   Objective tests' _____ in a relatively brief period and the _____ of scoring make them an attractive tool. One of the major criticisms directed at the objective test is its apparent emphasis on _____, _____ knowledge.

range of coverage, objectivity, fragmented, factual

28.   When writing supply items, don't be _____ with the wording of items, avoid writing items that use the _____ of the text, and avoid giving _____.

fancy, exact wording, clues

29.   The _____ type of item restricts the student's answers to those that are presented in the item. Some examples are alternative response, _____, and _____.

selection, multiple-choice, matching

30. When writing true/false items, be sure the statement is _____ either true or false, avoid using _____ statements, avoid textbook phrasing, avoid terms such as *always* and *never,* and keep the length of true and false statements _____.

definitely, negative, about equal

31. The _____ item presents students with a question or incomplete statement and several possible responses, one of which is correct. When writing multiple-choice items, present the problem in a clear and definite manner, avoid _____, make all the distractors _____, make the correct answer clearly _____, vary the _____ of the correct answer, avoid using "all of the above" or "none of the above" responses, and avoid clues.

multiple-choice, negative statements, plausible, distinguishable, position

32. The _____ test usually utilizes two columns, such that each item in the first column is to be matched with an item in the second column. When writing these items, include _____ directions, use _____ possible responses than items to be matched, keep _____ material in both columns, keep the response list _____, and arrange the list of responses _____.

matching, clear, more, homogeneous, short, logically

33. Performance assessments involve students' _____ of responses; direct observation of students' behavior on tasks resembling those commonly required for functioning in the _____; illumination of students' learning and thinking _____ along with their answers; and use predetermined _____ to score the student's performance and provide feedback.

construction, world outside school, processes, scoring criteria

34. The term _____ emphasizes a student's active generation of a response and highlights the fact that the response is observable, either directly or indirectly, via a permanent product. The term _____ refers to the nature of the task and context in which an assessment occurs.

performance, authentic

35. The authenticity dimension of assessment has become a very salient issue because most educators assume that the more _____ or _____ a task is, the more interesting and _____ it is to students. It is important for educators espousing an outcomes-oriented approach to education to focus assessments on skills and conditions like those to which they wish to _____ their educational efforts.

realistic, authentic, motivating, generalize

36. Three key dimensions to manipulate in assessments of achievement are student _____, _____ of the task, and _____ to instruction. Assessment tasks can be characterized as varying in the level of _____ they require, their _____, and their alignment with _____.

response, nature, relevance, performance, authenticity, curriculum outcomes

37.   What is new about current approaches to performance assessment is its use in _____, the use of scoring _____, and the encouragement of students to conduct _____. These new forms of performance assessment influence students' performances by selecting assessment tasks that are _____ with what has been taught, sharing the _____ for the assessment task with students prior to working on the task, providing students clear statement of standards and/or _____ of good performance, encouraging students to complete self-assessments of their performances, and interpreting students' performances by comparing them with _____.

core curricular areas, rubrics, self-assessments, clearly aligned, scoring criteria, models, consensus standards

38.   The power of alternative assessments lies in their ability to be constructed by _____ so they correspond to _____ instruction and provide information to learners and teachers about the learners' _____ of important competencies.

individual teachers, specific, accomplishment

39.   Performance spelling was designed to increase students' use of spelling words to _____ and to advance their _____ skills. This approach is _____, encourages active _____ involvement in selecting words and studying, has public _____, and has a scoring and progress monitoring systems that _____ manage. This program uses an _____ approach to scoring where a skill area is broken down into parts.

communicate, writing, individualized, parent, scoring criteria, students, analytic

40.   The first step in developing a performance assessment is to have a clear instructional _____ and vision of the _____ of the assessment. Then you need to identify the _____ of the outcome and describe them in _____ terms so they can be observed by two or more people. An evaluator must decide on which _____ to use to evaluate each component, such as frequency and quality. A balance must be established between _____ and _____ of the scoring criteria.

purpose, desired outcomes, subcomponents, objective, dimensions, specificity, practicality

41.   Stiggins (1994) said there are three critical issues in developing scoring criteria: the level of _____ needed in assessment results; the manner in which results will be _____, and _____ the observing and evaluating.

detail, recorded, who will do

42.   _____ characterize performances or products on a continuum of frequency or quality, allow scorers to record their _____ of a skill or dimension, and at the same time indicate their judgement of the _____. A less informative approach is to use a _____, which simply records whether the skill is observed and doesn't rate the quality of it.

Rating scales, observations, quality, checklist

43.   An _____ involves writing some detailed descriptions of the performance or product. This allows for richer portraits of the achievement but requires more _____. This is a good _____ to the others, and

should be encouraged when the purpose is to provide students _____ about a set of skills that are needed in subsequent learning activities.

anecdotal record, time, adjunct method, feedback

44.   The interpretation of any performance or project involves _____.

subjective judgements

45.   It is especially important to use other raters to monitor scoring so that _____ or _____ are discovered. Learners appear to benefit from scoring their own work because they _____ the characteristics of good work, gain a more personal sense of their _____, and get an opportunity to review and _____ on their work.

bias, inaccurate judgements, internalize, strengths and weaknesses, reflect

46.   A _____ is a revealing collection of a student's work that a teacher and/or a student judges to be important evidence of the student's learning. It often serves two purposes: _____ and _____. It encourages students to recognize their _____, seek opportunities to fill in _____, and to _____ what they do in school to the work world.

portfolio, documentation, evaluation, successes, gaps in skills, connect

47.   _____ require integration of a broad range of competencies and ever-increasing student initiative and responsibility.

Exhibitions

48.   In an authentic assessment approach, evaluative schemes are referred to as _____ and provide clearly articulated criteria that allow for reliable judgments about the students' demonstrated levels of proficiency.

profiles

49.   In a performance-oriented assessment system, learning outcomes are made explicit, and students are encouraged to review and analyze their performances, exhibitions, portfolios, and other activities that provide feedback about their learning. This is called _____.

student self-assessment

50.   _____ is the assessment of a test or an oral or written report; _____ is the evaluation of tests, reports, and essays; _____ is the manner in which the results are communicated to children and parents.

Marking, grading, reporting

51.   To improve your marking technique, be sure to mark any work you assign, return work
_____, _____ comment on the work, be _____, mark the work but not the _____, avoid _____
and belittling remarks, and decide whether to have students repeat their work and _____.

as soon as possible, personally, specific, student, sarcasm, correct errors

52.   The more variables included in a grade, the _____ it is as an indication of achievement. Grades
will represent true achievement to the extent that they reflect _____ and satisfactory _____. Teachers
should decide on what a grade is to represent, then share their criteria with _____.

less effective, objectives, test construction, students

53.   Other than informing parents and students of _____, a reporting system should _____ parents
and teachers so that they can combine efforts to encourage and help children.

progress, bring together

54.   When reporting student progress, study the _____ thoroughly, know exactly what constitutes
your evaluation of a student, beware of _____ in any objective reporting, use any subjective evaluation
cautiously but _____, and use _____ wisely.

school's system, personal opinion, honestly, parent-teacher conferences

55.   Gronlund suggested that schools and teachers adopt _____ for their grading and reporting
practices and then _____. The system should be sufficiently detailed to be helpful in diagnosis, but not
_____. It should reflect those educational objectives that guide learning, grading, and reporting.

guidelines, follow these procedures, overly complicated

56.   Hoge and Coladarci found _____ levels of agreement between teachers' judgments and
standardized achievement test scores. This review indicates that teachers can provide _____ of
their students.

high, valid performance judgments

57.   _____ refers to the ability of students to take all kinds of tests. It is different from
_____, which means preparing students to take a specific test.

Test-wiseness, coaching

58.   To help students improve their test-taking skills, suggest that they find out _____
beforehand, decide _____ for the test, and adjust test-taking _____ to fit the types of items on
the test.

what the test is like, how to study, strategies

59.   Seven standards for teacher competence in student assessment that teachers should be skilled in are: _____ assessment methods; _____ assessment methods; administering, scoring, and _____ of assessments; _____ assessment results; developing valid pupil _____; _____ assessment results; and recognizing unethical, illegal, and otherwise _____ assessment methods and uses of assessment information.

choosing, developing, interpreting the results, using, grading procedures, communicating, inappropriate

SUMMARIZE THE MAIN POINTS

This section of your study guide is designed to help you identify and understand the main points in each chapter. You've already reviewed the details using the Guided Review (above), and will consider the importance, relevance, and usefulness of the information in later sections. For now, focus on summarizing the main ideas.

For each major section in the chapter, summarize the main point and the evidence presented in the text to support and/or discuss it. If there are key terms presented in the section, define them. Some prompting questions are provided to help you structure your review.

The main sections of Chapter 11 are:

- Assessment: Terminology, assumptions, and purposes
- Methods and technical issues in the assessment of students
- Planning a teacher-constructed test
- Performance and portfolio assessment methods
- Using test data and teachers' roles and responsibilities for student assessment
- A comparative summary of teacher-constructed assessment methods

For each section, answer the following questions:

1. In two sentences or less, **summarize** what the **main point** of this section was.

2. Briefly **summarize the evidence** for and against each main point (a simple list of details they use to support each of their points is sufficient). If the authors discuss research studies to support the point, summarize the findings in one sentence. If the authors are presenting a logical argument to support the point (i.e., not citing data from research studies), briefly list the supporting points they made. Use the detailed chapter outline to help you identify the supporting points.

3. Briefly review the **definitions of any key terms** in each main section.

WHY SHOULD YOU CARE?

The purpose of this section of your study guide is to help you understand how and why the information in the chapter is relevant for you personally. You'll be asked to think more about the relevance and usefulness of the information in later sections of this study guide.

Look back at the work you did in summarizing the main points in the section above and answer the following questions:

1. For each section you summarized, why or how is the **main point** you identified **important to and/or relevant for teachers in general**? Try to limit your answer to only one or two sentences so you don't get bogged down in details, but focus on general usefulness.

2. Now think about the chapter as a whole. **Identify two specific events, contexts, or problems** for which the ideas presented in this chapter are relevant. Briefly discuss how they're relevant and how they could be useful.

3. Now **identify three concepts** from the chapter that **YOU find useful** in some way. Discuss how/why these concepts are useful, and specify how you will actually use them in your teaching and/or your daily life. (It's okay if there is some overlap between your answers for numbers 2 and 3.)

DISCUSSION QUESTIONS

The following "What do you think?" questions are printed in the margins of the text.

1. From your perspective as a student, what are the most important reasons for giving a test?

2. If you were responsible for assessing a student with a primary language other than English who was from a different culture than your own, what adjustments in your assessment would you make?

3. Based on your own experience with tests, what are two sources of error in the scores you have received?

4. Given your understanding of reliability, what steps can teachers take to ensure that the reliability of their tests is high?

5. If you could select the method by which you would be assessed in this class, what would it be like?

Additional discussion questions:

6. What considerations should you address when testing a multicultural student?

7. Compare the advantages of standardized and informal classroom achievement tests.

8. Define and discuss the importance of reliability. List three things a teacher can do to increase the reliability of his/her classroom assessments.

9. Define and discuss the importance of validity. List and define three kinds of validity. What can teachers do to increase the validity of classroom assessments?

10. What are two common alternative assessment methods? Briefly describe each, then list their advantages and disadvantages relative to more traditional assessment methods.

11. How can teachers help students to improve their test-taking skills?

12. Distinguish between assessments, tests, and grades. What is the purpose of each, and what are the limitations of each?

13. Define performance assessment and describe when it would be appropriate.

14. Define portfolio assessment and describe when it would be appropriate.

15. Why should teachers be good at assessment?

TAKE IT PERSONALLY!

The questions in this section are designed to help you personalize, integrate, and apply the information from the text. Personalization questions ask you to consider the personal relevance and usefulness of concepts, and consider how they might be useful in your life now and in the future. Integration questions ask you to pull together information from the text to evaluate it, summarize it or synthesize a recommendation on the basis of it, or express an opinion about it. Application questions ask you to think about how the concepts might be useful to address real problems or situations you may find yourself in. All three question types will help you consider the information at a deeper conceptual level, understand it more fully, and remember it.

1. Develop an essay test for tenth-graders to assess their knowledge of a history unit. What are some factors you should consider in writing the essay test? Discuss why an essay test is appropriate for this material, and discuss how you will score the essays. What information and/or advice should you give students to help them prepare for this test?

2. Refer to the learning objectives for this chapter. Design an assessment/assessment item to address each objective. Use Bloom's taxonomy to identify the level of thinking required in each item.

3. Distinguish between marking, grading, and reporting, and discuss the importance of each. List two guidelines and/or things to keep in mind about each.

4. The chapter states that all forms of assessment contain error. What does this mean? Why is it important for teachers to know this, and what effect should it have on teachers' assessment and interpretation practices?

5. Choose a topic, chapter, or section of this course. Develop a plan for assessing students' knowledge and/or skills for the chosen material. As you develop your plan, reflect on the type of assessment to be used, item types selected, scoring criteria, the range of information/skills assessed, and how the information from the assessment will be used. Why have you made the choices you have made? What other choices could you have made, and how would these different choices affect the knowledge/skills assessed, or the conclusions drawn?

6. If a test is unreliable, what does this mean? What are the implications for teaching and learning?

7. If a test is invalid, what does this mean? What are the implications for teaching and learning?

8. Write three essay questions that are appropriate for this course. Evaluate them: Are they well- or poorly written? How do you know? Now develop a plan for how you will score the answers. What difficulties might you have in scoring them?

9. Write two objective supply items and two objective selection items that are appropriate for this course. Evaluate them: Are they well- or poorly written? How do you know? Discuss any difficulties you might have in scoring these items.

10. Have you ever participated in an authentic/performance assessment? What is your opinion of such assessments—do you think they provide a better or worse measure of your knowledge and skills? Why? How could the use of this assessment have been improved?

11. Develop an authentic/performance assessment for some element of this course. What are the issues you must consider and the choices you must make in developing this assessment? Evaluate the assessment. Will it provide a valid assessment of students' skills? How will you evaluate, interpret, and report the results of the assessment?

12. Think about a teacher who you feel has/had good assessment practices. Analyze his or her practices and discuss why they were effective. What was the effect of these practices on your learning and motivation as a student?

CASE IN POINT...

Remember to use the cases from the text as contexts for identifying examples of concepts from the text and as contexts for solving educational problems. Also remember to use a consistent framework (like the DUPE model or the CASE NOTES in the text) to structure your "Mini-Case Report." Review the "Case in Point..." section of Chapter 1 in this study guide for more details.

SUGGESTED CONCEPTS TO IDENTIFY FOR CHAPTER 11

   achievement tests
   authentic/performance assessment
   criterion-referenced tests
   essay test
   extended vs. restricted response
   grading
   knowledge
   marking
   matching items
   multiple-choice items
   portfolio assessment
   reliability
   reporting
   standardized tests
   student self-assessment
   test-wiseness
   true/false question
   validity

Review Case #3 about Melissa Williams in your text and use the following questions to prompt your thinking about this case.

1. Is Melissa's emphasis on more performance-based and authentic assessment appropriate, given her situation? How can she balance her assessment approaches with those of her colleagues?

2. Why is Melissa dissatisfied with the emphasis her colleagues place on standardized test results? What information could she provide them that might help them see the reasons for her point of view?

3. Evaluate how well Melissa is assessing her students. What could she do better?

BIG IDEAS IN EDUCATIONAL PSYCHOLOGY

Thinking about the "big ideas" in educational psychology will help you organize and apply your newly acquired knowledge. Use the following steps to identify your own principles and strategies from the chapter and to relate them to the five main themes of the text (i.e., the "big ideas").

1. Review the TIPS from the text.

2. List some of the main concepts from the chapter. Use the work you did in prior sections of the study guide to help generate this list. Also look at the list of key terms from the chapter.

3. Select what you think are two or three of the most important concepts from your list.

4. For each concept you select, try to state it as a principle (use the TIPS format in the text and the example shown below as a guide for how to state principles).

5. Develop two or three specific teaching strategies that follow from each stated principle.

6. Relate your work to the five main themes from the text, identifying which theme(s) are relevant for each principle and strategy. This step will help you see how the information in each chapter contributes to improved teaching for each of these five critical aspects of instruction.

7. Think about and discuss with classmates how the principles and strategies you identify will help you improve your teaching for each theme you listed as relevant.

The five main themes from the text are:
ASSESSMENT, COMMUNICATION, LEARNING, MOTIVATION, AND TIME

Some example concepts, principles, and strategies for Chapter 11:

authentic/performance assessment
criterion-referenced tests
essay test (extended vs. restricted response)
grading
marking
matching items
multiple-choice items
portfolio assessment

reliability
reporting
standardized tests
student self-assessment
test-wiseness
true/false question
validity

Principle   *Grades based on several different assessments, and different types of assessments, usually provide a more valid indication of student learning and skill. (ASSESSMENT, COMMUNICATION, LEARNING, MOTIVATION)*

Strategy   Give students several opportunities to show what they have learned by giving more than just one or two assessments during a given unit. (ASSESSMENT, LEARNING, MOTIVATION)

Strategy   Vary the type of assessment used (i.e., use a mix of objective test items, essays, performance assessments, etc.) to give students the opportunity to show what they have learned in different formats. (ASSESSMENT, COMMUNICATION, LEARNING, MOTIVATION)

SUGGESTED READINGS

Bloom, B., Madaus, G., & Hastings, T. J. (1981). *Evaluation to improve learning.* New York: McGraw-Hill.

Dobbin, J. (1984). *How to take a test: Doing your best.* Princeton, NJ: Educational Testing Service.

Green, B. (1981). A primer of testing. *American Psychologist, 36,* 1001-1011.

Gronlund, N. (1985). *Measurement and evaluation in learning.* New York: Macmillan.

Herman, J. L., Aschbacher, P. R., & Winters, L. (1992). *A practical guide to alternative assessment.* Alexandria, VA: Association for Supervision and Curriculum Development.

Wiggins, G. (1998). *Educative assessment: Designing assessments to inform and improve student performance.* Jossey-Bass: San Francisco.

Witt, J. C., Elliott, S. N., Daly III, E. J., Gresham, F. M., & Kramer, J. J. (1998). *Assessment of at-risk and special needs children* (2nd ed.). Boston: McGraw-Hill.

PRACTICE TEST 1

1. What is the primary reason to conduct an assessment?
   a. to gather information for educational decision making
   b. to make decisions to improve curriculum
   c. to improve students' skills and achievement
   d. to improve teaching standards

2. Multicultural students' performance on tests may be affected by
   a. the language of the test.
   b. parental pressure.
   c. the types of items used on the test.
   d. All the answers are correct.

3. Which of the following is NOT one of the three possibilities to explain why a student has failed to attain objectives?
   a. the classroom environment
   b. the difficulty of the material
   c. the student
   d. the teaching method

4. While the quality of test items is _____ on standardized achievement tests, the quality of items is _____ on informal achievement tests.
   a. high; low
   b. low; high
   c. high; unknown
   d. low; unknown

5. Many teachers are careless in their test construction and interpretation because
   a. they believe that testing is not informative.
   b. they are confident about their ability to judge students.
   c. they have little confidence in the reliability and validity of most tests.
   d. they believe that by giving large numbers of tests, any error in their tests will be minimized.

6. If a test claims to measure extroversion and its results match judgments of people identified as extroverted, then the test is said to have
   a. reliability.
   b. content validity.
   c. construct validity.
   d. criterion-related validity.

7. What is the first step in test planning?
   a. Decide on the format of the test.
   b. Decide on the time allowed for the test.
   c. Review test methodology.
   d. Review objectives of the unit.

8. State what type of essay test item the following is: "How would you evaluate the characters in the novel?"
   a. supply item
   b. selection item
   c. extended response
   d. restricted response

9. Which of the following is a disadvantage of the essay test?
   a. It is difficult to construct.
   b. It is difficult to administer.
   c. Its reliability is questionable.
   d. All of the answers are correct.

10. Which of the following is suggested for writing supply items?
    a. Try to avoid giving obvious clues.
    b. Paraphrase, rather than directly copy, text material.
    c. Use precise phrasing.
    d. All of the answers are correct.

11. A teacher's evaluation of tests, reports, and essays is called
    a. marking.
    b. grading.
    c. reporting.
    d. assessing.

12. Why is the authenticity of an assessment important?
    a. Because the more authentic the assessment, the more interesting it will be to students.
    b. Because the more authentic the assessment, the more valid and reliable it will be.
    c. Because the more authentic the assessment, the less biased it will be.
    d. All of the answers are correct.

13. Hoge and Coladarci found _____ between teachers' judgmental measures and standardized achievement test scores.
    a. no agreement
    b. low levels of agreement
    c. moderate levels of agreement
    d. high levels of agreement

14. What is test-wiseness?
    a. Preparing students to take a specific test.
    b. Helping students to take all kinds of tests.
    c. Teaching students how to enhance study skills.
    d. Teaching students how to speed-test.

15. Which of the following must be considered when developing scoring criteria for performance assessments?
    a. The principle that simpler, less detailed scoring criteria are better.
    b. The need to always have scorers augment numerical ratings with an anecdotal record.
    c. The need to have and use good professional judgement in all aspects of criterion development and use.
    d. The fact that scoring criteria schemes are inherently subjective and therefore cannot yield reliable information about student knowledge and skills.

PRACTICE TEST 2

1. The process of gathering information about a student's abilities or behavior for the purpose of making decisions about the student is called
   a. assessing.
   b. grading.
   c. measuring.
   d. testing.

2. Ms. McArta has in her classroom students from several different cultural backgrounds. When testing these students, it is important for Ms. McArta to
   a. remember that these students typically are not interested in academic success.
   b. be careful not to provide too much information about the test ahead of time so that students will not become overly anxious.
   c. take time to explain the terms in the directions of the test.
   d. make certain she does not give these students any more time than students from the majority culture.

3. If a class as a whole has failed to attain lesson objectives, the teacher needs to examine three immediate possibilities. Which of the following is NOT one of the possible reasons?
   a. the student
   b. the difficulty of the material
   c. the classroom environment
   d. the teaching method

4. What is the reliability of standardized achievement tests?
   a. unknown
   b. .50
   c. .65
   d. .90

5. Reliability refers to which of the following?
   a. The appropriate use of the assessment information.
   b. The standardization of the assessment procedures.
   c. The degree to which an assessment measures what it is supposed to measure.
   d. The consistency of the assessment information.

6. If a student scores high on a test that measures mathematical ability, and likewise does well in mathematics class, the test has demonstrated
   a. reliability.
   b. content validity.
   c. construct validity.
   d. criterion-related validity.

7. Making hasty judgments based on inadequate data and testing with no definite purpose in mind are two major mistakes of which phase of test development?
   a. planning the test
   b. preparing the students for the test
   c. writing the test
   d. evaluating the test

8. State what type of essay test item the following is: "List the protagonists in each novel discussed in this course."
   a. supply item
   b. selection item
   c. extended response
   d. restricted response

9. Which of the following is an advantage of the essay test?
   a. It has high validity.
   b. It emphasizes wholes rather than parts.
   c. It is easy to score answers.
   d. All of the answers are correct.

10. Which of the following is NOT recommended to improve the scoring of essays?
   a. Identify ahead of time the ideas that must be included in the answer.
   b. Have students score their own answers to foster self-monitoring.
   c. Read all answers to a single question before moving on to the next question.
   d. Identify the answers by an identification number rather than by name.

11. Reports can be used to
   a. inform parents of student progress.
   b. inform students of their progress.
   c. bring teachers and parents together.
   d. All the answers are correct.

12. Why is it a good idea to use more than one rater when scoring a performance assessment?
   a. It ensures consistent bias in the scoring.
   b. It helps teachers justify why a low score is given.
   c. It ensures accurate use of the scoring criteria.
   d. It gives students an opportunity to revise their work.

13. What do the authors of the text conclude about Hoge and Coladarci's research on teachers' judgments of their students' academic performance?
   a. Teachers provide valid performance judgments of male students, but not of female students.
   b. Teachers provide valid performance judgments of female students, but not of male students.
   c. Teachers cannot provide valid performance judgments of their students.
   d. Teachers can provide valid performance judgments of their students.

14. Suppose a student is preparing to take the Scholastic Aptitude Test. How can a teacher help?
    a. by timing the student on various tests
    b. by explaining the importance of the test outcome to the student
    c. by explaining what the test is like beforehand
    d. by offering high expectations of his or her performance on the test

15. Which of the following best describes a portfolio?
    a. A portfolio serves to document a student's work.
    b. A portfolio can be used to help both teachers and students evaluate the student's work.
    c. A portfolio includes work selected to show evidence of what a student has learned.
    d. All of the above are true of portfolios.
    e. None of the above are true of portfolios.

ANSWER KEY

Practice Test 1

1.   ANSWER: A, Factual; OBJECTIVE: 1; PAGE: 420
2.   ANSWER: D, Factual; OBJECTIVE: 2; PAGE: 424
3.   ANSWER: A, Factual; OBJECTIVE: 6; PAGE: 425
4.   ANSWER: C, Factual; OBJECTIVE: 4; PAGE: 429
5.   ANSWER: B, Factual; OBJECTIVE: 3; PAGE: 427
6.   ANSWER: C, Conceptual; OBJECTIVE: 3; PAGE: 430
7.   ANSWER: D, Factual; OBJECTIVE: 4; PAGE: 434
8.   ANSWER: C, Conceptual; OBJECTIVE: 5; PAGE: 434
9.   ANSWER: C, Conceptual; OBJECTIVE: 5; PAGE: 436
10.   ANSWER: D, Factual; OBJECTIVE: 5; PAGE: 438-439
11.   ANSWER: B, Factual; OBJECTIVE: 8; PAGE: 460
12.   ANSWER: A, Factual; OBJECTIVE: 7; PAGE: 443
13.   ANSWER: D, Factual; OBJECTIVE: 8; PAGE: 464
14.   ANSWER: B, Factual; OBJECTIVE: 8; PAGE: 466
15.   ANSWER: C, Conceptual; OBJECTIVE: 7; PAGE: 454-455

Practice Test 2

1.   ANSWER: A, Factual; OBJECTIVE: 1; PAGE: 420
2.   ANSWER: C, Applied; OBJECTIVE: 2; PAGE: 425
3.   ANSWER: C, Factual; OBJECTIVE: 6; PAGE: 425
4.   ANSWER: D, Factual; OBJECTIVE: 3; PAGE: 429
5.   ANSWER: D, Factual; OBJECTIVE: 3; PAGE: 433
6.   ANSWER: D, Conceptual; OBJECTIVE: 3; PAGE: 430
7.   ANSWER: A, Factual; OBJECTIVE: 4; PAGE: 434
8.   ANSWER: D, Conceptual; OBJECTIVE: 5; PAGE: 434
9.   ANSWER: B, Factual; OBJECTIVE: 5; PAGE: 436
10.   ANSWER: B, Factual; OBJECTIVE: 5; PAGE: 438
11.   ANSWER: D, Factual; OBJECTIVE: 8; PAGE: 463
12.   ANSWER: C, Factual; OBJECTIVE: 7; PAGE: 455
13.   ANSWER: D, Factual; OBJECTIVE: 8; PAGE: 464
14.   ANSWER: C, Applied; OBJECTIVE: 8; PAGE: 466
15.   ANSWER: D, Factual; OBJECTIVE: 7; PAGE: 456

Chapter 12 STANDARDIZED TESTS AND BEHAVIOR RATING SCALES

LEARNING OBJECTIVES

After completing this chapter, you should be able to

1. Distinguish between the purposes of standardized tests and teacher-made tests.

2. Understand the content and format features of popular achievement, aptitude, and intelligence tests.

3. Discuss the interpretation and use of intelligence tests.

4. Describe the uses of behavior rating scales and state criteria for interpreting them.
5. Understand basic statistical techniques to interpret test results.

6. Interpret standardized test scores.

7. Understand the limitations of standardized testing toward the improvement of teaching and learning.

8. Make informed decisions concerning current testing issues that affect all students.

CHAPTER HIGHLIGHTS

A School's Testing Program

*   The use of standardized tests is integral to the educational purposes of the entire school system and should serve the needs of its students at all levels.
*   A well-designed standardized testing program serves three purposes: instructional, guidance, and administrative.
*   The value of standardized tests lies in their consistency or sameness, which provides a means of comparing students.
*   The norms that accompany standardized tests enable teachers, counselors, and other educators to interpret test scores by comparing them to the scores of other students, taken from a comparison sample.
*   A norm-referenced test enables the teacher to compare a student with a representative group of students who have already taken the test.
*   A criterion-referenced test enables the teacher to determine whether a student has achieved competence at one level of knowledge or skills before moving on to the next higher level of content.

Standardized Tests

- Standardized achievement tests are designed to assess the knowledge and skills taught by schools. The value of these tests is in their assessment of the development of individual learners at different ages and in different subjects.
- Standardized aptitude tests are used to predict what students can learn; they provide assessments of performance based on learning abilities.
- Although a clear definition of intelligence has remained elusive, attempts to measure it have produced some of psychology's most colorful, damaging, and useful insights into human behavior.
- Three important issues concerning the use of intelligence tests involve the stability of IQ test results, bias results for different ethnic groups, and the instructional validity or usefulness of the results. In general, researchers have found that well-constructed IQ tests yield stable results for children more than 7 years old, are generally relatively free from bias, and have limited instructional utility for educators. They are most useful in the process of classifying a student as mentally retarded or learning disabled, given current classification criteria.
- In spite of the problems that have been encountered in attempts to measure intelligence, several reasonable suggestions have been made as to fruitful uses of the results of intelligence testing. Properly interpreted, these scores can help teachers to improve their instruction; they are a good guide for initial efforts at grouping students; several of these tests can be used to identify students' needs; teachers can use test results to monitor school progress—to determine if these students are doing as well as possible, given what the tests indicate about their abilities.
- Behavior rating scales are commonly used to identify potential problem behaviors in students referred for special services. Teachers and parents are frequently asked to complete scales concerning a wide range of intrapersonal and interpersonal behaviors exhibited by children in situations at school and in the community.
- A behavior rating scale provides information about the frequency of potential problem behaviors and often compares the ratings of a student to those of a group of students of the same age and sex. Thus, some behavior rating scales are used to classify children's problems.

Interpreting Standardized Test Scores

- To utilize the results of standardized testing as fully as possible, the teacher must have some means of interpreting students' scores. Several meaningful techniques are available that can help to analyze scores and organize data so that the results of testing can be applied to classroom work. These include standard scores, percentile ranks, and knowledge of the normal distribution.

Using Standardized Tests

- The possible uses of standardized tests include student certification, special education placement, the testing of teachers, assessing the success of a school, and instructional assistance.
- Clear standards as guides to the best practices in test construction have been proposed for test developers.

DETAILED CHAPTER OUTLINE

I. A school's testing program
   A. Case Notes: Melissa Williams' class
   B. The selection, administration, and interpretation of standardized tests should be linked closely to the educational objectives of a particular school system.
   C. Purposes of a testing program
      1. Instructional. Achievement tests administered in the fall help teachers to commence instruction at a point where students can logically expect both challenge and success.
      2. Guidance. The results of some testing programs enable instructors to adapt the curriculum more efficiently to the student, and to aid students in choosing specialized courses.
      3. Administrative. Administrators are often interested in how groups of students are performing. Good tests can help them to make more suitable decisions about curriculum, placement, and how their students compare to others in the region or nation on the basis of substantial data.
   D. TIPS on assessment: The primary purpose of assessment is to improve student learning.

II. Standardized tests
   A. Standardized tests are commercially prepared and sample behavior under uniform procedures.
      1. There are two general categories.
         a. *Aptitude* tests are intended to assess students' general or specific abilities.
         b. *Achievement* tests measure accomplishment in such subjects as reading, arithmetic, language, and science.
      2. Standardization means the degree to which the observational procedures, administrative procedures, equipment and materials, and scoring rules have been fixed so that exactly the same testing procedure occurs at different times and in different places.
      3. A norm-referenced test (NRT) allows you to compare a given student with a representative group (referred to as a norm group) of students. There are several advantages of a norm-referenced test.
         a. It can assess a broad range of knowledge and understanding.
         b. It reflects common goals for learning.
         c. It can assess achievement at all levels of attainment.
         d. It can sample achievement more widely.
         e. It reflects the belief that achievement is more or less, not all or nothing.
         f. It often furnishes a single score that summarizes a student's general level of achievement.
         g. It provides summative evaluation information.
      4. Criterion-referenced tests (CRTs) provide a score informing teachers of the extent to which students have achieved predetermined objectives. Criterion-referenced tests are increasingly popular because of renewed emphasis on individualized instruction, behavior objectives, and mastery learning.
   B. Developing a standardized test
      1. Standardization offers consistency in administration and format of a test. If students' scores are to be compared, the test and the testing circumstances must remain uniform at all test administrations.
      2. The construction of the standardized test is an involved and complicated process. A standardized test is written by both subject-matter and measurement specialists. Considerable care is taken to ensure comprehensive coverage of a subject and to avoid ambiguity in the writing of the individual items. The test is initially given an experimental trial with representative groups to ascertain its suitability, reliability, and validity. Revisions are then made that result in a highly accurate instrument.
      3. Probably the most desirable aspect of standardized tests is the norms supplied with them. Norms provide the normal range of scores for a given population.

C. Current Issues and Perspectives: High standards for all students, and testing accommodations for students with disabilities.
D. Standardized achievement tests
1. Achievement tests attempt to assess the knowledge and skills taught by the schools.
2. A standardized achievement test has certain distinctive features, including a fixed set of test items designed to measure a clearly defined area of achievement, specific directions for administering and scoring the test, and norms based on representative groups of individuals like those for whom the test was designed.
3. The objective of achievement tests is to discover how much an individual has learned from educational experiences.
4. Desirable uses of standardized achievement tests
   a. They assess the accomplishment of learning objectives by individual learners.
   b. They aid both in the academic guidance of students and in planning of curriculum changes.
   c. They help in decisions about promotion and admission.
   d. They can stimulate an analysis of the effectiveness of the curriculum, materials, and instruction.
5. Two types of standardized achievement tests are currently popular: multilevel survey batteries that assess separate curricular topics over a wide range of grades and are group administered, and those designed to measure specific subjects, such as reading or mathematics, for an individual learner.
6. The Terra Nova Assessment Series is a series of achievement tests designed to assess K - 12th grade students' knowledge in reading/language arts, mathematics, science, and social studies. Each area is broken into subdomains, each of which has multiple test items. The items measure knowledge and skills in the subject areas and provide evidence about thinking skills and problem-solving processes.
7. Case Notes: Melissa Williams' class
E. Standardized aptitude tests
1. Aptitude tests are used to predict what students can learn. They do not measure innate capacity or learning potential directly, but measure performance based on learning abilities.
2. An aptitude test predicts an individual's performance in a certain task or in a particular job by sampling the cumulative effect of many experiences in daily living, including specific educational experiences.
3. TIPS on motivation and assessment: Creating fair assessments for all students
F. Intelligence, IQ tests, and fundamental assessment issues
1. Intelligence tests have been one of the most frequently used tests to understand children's cognitive functioning and are administered to nearly 20% of all school children each year. There is a wide range of opinion among educators and psychologists about the value of intelligence testing.
2. The Wechsler Intelligence Scale for Children III: An example of an aptitude test
   a. The WISC-III is individually administered and requires 60 to 90 minutes, and is designed for children from 6 to 17 years of age. It aims to provide a global measure of intelligence that taps "many different mental abilities, which all together reflect a child's general intellectual ability." It has 13 subtests, 6 in a Verbal Scale and 7 in a Performance Scale. Each subtest has specific rules about where to begin and end, depending on the age or assumed ability of the child.
   b. The WISC-III was standardized on 2,200 children selected to be representative of the U.S. population based on data gathered in 1988 by the U. S. Bureau of the Census.
   c. Scaled subtest scores are added and converted into deviation IQs (standard scores) for the Verbal, Performance, and Full Scales. Each has a mean of 100 and a standard deviation of 15. Verbal Comprehension, Perceptual Organization, Freedom from Distractibility, and Processing Speed scores can also be calculated.
   d. Much has been learned about the nature of cognitive abilities in the last 30 years, and yet the design and purpose of the WISC-III has changed little.

3. Stability of the IQ
   a. Misinterpretations of research on the stability of performances on intelligence tests has fed the misconception that infants are born with a certain amount of "intelligence," which does not change as the child grows.
   b. Most research has suggested that IQ tests tend to yield scores that are fairly stable, but IQs are more stable over shorter periods than over longer periods, and for older children and adults than for children under 6 years of age.
   c. It is not unusual for particular individuals to show a great deal of variability in their scores.
4. Bias in testing
   a. No issue related to the assessment of cognitive abilities has generated as much heated debate as the question of whether IQ tests are biased against individuals from minority cultures or different racial groups.
   b. A test can be considered biased if it differentiates between members of various groups on bases other than the characteristic being measured.
   c. The technical evidence overwhelmingly indicates that the vast majority of items used on tests like the WISC-R and Binet are not biased; these tests tend to measure the same factors and predict success equally well for all racial groups. Remember that IQ tests do not measure the amount of some innate, immutable ability that we all possess, but provide a general measure of expected school achievement.
   d. While it may be true that most intelligence tests are free of bias, it is also true that these tests have been used to discriminate.
5. Instructional validity and application of results
   a. Instructional validity is the ability of a test to lead to better treatments, such as more effective educational programs, or better counseling or teaching strategies.
   b. Intelligence tests were not created for the purpose of designing prescriptive instructional interventions, and attempts to make them into tools for specific instructional planning have failed miserably.
6. The intelligent use of intelligence tests
   a. People use intelligence tests because the concepts of intelligence and intellectual or cognitive functioning are central elements in the definition of several IDEA categories of disabilities. As long as classifications of disability are required for special education, it is likely that many service providers will feel the need to use IQ tests.
   b. It is important to remember that IQ tests should be used only after there has been a detailed assessment of classroom functioning and it is proven that teaching in the regular classroom will not help.
   c. IQ tests provide only one piece of evidence about how a child learns and the nature of any disability he/she may have.
7. TIPS on Communication: Best practices in reporting intelligence test results

III. Behavior rating scales: Summarizing observations of students' behavior
   A. A typical behavior rating scale includes a list of items that describe particular behaviors and indicates how frequently the child exhibits the behaviors. Some provide information about "how important" the behaviors are. Most rating scales also provide norms.
      1. Well-constructed rating scales have the potential to facilitate communication among individuals interested in the assessment of particular children and provide useful diagnostic information.
      2. Major factors affecting the increased use of rating scales include their ease of use, need for more teacher and parent involvement in assessment and intervention activities, and generally improved reliability and validity information.
   B. Uses of rating scales
      1. Rating scales have been used primarily as part of the screening and identification process for children referred for possible special education services.
      2. They have been used inappropriately to monitor behavior changes as a result of an intervention.

3. They have played a central role in the classification of childhood social/emotional disorders.
4. They have been used to address the validity of teachers' judgments of students' achievement.
5. Practitioners who emphasize a prereferral intervention and/or consultation approach to service delivery should find rating scales to be a primary assessment tool.
6. They are used for documentation and accountability regarding regular teacher and parent involvement in the identification of a child's problem.

C. Limitations or disadvantages of rating scales
1. They are measures of current or recent functioning but do not provide information on causes of problems.
2. Scores on existing problem-focused rating scales do not dictate choices for intervention.
3. They involve perceptions of problems rather than truly "objective" measures of such problems.

D. Case Notes: Melissa Williams' class

E. Characteristics and interpretation guidelines
1. In terms of reliability and validity characteristics and interpretation, rating scales are very complex.
2. Four issues influence use and interpretation of behavior rating scales.
   a. Ratings are summaries of observations of the relative frequency of specific behaviors.
   b. Ratings of social behavior are evaluative judgments affected by the subject's environment and the rater's standards for behavior.
   c. Multiple assessors of the same child's social behavior may agree only moderately.
   d. Many personal characteristics may influence the child's social behavior; however, the student's sex is a particularly salient variable.

IV.   Interpreting standardized test scores

A. Kinds of scores
1. Raw scores may be difficult to interpret. If an arithmetic test contains 50 items and a student scores 32, that student's raw score is 32.
2. Grade-equivalent scores are easily misinterpreted. A GE score of 7.2 on a test given to fifth-graders means the student's performance on fifth-grade material is equal to the performance of a student in the second month of the seventh grade on fifth-grade material.
3. Percentile rank indicates the percentage of students a given individual performed as well as or better than.
4. A frequency distribution tells us the frequency with which a particular score appears in a score category.
5. There are three measures of central tendency:
   a. The mode is that score obtained by the largest number of students.
   b. The median is that point in the distribution above which and below which exactly 50 percent of the cases lie.
   c. The mean is the average of the raw scores; add all the scores and divide by the number of scores.
6. Standard scores offer a constant definition and interpretation. Standard scores relate to the normal curve, a theoretical mathematical model based on the assumption that most human characteristics are distributed normally.
   a. Standard deviation units tell us how much a score varies from the mean.
   b. The Z score is the fundamental standard score, which tells us the distance of a student's raw score from the mean in standard deviation units.
   c. The t-score offers an alternative method of computing standard scores that avoids negative Z scores and decimals. A t-score is computed by multiplying the standard score by 10 and adding 50.
   d. Stanine scores are a quick means of classification and are easily understood. A stanine has a mean of 5 and a standard deviation of 2.

e. The standard error of measurement (SEM) is an estimate of the amount of error you can expect in a test score. It provides a range within which a student's true score is likely to fall.
7. Case Notes: Melissa Williams' class
8. TIPS on Assessment: Interpreting test results
B. Reporting test results
1. The Individual Profile Report provides a complete record of a student's test performance, including general information about the student's strengths and needs in major content areas and specific information about the student's mastery of objectives.
   a. The student's name and grade are listed along with a summary of the various norm-referenced scores for each subject matter area.
   b. The standard error of measurement is used to create a range for the national percentile scores. These are translated into a graphic picture of the student's performance.
   c. The scores on the graph can be transformed easily into national stanines by using a line graph presented on the report form.
   d. The student's performance is characterized in terms of the objectives measured by the test, resulting in an Objective Performance Index (OPI) for each subject matter area. This index estimates the number of times that a student could be expected to answer correctly if there had been 100 such items for the objective.
   e. A graphic portrayal of the OPI characterizes performance as non-mastery, partial mastery, or mastery.
   f. To identify skills and concepts on which to focus instruction and review, teachers might consider the areas for which partial or non-mastery is demonstrated.
2. A summary of the objectives mastered by an entire class is possible. Such an Objectives Performance Report for the class can be used to identify potential instructional priorities.
3. The report shows the average OPI on each objective for the students in the local and national norm groups. A positive difference indicates that the performance of the local group was higher than that of the national group.

V. Using standardized tests
   A. Educational applications of standardized testing
      1. special education placement
      2. student certification
      3. teacher testing
      4. educational assessment and accountability
      5. instructional guidance
   B. Common criticisms of standardized tests
      1. Testing limits teaching.
      2. Testing produces rigid grouping practices.
      3. Testing lowers student achievement.
      4. Tests lead to labeling students.
      5. Testing arouses negative emotional feelings.
      6. Testing may negatively affect a student's self-concept.
      7. Test scores do not directly influence teaching.
      8. Tests often do not measure what was taught.
   C. Case Notes: Melissa Williams' class
   D. Best practices
      1. The *Code of Fair Testing Practices in Education* (1988) contains standards for educational test developers and users in four categories: developing/selecting tests, interpreting scores, striving for fairness, and informing test-takers.
      2. The Code is meant for the general public and is limited to educational tests. It supplements the more technical *Standards for Educational and Psychological Testing* (AERA, APA, NCME, 1985).

VI.   Concluding thoughts about the value of standardized tests

VII.   Case reflections

VIII.   Chapter highlights

IX.   What do you think? questions

X.   Key terms

XI.   Appendix: The code of fair testing practices in education

KEY TERMS

achievement tests
aptitude tests
assessment
criterion-referenced test
frequency distribution
mean
measures of central tendency
median
mode
norm curve
norm group
norm-referenced test
norms
percentiles

raw score
social validity
standard deviation unit
standardized tests
stanine scores
t-score
Z score

GUIDED REVIEW

1.   Testing programs generally have three major purposes: _____, _____, and _____.

instruction on, guidance, administration

2.   _____ tests are commercially prepared and sample behavior under uniform procedures. _____ tests are intended to assess students' general or specific abilities. _____ tests measure accomplishments in such subjects as reading, arithmetic, language, and science.

Standardized, Aptitude, Achievement

3.   _____ is the degree to which the observational procedures, administrative procedures, equipment and materials, and scoring rules have been fixed so that exactly the same testing procedure occurs at different times and places.

Standardization

4.   A _____ test yields a score that enables you to compare it with the scores of others who took the same test. There are other tests that provide a score informing the rater of the extent to which a student has achieved predetermined objectives. These are called _____ tests, and their focus is on reaching particular _____.

norm-referenced, criterion-referenced, standards of performance

5.   Norm-referenced tests can assess a _____ of knowledge, reflect common _____ for learning, assess achievement at all levels of attainment, sample achievement more widely, reflect the belief that achievement is _____ rather than all or nothing, furnish a _____ that summarizes general level of achievement, provide _____ evaluation information, and identify learning as the primary responsibility of the _____.

broad range, goals, more or less, single score, summative, student

6.   _____ provide the normal range of scores for a given population.

Norms

7.   The objective of an _____ test is to discover how much an individual has learned from educational experiences.

achievement

8.   Standardized achievement tests assess the _____ of individual learners, aid in academic _____ of students and in planning of _____, help in decisions about _____ and _____, and can stimulate _____ of instructional issues.

accomplishment of learning objectives, guidance, curriculum changes, promotion, admission, analysis

9.   Two types of standardized achievement tests are currently popular: _____, which assess separate curricular topics over a wide range of grades, and those designed to measure _____ such as reading or mathematics.

multilevel survey batteries, specific subjects

10.   The Terra Nova Assessment Series is a series of _____ tests designed to assess K - 12th grade students' knowledge in reading/language arts, mathematics, science, and social studies. Each area is broken into _____, each of which has multiple test items. The items measure knowledge and skills in the subject areas and provide evidence about _____ skills and problem solving processes.

achievement, subdomains, thinking

11.   _____ tests are used to predict what students can learn. They do not measure native capacity or learning potential directly, but measure _____ based on learning abilities.

Aptitude, performance

12.   The WISC-III is individually administered, requires 60 to 90 minutes, and is designed for children from _____ years of age. It provides a global measure of _____ that taps "many different mental abilities, which all together reflect a child's general intellectual ability." It has 13 subtests, 6 in a Verbal Scale and 7 in a Performance Scale. Each subtest has specific _____ about where to begin and end, depending on the age or assumed ability of the child.

6 to 17, intelligence, rules

13.   On the WISC-III, scaled subtest scores are added and converted into _____ for the Verbal, Performance, and Full Scales. Each has a mean of _____ and a standard deviation of _____. Much has been learned about the nature of cognitive abilities in the last 30 years, and yet the _____ of the WISC-III has changed little.

deviation IQs, 100, 15, design and purpose

14.   Most research has suggested that IQ tests tend to yield scores that are fairly _____. However, IQs are more stable over _____ periods than over _____ periods and for _____ children and adults than for children under 6 years of age. It is not unusual for particular individuals to show a great deal of _____ in their scores.

stable, shorter, longer, older, variability

15. A test can be considered _____ if it differentiates between members of various groups on bases other than the characteristic being measured.

biased

16. The technical evidence overwhelmingly indicates that the vast majority of items used on tests like the WISC-R and Binet are _____; these tests tend to measure the same factors and predict success _____ for all racial groups. Remember that IQ tests do not measure the amount of some innate, immutable ability that we all possess, but provide a general measure of _____. Though most intelligence tests are free of bias, it is also true that these tests have been used to _____.

not biased, equally well, expected school achievement, discriminate

17. _____ is the ability of a test to lead to better treatments, such as more effective educational programs or better counseling or teaching strategies. Intelligence tests were not created for the purpose of designing prescriptive instructional _____, and attempts to make them into tools for specific instructional planning have _____.

Instructional validity, interventions, failed

18. It is important to remember that IQ tests should be used only after there has been a detailed assessment of _____ and it is proven that teaching in the regular classroom will not help. IQ tests provide only _____ about how a child learns and the nature of any disability he/she may have.

classroom functioning, one piece of evidence

19. A typical behavior rating scale includes a list of items that describe _____ and indicates how _____ the child exhibits the behaviors. Some provide information about the _____ of the behaviors. Most rating scales also provide _____. Well-constructed rating scales have the potential to facilitate _____ among individuals interested in the assessment of particular children and provide useful _____ information.

particular behaviors, frequently, importance, norms, communication, diagnostic

20. Rating scales have been used primarily as part of the screening and identification process for children referred for possible _____. They also have been used to monitor behavior _____ as a result of an intervention, in _____ childhood social/emotional disorders, to address the _____ of teachers' judgments of students' achievement by practitioners who emphasize a prereferral intervention and/or consultation approach to service delivery, and for documentation and accountability of _____ in the identification of a child's problem.

special education services, changes, classifying, validity, teacher and parent involvement

21. Rating scales are measures of current or recent functioning, but do not provide information on _____ of problems, do not dictate _____, and involve _____ of problems rather than truly "objective" measures of such problems.

causes, choices for intervention, perceptions

22.   _____ refers to the applied or social importance of exhibiting certain behaviors in particular situations.

Social validity

23.   Issues influencing the use and interpretation of behavior rating scales include these: Ratings are _____ of observations of the relative frequency of specific behaviors; they are _____ affected by the subject's environment and the rater's standards for behavior; multiple assessors of the same child's social behavior may agree only _____; and many characteristics of a student may influence his or her social behavior, but the student's _____ is a particularly salient variable.

summaries, evaluative judgments, moderately, gender

24.   If an arithmetic test contains 50 items and a student scores 32, that student's _____ is 32. Raw scores may be difficult to interpret, since you cannot _____ them to other students' scores.

raw score, compare

25.   _____ scores are easily misinterpreted. A GE score of 7.2 on a test given to 5th graders means that the student's performance on fifth-grade material is _____ the performance of a student in the second month of the seventh grade on fifth-grade material.

Grade equivalent, equal to

26.   _____ indicates the percentage of students a given individual performed as well as or better than.

Percentile

27.   _____ indicates the frequency with which a particular score appears in a score category.

Frequency distribution

28.   There are three measures of _____. The _____ is that score obtained by the largest number of students. The _____ is that point in the distribution above which and below which exactly 50 percent of the cases lie. The _____ is the average of the raw scores, found by adding all the scores and dividing by the number of scores.

central tendency, mode, median, mean

29.   _____ scores offer a constant definition and interpretation and relate to the normal curve, a theoretical mathematical model based on the assumption that most human characteristics are distributed normally.

Standard

30. _____ tell us how much a score varies from the mean.

Standard deviation units

31. _____ scores are the fundamental standard scores, which tell us the distance of a student's raw score from the mean in standard deviation units.

Z

32. The _____ score offers an alternative method of computing standard scores that avoids negative Z scores and decimals. It is computed by multiplying the standard score by 10 and adding 50.

t-

33. _____ scores are a quick means of classification and are easily understood. A _____ has a mean of 5 and a standard deviation of 2.

Stanine, stanine

34. It is important to remember that tests are only _____ of behavior and that all scores possess some _____.

samples, error

35. The _____ is an estimate of the amount of error you can expect in a test score. It provides a range within which a student's _____ is likely to fall.

standard error of measurement, true score

36. The Individual Profile Report provides a complete record of a student's test performance, including general information about the student's _____ in major content areas and specific information about the student's _____. It is a useful tool for general curricular planning and for organizing _____ about a student.

strengths and needs, mastery of objectives, feedback

37. The student's performance is characterized in terms of the _____ measured by the test, resulting in an Objective Performance Index (OPI) for each subject matter area. This index _____ the number of times that a student could be expected to answer correctly if there had been 100 such items for the objective. A graphic portrayal of the OPI characterizes performance as _____, _____, or _____.

objectives, estimates, non-mastery, partial mastery, mastery

38.	A summary of the objectives mastered by an entire class can be used to identify potential _____. This report shows the average OPI on each objective for the students in the local and national _____. A _____ difference indicates that the performance of the local group was _____ than that of the national group.

instructional priorities, norm groups, positive, higher

39.	Standardized tests have been used for _____, student _____, _____ testing, educational _____, and instructional _____.

special education placement, certification, teacher, assessment, guidance

40.	Standardized tests often are criticized on the grounds that testing _____ teaching, produces rigid _____, lowers student _____, leads to _____ students, arouses _____, may negatively affect a student's _____, and produces test scores that do not directly influence teaching, and that tests often _____ what was taught.

limits, grouping practices, achievement, labeling, negative emotions, self-concept, do not measure

41.	The Code of Fair Testing Practices in Education contains standards for educational test developers and users in four categories: _____ tests, _____ scores, striving for _____, and _____ test-takers.

developing/selecting, interpreting, fairness, informing

SUMMARIZE THE MAIN POINTS

This section of your study guide is designed to help you identify and understand the main points in each chapter. You've already reviewed the details using the Guided Review (above), and will consider the importance, relevance, and usefulness of the information in later sections. For now, focus on summarizing the main ideas.

For each major section in the chapter, summarize the main point and the evidence presented in the text to support and/or discuss it. If there are key terms presented in the section, define them. Some prompting questions are provided to help you structure your review.

The main sections of Chapter 12 are:

- A school's testing program
- Standardized tests
- Behavior rating scales: Summarizing observations of students' behavior
- Interpreting standardized test scores
- Using standardized tests
- Concluding thoughts about the value of standardized tests

For each section, answer the following questions:

1. In two sentences or less, **summarize** what the **main point** of this section was.

2. Briefly **summarize the evidence** for and against each main point (a simple list of details they use to support each of their points is sufficient). If the authors discuss research studies to support the point, summarize the findings in one sentence. If the authors are presenting a logical argument to support the point (i.e., not citing data from research studies), briefly list the supporting points they made. Use the detailed chapter outline to help you identify the supporting points.

3. Briefly review the **definitions of any key terms** in each main section.

WHY SHOULD YOU CARE?

The purpose of this section of your study guide is to help you understand how and why the information in the chapter is relevant for you personally. You'll be asked to think more about the relevance and usefulness of the information in later sections of this study guide.

Look back at the work you did in summarizing the main points in the section above and answer the following questions:

1. For each section you summarized, why or how is the **main point** you identified **important to and/or relevant for teachers in general**? Try to limit your answer to only one or two sentences so you don't get bogged down in details, but focus on general usefulness.

2. Now think about the chapter as a whole. **Identify two specific events, contexts, or problems** for which the ideas presented in this chapter are relevant. Briefly discuss how they're relevant and how they could be useful.

3. Now **identify three concepts** from the chapter that **YOU find useful** in some way. Discuss how/why these concepts are useful, and specify how you will actually use them in your teaching and/or your daily life. (It's okay if there is some overlap between your answers for numbers 2 and 3.)

DISCUSSION QUESTIONS

The following "What do you think?" questions are printed in the text.

1. What do you see as the advantages of a criterion-referenced test compared to a norm-referenced test?

2. Intelligence is a complex and controversial construct. What is your definition of intelligence and what is the best way to measure it?

3. From your perspective, what is the most salient criticism of standardized tests?

4. What kind of information would you need to use the results of a standardized achievement test to inform your teaching of students?

5. From your perspective, what are the major limitations in using behavior rating scales to evaluate students?

Additional discussion questions:

6. List and discuss the three major purposes of testing programs.

7. What is an aptitude test? An achievement test? What are the purposes of each?

8. What is the main difference between norm-referenced tests and criterion-referenced tests? List two examples of norm-referenced tests, then two examples of criterion-referenced tests.

9. What is standardization? What advantages and disadvantages does it offer relative to teacher-made tests?

10. List and discuss two educational applications of standardized testing.

11. Why is stability of IQ an important factor to consider when evaluating IQ tests?

12. Define instructional validity. Why is this important to teachers?

13. What is a behavior rating scale and how can teachers use them in classrooms?

TAKE IT PERSONALLY!

The questions in this section are designed to help you personalize, integrate, and apply the information from the text. Personalization questions ask you to consider the personal relevance and usefulness of concepts, and consider how they might be useful in your life now and in the future. Integration questions ask you to pull together information from the text to evaluate it, summarize it or synthesize a recommendation on the basis of it, or express an opinion about it. Application questions ask you to think about how the concepts might be useful to address real problems or situations you may find yourself in. All three question types will help you consider the information at a deeper conceptual level, understand it more fully, and remember it.

1. What kind of "testing program" did your high school have? What was the purpose of each element? What changes would you make in the testing program, and why?

2. Identify an example of a norm-referenced test that you have taken. What useful information did the test provide? Identify an example of a criterion-referenced test that you have taken. What useful information did this test provide? Compare the types of information each test provided, and consider how the results were or could have been used.

3. If you were designing an intelligence test, what would the focus be? What would the underlying theory of intelligence be: a general-factor, specific-abilities, or cognitive process approach? What problems do you think you would encounter in your attempts to measure intelligence? How would you ensure that your test was used responsibly?

4. Find an example of a behavior rating scale and analyze it. What is its purpose? What behaviors does it focus on, and how does it operationally define them? What guidance is provided for interpretation and communication of the results? For what uses is this scale appropriate?

5. For each type of score covered in the text (raw, grade equivalent, percentile, Z, t, and stanine), define the score, give an example, and provide suggestions for valid interpretation of the score. What problems might be encountered in communicating the meaning of each type of score?

6. Using the following classroom test scores, create a frequency distribution and find the mean, median, and mode of the test scores: 7, 8, 8, 10, 12, 14, 17, 18, 18, 18, 18, 19, 19, 19, 19, 20, 20, 20, 20, 20, 20, 21, 21, 21, 21, 23, 23, 23, 28.

7. How can you as a teacher help ensure that assessments of multicultural students are valid?

8. List the common criticisms of standardized tests. For each, summarize the argument being made, then say whether you agree or disagree with the criticism.

9. Summarize the pros and cons of intelligence testing. In your opinion, are these tests helpful or harmful overall? Why?

CASE IN POINT...

Remember to use the cases from the text as contexts for identifying examples of concepts from the text and as contexts for solving educational problems. Also remember to use a consistent framework (like the DUPE model or the CASE NOTES in the text) to structure your "Mini-Case Report." Review the "Case in Point..." section of Chapter 1 in this study guide for more details.

SUGGESTED CONCEPTS TO IDENTIFY FOR CHAPTER 12

    achievement tests
    aptitude tests
    frequency distribution
    mean
    median
    mode
    norms
    percentile score
    social validity
    standardized tests
    stanine scores
    t-score
    Z score

Review Case #3 about Melissa Williams in your text and use the following questions to prompt your thinking about this case.

1. Why is Melissa dissatisfied with the emphasis her colleagues place on standardized test results? How might such tests be useful to Melissa?

2. If Melissa gave her students a test like the Terra Nova assessment, what kinds of information could she gain from it? How could she use this information to improve her teaching?

3. Should Melissa be concerned about the issue of bias in standardized tests for her students? If so, what bias issues might there be, and how could she deal with them?

BIG IDEAS IN EDUCATIONAL PSYCHOLOGY

Thinking about the "big ideas" in educational psychology will help you organize and apply your newly acquired knowledge. Use the following steps to identify your own principles and strategies from the chapter and to relate them to the five main themes of the text (i.e., the "big ideas").

1. Review the TIPS from the text.

2. List some of the main concepts from the chapter. Use the work you did in prior sections of the study guide to help generate this list. Also look at the list of key terms from the chapter.

3. Select what you think are two or three of the most important concepts from your list.

4. For each concept you select, try to state it as a principle (use the TIPS format in the text and the example shown below as a guide for how to state principles).

5. Develop two or three specific teaching strategies that follow from each stated principle.

6. Relate your work to the five main themes from the text, identifying which theme(s) are relevant for each principle and strategy. This step will help you see how the information in each chapter contributes to improved teaching for each of these five critical aspects of instruction.

7. Think about and discuss with classmates how the principles and strategies you identify will help you improve your teaching for each theme you listed as relevant.

The five main themes from the text are:
ASSESSMENT, COMMUNICATION, LEARNING, MOTIVATION, AND TIME

Some example concepts, principles, and strategies for Chapter 12:

achievement tests	error in measurement
aptitude tests	norms
assessment	social validity
behavior rating scales	standardized tests

Principle   *Every assessment contains some error. (ASSESSMENT, COMMUNICATION, LEARNING)*

Strategy   Remember that NO assessment, teacher-developed or other, is perfect. Base decisions about students and teaching on multiple sources of information, not just on one assessment. (ASSESSMENT, COMMUNICATION)

Strategy   Because all assessments have error, think carefully about the conclusions a given assessment seems to indicate to determine whether they make sense given everything else you know about the student. If not, try to figure out why before drawing any firm conclusions. (ASSESSMENT, COMMUNICATION, LEARNING)

SUGGESTED READINGS

Gould, S. (1980). *The mismeasure of man.* Cambridge, MA: Harvard.

Linn, R. (1986). Educational testing and assessment. *American Psychologist, 41,* 1153-1160.

Lyman, H. (1998). *Test scores and what they mean.* Boston: Allyn & Bacon.

Wiggins, G. (1994). *Assessing Students' Performance.* San Francisco: Jossey-Bass.

Wiggins, G. (1998). *Educative assessment: Designing assessments to inform and improve student performance.* San Francisco: Jossey-Bass.

PRACTICE TEST 1

1. When compared to teacher-made tests, standardized tests
    a. are less consistent.
    b. usually have less comprehensive coverage of material.
    c. are less valid assessment instruments.
    d. are less ambiguous in the wording of test items.

2. Behavior rating scales are typically used to
    a. assess a student's general or specific abilities.
    b. screen children for possible special education placement.
    c. assess mastery of material covered.
    d. predict occupational skills and success.

3. "My son got a grade equivalent score of 8.5 in mathematics, and he's only in sixth grade! His teacher said that score indicates he is gifted in mathematics and should probably skip a couple of grades in math." This teacher
    a. is correctly interpreting the grade equivalent score.
    b. is understating the degree of ability this student has in mathematics.
    c. is incorrectly interpreting the grade equivalent score.
    d. None of the answers are correct.

4. One use of standardized testing is to make decisions about a school's curriculum based on testing students. Which purpose of a testing program does this illustrate?
    a. instructional
    b. guidance
    c. administrative

5. When teachers teach for the test, testing
    a. lowers student achievement.
    b. limits teaching.
    c. produces rigid grouping practices.
    d. arouses negative feelings.

6. A teacher grades a test, compares each student's answers and decides that a given student's answers, compared to the others, should receive a C. What is such a test called?
    a. aptitude test
    b. achievement test
    c. norm-referenced test
    d. criterion-referenced test

7. Which of the following does NOT characterize both norm-referenced and criterion-referenced tests?
   a. Both use the same types of test items.
   b. Both are useful in educational achievements.
   c. Both require specification of the achievement domain to be measured.
   d. Both are used primarily for mastery testing.

8. What is the objective of the standardized achievement test?
   a. to determine a student's grade entry level
   b. to find out how much a student has learned from educational experiences
   c. to determine a student's potential for a given school subject
   d. to find out how much a student has learned from experiences other than in the educational environment

9. IQ scores obtained before children enter kindergarten or first grade are
   a. highly reliable.
   b. not reliable.
   c. aptitude tests.
   d. achievement tests.

10. If a geography test contains 100 items and a student scores 70, what is that student's raw score?
    a. 7
    b. 30
    c. 70
    d. 100

11. The statistical average is called the
    a. mode.
    b. percentile.
    c. mean.
    d. median.

12. Which of the following tell(s) us how much a score varies from the mean?
    a. frequency distribution
    b. median
    c. mode
    d. standard deviation units

13. Instructional validity refers to which of the following?
    a. the ability of a test to accurately predict academic achievement
    b. the degree of bias against minority groups that exists in a test
    c. how important a test is in making educational placement decisions
    d. the ability of a test to lead to better treatments

14. Which of the following is true about behavior rating scales?
    a. The ratings give a precise measure of behavior frequency that can be generalized to other classroom contexts.
    b. The ratings are less subjective than most other measures available.
    c. Multiple assessments of the same child's social behavior typically show high levels of agreement.
    d. All of the above statements are true.
    e. None of the above statements are true.

15. What is the general purpose of the *Code of Fair Testing Practices in Education*?
    a. To provide guidelines to those developing, using, and taking tests.
    b. To provide details to teachers as to how to develop standardized tests.
    c. To summarize how to compute various kinds of standardized test scores.
    d. To inform test-takers and their parents of their legal rights when taking standardized tests.

PRACTICE TEST 2

1. A main difference between teacher-made and standardized tests is that
   a. standardized tests allow meaningful comparisons between students.
   b. standardized tests provide unbiased estimates of students' knowledge.
   c. standardized tests allow greater variability in the testing procedures.
   d. standardized tests can be developed more quickly.

2. One limitation of behavior rating scales is that they
   a. are too limiting in the interventions prescribed.
   b. are not easily adaptable for classroom use.
   c. do not provide information on causes of problems.
   d. do not include subjective perceptions of problems.

3. A percentile rank of 92 means that
   a. this student performed as well as or better than 92% of the students taking the test.
   b. this student answered correctly 92% of the items on the test.
   c. this student performed worse than 92% of the students taking the test.
   d. this student scored in the top 2% of those students taking the test.

4. One use of standardized testing is to diagnose special needs. Which purpose of a testing program does this illustrate?
   a. instructional
   b. guidance
   c. administrative

5. One criticism of standardized tests is that when students are assessed, the resulting label produces
   a. rigid grouping practices.
   b. lower student achievement.
   c. lower teacher expectations.
   d. All of the answers are correct.

6. According to the text, what is the most desirable feature of the standardized test for many test users?
   a. the detailed diagnostic information obtained.
   b. the norms supplied
   c. their consistency with local curriculum
   d. their detailed prescriptive information for curriculum development

7. While norm-referenced tests are used primarily for _____, criterion-referenced tests are used primarily for _____.
   a. achievement; aptitude
   b. aptitude; achievement
   c. mastery testing; survey testing
   d. survey testing; mastery testing

8. Multilevel survey batteries assess
   a. separate curricular topics over a wide range of goals.
   b. children with problems early in order to establish intervention methods to improve their lives at school.
   c. how much a student has learned from experiences other than educational ones.
   d. a student's mastery of a school subject.

9. Which of the following statements regarding IQ tests is true?
   a. IQ tests tend to yield unstable scores.
   b. IQ tests tend to yield scores that are fairly stable.
   c. IQ tests are more stable over longer as opposed to shorter periods.
   d. IQ tests are more stable for children under 6 years of age than for older children and adults.

10. If David gets 42 correct answers out of 50 items on a math test, 42 is his
    a. standard score.
    b. raw score.
    c. percentile.
    d. Z-score.

11. That point in the distribution above which and below which exactly 50 percent of the cases lie is the
    a. mode.
    b. mean.
    c. median.
    d. percentile.

12. The standard score that tells us the distance of a student's raw score from the mean in standard deviation units is the
    a. Z-score.
    b. t-score.
    c. stanine score.
    d. grade-equivalent score.

13. The Wechsler Intelligence Scale for Children-III (WISC-III) provides which of the following intelligence scores?
    a. verbal score
    b. performance score
    c. total IQ score
    d. All of the answers are correct.

14. In interpreting information gained from behavior rating scales, it is important to remember that the ratings
    a. can be reliably used as the single source of information for decision making.
    b. can be heavily influenced by several characteristics of the person doing the rating.
    c. are generally not very reliable and so are not very useful for making decisions about the student.
    d. give a precise measure of behavior frequency that can be generalized across classroom contexts.

15. Which of the following best summarizes the text's overall recommendation regarding the use of standardized tests?
    a. Standardized tests have been found to show a fair degree of bias; therefore, these tests should not play a major role in making decisions about students.
    b. Standardized tests should play a major role in classroom decision making because they are more reliable and objective than teacher-made tests.
    c. Standardized tests must be used with caution, with good judgement, and in conjunction with multiple sources of information.
    d. Classroom teachers should play a bigger role in developing standardized tests for their districts and states since they are more familiar with the local curriculum.

ANSWER KEY

Practice Test 1

1. ANSWER: D, Factual; OBJECTIVE: 1; PAGE: 482
2. ANSWER: B, Factual; OBJECTIVE: 4; PAGE: 496
3. ANSWER: C, Applied; OBJECTIVE: 6; PAGE: 499
4. ANSWER: C, Factual; OBJECTIVE: 1; PAGE: 476
5. ANSWER: B, Factual; OBJECTIVE: 7; PAGE: 509
6. ANSWER: C, Applied, OBJECTIVE: 2; PAGE: 478
7. ANSWER: D, Conceptual; OBJECTIVE: 2; PAGE: 478
8. ANSWER: B, Factual; OBJECTIVE: 2; PAGE: 482
9. ANSWER: B, Factual; OBJECTIVE: 3; PAGE: 491
10. ANSWER: C, Applied; OBJECTIVE: 6; PAGE: 498
11. ANSWER: C, Factual; OBJECTIVE: 5; PAGE: 499
12. ANSWER: D, Factual; OBJECTIVE: 5; PAGE: 501
13. ANSWER: D, Factual; OBJECTIVE: 3; PAGE: 493
14. ANSWER: E, Factual; OBJECTIVE: 4; PAGE: 497-498
15. ANSWER: A, Factual; OBJECTIVE: 8; PAGE: 511

Practice Test 2

1. ANSWER: A, Conceptual; OBJECTIVE: 1; PAGE: 482
2. ANSWER: C, Factual; OBJECTIVE: 4; PAGE: 497
3. ANSWER: A, Applied; OBJECTIVE: 6; PAGE: 499
4. ANSWER: B, Factual; OBJECTIVE: 1; PAGE: 476
5. ANSWER: D, Factual; OBJECTIVE: 7; PAGE: 510
6. ANSWER: B, Factual; OBJECTIVE: 1; PAGE: 482
7. ANSWER: D, Conceptual; OBJECTIVE: 2; PAGE: 479
8. ANSWER: A, Factual; OBJECTIVE: 2; PAGE: 483
9. ANSWER: B, Factual; OBJECTIVE: 3; PAGE: 491
10. ANSWER: B, Applied; OBJECTIVE: 6; PAGE: 498
11. ANSWER: C, Factual; OBJECTIVE: 5; PAGE: 499
12. ANSWER: A, Factual; OBJECTIVE: 5; PAGE: 501
13. ANSWER: D, Factual; OBJECTIVE: 2; PAGE: 491
14. ANSWER: B, Factual; OBJECTIVE: 4; PAGE: 497-498
15. ANSWER: C, Factual; OBJECTIVE: 8; PAGE: 511

Chapter **13** EFFECTIVE TEACHING STRATEGIES AND THE DESIGN OF INSTRUCTION

LEARNING OBJECTIVES

After completing this chapter, you should be able to

1. Identify the common features of teaching.

2. Identify the key features of effective teachers.

3. Describe the effective use of praise.

4. Distinguish between direct and inquiry teaching.

5. Write clear and concise learning objectives and describe their role in the design and management of instruction.

6. Describe Skinner's, Markle's, and Gagne's approaches to instructional design.

7. Discuss ways in which technology-based teaching strategies can be used in classrooms.

8. Identify ways to teach the "big ideas" in Reading and Mathematics.

9. Cite examples of how you could adapt teaching to the needs of your students.

CHAPTER HIGHLIGHTS

The Meaning of Teaching

- Effective teaching is characterized by identifiable behaviors: Lesson clarity, instructional variety, task orientation and engagement in the learning process, praising students appropriately, and reflection.

Approaches to Instruction

- Direct and indirect, or inquiry, instruction must be compatible with both objectives and materials.
- A well-known example of direct instruction is Madeline Hunter's Clinical Theory of Instruction.
- A well-known example of inquiry instruction is Jerome Bruner's cognitive theory.
- Teachers' use of praise has been carefully analyzed in attempts to make it a more meaningful and forceful element in the classroom.

The Design of Instruction

- Clearly articulated objectives make learning more meaningful and useful by providing a structure for planning, delivering, and assessing instruction.
- A well-written objective specifies the behavior to be acquired or demonstrated, the conditions under which the behavior occurs, and the criteria for evaluating the behavior.
- B. F. Skinner applied the principles of operant conditioning to the classroom as he consistently advocated a technology of teaching. He encouraged teachers to first decide what their students should be able to do after instruction, carefully determine the steps needed to achieve that behavior, and skillfully use appropriate reinforcers.
- Susan Markle used a programed instruction model ("programed" with one *m*) that featured three principles of instruction: a student's active responding, errorless learning, and immediate feedback.
- Robert Gagne formulated an instructional design technique that accounts for learning outcomes as they are related to specific conditions for that learning. Gagne outlined what he believed to be the "optimal conditions" for learning. These included gaining the attention of a student, learning objectives, stimulating prior knowledge, presenting material in an interesting manner, providing learning guidance, eliciting a performance, providing feedback, assessing the performance, and enhancing retention and transfer.

Technology-Based Teaching Strategies

- Researchers indicate that using technology in classrooms can significantly improve instruction and students' learning. Educational technology offers a number of advantages for instruction, from providing simple audiovisual demonstrations of concepts to allowing students to interact with concepts and materials in a way that would otherwise be difficult, dangerous, or impossible, and to collaborate with students across the world.
- Computer-assisted instruction uses technology to present material to students or assist them in mastering it. Examples are computerized programmed instruction and drill-and-practice software.
- Multimedia uses technology to integrate and simultaneously use several different types of technology. Laser videodiscs and CD-ROMs are examples.
- Intelligent tutoring systems use technology to provide an individualized tutor for each student.
- Finally, the use of web-based learning and virtual reality are connecting learners with others across the world and exposing students to many subjects in a personal way that only five years ago was not possible. These advances are encouraging discovery learning for many students.

Teaching the Big Ideas in Reading and Mathematics

- Subject matter knowledge is one of the fundamental characteristics of an effective teacher.
- Pedagogical knowledge refers to how the basic principles and strategies of a subject are best acquired and retained.
- Fundamental concepts, or big ideas, are critical elements to stress in instruction. In reading, the big ideas are phonological awareness, alphabetic understanding, and automaticity with the code. In mathematics, big ideas include proportions, estimation, area, and fractions.
- Subject matter experts agree that effective delivery of the big ideas include the use of a conspicuous strategy, strategically integrated training, scaffolding, and structured review sessions.
- High-quality review sessions involve introducing information into activities cumulatively, distributed practice that emphasizes relationships between new and old material, quick response times, and varied examples for practice and generalization.

- Benjamin Bloom believes that studies of teaching must take into account the time pupils need for a task, their cognitive entry behaviors, and the proper use of testing, among other aspects. Bloom's concern with mastery learning led him to propose a model of school learning with such core concepts as cognitive entry behaviors, affective entry characteristics, and quality of instruction.
- Study skills and homework are part of effective instruction and help students improve their achievement.
- The "Pygmalion in the classroom" effect, i.e., a self-fulfilling prophecy about students, although not as great an influence on students' learning as originally thought, still should be a concern for educators.

DETAILED CHAPTER OUTLINE

I. What makes a teacher effective?
   A. There are four common features of teaching: teachers, learners, subject matter, and context.
   B. Outstanding teachers have several characteristics that make them great, including the way in which they use language and the knowledge they possess.
      1. Key behaviors of effective teachers
         a. Lesson clarity refers to how clear you make your presentations to your class.
         b. Instructional variety means that your teaching techniques remain flexible during the presentation of a lesson.
         c. Task orientation and engagement in the learning process refer to the time spent in learning academic subjects.
         d. Success rate means the rate at which students understand and correctly complete their work.
      2. Case Notes: Melissa Williams' Class
   C. Be careful how you use praise. Teacher praise usually is infrequent, noncontingent, global, and determined more by students' personal qualities than by students' achievements.
   D. Engage in reflection by stepping back occasionally to think about what you are doing, and whether it is worthwhile.
   E. TIPS on communicating: Using praise effectively

II. Approaches to instruction
   A. Direct instruction
      1. With direct instruction, teachers tell, demonstrate, explain, and assume the major responsibility for the lesson's progress and adapt the work to their students' age and abilities.
      2. Student achievement seems to be superior with direct instruction, particularly with regard to factual information.
      3. Madeline Hunter's Clinical Theory of Instruction
         a. Working on the assumption that the teacher is a decision-making professional, Hunter's Clinical Theory of Instruction (CTI) claims universal application, regardless of content, school organization, learner's age, or socioeconomic status.
         b. CTI is derived from research on human learning and based on the notion that instructional decisions are made consciously or by default.
         c. Seven steps in planning for effective instruction are establish an anticipatory set; present the objective and its purpose; decide on the instructional input; model the essential features; check for understanding; provide guided practice; provide independent practice such as homework.
      4. Some dos and don'ts for direct instruction
         a. Begin your teaching by using an advance organizer, define new words, present ideas in a carefully prepared and logical sequence, use questions to keep the class motivated and

check their understanding, watch for signs of wandering attention or boredom, and follow up with activities designed to help retention and transfer.

    b. Guard against too much talking, constantly check for misinterpretations, and be sure that the material lends itself to direct instruction.

    c. Constantly check for misinterpretations.

    d. Make sure the material lends itself to direct instruction.

    e. TIPS on learning: Asking questions of students during instruction

  5. Case Notes: Melissa Williams' class

B. Indirect instruction

  1. Acquisition of facts and knowledge, as the sole tools of teaching and learning, are not enough. Teaching that encourages inquiry learning is less structured and more informal.

  2. Help students actively explore by providing advance organizers, conceptual frameworks. Ask guiding questions, help students become responsible for their own learning, and provide cues to draw attention to inappropriate responses.

  3. Bruner and inquiry teaching

    a. Bruner identifies three sources of teacher behavior.

      (1) Communicators of knowledge, including mastery of both knowledge and methods of communication.

      (2) Models.

      (3) Symbols representing "education."

    b. A theory of instruction prescribes how teachers can help a child acquire cognitive abilities, outlining the materials and methods best suited to help students move to a higher cognitive level.

    c. Bruner developed four major themes in analyzing learning: structure, readiness, intuition, and motivation.

      (1) Understanding a subject's structure allows one to learn how things are related.

      (2) In a spiral curriculum, a subject is taught at successively higher grade levels in an increasingly abstract manner.

      (3) Once students obtain a detailed knowledge of a subject, they can begin to expand their hypothetical abilities.

      (4) Motivation is Bruner's final indispensable learning ingredient.

    d. Modes of representation. Bruner believes that if teachers understand the mental stages that a child passes through, they can adapt their teaching accordingly. He calls these stages modes of representation.

      (1) Enactive mode (first level). The infant knows the world only by acting on it; otherwise the object does not exist for the child.

      (2) Iconic mode (second level). Bruner's term for perceptual organization.

      (3) Symbolic mode (third level). Here the child engages in symbolic activities, such as language and mathematics.

      (4) Students learn according to their mode of representation; for Bruner, learning a subject involves three almost simultaneous processes: acquisition of new information, transformation, and evaluation.

    e. Bruner believes that if teachers respect a student's thinking process and translate material into meaningful units, they can introduce great ideas to children at different times and with increasing abstractness. This is the spiral curriculum.

    f. To teach effectively, you must master the material to be taught, and remember that you are a model.

  4. Some dos and don'ts for indirect instruction

    a. The content and situation must be appropriate.

    b. Considerable time and effort are required.

    c. Results may be unexpected.

    d. Be supportive.

e. Reinforce what your students did correctly.

f. Be sure that you have provided adequate clues for your students to use.

g. Encourage your students to work cooperatively.

III. The design of instruction
   A. Classroom objectives
      1. Teachers should formulate specific objectives that will encompass their daily concerns and communicate with students what is expected.
      2. If there is one indispensable guideline for formulating objectives, it is to be precise.
      3. Statements of educational objectives describe what a student should be able to produce or do, or what characteristics students should possess after the learning.
      4. Why bother with objectives?
         a. Given the current decrease in dependence on textbooks and curriculum guides for the identification of objectives, teachers' planning is assuming greater importance.
         b. Teachers must make decisions based on the needs of the individual learners in their classrooms.
         c. By writing clearly stated objectives, teachers keep their instruction focused, and students quickly learn what is expected of them.
         d. Many school districts have established expected learner outcomes (ELOs) for each primary grade, and use their ELOs to make decisions about school entry and grade retention.
         e. Task analysis links objectives to content. It requires deciding how the lessons relate to the unit's objectives, ensuring that the pupils have the skills to carry out the assignment, and helping students understand the logical sequence and the necessity to integrate all components of the task.
      5. TIPS on Assessment: Conducting a task analysis
      6. What are good objectives?
         a. Once you have determined the type of objectives needed, you must express them in such a way that they are clearly understood by all.
         b. An instructional objective is an intent communicated by a statement describing a proposed change in the learner, a statement of what the learner is to be able to do upon completion of the learning experience. It is student-centered, involves learning outcomes and observable behavior.
      7. Evaluating and writing objectives
         a. Desirable objectives have three characteristics.
            (1) Specify an acceptable level of the desired behavior.
            (2) Specify the conditions under which the specific behavior should occur.
            (3) Specify the criteria that inform you that students have achieved an objective at the proper level.
      8. TIPS on Communication: Objectives clarify expectations
      9. Choose action verbs for objectives that clearly convey your instructional intent and that precisely state the behavior and level of performance expected of students.
      10. Armstrong and Savage (1983) suggested the ABCD format for writing objectives.
         (1) A: The audience for which the objectives are intended
         (2) B: The behavior that indicates learning
         (3) C: The conditions under which the behavior is to appear
         (4) D: The degree of competency that will be accepted
      11. Sources of objectives
         a. Published materials, subject area yearbooks, and state departments of education
         b. Specialized sources, such as *The Taxonomy of Educational Objectives*

      (1)   Bloom's taxonomy tries to clarify vague terminology.

      (2)   There are three taxonomies: cognitive, affective, and psychomotor.

      (3)   The cognitive taxonomy has six major classes: knowledge, comprehension, application, analysis, synthesis, and evaluation.

      (4)   The great value of the taxonomy is its general application.

    c.   Bloom's taxonomy is remarkably flexibley, offering insights into the formation of acceptable objectives and providing a basis for teaching thinking skills.

B.   Skinner and the technology of teaching

    1.   Skinner applied the principles of operant conditioning to both learning and teaching, in a procedure called programmed instruction.

    2.   General characteristics of teaching that cultivate both teaching and learning:

      a.   Define the terminal behavior.

      b.   Solve the problem of the first instance.

      c.   Decide what you will use to prompt behavior.

      d.   Program complex behavior.

      e.   Decide the proper size and most effective sequence of steps for the program.

    3.   An example that reflects these principles is the Bereiter-Englemann program, designed to prescribe teaching procedures for disadvantaged children. The teaching strategies devised include these:

      a.   Be careful when you vary your presentation methods.

      b.   Give children sufficient time to respond.

      c.   Use questions liberally.

      d.   Try using multiple examples.

      e.   Try to prevent incorrect responses.

      f.   Be clear in responding to correct and incorrect answers.

C.   Markle and programed instruction

    1.   The principle of active responding refers to meaningful responses that are overt, psychomotor, or verbal. What the student is asked to do determines what information the student will notice and retain.

    2.   The principle of errorless learning. Errors can be a signal that instruction needs improvement, or a reliable guide for diagnosis, and they can aid programers in shaping the final form of a program.

    3.   The principle of immediate feedback. The need for feedback is related to the way a statement is framed. Challenging situations produce more errors and a greater need for feedback.

    4.   Case Notes: Melissa Williams' class

D.   Gagne and instructional design

    1.   Gagne described five learning outcomes: verbal information, intellectual skills, cognitive strategies, attitudes, and motor skills. Each outcome demands a different set of conditions for optimizing learning, retention, and transferability.

    2.   Gagne identified several instructional events that he believes help students to learn meaningfully.

      a.   Gain the attention of your students.

      b.   Inform learners of the objective.

      c.   Stimulate recall of prerequisites.

      d.   Present the stimulus material.

      e.   Provide learning guidance.

      f.   Elicit the performance.

      g.   Provide appropriate feedback.

      h.   Assess the performance in an accurate manner.

      i.   Enhance retention and transfer.

    3.   Gagne believes this nine-step model can function as a theory of learning and memory. It also provides an instructional basis for analyzing the interaction of internal events with external events, so it is applicable to many instructional forms, settings, and learners.

IV. Technology-based teaching strategies
  A. Technology-based teaching strategies use the unique properties of technology to help students master material and skills. The technology varies with the teacher's instructional goals, students' levels and needs, and available resources.

  B. Advantages of technology-based teaching strategies
    1. Students can work on problems that would be difficult or impossible otherwise.
    2. Students can see the dynamics of processes and changes over time and precisely control how quickly the changes progress, which allows more careful exploration of causes and results.
    3. Computer networks allow communication with others in distant locations and access to resources and expertise that otherwise would not be available.
  C. Differences between technology-based and traditional teaching strategies
    1. Technology-based strategies are often based on cognitive constructivist views, which places both teachers and students in new roles.
    2. Complex student-developed projects are common, relatively long-term in duration, usually involve collaboration between students, and often emphasize problem-solving and research skills.
    3. Different kinds of assessments are often needed. They are often more project and/or performance oriented and include assessment of content; problem solving, thinking, and research skills acquired; and sometimes changes in motivation and the degree to which students take responsibility for their own learning.
  D. Web-Based Instruction
    1. The "WorldWideWeb" is an organized system of computer networks that allows users to transmit and search information using many different branching pathways. Information can be found quickly.
    2. Web-based instruction (WBI) uses the information search and transmitting capabilities of the WWW and the vast array of resources available on it to provide instruction to students.
      a. Sometimes WBI is very structured, as when colleges offer entire courses on-line.
      b. WBI at the K-12 level is usually less integrated and less comprehensive, often using the WWW as an information resource. It is increasingly used to allow students to collaborate with experts and other students in different locations and to actively participate in activities that would otherwise not be possible.
    3. Advantages of WBI
      a. Potential to increase the accessibility of learning
      b. Potential for increased interaction with students of different backgrounds and races, allowing students to move away from an "ethnocentric" perspective, learn tolerance and respect for others, and gain greater self-understanding.
      c. Potential to encourage the development of problem solving, information evaluation, and information search skills.
      d. Greater learner control of the learning process and products, with the potential for more detailed, thoughtful, and creative student learning and products.
      e. Can allow for greater accommodation of different learning styles through learner control of the pace, number of repetitions, and sometimes the media format of learning.
    4. Problems and Prerequisites
      a. Different thinking, learning, and study skills are often emphasized. Teachers, students, and parents need to understand and communicate about the goals, skills, and assessments of WBI.
      b. Students need to learn web-navigating skills so they do not get lost or too distracted as they work their way through Web sites.
      c. Money is needed to provide computers with adequate memory, processing capacity, and modem speed.

      d.   Effect on the "technology gap" between higher and lower SES schools.
         (1)   Some argue that lower SES schools will be less able to get equipment and help and become more disadvantaged for college entrance and job competition.
         (2)   Others argue that WWW access will DECREASE the gap because lower SES schools will gain access to information, instructional materials, expertise, and experiences that would otherwise be impossible.

   5. Effectiveness of WBI
      a.   There are few studies that assess the effectiveness of WBI, especially for K-12 students.

E. Multimedia
   1. Multimedia instruction is the integration and simultaneous use of several different types of technology to improve instruction. Many are interactive in that the user manipulates them in some way, designed to encourage integration of different types of content, and emphasize problem-solving.
   2. Laser videodiscs
      a.   One example of a multimedia project designed to integrate several content areas is a series of laser videodiscs about a character named Jasper Woodbury solving complex, realistic problems.
      b.   Several aspects of the videodiscs are useful for learning content, problem solving, and integrating knowledge.
         (1)   The problems are complex
         (2)   The problems are realistic
         (3)   There is an embedded data design in which students view the videodisc, generate subproblems, then go back and find the relevant information embedded in the story. This helps students develop information search and evaluation skills.
         (4)   Students are encouraged to integrate content areas like mathematics and science
         (5)   Students are encouraged to view scientific and mathematical skills as tools to be used in the service of solving a problem, rather than just as facts and formulas to be memorized.
   3. Effectiveness of teaching with multimedia. Research indicates that multimedia instruction results in more creative problem solving; positive effects on student comprehension, retention, and use of new knowledge; and a greater sense of ownership and greater involvement in project design and production.
   4. Disadvantages of multimedia instruction
      a.   Cost can be a problem. Different types of technology and software are needed.
      b.   There can be a loss of control over what students are learning when control and responsibility for learning is given to the students themselves.

F. CD-ROM (Compact disc-read only memory)
   1. CD-ROM is an optical disc technology that allows the storage of large amounts of digital data including text, digital sound and graphics, and digital movies. They include both static and dynamic visual information and sound and give richer information than a printed text can.
   2. CD-ROMs focused on initial instruction of skills are being developed at an astonishing pace. They include animation, music, narration, bilingual options, teacher/parent "edit pages," and progress reports.
   3. Assessments of CD-ROMs so far show positive effects on such measures as reading achievement, comprehension, and enjoyment.

G. Intelligent tutoring systems (ITSs)
   1. The goal of an ITS is to provide an individual tutor for each student for a given subject area. It must present new material, provide examples, provide appropriate problems, track performance, identify errors and misconceptions, and provide appropriate guidance and feedback.
   2. ITSs typically have three components: an expert component to solve the problems presented; a diagnostician to track performance and diagnose misconceptions and errors; and a tutorial component that provides appropriate feedback and guidance.

3. Advantages of ITSs
    a. They can individualize instruction to a degree not seen before in educational technology.
    b. They can often allow a type of instruction that would otherwise be difficult if not impossible, using examples that are either rarely occurring but important, or dangerous.
    c. The level of content expertise programmed into an ITS can far exceed what a classroom teacher can be expected to have. This becomes especially important when trying to identify misconceptions.
4. Disadvantages of ITSs
    a. Cost and availability
    b. The tutorial component tends to focus almost exclusively on cognitive aspects of the tutoring process, and does not consider motivational components.
    c. Most ITSs are based on a cognitive theory of learning, but they do not consider the social context of learning and the role of social interactions.
5. There are few systematic evaluations of ITSs. Those available show that ITSs increase the pace of learning without causing decreases in performance; produce changes in teachers' and students' classroom roles; and that students enjoy using ITSs.
H. Virtual reality (VR)
    1. VR is a three-dimensional computer-generated environment that involves the user in real-time, multi-sensory interactions.
    2. VR systems allows interactive learning that combines cognitive, affective, and psychomotor skills
    3. Few elementary and secondary schools have VR systems available as of yet. Data on mastery of skills and information, pace of learning, and student attitudes are not yet available for K-12 levels.

V. Teaching the big ideas in reading and mathematics
A. Subject matter knowledge
    1. Shulman distinguished three types of content knowledge.
        a. Subject matter knowledge refers to a teacher's comprehension of a subject when compared to that of a specialist.
        b. Pedagogical knowledge refers to how the basic principles and strategies of a subject are best acquired and retained.
        c. Curriculum knowledge refers to the optimal manner in which knowledge of a subject can be organized and presented.
    2. Research indicates that knowledgeable teachers can better detect student misconceptions and exploit opportunities for meaningful learning.
    3. Know as much as possible about your subject, present it as dynamically as possible, and be prepared to answer all kinds of questions about what you teach. A teacher's task is to help students learn as much as their potential permits.
B. Reading
    1. Research on visual perceptual abilities and on linguistic basis of reading delay revealed that good and poor readers differ on virtually every dimension of language, but the basis of early reading delay is largely due to phonological processing difficulties (the use of the sounds of one's language).
    2. Three critical features of early reading are apparent
        a. Phonological awareness, or awareness of the sounds of a language. This can be difficult because individual sounds in words are often merged and not pronounced as separate parts. The best interventions combine phonological awareness and letter-sound instruction.
        b. Alphabetic understanding, the connection between the letter code and reading words. The first step is to teach individual letter-sound correspondences, then teach blending isolated sounds into meaningful words.
        c. Automaticity with the code, or rapid recognition and performance of a skill. Word identification becomes less capacity-demanding as experience with words increases. Students should be given frequent practice at blending words with patterns previously practiced.

C. Mathematics
   1. Porter (1989) noted several weaknesses related to difficulties in acquiring complex problem-solving skills.
      a. Excessive time is spent on computational skills with little emphasis on concept understanding and application.
      b. Time allocated for instruction is not adequate for many students.
      c. The rate at which students are taught new content as they proceed through grades is slow because of redundancy.
   2. The current mathematics standards suggest that instruction in mathematics needs to be characterized by more teacher and student interactions in meaningful contexts, with less attention to rote practice. Students must acquire knowledge of the important key mathematics concepts, such as proportions, estimation, and area.
D. Instructional principles for improving reading and mathematics
   1. Instructions should be characterized by four principles: a conspicuous strategy, strategically integrated training, scaffold activities, and structured reviews.
   2. The role of structured review is particularly important. Carnine (1989) identified six guidelines for designing review and practice activities.
      a. Introduce information into review activities cumulatively.
      b. Distribute practice to build retention.
      c. Emphasize relationships to make learning more meaningful.
      d. Reduce processing demands by preteaching components of a strategy.
      e. Require quicker response times.
      f. Use varied examples for review.

VI. Adapting instruction to the individual differences of learners
   A. Bloom identified several variables that influence the teaching-learning process.
      1. Time on task has always been recognized as a critical factor in learning. Studies of cues, reinforcement, and participation provide valuable clues as to just what teachers are doing with their time. Bloom stresses that time on task can be altered.
         a. Gettinger (1990) identified three aspects of learning time that could be increased: time used for instruction, engaged time, and productive learning time.
      2. Intelligence versus cognitive entry behaviors. Although researchers repeatedly have demonstrated a link between intelligence and aptitude tests and later achievement, Bloom argues that these findings do not determine a student's potential for learning. Cognitive entry characteristics also show a close relationship with achievement, and can be altered.
      3. Summative versus formative testing. Summative evaluation involves using classroom tests to measure a student's achievement at the completion of a block of work. Formative evaluation is primarily intended to aid in the formation of learning by providing feedback about what has been and remains to be learned. Bloom believes that when tests are used in this manner, the number of students who achieve mastery increases dramatically.
      4. TIPS on time: Methods for increasing academic learning time
   B. Mastery learning
      1. Mastery learning is the key to Bloom's work, for it is this goal that all other means are intended to achieve. He believes that about 90 percent of all students can learn to mastery if properly instructed.
      2. Quality of instruction. Mastery learning is tied closely to the quality of instruction, which must be considered in light of individual learners and not groups.
      3. Students' ability to understand instruction. Because our schools are highly verbal, ability to understand is likened to language ability and reading comprehension.
      4. Perseverance. Bloom emphasizes the significance of perseverance by commenting on students' variability in the amount of time they are willing to spend on a task and believes that the key to increasing perseverance is appropriately designed instruction and learning materials.

5. Time allowed for learning. If aptitude determines the rate of learning, then time allowed for learning can produce mastery. Teachers can alter the time spent on task by following mastery principles and allowing students the time they need to reach mastery in a particular subject.
6. With mastery learning, students usually show increased interest in subject matter, an increased sense of self-worth, and improved retention and transfer of material. Teachers gain a sense of professional renewal.
7. Bloom's theory addresses student characteristics, instruction, and learning outcomes.
   a. Student characteristics significant for learning are cognitive entry behaviors and affective entry characteristics.
      (1) Cognitive entry behavior is the prerequisite learning needed for mastery of new tasks. The critical point is the availability of the prerequisite learning at the time it is required for the specific new learning task. These behaviors fall into two categories: those specific to a subject, and those that are general.
      (2) Affective entry characteristics refer to the differences among students in what they are emotionally prepared to learn as expressed in their interests, desires, and attitudes. Affect toward school accounts for as much as 25 percent of the variation in achievement. Affect toward both school and subject can be altered.
      (3) Cognitive entry behaviors and affective entry characteristics can account for about 65 percent of the achievement variation on a new learning task.
   b. Affective entry characteristics can be altered by the quality of instruction; in spite of the significant contribution made by cognitive entry behaviors, quality of instruction can have a powerful effect on learning.
C. Study skills
   1. Students with good study skills are more likely to experience increased feelings of competence and confidence, and tend to approach schoolwork with a positive attitude.
   2. Study skills are basic learning tools; they enable students to acquire and retain information presented in textbooks and classrooms.
   3. Study skills may be organized into four general stages of learning that are common to all students.
      a. The first stage of studying involves taking in information from books, lectures, or presentations. Study behaviors that are associated with success at this stage include listening and reading.
      b. The second stage involves organizing the information. Study behaviors that facilitate organization of the information include underlining, notetaking, outlining, making lists, or asking oneself questions about the material.
      c. Stage three involves practicing or rehearsing the organized material and requires some type of review or discussion.
      d. The final stage is the actual remembering or application of information. Skills in taking tests, writing, or preparing reports are used in this stage.
   4. Developing a system that works for a given child and using the system effectively and consistently is more important than following any particular method.

   5. Parents can help by encouraging children to
      a. Establish a study routine.
      b. Make sure study surroundings allow children to concentrate.
      c. Keep assignments in one folder.
      d. Work out a study system.
      e. Expand concentration time.
      f. Develop time estimation skill, which means being able to estimate how long it will take to complete each assignment.
      g. Plan ahead.
      h. Set goals.
      i. Reward achievement.

6. Case Notes: Melissa Williams' class
D. Homework
   1. Another means of adapting your instruction to the needs of your students is by the use of carefully assigned homework, or tasks assigned to students and meant to be carried out during non-school hours.
   2. Homework has positive effects on achievement, especially for junior and senior high school students. It also is seen as having important "side effects" on student-parent relations and self-management.
   3. Cooper identified over 20 specific factors that influence homework outcomes and organized these into six general factors.
      a. Cooper found the effect of homework on achievement was negligible for elementary students, moderately important for junior high students, and very important for high school students.
      b. Cooper still recommends homework for elementary students to help them develop good study habits and positive attitudes toward school, and to communicate the idea that learning takes place at home as well as at school.
   4. Research indicates several effective instructional practices regarding homework.
      a. The benefits of homework for young children may not be immediately evident, but they exist nonetheless.
      b. Homework in the early grades can have a long-term developmental effect that reveals itself when the student moves into secondary school.
      c. Parental attitudes play a significant and stable role in shaping students' attitudes toward homework and grades.
   5. Current Issues and Perspectives: Can homework bring home and school closer together?
E. Multicultural education
   1. Multicultural education is a concern affecting every phase and aspect of teaching.
   2. In a multicultural curriculum, students learn about themselves and others as they study various cultures. Multicultural students, like all students, respond best to teacher support and warmth and to appropriate, challenging standards.
   3. In presenting multicultural topics, teachers proceed in exactly the same manner as with their other subjects: They establish the necessary knowledge base, utilize effective instructional methods, and base their instruction on their students' needs.
   4. Minority students may bring differences in behavioral and communication styles to a classroom that a teacher must recognize if these students are to achieve as well as possible.
F. Teacher's expectations and how they influence interactions with students
   1. In 1968, Rosenthal and Jacobson reported that when teachers expected more of children, the youngsters met their expectations—a self-fulfilling prophecy referred to as Pygmalion in the classroom.
   2. Attempts to replicate the Rosenthal and Jacobson findings produced conflicting evidence.
   3. Perhaps it is safest to conclude that teachers' expectations make a difference, but not as uniformly as, and in a much more complex manner than, they were originally believed to.
   4. These expectations can translate into teacher behavior in the classroom, in that teachers often tend to
      a. seat low-expectation students farther from the teacher.
      b. pay less attention to low-expectation students in academic activities.
      c. call on these students less often to answer questions.
      d. wait less time for and then interrupt those students whom they perceive as less capable.
      e. criticize those students for whom they have low expectations more frequently, praising them less often.
      f. provide lower-quality feedback to their low expectation students.

VII. The eleven big ideas in effective teaching
    A. Features of effective teaching
       1. It has a clear focus and explicit learning outcomes that students understand and are held accountable for learning.
       2. Instruction is delivered under conditions like those described by Gagne as optimal.
       3. Students often benefit from direct instruction in how to study and complete homework. Parent involvement in homework provides enhanced effects on learning.
       4. Effective teachers have a strong understanding of the big ideas in subject matter areas.
    B. The eleven big ideas
       1. Teachers communicate clear and high expectations for student learning.
       2. Standards for classroom behavior are explicitly communicated.
       3. Classroom routines are smooth and efficient.
       4. Students are carefully oriented to lessons.
       5. Instruction is clear and developmentally appropriate.
       6. Instructional groups are based on instructional needs of students.
       7. Learning progress is monitored frequently.
       8. Review and reteaching are utilized.
       9. Learning time must be increased.
       10. Personal interactions between teachers and students are positive.
       11. Incentives and rewards are used to promote excellence.

VIII. Case reflections

IX. Chapter highlights

X. What do you think? questions

XI. Key terms

KEY TERMS

academic content standards
affective entry characteristics
beginning teacher evaluation studies (BTES)
Bloom's taxonomy
clinical theory of instruction (CTI)
cognitive entry behaviors
enactive mode of representation
expected learner outcomes (ELOs)
formative evaluation
iconic mode of representation
inquiry teaching
instructional objective

intelligent tutoring system (ITS)
mastery learning
modes of representation
programmed instruction (Skinnerian)
quality of instruction
self-fulfilling prophecy
spiral curriculum
summative evaluation
symbolic mode of representation
task analysis
terminal behavior
Web-based instruction (WBI)

GUIDED REVIEW

1.   The four "common features" of teaching include _____, _____, _____, and _____.

teachers, learners, subject matter, context

2.   Effective teachers show several key behaviors. Lesson _____ refers to how clear you make your presentations to your class. _____ means that your teaching techniques remain flexible during the presentation of a lesson. Task _____ and _____ in the learning process refer to the time spent in learning academic subjects. _____ means the rate at which students understand and correctly complete their work.

clarity, Instructional variety, orientation, engagement, Success rate

3.   The beginning teacher evaluation studies (BTES) were inspired by _____ model of school learning and represented an effort to identify a _____ variable between teaching behavior and student performance. Carroll's model shifted the research emphasis from _____ behavior to _____ activities.

Carroll's, mediating, teacher, student

4.   Be careful how you use _____. Teacher praise usually is infrequent, _____, global, and determined more by students' _____ than by students' achievements.

praise, noncontingent, personal qualities

5.   Engage in _____ by stepping back occasionally to think about what you are doing, and whether it is _____.

reflection, worthwhile

6.   With _____, teachers tell, demonstrate, explain, and assume the major responsibility for the lesson's progress and adapt the work to their students' ages and abilities. Student _____ seems to be superior with direct instruction, especially for _____ information.

direct instruction, achievement, factual

7.   Hunter's Clinical Theory of Instruction (CTI) assumes that the teacher is a _____ professional and is based on the notion that instructional decisions are made _____ or by _____.

decision-making, consciously, default

8.   Hunter's program includes seven steps: _____ set, the _____ and its purpose, instructional _____, _____, checking for _____, _____ practice, and _____ practice.

Anticipatory, objective, input, modeling, understanding, guided, independent

9.   When using direct instruction, begin by using an _____, define new _____, present ideas in a carefully prepared and logical _____, use _____ to keep the class motivated and check their understanding, watch for signs of wandering attention or _____, and follow up with activities designed to help retention and _____. Guard against too much _____, constantly check for _____, and be sure that the material lends itself to direct instruction.

advance organizer, words, sequence, questions, boredom, transfer, talking, misinterpretations

10.   Teaching that encourages _____ learning is less structured and more informal than direct teaching methods. Help students _____ by providing advance organizers and conceptual frameworks. Ask _____ questions, help students become responsible for their own learning, use examples from students' _____, _____ ideas to past learning and current interests, and provide _____ to draw attention to inappropriate responses.

inquiry, actively explore, guiding, experiences, relate, cues

11.   According to Bruner, teachers are communicators of _____, _____, and _____.

knowledge, models, symbols

12.   Bruner noted that theories of learning and development are _____ rather than prescriptive; that is, they tell us what happened after the fact. A theory of _____ prescribes how teachers can help a child acquire cognitive abilities.

descriptive, instruction

13.   Bruner developed four major themes in analyzing learning: _____, _____, _____, and _____.

structure, readiness, intuition, motivation

14.   The _____ is closely linked to Bruner's theme of readiness, and is an example of an attempt to develop structure. Bruner said that any subject can be taught effectively in some _____ form to any child at any stage of development. This means that the basic ideas of any subject area are both _____ and _____. Pupils can learn important basics at any stage of mental development, then the principles of the spiral curriculum can be used to help them proceed to _____ of the subject.

spiral curriculum, intellectually honest, simple, powerful, more complex forms

15.   Bruner believes that if teachers understand the mental stages that a child passes through, they can adapt their teaching accordingly. He calls these stages _____. The first level is the _____ mode of representation. The infant knows the world only by acting on it; otherwise the object does not exist. The second level is the _____ mode of representation, Bruner's expression for perceptual organization. When human beings face a series of apparently unrelated tasks, discovering a pattern makes the work easier. The third level is the _____ mode of representation. Here the child engages in symbolic activities, such as language and mathematics.

modes of representation, enactive, iconic, symbolic

16. Students learn according to their mode of representation, and for Bruner, learning a subject involves three almost simultaneous processes. _____, which replaces or expands what the student already knows, is the initial phase. Here the child incorporates environmental stimuli according to the existing mode of representation. _____ is the second phase. Once youngsters or adults acquire new information, then they must manipulate or change it to meet new tasks. _____ is the final phase.

Acquisition of new information, Transformation, Evaluation

17. When using indirect instruction, be _____, _____ what your students did correctly, be sure that you have provided adequate _____ for your students to use, and encourage your students to work _____.

supportive, reinforce, clues, cooperatively

18. If there is one indispensable guideline for formulating objectives, it is to _____.

be precise

19. Statements of educational objectives describe what a student should be able to _____ or _____, or what _____ students should possess after the learning. Teachers should have _____ instructional objectives that form an integrated whole to _____ all aspects of teaching.

produce, do, characteristics, clearly defined, guide

20. When clearly stated objectives are written, teachers keep their instruction _____, and students quickly learn what is _____.

focused, expected of them

21. Many school districts use _____ to make decisions about school entry and grade retention. Well-written ELOs list curriculum-referenced cognitive and behavior _____ that can be empirically _____.

expected learner outcomes, objectives, assessed

22. _____ links objectives to content. It requires deciding how the lessons relate to the unit's _____, ensuring that the pupils have the _____ to carry out the assignment, and helping students understand the _____ and the necessity to _____ all components of the task.

Task analysis, objectives, skills, logical sequence, integrate

23. An _____ is an intent communicated by a statement describing a proposed _____ in the learner: a statement of what the learner is to be able to _____ upon completion of the learning experience. It is _____, and involves learning _____ and _____ behavior.

instructional objective, change, do, student-centered, outcomes, observable

24. Desirable objectives specify the _____ that should result, an acceptable _____, the _____ under which the specific behavior should occur, and the _____ for determining when students have achieved an objective at the proper level.

behavior, level, conditions, criteria

25. Gronland states that the action verbs you use in objectives should clearly convey your _____, and they should precisely state the _____ and _____ expected of pupils.

instructional intent, behavior, level of performance

26. Writing objectives using The ABCD format includes four elements: A—the _____ for which the objectives are intended; B—the _____ that indicates learning; C—the _____ under which the behavior is to appear; D—the _____ that will be accepted.

audience, behavior, conditions, degree of competency

27. Some sources of objectives include _____ materials, subject area _____, and state departments of _____; specialized sources, such as *The Taxonomy of Educational Objectives.*

published, yearbooks, education

28. Benjamin Bloom and his colleagues devised the taxonomy of _____. The main purpose of the taxonomy is to provide a classification of the goals of our _____. There are three taxonomies: _____, _____, and _____.

educational objectives, educational system, cognitive, affective, psychomotor

29. Bloom's cognitive taxonomy is divided into six major classes: _____—the recall of pertinent facts when needed; _____—understanding the meaning of what is presented; _____—use of ideas and rules where needed; _____—separating a unit into its parts; _____—constructing a whole from parts; and _____—making judgments.

knowledge, comprehension, application, analysis, synthesis, evaluation

30. Bloom's taxonomy is valuable because it is applicable to many situations and content areas, offers reliable _____ into the formation of acceptable objectives, and can be used as the basis for teaching _____.

insights, thinking skills

31. Skinner has applied the principles of operant conditioning to both learning and teaching in a procedure called _____.

programmed instruction

32.   Using programmed instruction, the teacher must decide what students should be able to do after teaching. This is called defining the _____ behavior.

terminal

33.   Once terminal behavior has been determined, it must be strengthened by reinforcement. But you cannot reinforce what does not appear. The problem of the _____ means that students must exhibit some aspect of the desired behavior.

first instance

34.   Skinner recommends that teachers _____ complex behavior. It is important to decide on the proper _____ and most effective _____ for the program.

program, size, sequence of steps

35.   The Bereiter-Englemann program is designed to prescribe teaching procedures for _____. It is an example of programmed instructional principles.

disadvantaged children

36.   Susan Markle built her concept of _____ around the principle of active responding.

programed instruction

37.   Three programming principles—_____, _____, and _____—form the basis of Markle's model of instructional design.

active responding, errorless learning, immediate feedback

38.   The principle of _____ refers to meaningful responses that are covert, overt, psychomotor, or verbal.

active responding

39.   According to the principle of errorless learning, _____ serve many functions. They can be a signal that instruction needs improvement, they are a reliable guide for _____, and they aid programmers in shaping the final form of a program.

errors, diagnosis

40.   According to the principle of _____, challenging situations, however, cause students to make more errors and learn less when feedback is lacking.

immediate feedback

41.   In 1979, Gagne and Briggs published one of the first major entries in the field of instructional design, *Principles of Instructional Design.* This influential work was based upon Gagne's views of five learning outcomes: _____, _____, _____, _____, and _____.

verbal information, intellectual skills, cognitive strategies, attitudes, motor skills

42.   Gagne identified several instructional events that he believes help students to learn meaningfully: gain _____, inform learners of the _____, stimulate _____ of prerequisites, _____ the stimulus material, provide learning _____, _____ the performance, provide appropriate _____, _____ the performance in an accurate manner, and enhance _____ and _____.

attention, objective, recall, present, guidance, elicit, feedback, assess, retention, transfer

43.   Technology-based teaching strategies use the unique properties of technology to help students master _____ and _____. The technology varies with the teacher's instructional _____, students' levels and _____, and available _____.

material, skills, goals, needs, resources

44.   Some advantages of technology-based teaching strategies are that students can work on problems that would be _____ or _____ otherwise; students can see the _____ of processes and changes over time and precisely _____ how quickly the changes progress, which allows more careful exploration of _____; and computer networks allow communication with others in _____ and _____ to resources and expertise that otherwise would not be available.

difficult, impossible, dynamics, control, causes and results, distant locations, access

45.   Technology-based and more traditional teaching methods differ in several ways. Technology-based strategies are often based on cognitive _____ views, which places both teachers and students in new _____. Complex student-developed _____ are common, relatively _____ in duration, usually involve _____ between students, and often emphasize _____ and _____ skills. Different kinds of _____ are often needed.

constructivist, roles, projects, long-term, collaboration, problem-solving, research, assessments

46.   The _____ is an organized system of computer networks that allows users to _____ and _____ information using many different branching pathways. Information can be found quickly. _____ uses the information search and transmitting capabilities of the WWW and the vast array of resources available on it to provide instruction to students. WBI at the K-12 level is increasingly used to allow students to _____ with experts and other students in different locations and to actively participate in activities that would otherwise not be possible.

WorldWideWeb, transmit, search, Web-based instruction, collaborate

47.   Some advantages of WBI are the potential to increase the _____ of learning; potential for increased _____ with students of different backgrounds and races; potential to encourage the development of problem solving, information _____, and information _____ skills; greater learner _____ of the learning process and products; and it can allow for greater accommodation of different learning _____.

accessibility, interaction, evaluation, search, control, styles

48.   Different thinking, _____, and _____ skills are often emphasized in WBI. Teachers, students, and parents need to understand and communicate about the _____, skills, and _____ of WBI. Students need to learn _____ skills so they do not get lost or too distracted as they work their way through Web sites. _____ is needed to provide computers with adequate memory, processing capacity, and modem speed. The _____ between higher and lower SES schools may _____ because lower SES schools will be less able to get equipment and help, or decrease because lower SES schools will gain _____ to information, instructional materials, expertise, and experiences that would otherwise be impossible. There are _____ that assess the effectiveness of WBI, especially for K-12 students.

learning, study, goals, assessments, Web-navigating, Money, technology gap, increase, access, few studies

49.   _____ is the integration and simultaneous use of several different types of technology to improve instruction. Many are _____ in that the user manipulates them in some way, designed to encourage _____ of different types of content, and emphasize _____.

Multimedia, interactive, integration, problem-solving

50.   Several aspects of the videodiscs are useful for learning content, _____, and _____ knowledge. The problems are _____ and realistic; there is an _____ design that helps students develop information _____ and evaluation skills; students are encouraged to _____ content areas; and students are encouraged to view scientific and mathematical skills as _____ to be used in the service of solving a problem, rather than just as facts and formulas to be _____.

problem solving, integrating, complex, embedded data, search, integrate, tools, memorized

51.   Research indicates that multimedia instruction results in more _____ problem solving; positive effects on student _____, retention, and _____ of new knowledge; and a greater sense of _____ and greater _____ in project design and production. However, _____ can be a problem and there can be a loss of _____ over what students are learning when responsibility for learning is given to the students themselves.

creative, comprehension, use, ownership, involvement, cost, control

52.   Compact disc-read only memory (CD-ROM) is an _____ technology that allows the storage of _____ amounts of digital data including text, digital sound and graphics, and digital movies. They include both static and _____ visual information and sound and give _____ than a printed text can. CD-ROMs focused on initial instruction of skills are being developed at an astonishing pace. They include _____, music, narration, _____ options, teacher/parent "edit pages", and _____ reports. Assessments of CD-ROMs so far show _____ effects on such measures as reading achievement, _____, and _____.

optical disc, large, dynamic, richer information, animation, bilingual, progress, positive, comprehension, enjoyment

53.   The goal of an intelligent tutoring systems (ITS) is to provide an _____ for each student for given subject area. ITSs typically have three components: an _____ component to solve the problems presented, a _____ to track performance and diagnose misconceptions and errors, and a _____ component that provides appropriate feedback and guidance.

individual tutor, expert, diagnostician, tutorial

54. ITSs can _____ instruction to a degree not seen before in educational technology. They can often allow a type of instruction that would otherwise be _____ if not impossible, using examples that are either _____ or _____. The level of _____ programmed into an ITS can far exceed what a classroom teacher can be expected to have. This becomes especially important when trying to identify _____.

individualize, difficult, rarely occurring but important, dangerous, content expertise, misconceptions

55. Some of the disadvantages of ITSs include _____ and availability, the tutorial components do not usually consider _____ components of learning, and most do not consider the _____ of learning and the role of _____ interactions. The few systematic evaluations of ITSs available show that ITSs increase the _____ of learning without causing decreases in performance, produce changes in teachers' and students' classroom _____, and that students _____ using ITSs.

cost, motivational, social context, social, pace, roles, enjoy

56. _____ is a three-dimensional computer-generated environment that involves the user in real-time, multi-sensory interactions. These systems allow _____ learning that combines cognitive, _____, and _____ skills. Few elementary and secondary schools have these systems available as of yet. Data on mastery of skills and information, pace of learning, and student attitudes are _____ for K-12 levels.

Virtual reality (VR), interactive, affective, psychomotor, not yet available

57. There are three types of content knowledge: _____ knowledge refers to a teacher's comprehension of a subject when compared to that of a specialist; _____ knowledge refers to how the basic principles and strategies of a subject are best acquired and retained; _____ knowledge refers to the optimal manner in which knowledge of a subject can be best organized and presented.

Subject matter, pedagogical, curriculum

58. Research on visual perceptual abilities and on linguistic basis of reading delay revealed that good and poor readers differ on _____ of language, but the basis of early reading delay is largely due to _____ difficulties.

virtually every dimension, phonological processing

59. Three critical features of early reading are apparent: _____, or awareness of the sounds of a language; _____, the connection between the letter code and reading words; and _____, or rapid recognition and performance of a skill.

Phonological awareness, alphabetic understanding, automaticity with the code

60. Porter (1989) noted several weaknesses related to difficulties in acquiring complex _____ skills. Excessive time is spent on _____ skills with little emphasis on concept understanding and _____. _____ for instruction is not adequate for many students. The _____ at which students are taught new content as they proceed through grades is slow because of _____.

problem-solving, computational, application, Time allocated, rate, redundancy

61.   The current mathematics standards suggest that instruction in mathematics needs to be characterized by more teacher and student interactions in _____, with less attention to _____ practice. Students must acquire knowledge of the important _____, such as proportions, estimation, and area.

meaningful contexts, rote, key mathematics concepts

62.   Instruction for improving reading and mathematics should be characterized by four principles: a _____ strategy, strategically _____ training, _____ activities, and structured _____.

conspicuous, integrated, scaffold, reviews

63.   Carnine (1989) identified six guidelines for designing review and practice activities, including introduce information into review activities _____; _____ practice to build retention; emphasize _____ to make learning more meaningful; reduce processing demands by _____ components of a strategy; require _____ response times; and use _____ examples for review.

cumulatively, distribute, relationships, preteaching, quicker, varied

64.   Bloom identified several variables that influence the teaching-learning process: _____, intelligence versus _____, and summative versus _____ testing.

time on task, cognitive entry behaviors, formative

65.   Gettinger (1990) identified three aspects of learning time that could be increased: time used for _____, _____ time, and _____ learning time.

instruction, for engaged, for productive

66.   _____ refers to knowledge essential for learning a particular subject. This prior knowledge shows a close relationship with _____, and it can be altered.

Cognitive entry behavior, achievement

67.   _____ evaluation refers to measuring a student's achievement at the completion of a block of work. _____ evaluation is intended to provide feedback about what has been learned and what remains to be learned.

Summative, Formative

68.   _____ learning is probably the key element in Bloom's work, for it is this goal that all other means are intended to achieve.

Mastery

69.   _____ refers to needed cues, practice, and reinforcement necessary to make learning meaningful for students.

Quality of instruction

70.   Bloom emphasizes the significance of _____ by commenting on students' variability in the amount of time they are willing to spend on a task, and believes that the key to increasing perseverance is _____ instruction and learning materials.

perseverance, appropriately designed

71.   With mastery learning, students usually show increased _____ in subject matter, an increased sense of _____, and improved _____ and _____ of material. Teachers gain a sense of professional _____.

interest, self-worth, retention, transfer, renewal

72.   Cognitive entry behaviors fall into two categories: those that are _____ to a subject, and those that are _____, such as verbal ability and reading comprehension.

specific, general

73.   _____ characteristics refer to the differences among students in what they are emotionally prepared to learn as expressed in their interests, attitudes, and self-views.

Affective entry

74.   Study skills may be organized into four general stages of learning that are common to all students. The first stage of studying involves taking in information from books, lectures, or presentations. Study behaviors that are associated with success at this stage include _____ and _____. The second stage entails some _____. Study behaviors that facilitate organization of the information include underlining, notetaking, outlining, making lists, and asking oneself questions about the material. Stage three involves _____ the organized material and requires some type of review or discussion on the part of the learner. The final stage is the _____ of information. Skills in taking tests, writing, or preparing reports are used in this stage.

listening, reading, organization of the information, practicing or rehearsing, actual remembering or application

75.   Parents can help by encouraging children to establish a study _____, make sure study surroundings allow children to _____, keep assignments in one folder, work out a _____, expand _____ time, develop _____ skills, plan ahead, set _____, and reward _____.

routine, concentrate, study system, concentration, time estimation, goals, achievement

76.   _____ refers to tasks assigned to students by school teachers that are meant to be carried out during non-school hours.

Homework

77.   Cooper formulated a "model" of the factors that influence homework outcomes. Of all the factors, _____ was the most significant. The effect of homework on achievement was _____ for elementary students, moderately important for _____ students, and _____ for high school students.

grade level, negligible, junior high, very important

78.   The benefits of homework for young children may not be immediately evident, but they exist nonetheless in such things as developing good _____. Homework in the early grades can have a long-term developmental effect that reveals itself when the student moves into secondary school. _____ play a significant and stable role in shaping students' attitudes toward homework and grades.

study habits, Parental attitudes

79.   In presenting multicultural topics, teachers proceed in exactly the same manner as with their other subjects: Establish the necessary _____, utilize effective instructional methods, and base their instruction on their students' _____.

knowledge base, needs

80.   Minority students may bring differences in _____ and _____ styles to your classroom that you must recognize if these students are to achieve as well as possible.

behavioral, communication

81.   Rosenthal and Jacobson (1968) found that when teachers expected more of children, the youngsters met their expectations—a _____ referred to as Pygmalion in the classroom. Attempts to replicate the study have produced _____ evidence.

self-fulfilling prophecy, conflicting

82.   Teacher expectations translate into teacher behavior in the classroom, in that teachers often tend to seat low-expectation students _____ from the teacher, pay _____ to low-expectation students in academic activities, call less often on these students to answer questions, _____ less time and then _____ those students whom they perceive as less capable, _____ those students for whom they have low expectations more frequently, praise them _____ often, and provide _____ to their low-expectation students.

farther, less attention, wait, interrupt, criticize, less, lower quality feedback

83.   Effective teaching has a clear _____ and explicit _____ that students understand and are held accountable for learning; is delivered under conditions like those described by Gagne as _____; and has direct instruction in how to _____ and do _____. _____ involvement in homework provides enhanced effects on learning, and effective teachers have a strong understanding of the _____ in subject matter areas.

focus, learning outcomes, optimal, study, homework, Parent, big ideas

84.   The eleven big ideas in educational psychology identified and discussed throughout the text are: Teachers communicate clear and high _____ for student learning; standards for classroom behavior are _____; classroom _____ are smooth and efficient; students are carefully _____ to lessons; instruction is clear and _____; instructional groups are based on instructional _____ of students; learning progress is _____ frequently; review and _____ are done as frequently as needed; learning _____ is increased as much as possible; personal interactions between teachers and students are _____; and _____ are used to promote excellence.

expectations, explicitly communicated, routines, oriented, developmentally appropriate, needs, monitored, reteaching, time, positive, incentives and rewards

SUMMARIZE THE MAIN POINTS

This section of your study guide is designed to help you identify and understand the main points in each chapter. You've already reviewed the details using the Guided Review (above), and will consider the importance, relevance, and usefulness of the information in later sections. For now, focus on summarizing the main ideas.

For each major section in the chapter, summarize the main point and the evidence presented in the text to support and/or discuss it. If there are key terms presented in the section, define them. Some prompting questions are provided to help you structure your review.

The main sections of Chapter 13 are:

- What makes a teacher effective?
- Approaches to instruction
- The design of instruction
- Technology-based teaching strategies
- Teaching the big ideas in reading and mathematics
- Adapting instruction to the individual differences of learners
- The eleven big ideas in effective teaching

For each section, answer the following questions:

1. In two sentences or less, **summarize** what the **main point** of this section was.

2. Briefly **summarize the evidence** for and against each main point (a simple list of details they use to support each of their points is sufficient). If the authors discuss research studies to support the point, summarize the findings in one sentence. If the authors are presenting a logical argument to support the point (i.e., not citing data from research studies), briefly list the supporting points they made. Use the detailed chapter outline to help you identify the supporting points.

3. Briefly review the **definitions of any key terms** in each main section.

WHY SHOULD YOU CARE?

The purpose of this section of your study guide is to help you understand how and why the information in the chapter is relevant for you personally. You'll be asked to think more about the relevance and usefulness of the information in later sections of this study guide.

Look back at the work you did in summarizing the main points in the section above and answer the following questions:

1. For each section you summarized, why or how is the **main point** you identified **important to and/or relevant for teachers in general**? Try to limit your answer to only one or two sentences so you don't get bogged down in details, but focus on general usefulness.

2. Now think about the chapter as a whole. **Identify two specific events, contexts, or problems** for which the ideas presented in this chapter are relevant. Briefly discuss how they're relevant and how they could be useful.

3. Now **identify three concepts** from the chapter that **YOU find useful** in some way. Discuss how/why these concepts are useful, and specify how you will actually use them in your teaching and/or your daily life. (It's okay if there is some overlap between your answers for numbers 2 and 3.)

DISCUSSION QUESTIONS

The following "What do you think?" questions are printed in the text.

1. You have read a significant amount of information about effective teaching. In your words, what is an effective teacher? Identify at least five characteristics of an effective teacher you had when you were in high school.

2. What is the difference between an objective, a goal, and a standard? Many people seem to use these terms interchangeably. Do you?

3. Time on task has consistently been shown to be an important aspect of effective learning. What could you do as a teacher or parent that would increase the amount of time a learner spends actively engaged in learning?

4. What do you think about the use of praise? Do you like to be praised? If so, why? What effect does it have on your learning when somebody praises you?

5. Homework often stimulates many negative reactions from learners, yet it has consistently been shown to be part of effective teaching and learning, especially for middle and high-school-aged students. If it enhances learning, why don't more learners like it? Why don't more parents stress it?

Additional discussion questions:

6. List the characteristics and strategies that are associated with "effective" teaching. For each thing listed, explain how/why that characteristic or strategy contributes to effectiveness.

7. Should teachers praise their students? Why or why not? How should they use praise, and when?

8. Define direct instruction and indirect instruction, and identify specific differences between the two.

9. List the major points of the theories of Bloom, Bruner, Gagne, Hunter, Skinner, and Markle. Identify the similarities and differences among them and the educational applications of each.

10. List and discuss the elements of Hunter's Clinical Theory of Instruction. Give an example of each element.

11. Summarize Bruner's theory of inquiry teaching. What elements of this approach do you think you will use in your teaching? Why?

12. What are Bruner's modes of representation? Define and give an example of each. How is each one relevant for teachers?

13. What are objectives, and why are they important to teachers and students?

14. List and explain the characteristics of good objectives. Give suggestions for how to write good objectives.

15. What specific sources of objectives will you use in your own teaching?

16. List and define each step of the ABCD model for writing objectives. Write or find an objective, then identify an example of how the information in each step of the ABCD model was considered or addressed in that objective.

17. List and give an example of each of Skinner's characteristics of teaching that cultivate teaching and learning. Explain how each characteristic contributes to good teaching and learning.

18. Define and give an example of each of Markle's three programming principles. How could you use each?

19. What are the steps in Gagne's model of instruction? Identify each of the steps in a lesson you have experienced or taught. Give suggestions for how to improve at each step.

20. Describe the types of technology-based teaching strategies presented in the text. List two advantages and two disadvantages of each. For each type, identify when and how it might be helpful for teaching and learning.

21. How do technology-based teaching strategies differ from non-technology-based teaching strategies?

22. Define and give an example of the three types of content knowledge (subject matter knowledge, pedagogical knowledge, and curriculum).

23. Based on the information presented in your text, state two things teachers can do to become more effective in teaching the content area of reading. Do the same for mathematics. Then describe why each suggestion is important and why/how it is likely to improve instruction in those content areas.

24. What is structured review, and why is it important? List and explain Carnine's six guidelines for designing review and practice activities.

25. What is mastery learning, and how is it supposed to improve teaching and learning?

26. List and define the four general stages of learning as presented in Chapter 13 of your text. List the study skills relevant to each stage. What can teachers do to foster the study skills listed for each stage?

27. What are teacher expectations? How can they affect students' achievement?

28. List each of the five themes from the text. Discuss why each is seen as so important for effective teaching and learning. List three specific instructional strategies that would increase effectiveness for each of the five major themes.

TAKE IT PERSONALLY!

The questions in this section are designed to help you personalize, integrate, and apply the information from the text. Personalization questions ask you to consider the personal relevance and usefulness of concepts, and consider how they might be useful in your life now and in the future. Integration questions ask you to pull together information from the text to evaluate it, summarize it or synthesize a recommendation on the basis of it, or express an opinion about it. Application questions ask you to think about how the concepts might be useful to address real problems or situations you may find yourself in. All three question types will help you consider the information at a deeper conceptual level, understand it more fully, and remember it.

1. Identify a teacher you think is or was effective. Identify the characteristics and behaviors that made this teacher effective and explain how these characteristics contributed to his or her effectiveness.

2. As a student, do you prefer a more direct or more indirect approach to teaching and learning? Why?

3. Define and describe inquiry teaching. Evaluate its pros and cons. Do you think you would like this type of instruction as a teacher? As a student?

4. What are the goals and objectives of this course? How does knowledge of these things affect your studying?

5. Choose one chapter from this text. Write objectives for it. Evaluate the objectives you have written. Are they well written or poorly written? How could they be improved?

6. Define task analysis. Choose a skill you will teach and do a detailed task analysis, then develop instructional objectives based on this analysis. How is task analysis helpful in the development of objectives?

7. Classify the instructional objectives of a selected chapter in this text according to Bloom's taxonomy. How could you increase the number of objectives reflecting the higher levels of the taxonomy?

8. Select a content area (e.g., reading, math, science, etc.) you plan to teach someday, and choose a topic or unit in this area. Devise objectives for that topic or unit. Use the ABCD model if you like. Evaluate your objectives according to the criteria in the text.

9. Describe Skinner's programmed instruction. Apply it to a topic or unit you will teach. Is it helpful in organizing your instruction? Do you agree or disagree with the underlying theory?

10. Pretend you are B. F. Skinner. Write a summary of your views on education and how to improve it. What are the problems, and what are the solutions?

11. Suppose that you are teaching a tenth-grade course in American Literature. Using Gagne's instructional design, identify nine instructional events that should occur during the teaching of the course.

12. Identify examples of educational technology that you have used in your classes. What type of technology-based teaching strategy was used? Was it used effectively, and did it enhance your learning? How could it have been used more effectively?

13. How do you feel about the different role for teachers that many of the newer forms of technology are based upon? How will your ease or discomfort with this role affect the technologies you use in your teaching, and the ways in which you use them?

14. What recent developments in educational technology are you familiar with? How are they or will they be useful in teaching? What problems and possibilities do they offer?

15. Examine the three types of content knowledge for your subject of teaching expertise. To what degree do you possess each type? How does each type contribute to improving your teaching?

16. Describe ways to increase your students' academic learning time.

17. Discuss Bloom's concept of mastery learning. How is this concept useful to you? How could you use a mastery learning approach in this course?

18. Describe Bloom's model of school learning, including his ideas of cognitive entry behaviors and affective entry characteristics. How could you use this to individualize instruction?

19. Which study skills do you see as most fundamental for students to develop? What can you do to help students develop these skills?

20. Summarize the positive and negative effects of homework. What will your policies be regarding homework when you are a teacher, and why?

21. Analyze your experiences in multicultural classrooms. Were the instructional techniques different than those used in less multicultural classrooms? Should they be? Why or why not? How should they differ?

22. Have you ever experienced the benefits or detriments of a teacher's expectations? How did it affect your learning, and your attitudes toward school, learning, and yourself?

23. List and discuss the five themes from the text. Would you add or delete any from this list? Why?

24. Review each of the eleven "big ideas" from Chapter 13. Do you agree that each is an important major idea for teachers? Would you add any? For each of the eleven "big ideas," list two ways to apply or achieve it in a classroom.

25. Identify the two MOST important ideas to you personally that you have learned from this course. How/why are they so important to you? Identify the two LEAST important ideas to you personally. Why are they not important?

CASE IN POINT....

Remember to use the cases from the text as contexts for identifying examples of concepts from the text and as contexts for solving educational problems. Also remember to use a consistent framework (like the DUPE model or the CASE NOTES in the text) to structure your "Mini-Case Report." Review the "Case in Point..." section of Chapter 1 in this study guide for more details.

SUGGESTED CONCEPTS TO IDENTIFY FOR CHAPTER 13

> affective entry characteristics
> Bloom's taxonomy
> cognitive entry behaviors
> formative evaluation
> inquiry teaching
> instructional objective
> intelligent tutoring system (ITS)
> mastery learning
> programmed instruction (Skinnerian)
> self-fulfilling prophecy
> summative evaluation
> task analysis
> Web-based instruction (WBI)

Review Case #3 about Melissa Williams in your text and use the following questions to prompt your thinking about this case.

1. What approach(es) to instruction does Melissa seem to take (inquiry, mastery, etc.)? Are the approaches evident in her teaching plans? Does her approach seem appropriate?

2. What conflicts do there seem to be between Melissa's philosophy, goals, and objectives and those of the school? What impact do these differences have for Melissa's instructional planning and approach?

3. Would technology-based teaching strategies be helpful to Melissa? Which specific technology-based strategies might be useful?

CASE WRAPUP

This chapter is the last on in the text dealing specifically with Melissa Williams. Take a moment to review your thoughts, "mini-case reports," and suggestions for Melissa. Jot down a brief summary of your suggestions for her, highlighting what you think are the main issues/problems she must address and the actions that you think would be most successful for her. Reflect on what you have learned about teaching and learning interactions by analyzing this case and which ideas you think will be most useful to you in your teaching career.

Also think about the content covered in Sections 1 and 2 of the text dealing with the development of students and learning theories. Take a moment to consider whether and how any of this information might be helpful to Melissa, then make a brief list of the relevant concepts.

Finally, use this chapter as an opportunity to revisit each of the cases. Take a moment to review Case #1 about Marsha Warren and Case #2 about Mark Siegel. Would any of the information covered in the last section of the text be useful for Marsha or for Mark? Make a brief list of which concepts from Section 3 might be helpful to Marsha or Mark.

BIG IDEAS IN EDUCATIONAL PSYCHOLOGY

Thinking about the "big ideas" in educational psychology will help you organize and apply your newly acquired knowledge. Use the following steps to identify your own principles and strategies from the chapter and to relate them to the five main themes of the text (i.e., the "big ideas").

1. Review the TIPS from the text.

2. List some of the main concepts from the chapter. Use the work you did in prior sections of the study guide to help generate this list. Also look at the list of key terms from the chapter.

3. Select what you think are two or three of the most important concepts from your list.

4. For each concept you select, try to state it as a principle (use the TIPS format in the text and the example shown below as a guide for how to state principles).

5. Develop two or three specific teaching strategies that follow from each stated principle.

6. Relate your work to the five main themes from the text, identifying which theme(s) are relevant for each principle and strategy. This step will help you see how the information in each chapter contributes to improved teaching for each of these five critical aspects of instruction.

7. Think about and discuss with classmates how the principles and strategies you identify will help you improve your teaching for each theme you listed as relevant.

The five main themes from the text are:
ASSESSMENT, COMMUNICATION, LEARNING, MOTIVATION, AND TIME

Some example concepts, principles, and strategies for Chapter 13:

affective, cognitive entry characteristics	mastery learning
Bloom's taxonomy	modes of representation
clinical theory of instruction (CTI)	programmed instruction (Skinnerian)
formative vs. summative evaluation	self-fulfilling prophecy
indirect (inquiry) teaching	task analysis
instructional objective	technology-based teaching strategies
intelligent tutoring system (ITS)	Web-based instruction (WBI)

Principle	Indirect (inquiry) instruction can help students learn concepts and move beyond memorization to draw conclusions and form generalizations, resulting in more meaningful knowledge. (LEARNING, MOTIVATION)
Strategy	Structure the learning environment so that students can succeed with indirect instruction. Make sure they have access to needed materials and resources, allow enough time for students to be able to work through the issues or problems, and provide additional information, materials, and support as the needs arise. (LEARNING, MOTIVATION)
Strategy	Be supportive, specific in your feedback, and honest. Make sure to point out what students are doing well, when they are on a good track (even though they haven't completed the work yet), but also make sure to correct misunderstandings and mistakes. (LEARNING, MOTIVATION)

SUGGESTED READINGS

Ahlgren, A. (1993). Creating benchmarks for science education. *Educational Leadership, 50*(5), 46-49.

Airasian, P. W. (1994). *Classroom assessment.* New York: McGraw-Hill.

Bloom, B. (Ed.). (1956). *Taxonomy of educational objectives. Handbook 1: Cognitive domain.* New York: McKay.

Bloom, B. (Ed.). (1981). *All our children learning.* New York: McGraw-Hill.

Brophy, J. (1987). Teacher influences on student achievement. *American Psychologist, 41,* 1069.

Bruner, J. (1960). *The process of education.* Cambridge, MA: Harvard University Press.

National Council of Teachers of Mathematics. (1989). *Curriculum and evaluation standards for school mathematics.* Reston, VA: NCTM.

Shulman, L. (1986). Paradigms and research programs in the study of teaching. In M. Wittrock (Ed.), *The Handbook of Research on Teaching.* New York: Macmillan.

Romberg, T. (1993). NCTM's Standards: A rallying flag from mathematics teachers. *Educational Leadership, 50*(5), 36-41.

Science for All Americans. (1989). Washington, DC: American Association for the Advancement of Science.

PRACTICE TEST 1

1. The four common features of teaching are
   a. tasks, materials, objectives, and goals.
   b. tasks, assessments, feedback, and instruction.
   c. teachers, learners, subject matter, and context.
   d. teachers, students, parents, and administrators.

2. Sandra assumes that students should be active in their learning and seek out information. Students are encouraged to solve problems, and the classroom atmosphere is very informal. Sandra uses
   a. direct instruction.
   b. indirect instruction.
   c. Hunter's Clinical Theory of Instruction.
   d. a spiral curriculum.

3. To be *effective*, praise
   a. should be delivered unsystematically.
   b. should be restricted to global positive reactions.
   c. should orient students toward competition.
   d. should be delivered contingently.

4. Mr. Jenkins organizes his material carefully, uses terms and language he knows his students will understand, and links his lessons to past work. Which key behavior of effective teachers is Mr. Jenkins exhibiting?
   a. lesson clarity
   b. instructional variety
   c. task orientation
   d. engagement in the learning process

5. The first step in Hunter's Clinical Theory of Instruction is
   a. anticipatory set.
   b. the objective and purpose.
   c. instructional input.
   d. modeling.

6. A principal observed a teacher's comfort level in answering students' questions accurately and in a relaxed manner. This illustrates which type of content knowledge?
   a. subject matter knowledge
   b. curriculum knowledge
   c. pedagogical knowledge
   d. All of the answers are correct.

7. Preschoolers count apples one by one in learning how to count numbers. This illustrates learning
   a. symbolically.
   b. enactively.
   c. iconically.
   d. intuitively.

8. The spiral curriculum is closely related to which of Bruner's themes in analyzing learning?
   a. readiness
   b. structure
   c. intuition
   d. motivation

9. Which of the following is the correct sequence in the development of modes of representation?
   a. enactive, symbolic, iconic
   b. enactive, iconic, symbolic
   c. iconic, symbolic, enactive
   d. symbolic, iconic, enactive

10. Programmed instruction is based on the principles of
    a. Piagetian development.
    b. operant conditioning.
    c. classical conditioning.
    d. social cognitive learning.

11. According to Bloom, what percentage of students can learn to mastery if properly instructed?
    a. less than 50%
    b. about 75%
    c. about 90%
    d. 100%

12. According to Gagne, what is the first thing teachers must do to help students learn meaningfully?
    a. gain students' attention
    b. stimulate recall of students' prior knowledge
    c. provide learning guidance
    d. provide feedback

13. Which of Markle's programming principles refers to meaningful responses that are covert, overt, psychomotor, or verbal?
    a. errorless learning
    b. immediate feedback
    c. active responding
    d. None of the answers is correct.

14. What does the first stage of studying involve?
    a. organization of the information
    b. practicing or rehearsing
    c. actual remembering or application of information
    d. taking in information from books, lectures, or presentations

15. Allison's parents encouraged her to study in her bedroom following dinner every evening. What are Allison's parents encouraging her to do?
    a. develop time estimation skill
    b. expand concentration time
    c. establish a study routine
    d. work out a study system

16. Greater self-direction and self-discipline, better time organization, and more inquisitiveness are _____ effects of homework.
    a. short-term academic
    b. long-term academic
    c. nonacademic
    d. satiation

17. In a study of teacher expectations, Rosenthal and Jacobson (1968) found that when teachers expected more of children, the students
    a. failed.
    b. made more errors.
    c. attributed their achievement to luck.
    d. met their expectations.

18. Sam was planning to teach his Boy Scout troop how to pitch a tent. He thought through all the steps involved in pitching a tent and identified subtasks to teach. He also considered what skills each scout would need for each subtask, and ways to help them integrate all the subcomponents. Finally, he carefully considered the best way to sequence his instruction. Sam was using
    a. static schema.
    b. task analysis.
    c. synthesis levels of questioning.
    d. delivery standards.

19. One objective of a statistics unit stated "The student will correctly solve 70% of the applications problems for each section of this unit." This objective
    a. is vague concerning the expected behavior.
    b. is inappropriate for the content.
    c. provides a general statement of content to be covered.
    d. provides the criterion level required.

20. In the following objective, "Each student will be able to identify 40 of the 50 states in the United States," which part of the objective specifies the "A" in the ABCD format for writing objectives?
   a. in the United States
   b. identify
   c. 40 of the 50 states
   d. each student

21. Students in a political science class are asked to write a position paper justifying their particular presidential candidate's policies. This illustrates which category of Bloom's cognitive taxonomy?
   a. evaluation
   b. application
   c. analysis
   d. synthesis

22. One reason to use technology in the classroom is that it
   a. ensures individualized instruction for every student.
   b. prevents students from developing misconceptions about the content.
   c. allows students to work safely on rare or dangerous problems.
   d. eliminates the need to track student progress.

23. "I do not use technology a great deal in my teaching. It seems that whenever I have tried it, things became chaotic. I couldn't tell who had covered what parts of the lesson, and it was impossible for me to keep everyone on track." This comment exemplifies which of the following reasons for not using technology?
   a. belief that computers don't help
   b. different role for teachers
   c. societal resistance
   d. the computer as competitor

24. Web-based instruction offers the advantage of allowing students
   a. to work cooperatively with different sites.
   b. easy access to materials and expertise.
   c. greater control over their learning.
   d. All of the above are advantages of web-based instruction.

PRACTICE TEST 2

1. Which of the following is NOT one of the four common features of teaching?
   a. teachers
   b. learners
   c. context
   d. parents

2. Student _____ is superior with direct instruction as opposed to inquiry.
   a. motivation
   b. achievement
   c. attitude
   d. reaction

3. To be *effective,* praise should
   a. be used very sparingly.
   b. be general in nature.
   c. be based on whether the student usually tries hard.
   d. be offered immediately after the behavior.

4. Mrs. Freedman makes sure her students know the classroom rules, monitors seatwork carefully, and gives interesting independent assignments. Which key behavior of effective teachers is Mrs. Freedman exhibiting?
   a. lesson clarity
   b. instructional variety
   c. engagement in the learning process
   d. student success

5. Which of the following theorists believes that the teacher is a decision-making professional and that, if instructional decisions are not made consciously, they will be made by default?
   a. Bloom
   b. Bruner
   c. Gagne
   d. Hunter

6. The optimal manner in which knowledge of a subject can be organized and presented defines
   a. subject matter knowledge.
   b. pedagogical knowledge.
   c. curriculum knowledge.
   d. metacognitive knowledge.

7. Searching for patterns in information is an example of learning
   a. iconically.
   b. enactively.
   c. intuitively.
   d. symbolically.

8. The spiral curriculum exemplifies an attempt to develop
   a. intuition.
   b. structure.
   c. readiness.
   d. motivation.

9. Which of Bruner's modes of representation involves information representation and considering possibilities?
   a. symbolic mode
   b. iconic mode
   c. enactive mode
   d. None of the answers is correct.

10. In programed instruction, deciding what students should be able to do after teaching is called defining the
    a. first instance.
    b. prompt behavior.
    c. complex behavior.
    d. terminal behavior.

11. What is the key element in Bloom's work?
    a. mastery learning
    b. learning outcomes
    c. the spiral curriculum
    d. the principle of active responding

12. In Gagne's instructional design, each of five learning outcomes demands a different set of optimal conditions. What does optimal conditions mean?
    a. the classroom atmosphere
    b. the text used
    c. the test method used
    d. the instruction that students receive

13. Markle links the need for feedback to the
    a. manner in which the statement is framed.
    b. importance of the material.
    c. interest of the students.
    d. anxiety of the students.

14. What is the final stage of studying?
    a. organization of the information
    b. practicing or rehearsing
    c. actual remembering or application of information
    d. taking in information from books, lectures, or presentations

15. Margot studies every night after dinner in her room. She keeps the room quiet so she can concentrate, and uses the SQ3R method to guide her studying. She sets realistic goals and keeps her assignments organized in one notebook so she can quickly see what she must accomplish. However, Margot often is late in turning in her work and spends hours the night before something is due "cramming" to finish. What could Margot do to improve her study skills?
    a. Develop time estimation skills.
    b. Plan ahead.
    c. Set goals.
    d. All of the suggestions should help Margot improve.

16. Cooper found that the effect of homework on achievement was especially important for
    a. lower elementary students.
    b. upper elementary students.
    c. middle school students.
    d. high school students.

17. What does the self-fulfilling prophecy mean for teachers?
    a. Students' expectations affect their achievement.
    b. Teacher expectations affect students' achievement.
    c. How teachers present material affects students' achievement.
    d. Teacher expectations affect their classroom performance.

18. Joan was teaching a mathematics unit on two-step addition, but her students were not performing well. They often became confused about which numbers to add first, and which columns to "carry" to. Joan decided to identify all the subparts of this skill and review which ones students needed help with, making sure everything was carefully sequenced. Joan was using
    a. dynamic schema.
    b. mathematics as problem solving.
    c. task analysis.
    d. error analysis.

19. Expected learner outcomes are used to determine
    a. teacher competency.
    b. school entry and grade retention.
    c. mastery of a specific school subject.
    d. minimum competency.

20. In the ABCD format for writing objectives, what does the D represent?
    a. determining the instructional goals
    b. the decision to move a student to the next grade level
    c. determining the student's learning deficits
    d. the acceptable degree of competency

21. Students are quizzed on recalling the basic facts of their current science unit. This relates to which of Bloom's taxonomy categories?
    a. knowledge
    b. synthesis
    c. comprehension
    d. application

22. Technology can be helpful to teachers by
    a. allowing activities that otherwise would be impossible.
    b. eliminating the dynamics of processes so students can study each aspect of the processes in isolation.
    c. preventing unauthorized access to student records.
    d. None of the answers are correct.

23. The diagnostician component of an ITS
    a. solves the problems presented to students.
    b. tracks performance and identifies errors.
    c. provides feedback and guidance to students.
    d. contains rules for deciding whether and how to intervene in students' performance.

24. Multimedia uses of technology allow students to
    a. view content skills as cognitive tools rather than memorized information.
    b. focus on the problems presented without having to expend cognitive effort on problems generation.
    c. solve problems in a simple, controlled environment.
    d. keep content areas separate so they can better master the basics of the areas.

ANSWER KEY

Practice Test 1

1. ANSWER: C, Factual; OBJECTIVE: 1; PAGE: 520
2. ANSWER: B, Applied; OBJECTIVE: 4; PAGE: 527
3. ANSWER: D, Factual; OBJECTIVE: 3; PAGE: 523
4. ANSWER: A, Applied; OBJECTIVE: 2; PAGE: 520
5. ANSWER: A, Factual; OBJECTIVE: 4; PAGE: 524
6. ANSWER: A, Applied; OBJECTIVE: 8; PAGE: 555
7. ANSWER: B, Conceptual; OBJECTIVE: 4; PAGE: 529
8. ANSWER: A, Conceptual; OBJECTIVE: 4; PAGE: 528
9. ANSWER: B, Conceptual; OBJECTIVE: 4; PAGE: 529
10. ANSWER: B, Factual; OBJECTIVE: 6; PAGE: 541
11. ANSWER: C, Factual; OBJECTIVE: 9; PAGE: 560
12. ANSWER: A, Factual; OBJECTIVE: 6; PAGE: 545
13. ANSWER: C, Factual; OBJECTIVE: 6; PAGE: 541
14. ANSWER: D, Conceptual; OBJECTIVE: 9; PAGE: 563
15. ANSWER: C, Applied; OBJECTIVE: 9; PAGE: 564
16. ANSWER: C, Factual; OBJECTIVE: 9; PAGE: 567
17. ANSWER: D, Factual; OBJECTIVE: 9; PAGE: 570
18. ANSWER: B, Applied; OBJECTIVE: 5; PAGE: 532
19. ANSWER: D, Applied; OBJECTIVE: 5; PAGE: 535
20. ANSWER: D, Applied; OBJECTIVE: 5; PAGE: 536
21. ANSWER: A, Applied; OBJECTIVE: 5; PAGE: 538
22. ANSWER: C, Factual; OBJECTIVE: 7; PAGE: 546
23. ANSWER: B, Applied; OBJECTIVE: 7; PAGE: 547
24. ANSWER: D, Factual; OBJECTIVE: 7; PAGE: 548-549

Practice Test 2

1. ANSWER: D, Factual; OBJECTIVE: 1; PAGE: 520
2. ANSWER: B, Factual; OBJECTIVE: 4; PAGE: 523
3. ANSWER: D, Factual; OBJECTIVE: 3; PAGE: 523
4. ANSWER: C, Applied; OBJECTIVE: 2; PAGE: 521
5. ANSWER: D, Factual; OBJECTIVE: 4; PAGE: 524
6. ANSWER: C, Factual; OBJECTIVE: 8; PAGE: 555
7. ANSWER: A, Factual; OBJECTIVE: 4; PAGE: 529
8. ANSWER: B, Factual; OBJECTIVE: 4; PAGE: 528
9. ANSWER: A, Factual; OBJECTIVE: 4; PAGE: 529
10. ANSWER: D, Factual; OBJECTIVE: 6; PAGE: 538
11. ANSWER: A, Factual; OBJECTIVE: 9; PAGE: 559
12. ANSWER: D, Factual; OBJECTIVE: 6; PAGE: 545
13. ANSWER: A, Factual; OBJECTIVE: 6; PAGE: 544
14. ANSWER: C, Conceptual; OBJECTIVE: 9; PAGE: 563
15. ANSWER: D, Applied; OBJECTIVE: 9; PAGE: 564-565
16. ANSWER: D, Factual; OBJECTIVE: 9; PAGE: 566
17. ANSWER: B, Factual; OBJECTIVE: 9; PAGE: 570
18. ANSWER: C, Applied; OBJECTIVE: 5; PAGE: 532
19. ANSWER: B, Factual; OBJECTIVE: 5; PAGE: 532
20. ANSWER: D, Factual; OBJECTIVE: 5; PAGE: 536
21. ANSWER: A, Conceptual; OBJECTIVE: 5; PAGE: 537
22. ANSWER: A, Factual; OBJECTIVE: 7; PAGE: 546
23. ANSWER: B, Factual; OBJECTIVE: 7; PAGE: 552
24. ANSWER: A, Conceptual; OBJECTIVE: 7; PAGE: 551

Appendix A RESEARCH METHODS AND THE PRACTICE OF EDUCATION

LEARNING OBJECTIVES

After completing this chapter, you should be able to

1. Identify the sources of knowledge that lead to educational decisions.

2. Explain reasons that baby biographies and case studies are generally considered unreliable research procedures.

3. Relate the five steps of the scientific method to an educational problem.

4. Name two criteria for experimental research.

5. Describe surveys, interviews, and observations as techniques used by researchers to gather data, and explain advantages and disadvantages of each.

6. Compare advantages and disadvantages of cross-sectional and longitudinal methods and cite examples of each.

7. Explain the importance of cross-cultural research.

8. Describe the use of single-case research.

9. Define primary, secondary, and meta-analysis.

10. Highlight ethical and legal considerations in research in education.

APPENDIX HIGHLIGHTS

Research and Effective Schooling

- One of the most important sources of knowledge about human behavior is scientific research.
- Research answers questions about the effectiveness of educational practices.
- Scientific research is systematic, controlled, empirical, and involves a critical study of some issue or problem.
- Scientific research has been subjected to many and varied influences.
- Scientific research typically follows a series of steps that consists of identifying, clarifying, implementing, evaluating, and interpreting procedures.

Major Research Methods

- Research into educational problems may be historical, descriptive, correlational, comparative, or experimental.
- Historical research involves studying, understanding, and explaining past events.

- Descriptive, or qualitative, research involves collecting data to test hypotheses or answer questions related to the current status of a problem.
- Correlational research involves the process of determining whether, and to what degree, a relation exists between two or more variables.
- Comparative research involves establishing a direct relation between variables that the researcher compares, but does not directly manipulate.
- Experimental research involves a study in which the researcher actually manipulates at least one independent variable to observe the effect on one or more dependent variables.

Techniques Used by Researchers

- The more common research techniques used today are surveys, interviews, observations, and cross-sectional and longitudinal studies.
- Research can be conducted with large groups of subjects or with a single subject.
- Cross-cultural research helps to explain differences in how individuals behave, think, and attempt to solve problems.
- Meta-analysis, the analysis of the results of a large number of individual studies, is increasingly popular today.
- No one research method is always best; the research question and issues investigated often determine the method that the researcher will use.

DETAILED APPENDIX OUTLINE

I. Research and effective schooling
   A. Sources of knowledge
      1. Authority. People in positions of status have provided people or societies with the so-called "truth."
      2. Tradition. Knowledge is also obtained from tradition. This knowledge may no longer be relevant and can be inaccurate.
      3. Expert opinion. Certain individuals may take positions that dramatically influence people's beliefs.
      4. Personal experience. We gain a lot of knowledge from our experiences, though not all of it is accurate.
      5. Documentation of events. These are records kept of various events or phenomena.
      6. Scientific research. This is the systematic, controlled, empirical, and critical investigation of hypothetical propositions about the presumed relations among natural phenomena. It is orderly so that the researcher can have confidence in the outcomes, carried out under controlled conditions, and both the procedures and findings are available for outside evaluation.
   B. Current Issues and Perspectives: Piaget's modeling clay conservation task

II. The emergence of research on children.
   A. Baby biographies
      1. Publications by Charles Darwin and by William Preyer popularized the baby biography as a method of child study and created interest in child study in general.
      2. Problems with the baby biography
         a. It represents a subjective description of events and cannot be independently evaluated and replicated by others.
         b. Typical observations made by individuals are unsystematic and may be taken at irregular intervals.

       c.   Descriptions of behavior may represent the bias of the individual who holds certain conceptions of human development.

       d.   It is difficult to generalize data from the biographies.

  B. Case studies

    1.   Case studies commonly are used in reporting therapeutic interventions with children and adults, and also have been used widely in psychology and education.

    2.   Case studies can foster clinical innovation, cast doubt on certain theoretical positions, permit study of uncommon problems, develop new technical skills, support theoretical views, promote refinement in various techniques, and provide data that can be used to design more highly controlled research.

    3.   Case studies generally are not regarded as reliable because they are characterized by subjective impression, bias, inadequate description of the procedures used to treat a person, and replication difficulty.

  C. Scientific influences

    1.   Scientific research generally is guided by five steps:

       a.   research problem identification

       b.   research problem clarification

       c.   implementation of research plan

       d.   research plan evaluation

       e.   data interpretation and generalization

III. Major research methods

  A. Historical research

    1.   Involves studying, understanding, and explaining past events.

    2.   Purpose is to formulate conclusions about causes, effects, or trends of past events that either help explain current events or anticipate future events.

    3.   Data that are already available are used.

  B. Descriptive research (qualitative research)

    1.   Investigator examines and reports things the way they are, to understand and explain them.

    2.   Involves collecting data to test hypotheses or answer questions related to the current status of a problem using instruments such as surveys, questionnaires, interviews, and observations.

  C. Correlational research

    1.   Involves the process of determining whether a relation exists between two or more variables.

    2.   The finding that two variables are highly related (correlated) does not mean that one caused the other; a third variable may cause or strongly influence the variables.

    3.   The degree of relation between two or more variables generally is expressed as a correlation coefficient that is represented by a number between -1.00 and +1.00.

    4.   The closer two variables are to +1.00 or -1.00, the better the researcher is able to make a prediction.

  D. Comparative research

    1.   Involves searching for causal relations among variables that are compared but not manipulated by the researcher.

    2.   Typically involves the comparison of groups that are different before the study begins.

    3.   Because there is no manipulation or control over extraneous events, the relations established in comparative research must remain tentative.

    4.   Though not as predictable as experimental research, comparative research offers an option to doing no study when the variables involved cannot be manipulated or controlled by the researcher.

  E. Experimental research

    1.   Experimental research involves the manipulation of an independent variable to observe changes in the dependent variable(s).

    2.   The independent variable frequently is called the experimental or treatment condition.

    3.   Treatment conditions may be compared with each other or to a control condition.

4. The most important feature is that researchers are able to manipulate variables and control sources of influence that could affect the results.
5. Random assignment is when any individual going into one of the two groups has an equal chance of ending up in either group. No bias is introduced by having more participants with specific characteristics in one group than in the other.
6. The two criteria of experimental research are control of the independent variable and random assignment of subjects. When these two criteria are met, a cause-effect relationship can be established.
7. The way in which subjects respond is the dependent variable.
8. To determine if a relationship exists between the independent and dependent variables, internal validity is examined.
9. To determine how widely the relationship between the independent and dependent variables applies, external validity is examined. It represents the generality of the research findings.
10. Research credibility refers to a study that is methodologically sound and is a function of internal validity characteristics. Creditable educational intervention research refers to work that addresses important issues and problems.
11. Many factors must be examined to decide which research method is best under what circumstances; no single research method is always the best.

IV. Techniques used by researchers
   A. Surveys
      1. The investigator asks a group of individuals questions about a particular issue.
      2. Surveys are conducted through methods such as interviews, questionnaires, the telephone, and mail.
      3. The heart of good survey research is the development of a meaningful survey tool.
      4. Advantages
         a. A great deal of information can be obtained from a large population.
         b. A good representation of sources of information is provided.
      5. Disadvantages
         a. May not allow very detailed information on the issue being researched.
         b. Expensive and time-consuming.
         c. Introduction of an error into the study sampling can bias the results.
         d. Subject to faking responses and bias in responding to questions.
   B. Interviews
      1. Procedure involves a face-to-face situation in which an interviewer asks questions relevant to the research problem.
      2. Standardized, structured interview is a closed format. The interviewer asks questions in which the sequence and wording are fixed.
      3. Unstandardized, nonstructured interview is an open format. Unstandardized interviews are more flexible and open because the interviewer determines what will be asked.
      4. Advantages
         a. Allow the interviewer to obtain a great deal of information, particularly when the situation is open.
         b. Can be made flexible to meet the need of situation, problem, person.
      5. Disadvantages
         a. Interviewee responses can be faked.
         b. Interviewee responses are subject to interpretation.
         c. Time-consuming.
   C. Observation
      1. Most common way we obtain information.
      2. Ecological psychology developed out of naturalistic observational techniques. In this form of observation, teams of observers view children throughout a typical day's activities.
      3. Advantages
         a. Has opened many new possibilities in the field of educational psychology.
         b. Useful for studying children and adolescents in their natural environments.

4. Disadvantages
   a. Expensive and time-consuming, both in training observers and in conducting the observations in the natural environments.
D. Cross-sectional and longitudinal research
   1. A main feature of the cross-sectional approach is the selection of different groups of children at a variety of age levels for study. Typically, a researcher separates the children into different age levels and studies the problem of interest.
   2. Advantages of cross-sectional approach
      a. Data can be collected across a wide age range in a relatively short time period.
   3. Disadvantages of cross-sectional approach
      a. Yields no information about the history of age-related changes.
   4. Longitudinal research involves subjects assessed repeatedly over a longer period of time.

   5. Advantages of longitudinal approach
      a. Researcher can study the same subjects at each stage or age interval so that he or she can record the patterns of an individual's behavior.
   6. Disadvantages of longitudinal approach
      a. Expensive and time-consuming.
      b. Subjects may leave the study for a variety of reasons, which can bias the results.
E. Cross-cultural research
   1. Determines which factors are related to a particular culture.
F. Single-case research
   1. Emphasizes the repeated analysis of a group or individual subject over a definite time period, but the repeated measurement is taken at frequent intervals over a relatively short period of time. At some point, an intervention is introduced and the researcher evaluates the effect.
   2. The major advantage of single-case research is that formal measurement takes place, some credible design is used to evaluate treatments, and reliable data are gathered.
   3. Single-case designs are used in research as well as in applied settings where the researcher wishes to demonstrate that some intervention was effective with an identified problem.
V. Primary, secondary, and meta-analysis
A. Primary analysis is the first, or original, analysis of the data and is usually done by the individual who designed and conducted the research.
B. Secondary analysis refers to the reanalysis of data to clarify the original research questions with better statistical procedures or to answer new questions with old data.
C. Meta-analysis refers to the statistical analysis of a large collection of analysis results from individual studies for the purpose of integrating the findings.
D. Applications of meta-analysis have been quite controversial. Some have criticized meta-analyses because in making general statements about a particular research topic, it does not discriminate between good and poor studies. Some authors recommend combining meta-analysis with other literature review methods.
VI. Ethical and legal considerations in research in education
A. APA Guidelines
   1. The American Psychological Association (APA) has developed guidelines for research with human subjects to provide researchers with direction when undertaking scientific investigation.

VII. Chapter highlights

KEY TERMS

(Note: The following key terms are NOT published in the text.)

case studies	historical research
comparative research	independent variable
correlational research	interviews
cross-cultural research	longitudinal research
cross-sectional research	meta-analysis
dependent variable	observation
descriptive research	single-case research
experimental research	surveys

GUIDED REVIEW

1.   Research _____, usually about _____, _____ among variables, or effectiveness.

answers questions, causation, relationships

2.   Individuals in a position of _____ have provided societies with the so-called "truth," such as the belief that the earth was flat.

authority

3.   Knowledge can be obtained from _____, as in the practice of starting formal education around the age of 6 years. Another source of knowledge comes from _____, in which certain individuals take positions that dramatically influence people's beliefs. We gain a considerable amount of knowledge from _____, although not all of it is accurate, as when a teacher uses a technique that worked for him or her when he or she was a student.

tradition, expert opinion, personal experience

4.   Another knowledge source comes through the_____ of events, in which a record is kept of various events or phenomena. The final means of gaining information is the use of _____, which typically is carried out under controlled conditions.

documentation, scientific research

5.   Records maintained about one's children are known as_____. The method is not held in high regard in the scientific community. There are several reasons for this. First, it represents a _____ description of events and cannot be independently evaluated and replicated by others. Second, typical observations made by individuals are _____ and may be taken at irregular intervals. Third, the descriptions of behavior may represent the _____ of the individual, who holds certain conceptions of human development. Fourth, it is difficult to _____ data from biographies.

baby biographies, subjective, unsystematic, bias, generalize

6.   As a form of research methodology, _____ evolved as individuals from various theoretical orientations began to treat people with personality and behavior problems. They have been used widely in psychology and education. Such methods remained a primary form of methodology of clinical investigations through the first half of this century.

case studies

7.   Neither case studies nor baby biographies generally are regarded as _____ research procedures.

reliable

8.   Case studies are typically characterized by _____ impression, bias, inadequate description of the _____ used, and they are difficult to _____. They are being replaced by single-case _____ research strategies that are designed to make replication possible.

subjective, procedures, replicate, time-series

9.   Step 1: _____. A first step in conducting scientific research involves the problem or question. Step 2:_____. The specific aspects of the problem must be analyzed and the nature, scope, and specifics of the situation identified. Step 3: _____. In this step the researchers state the problem and test the plan and program implemented to answer the question. Step 4: _____. This step involves making decisions based upon the data collected from the study. Step 5: _____. The final step involves interpretation and generalization of the researcher's findings into a larger body of knowledge related to the problem under study.

Research problem identification, Research problem clarification, Implementation of research plan, Research plan evaluation, Data interpretation and generalization

10.   _____ research involves studying, understanding, and explaining past events. A major purpose is to formulate conclusions about causes, effects, or trends of _____ that either help explain current events or anticipate future events. Typically, individuals conducting historical research use data that are already_____.

Historical, past events, available

11.   In _____ research, the investigator examines and reports things the way they are. The researcher collects data to test a hypothesis or answer questions concerning the status of some issue or problem. Instruments such as surveys, questionnaires, interviews, and observational codes may be developed for this type of investigation.

descriptive

12.   In _____ research, the researcher attempts to determine if a relation exists between two or more variables. _____ can refer to a range of human characteristics, such as height, weight, sex, intelligence, and so forth.

correlational, Variables

13.   The finding that two variables are highly related (correlated) does not mean that one _____ the other. The degree of relation between two or more variables is generally expressed as a _____ that is represented by a number between _____ and _____. The more closely two variables approach +1.00 or -1.00, the better the researcher is able to make a _____.

caused, correlation coefficient, .00 (no relation), 1.00 (perfect relation), prediction

14.   In _____ research, the investigator searches for causal relations among variables that are compared with each other. Since there is no manipulation or control over extraneous events, the causal relations established in this type of research must remain _____.

comparative, tentative

15.   _____ research involves the active manipulation of an independent variable to observe changes in the dependent variable. In this type of research, the _____ is the experimental or treatment condition. A _____ is a condition in which no treatment is administered, although the group is the same as the treatment group in all other respects.

Experimental, independent variable, control condition

16.   The criteria for experimental research include control of the _____ and _____ assignment of subjects. The way in which the subjects respond is the _____.

independent variable, random, dependent variable

17.   To determine if a relationship exists between the independent and the dependent variables, _____ is examined.

internal validity

18.   To determine how widely the relationship between the independent and dependent variables applies, _____ is examined, which represents the _____ of the research findings.

external validity, generality

19.   _____ refers to a study that is methodologically sound and is a function of internal _____ characteristics. Credible _____ research refers to work that addresses important issues and problems. Research that has credibility has impact potential.

Research credibility, validity, educational intervention

20.   Many educational researchers believe that _____ research is the most useful form of scientific investigation. Many factors must be examined, however, and _____ is always the best.

experimental, no single research method

21.   In _____ research, the investigator asks a group of individuals questions about a particular issue. The heart of good survey research is a meaningful _____.

survey, survey tool

22.   With surveys, a _____ of information can be obtained from a large sample and a good representation of _____ is provided. Surveys may not allow collection of _____ on the issue being researched, however. They also can be _____, _____, and _____ due to introduction of an error into the study sampling or faking of responses by subjects.

great deal, sources of information, detailed information, expensive, time-consuming, biased

23.   The _____ procedure involves a face-to-face situation in which an interviewer asks another individual questions designed to obtain answers relevant to the research problem.

interview

24.   In a _____ interview, the interviewer asks questions in which the sequence and wording are fixed. In contrast, _____ interviews are more flexible and open, in that the interviewer determines what will be asked.

standardized, unstandardized

25.   Interviews can provide a great deal of information, particularly when the situation is _____. However, responses can be _____ and are subject to _____. Interviews also can be _____.

open, faked, interpretation, time-consuming

26.   A special branch of psychology called _____ was developed out of naturalistic observational techniques. In this approach, teams of observers view children throughout a _____. Observational research has been useful for studying children in their _____, but is expensive and _____.

ecological psychology, typical day's activities, natural environments, time-consuming.

27.   The _____ approach involves the selection of different groups of children at a variety of age levels for study. Typically, a researcher separates the children into different age levels and studies the problem of interest.

cross-sectional

28.   Use of a cross-sectional approach means that data can be collected across a _____ in a relatively _____, but this approach does not provide information about the _____ of age-related changes.

wide age range, short time period, history

29. _____ research involves assessment of the same participants repeatedly over a longer period of time.

Longitudinal

30. In the longitudinal approach, the _____ subjects are studied at each age interval, and patterns of an individual's behavior can be studied. This approach is _____ and _____, however, and the results may be _____ by subjects leaving the study.

same, expensive, time-consuming, biased

31. _____ studies should be conducted to determine which factors are related to a particular culture.

Cross-cultural

32. _____ research emphasizes the repeated analysis of a group or individual subject over a definite time period, but the repeated measurement is taken at _____ intervals over a relatively _____ period of time. At some point, an intervention is introduced, and the researcher evaluates the effect.

Single-case, frequent, short

33. The major advantages of single-case research are that _____ takes place, some _____ is used to evaluate treatments, and _____ data are gathered.

formal measurement, credible design, reliable

34. The first or original analysis of the data that takes place is called _____, and is usually done by the individual who designed and conducted the research.

primary analysis

35. _____ refers to the reanalysis of data to clarify the original research questions with better statistical procedures, or to answer new questions with old data.

Secondary analysis

36. _____ refers to the statistical analysis of a large collection of analysis results from individual studies for the purpose of integrating the findings. Some authors have recommended the use of _____, in which traditional _____ review is combined with meta-analysis.

Meta-analysis, best-evidence synthesis, narrative

37.   Applications of meta-analysis have been quite controversial. Some have criticized meta-analysis because in making general statements about a particular research topic, it does not discriminate between _____ studies.

good and poor

_____ and quality _____. Ethical and legal guidelines have been advanced for doing research with children and adults. The APA *Ethical Standards for Research with Human Subjects* provides researchers with _____ when undertaking scientific investigation.

human condition, education, direction

SUMMARIZE THE MAIN POINTS

This section of your study guide is designed to help you identify and understand the main points in each chapter. You've already reviewed the details using the Guided Review (above), and will consider the importance, relevance, and usefulness of the information in later sections. For now, focus on summarizing the main ideas.

For each major section in the chapter, summarize the main point and the evidence presented in the text to support and/or discuss it. If there are key terms presented in the section, define them. Some prompting questions are provided to help you structure your review.

The main sections of the Appendix are:

- Research and effective schooling
- The emergence of research on children
- Major research methods
- Techniques used by researchers
- Primary, secondary, and meta-analysis
- Ethical and legal considerations in research in education

For each section, answer the following questions:

1. In two sentences or less, **summarize** what the **main point** of this section was.

2. Briefly **summarize the evidence** for and against each main point (a simple list of details they use to support each of their points is sufficient). If the authors discuss research studies to support the point, summarize the findings in one sentence. If the authors are presenting a logical argument to support the point (i.e., not citing data from research studies), briefly list the supporting points they made. Use the detailed chapter outline to help you identify the supporting points.

3. Briefly review the **definitions of any key terms** in each main section.

WHY SHOULD YOU CARE?

The purpose of this section of your study guide is to help you understand how and why the information in the chapter is relevant for you personally. You'll be asked to think more about the relevance and usefulness of the information in later sections of this study guide.

Look back at the work you did in summarizing the main points in the section above and answer the following questions:

1. For each section you summarized, why or how is the **main point** you identified **important to and/or relevant for teachers in general**? Try to limit your answer to only one or two sentences so you don't get bogged down in details, but focus on general usefulness.

2. Now think about the chapter as a whole. **Identify two specific events, contexts, or problems** for which the ideas presented in this chapter are relevant. Briefly discuss how they're relevant and how they could be useful.

3. Now **identify three concepts** from the chapter that **YOU find useful** in some way. Discuss how/why these concepts are useful, and specify how you will actually use them in your teaching and/or your daily life. (It's okay if there is some overlap between your answers for numbers 2 and 3.)

DISCUSSION QUESTIONS

1. Discuss the importance of educational research in the teaching and learning process.

2. Identify the sources of knowledge that lead to educational decisions. For each source, discuss the advantages and disadvantages of relying on this as a source of information.

3. List and briefly define the five major research methods discussed in your text. Then evaluate the pros and cons of each.

4. Compare and contrast the cross-sectional and longitudinal strategies for conducting research.

5. Why are baby biographies and case studies considered less reliable research procedures than scientific research?

6. Describe and explain the criteria for experimental research. Why are they so important?

7. Describe and explain internal and external validity. Why are they important? What are some of the possible effects of low validity?

8. What are the five steps of the scientific method? Pretend that you wanted to assess the effectiveness of your math text's new approach to teaching problem solving. Briefly describe how you would implement each of the five steps to address this question.

TAKE IT PERSONALLY!

The questions in this section are designed to help you personalize, integrate, and apply the information from the text. Personalization questions ask you to consider the personal relevance and usefulness of concepts, and consider how they might be useful in your life now and in the future. Integration questions ask you to pull together information from the text to evaluate it, summarize it or synthesize a recommendation on the basis of it, or express an opinion about it. Application questions ask you to think about how the concepts might be useful to address real problems or situations you may find yourself in. All three question types will help you consider the information at a deeper conceptual level, understand it more fully, and remember it.

1. Think about the cases presented in your textbook. Identify an educational research question that would be relevant for Marsha, Mark, or Melissa from the cases. Using the five steps, describe how you'd design and implement a research study to address their question. What problems might you have in implementing the five steps?

2. What is the purpose of research in education? Do you use research in your teaching and learning? How?

3. Identify a research question in which you are interested. What method would you use to address this question? Why would you select that method? How else could you address it?

4. Identify an example of a misinterpreted or over-interpreted correlation. How does this mis- or over-interpretation affect thinking and/or behavior?

5. List, define, and give examples of each of the research techniques. Identify a research question you would or could use each technique for, or describe how each could be used to address one specific question. How does one decide which technique is the best one for a given research question?

6. How will you use cross-cultural research in your teaching?

7. What is single-case research? Should teachers use it in their classrooms? Why and how should they use it? Identify a question you could use this technique for and outline how you would go about applying it.

8. Define meta-analysis and find an example of its use in the literature. How is this technique useful for teachers? What are some of the problems with meta-analysis?

9. Why do educational researchers need ethics guidelines? How do these guidelines apply to you as a student? To you as a teacher?

CASE IN POINT...

Remember to use the cases from the text as contexts for identifying examples of concepts from the text and as contexts for solving educational problems. Also remember to use a consistent framework (like the DUPE model or the CASE NOTES in the text) to structure your "Mini-Case Report." Review the "Case in Point..." section of Chapter 1 in this study guide for more details.

SUGGESTED CONCEPTS TO IDENTIFY FOR THE APPENDIX

   case studies
   comparative research
   correlational research
   cross-cultural research
   cross-sectional research
   dependent variable
   descriptive research
   experimental research
   historical research
   independent variable
   interviews
   longitudinal research
   meta-analysis
   observation
   single-case research
   surveys

Review Cases #1, #2, and #3 in your text and use the following questions to prompt your thinking about this case.

1. For one or all of the cases, identify a specific instructional question you think is interesting. If you were the teacher in the case, how would you address this question? What research methods seem most appropriate and feasible? How would using this method help you answer your question?

2. How could Marsha, Mark, and Melissa benefit from knowing about the research methods described in the Appendix? For example, could they make use of a case study approach, interviews, observations, surveys, or single-case research designs to gather information and improve their teaching?

3. Can the teachers in these cases (and classroom teachers in general) implement a true experimental design to answer instructional questions in their classrooms? How would they go about doing so, and what advantages would this kind of design give them over other possible methods they might consider?

BIG IDEAS IN EDUCATIONAL PSYCHOLOGY

Thinking about the "big ideas" in educational psychology will help you organize and apply your newly acquired knowledge. Use the following steps to identify your own principles and strategies from the chapter and to relate them to the five main themes of the text (i.e., the "big ideas").

1. (The Appendix does not list any TIPS in the text.)

2. List some of the main concepts from the chapter. Use the work you did in prior sections of the study guide to help generate this list. Also look at the list of key terms from the chapter.

3. Select what you think are two or three of the most important concepts from your list.

4. For each concept you select, try to state it as a principle (use the TIPS format in prior chapters of the text and the example shown below as a guide for how to state principles).

5. Develop two or three specific teaching strategies that follow from each stated principle.

6. Relate your work to the five main themes from the text, identifying which theme(s) are relevant for each principle and strategy. This step will help you see how the information in each chapter contributes to improved teaching for each of these five critical aspects of instruction.

7. Think about and discuss with classmates how the principles and strategies you identify will help you improve your teaching for each theme you listed as relevant.

The five main themes from the text are:
ASSESSMENT, COMMUNICATION, LEARNING, MOTIVATION, AND TIME

Some example concepts, principles, and strategies for the Appendix:

case studies	historical research
comparative research	independent variable
correlational research	interviews
cross-cultural research	longitudinal research
cross-sectional research	meta-analysis
dependent variable	observation
descriptive research	single-case research
experimental research	surveys

Principle	Teachers who are alert to the latest research on teaching become increasingly more skillful in their classroom instruction. (COMMUNICATION, LEARNING)
Strategy	Subscribe to (or regularly read) one research-oriented journal that is geared toward your content area and/or grade level. Read the articles with a critical eye, questioning the quality of the methods and thinking, and the soundness of the conclusions. Talk with other teachers about the research, the teaching methods, etc. (COMMUNICATION, LEARNING)
Strategy	Attend one or two teacher in-services or conferences each year that present information on teaching and/or assessment strategies relevant to your grade level or subject areas. Try one of the ideas in your teaching. (COMMUNICATION, LEARNING)

SUGGESTED READINGS

Agnew, N. M., & Pyke, S. W. (1987). *The science game* (4th ed.). Englewood Cliffs, NJ: Prentice Hall.

Best, J. W., & Kahn, J. V. (1989). *Research in education* (6th ed.). Englewood Cliffs, NJ: Prentice Hall.

Cook, T. D., & Campbell, D. T. (1979). *Quasi-experimental design and analysis issues for field settings.* Chicago: Rand McNally.

Glass, G. V., McGraw, B., & Smith, M. L. (1981). *Meta-analysis in social research.* Beverly Hills, CA: Sage Publications.

Kazdin, A. E. (1991). *Research design in clinical psychology.* New York: Pergamon Press.

PRACTICE TEST 1

1. When Jack was student teaching, he adopted a classroom organization style that his mentor used. When Jack taught a class of his own, he continued to use this style of classroom organization. What was Jack's source of knowledge?
   a. authority
   b. expert opinion
   c. personal experience
   d. tradition

2. What is the purpose of research?
   a. to answer questions
   b. to guide practice
   c. to assess the relationship between variables
   d. All of the answers are correct.

3. Why are case studies difficult to replicate?
   a. Because they involve too few subjects.
   b. Because they are not always accurate.
   c. Because the cost of replicating a case study can be prohibitive.
   d. Because they are subjective accounts of an individual with procedures unique to the given situation.

4. A researcher studies the data he has gathered on the study of environmental noise and learning disabilities. He finds no differences between the conditions of noise and learning disabilities. Which step of the scientific method involves this decision making?
   a. Research problem identification.
   b. Research plan evaluation.
   c. Research problem clarification.
   d. Data interpretation and generalization.

5. Which correlation coefficient indicates the strongest relationship between two variables?
   a. +.77
   b. -1.00
   c. +.85
   d. -.30

6. Internal validity refers to
   a. determination of whether a relationship exists between the independent and dependent variables.
   b. determination of how widely a relationship between an independent and dependent variable applies.
   c. the degree of relationship between two variables.
   d. the generality power of the relationship between two variables.

7. External validity refers to
   a. determination of whether a relationship exists between the independent and dependent variables.
   b. determination of how widely a relationship between an independent and dependent variable applies.
   c. the degree of relationship between two variables.
   d. the generality power of the relationship between two variables.

8. A researcher is interested in studying the effects of whole language for reading and writing. The whole language method is the
   a. random assignment.
   b. independent variable.
   c. dependent variable.
   d. control group.

9. What is the difference between the standardized and the unstandardized interview?
   a. The standardized interview has a closed format, whereas the unstandardized has an open format.
   b. The standardized interview has an open format, whereas the unstandardized has a closed format.
   c. The standardized interview is graded.
   d. The unstandardized interview is graded.

10. Surveys allow researchers to
    a. obtain very detailed information.
    b. eliminate sampling error.
    c. obtain information from a large sample.
    d. conduct research inexpensively.

11. Marcia interviewed teachers as part of her master's degree thesis work. While she had a set of prepared questions for each teacher, she was able to alter the questions depending on what each teacher said. This exemplifies
    a. the unreliability of interviews.
    b. that subjects often fake responses.
    c. the flexibility of interviews.
    d. the degree to which experimenter interpretation often is involved in analyzing interview responses.

12. The Fels Study begun in 1929 is an example of
    a. cross-sectional research.
    b. longitudinal research.
    c. standardized research.
    d. statistical research.

13. Cross-sectional research has the major advantage of
    a. collecting data across a wide age range in a short time period.
    b. providing information on the history of age-related changes.
    c. obtaining multiple responses from the same subjects.
    d. recording patterns of an individual's behavior at different intervals of time.

14. One major disadvantage of longitudinal research is that
    a. multiple responses cannot be obtained from the same subjects.
    b. results may be biased due to subjects dropping out.
    c. it yields no information about the history of age-related changes.
    d. patterns of an individual's behavior are not assessed.

15. What is the purpose of cross-cultural studies?
    a. to measure cultural prejudices
    b. to understand Third World cultures
    c. to determine which factors are related to a particular culture
    d. to understand our own heritage

16. Repeated analysis of a group or individual at frequent intervals over a relatively short time period is called
    a. single-case research.
    b. longitudinal research.
    c. cross-sectional research.
    d. meta-analysis.

17. What term is used to describe the reanalysis of data to clarify the original research questions with better statistical procedures or to answer new questions with old data?
    a. secondary analysis
    b. meta-analysis
    c. reformatted analysis
    d. second generation analysis

18. Who retains the responsibility for ensuring ethical practice in research?
    a. the American Psychological Association
    b. the participants in the study
    c. the ethics committee involved in the research project
    d. the investigator

PRACTICE TEST 2

1. Fred's knowledge that formal education begins around the age of 6 years comes from
   a. authority.
   b. tradition.
   c. expert opinion.
   d. documentation.

2. Research
   a. guides practice, but is not affected by practice.
   b. answers questions about causation, relationships, or effectiveness.
   c. helps further our understanding of educational processes, but is not useful for improving educational practice.
   d. cannot be effectively conducted in real-life settings like the classroom.

3. The fact that William Preyer maintained a baby biography of his own son's first four years of life makes it unreliable as a method because
   a. it should extend at least six years to be reliable.
   b. it is a subjective description of events.
   c. it would have to be repeated to be considered reliable.
   d. it is an objective description of events.

4. A researcher who wishes to study the long-term effects of Head Start programs addresses the problem of how to examine variables that might influence learning. This relates to which step of the scientific method?
   a. Research problem identification.
   b. Implementation of research plan.
   c. Research plan evaluation.
   d. Research problem clarification.

5. Which research method involves examining and reporting things the way they are?
   a. descriptive
   b. historical
   c. experimental
   d. correlational

6. The existence of a relationship between independent and dependent variables is called
   a. internal validity.
   b. correlational validity.
   c. external validity.
   d. random assignment.

7. How widely a relationship between independent and dependent variables applies is called
   a. internal validity.
   b. correlational validity.
   c. external validity.
   d. random assignment.

8. Random assignment occurs
   a. when subjects have an equal chance of being assigned to the experimental and the control groups.
   b. when people have an equal chance of being selected for a study in a given population.
   c. when subjects are selected to determine which factors are related to a particular culture.
   d. when research interviews are conducted.

9. Ecological psychology developed out of which technique?
   a. surveys
   b. experiments
   c. observations
   d. interviews

10. One disadvantage of using surveys is that
    a. they are expensive and time-consuming.
    b. subjects can fake responses.
    c. they can be biased due to sampling error.
    d. All the answers are correct.

11. Jarrod interviewed teachers as part of his master's degree thesis work. He had a set of prepared questions and asked each subject the same questions in the same order. This type of interview strategy is called
    a. a standardized interview.
    b. an unstandardized interview.
    c. an unstructured interview.
    d. a flexible interview.

12. Which of the following characterizes cross-sectional research?
    a. It is typically inexpensive.
    b. It takes a long time to conduct.
    c. Typically, many research teams are needed.
    d. It involves repeated measurement of the same group over long periods of time.

13. One major disadvantage of cross-sectional research is that
    a. it is very expensive and time-consuming.
    b. results may be biased due to subjects dropping out.
    c. it yields no information about the history of age-related changes.
    d. wide age ranges cannot be sampled.

14. Longitudinal research has the major advantage of
    a. collecting data across a wide age range in a short time period.
    b. providing information on the history of age-related changes.

c. sampling wide age ranges.
d. easy and quick administration.

15. The difference found between American children and Sarawak children in determining the characteristics of age judgments is explained by
    a. observational differences.
    b. reporting differences.
    c. language differences.
    d. cultural differences.

16. A major advantage of single-case research is that
    a. formal measurement takes place.
    b. trained observers are used.
    c. students record their own behavior.
    d. teachers identify and record the behaviors of interest.

17. Campbell and Erlebacher reexamined the original data analysis of the Westinghouse/Ohio University report on the effectiveness of Head Start. What is this procedure called?
    a. primary analysis
    b. meta-analysis
    c. secondary analysis
    d. tertiary analysis

18. The American Psychological Association's code of "Ethical Standards for Research with Human Subjects" attempts to
    a. provide protection for the rights of investigators in experiments.
    b. provide researchers with guidance on ethical issues when conducting studies.
    c. provide a way to insure that the knowledge gained is useful.
    d. provide a way to ensure that the knowledge gained will be used in appropriate ways.

ANSWER KEY

Practice Test 1

1. ANSWER: C, Applied; OBJECTIVE: 1; PAGE: 582
2. ANSWER: D, Factual; OBJECTIVE: 3; PAGE: 581
3. ANSWER: D, Conceptual; OBJECTIVE: 2; PAGE: 584
4. ANSWER: B, Applied; OBJECTIVE: 3; PAGE: 585
5. ANSWER: B, Applied; OBJECTIVE: 4; PAGE: 587
6. ANSWER: A, Factual; OBJECTIVE: 4; PAGE: 588
7. ANSWER: B, Factual; OBJECTIVE: 4; PAGE: 588
8. ANSWER: B, Applied; OBJECTIVE: 5; PAGE: 588
9. ANSWER: A, Conceptual; OBJECTIVE: 5; PAGE: 590
10. ANSWER: C, Factual; OBJECTIVE: 5; PAGE: 589
11. ANSWER: C, Applied; OBJECTIVE: 5; PAGE: 590
12. ANSWER: B, Factual; OBJECTIVE: 6; PAGE: 591
13. ANSWER: A, Factual; OBJECTIVE: 6; PAGE: 591
14. ANSWER: B, Factual; OBJECTIVE: 6; PAGE: 592
15. ANSWER: C, Factual; OBJECTIVE: 7; PAGE: 592
16. ANSWER: A, Factual; OBJECTIVE: 8; PAGE: 594
17. ANSWER: A, Factual; OBJECTIVE: 9; PAGE: 594
18. ANSWER: D, Factual; OBJECTIVE: 10; PAGE: 596

Practice Test 2

1. ANSWER: B, Factual; OBJECTIVE: 1; PAGE: 581
2. ANSWER: B, Factual; OBJECTIVE: 3; PAGE: 581
3. ANSWER: B, Factual; OBJECTIVE: 2; PAGE: 584
4. ANSWER: D, Conceptual; OBJECTIVE: 3; PAGE: 585
5. ANSWER: A, Factual; OBJECTIVE: 5; PAGE: 587
6. ANSWER: A, Factual; OBJECTIVE: 4; PAGE: 588
7. ANSWER: C, Factual; OBJECTIVE: 4; PAGE: 588
8. ANSWER: A, Factual; OBJECTIVE: 4; PAGE: 588
9. ANSWER: C, Factual; OBJECTIVE: 5; PAGE: 591
10. ANSWER: D, Factual; OBJECTIVE: 5; PAGE: 589
11. ANSWER: A, Applied; OBJECTIVE: 5; PAGE: 590
12. ANSWER: A, Factual; OBJECTIVE: 6; PAGE: 591
13. ANSWER: C, Factual; OBJECTIVE: 6; PAGE: 591
14. ANSWER: B, Factual; OBJECTIVE: 6; PAGE: 592
15. ANSWER: D, Factual; OBJECTIVE: 7; PAGE: 593
16. ANSWER: A, Factual; OBJECTIVE: 8; PAGE: 594
17. ANSWER: C, Conceptual; OBJECTIVE: 9; PAGE: 594
18. ANSWER: B, Factual; OBJECTIVE: 10; PAGE: 596